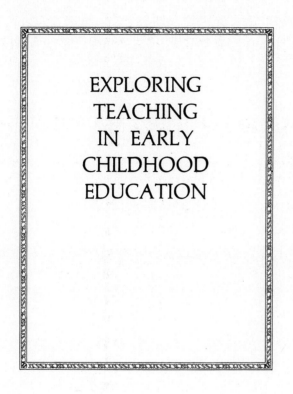

EXPLORING
TEACHING
IN EARLY
CHILDHOOD
EDUCATION

EXPLORING TEACHING IN EARLY CHILDHOOD EDUCATION

HELEN F. ROBISON

Bernard M. Baruch College
City University of New York

Allyn and Bacon, Inc.   Boston   London   Sydney   Toronto

To Naomi and Ezra, my grandchildren,
who have renewed my trust in
the future of humanistic education

Copyright © 1977 by Allyn and Bacon, Inc.
470 Atlantic Avenue, Boston, Massachusetts 02210

Library of Congress Cataloging in Publication Data

Robison, Helen F
Exploring teaching in early childhood education.

Includes bibliographies and index.
1. Education, Preschool—Hand books, manuals, etc. I. Title.
LB1140.2.R614   372.21   76-49642
ISBN 0-205-05550-8

CONTENTS

PREFACE

This book is an exploration of what we know about teaching young children. It assumes that the teaching profession has unique functions and requirements and that young children are qualitatively different from older children; therefore, it concentrates on those teaching strategies and understandings that are most closely related to the teaching of the young.

Written at an introductory level, the book is addressed primarily to preservice students who are preparing to teach and to inservice teachers who keep in touch with the field and try out new approaches that show promise. Reflecting my own humanistic commitment and optimistic expectations of young children, teachers, and teaching, it also reflects the fundamental view that well-prepared teachers are central to excellence in early childhood education.

Each chapter contains a contemporary view of major teaching functions, their theoretical bases, application of theories, current trends, and many suggestions for sources, materials, activities, and teaching procedures.

Realistic skill development exercises for teachers—compiled separately for preservice students and inservice teachers—will be found at the end of each chapter. Teacher educators will find these are readily translated into modular units of instruction leading to student independence in working toward mastery.

Bibliographic resources for each chapter are broad but have been carefully controlled, and five case studies will be found in Chapter 4 dealing with self-esteem.

Responding to the national movement toward competency-based teacher education, this book offers a conception of CBTE that firmly supports a humanistic system and contains what may be the most specific and detailed descriptions of teaching skills and competencies to be found in contemporary literature on early childhood education. Faculty moving toward competency-based programs will find extensive descriptions, analyses, and assessment options for skills and knowledge required for teaching young children, especially in humanistically oriented programs.

Educational and social changes are also identified and analyzed for their contributions to and pressures upon early childhood education. In addition to the CBTE movement, they include accountability, intensified studies of teaching behaviors, demands for cultural pluralism by many minorities, women's liberation trends, and changing family lifestyles.

Research and theory are cited to illuminate and support approaches to teaching and to program design. Examples of teaching illustrate many aspects of skill and knowledge application in the classroom. This authentic material is based on classroom observations, students' reports and videotaped teaching samples, and student teacher logs. Used extensively in workshops, seminars, and teacher conferences, the material has been enriched by the experiences of many teachers.

Readers will find an open-ended brainstorming type of approach to creative solutions: How many different ways, for example, are there to resolve a problem within clearly defined value commitments? The methods suggested in this book feature personalized processes, not pat answers and gimmicks.

The book also emphasizes the community relationships of early childhood education, as there is much stress on the interactions among the various forces in American history and culture that contribute to shaping our educational programs (often most clearly seen in the education of our youngest).

Rich curriculum possibilities are detailed for children from ages three to eight, the traditional range of early childhood education. Varieties of programs, philosophies, schedules, and teaching methods are included. Music and the arts are featured in unusual detail as areas of special interest for teachers of young children, and theoretical support will be found for the prominence given to these prime areas of children's learning. Equal importance is given to many forms of intellectual challenge, including games, constructions, scientific explorations, and social learnings. Many suggestions are made for integrating a Piagetian view of intellectual development with an activist but open-ended teaching methodology.

Since my students usually insist upon hearing my preferences among the competing theories and belief systems they have learned, I have communicated to readers some of the commitments children have helped me to accept. Readers, however, are encouraged to reach their own conclusions.

My husband, Joseph B. Robison, made this book possible by his unfailing cooperation and support. My students—preservice and inservice—at Bernard M. Baruch College of The City University of New York have contributed significantly to my understanding of contemporary teaching problems in early childhood education.

I am indebted to many people who in many ways helped to complete the book: Dr. Gerald Leinwand, Dean, Baruch School of Education, for continuous encouragement; my colleague, Dr. Arline Julius, for reviewing several chapters and making helpful suggestions; Alan Pearlman for his contribution of photographic skill; Little Star of Broome and Aguadilla en Borinquen, day care centers where the children were photographed; Steven Mathews, editor, for his great skill and helpfulness from beginning to end; and to Shirley Davis, production editor, whose detailed and thoughtful editing of the manuscript contributed in countless ways to its improvement and final form.

Helen F. Robison

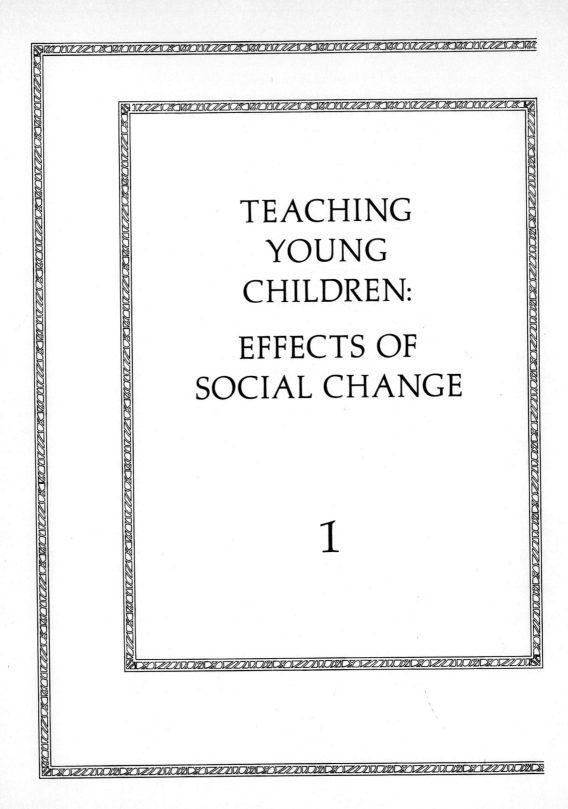

TEACHING YOUNG CHILDREN:

EFFECTS OF SOCIAL CHANGE

1

The education of young children has become an issue of national importance in our time. Never before has there been so much research, ferment, and concern about how the young shall be reared and educated in the United States. Many recent developments are focusing on the need to change educational beginnings at home and in group settings in schools. The expectation of increasing demand for day care facilities and the likelihood that more infants and toddlers will be placed in such settings, are major factors in the growing emphasis upon early childhood education. Students who plan to teach children in the age range from birth to eight years choose a specialized area of education which is critical to development at all subsequent levels.

The importance of children's earliest educational experiences makes the field of early childhood education an inevitable target and beneficiary of the effects of the great social and political movements of our time. Teacher candidates need understanding and skills in order to cope with ambiguity and change in a world of conflicting ideas and approaches to education. To ignore politics in education is to ignore the sources of decisions which eventually determine the distribution of funds for education and the options for attainment of goals. Politics, in the broadest sense, must necessarily be the arena in which conflicting demands for educational policies are resolved.

Integrating broad social trends with ideas about teaching and learning helps us to understand the contemporary turmoil about school objectives and programs and to resolve our own dilemmas about values. History of educational development teaches us how current issues and philosophical conflicts have come about and how they have been resolved in the past. Teacher candidates need preparation to identify undefined, implicit philosophical arguments which mask preferences for particular objectives in the guise of common sense. Contrary positions by parents and community representatives about educational goals can only be dealt with by teachers when they understand the real implications of the beliefs expressed. Adequate foundations for teaching young children, in addition to history of education and studies of educational philosophies, include sociological studies in order to sensitize us to the differentiating effects of socioeconomic level, race, ethnicity, and sex. Psychological research and theory are fundamental for helping us to understand human development and motivation in ways that offer disciplined frameworks for scientific and artistic teaching.

The nuclear family is slowly changing in our society. Communes are exploring alternatives as they try to create more flexible ways of meeting the needs of children and adults. Variations of the extended family are developing, some of which have long been a necessary alternative for various minority groups in order to insure survival of the young in a world of economic uncertainties.

Sociological, historical, and philosophical studies and psychological research and theory provide valuable backgrounds for scientific and artistic teaching.

Parents and communities are trying to reshape the schools to serve their needs better, but consensus is lacking about which needs are most important and how they could better be served. While parents want their children to be successful and happy members of their society, many people are questioning the values and the priorities of this society. Fundamental values are being disputed, including such issues as: money for arms and money for health, education and welfare; material goods accumulation and human spiritual and esthetic needs; private profit and public or human needs, as well as energy exploitation and conservation.

Observe the brief exchanges between teacher and parent in public school kindergartens, and hear the value questions. "Was he good today?" many mothers ask. The lower the economic scale, the more likely the value question concerns behavior. Where juvenile delinquency has high visibility, farsighted parents stress early training *by the school* in good behavior. Some parents even urge teachers to use physical punishment. "Is he learning his letters?" is an increasingly frequent question parents ask in classes for three-, four- and five-year-olds. Again, in low income areas, knowing how to read has risen to the top of the value list because it may provide insurance against future failure.

More affluent parents are equally concerned with early literacy for their children, but they often provide their own insurance by starting to teach their children to read at home. These parents are more likely to inquire about values of socialization, independence, and creativity.

*Table 1.1
presents four
contrasting
philosophies.*

A sharply etched picture of how different philosophies view the child and teachers is provided by Venable in Table 1.1 which follows. Venable depicts contrasting views of the child as seen by (1) essentialists who see the child as an unwilling learner requiring discipline so that he will learn even though it may be unpleasant; (2) idealists who see the child in a developmental continuum as one who can be trusted to attempt to fill his own needs; (3) pragmatists who picture the child in a struggle to adjust to his social environment in problem-solving social situations; and (4) realists who view the child as naturally inclined to learn and to seek knowledge. Views of teachers and teaching are congruent with views of the child: teachers are masters and scholars for essentialists, friends and guides for idealists, organizers of the learning experiences for pragmatists, and scholars who are continually seeking knowledge for realists.[1] Most parents are not conscious of the broad philosophic group with which their ideas are most in harmony but they are usually well aware of their current value preferences.

Most Americans seem to think that very young children belong in the home, and it is difficult to counter this argument successfully. Yet in 1973 there were about 6.6 million families headed by women in the United States, an increase of one million over 1970.[2] This meant that, in 1973, 14 percent of all children under eighteen were in single-parent families headed by women. The proportion was higher in black than in white families. According to the census figures, female family heads are younger than before and include fewer widows, more divorcees, and a growing percentage of unmarried women. More women are working because they have to support their young children, being without partners to share the financial and personal burdens of rearing them. These statistics indicate to teachers some of the reasons for current pressures to work closely with parents and, in many cases, to offer more services than ever before.

Many families are finding different ways to share or distribute parental roles. Some men claim the right to be "househusbands." Some husbands request paternity leave after the birth of a child when the mother chooses to stay on her job. A *New York Times* article, July 9, 1975, indicated that eight men had requested paternity leave since the spring of 1973 when the New York City Board of Education

1. Tom C. Venable, *Philosophical Foundations of the Curriculum* (Chicago: Rand McNally, 1967), pp. 110–11.
2. *New York Times*, August 8, 1974, p. 14.

TABLE 1.1

	VIEW OF THE CHILD	VIEW OF THE SUBJECT MATTER	VIEW OF THE LEARNING PROCESS	VIEW OF THE TEACHING AGENCY
Essentialism	Theory of Natural Evil: The child a fugitive from learning.	Correspondence Theory of Truth: Subject matter the prime concern in curriculum development.	Faculty Psychology or Associational Theory: Learning through drill on particulars.	Custodial View of School and Society: Teacher as master scholar. Separate subjects curriculum.
Idealism	Theory of Natural Good: The child a developing organism who is aware of his own needs.	Intuitive Theory of Truth: Child's felt needs the starting point in curriculum development.	Genetic Phychology: Learning and development are synonymous.	Creative View of School and Society: Teacher as friend and guide. Child-centered curriculum.
Pragmatism	Theory of Evolving Man: The child an organism struggling to achieve adjustment.	Pragmatic Theory of Truth: Content must be the result of what is needed to solve problems.	Field Theory: Emphasis on problem solving.	Interactional View of School and Society: Teacher as the organizer of learning experiences. Experience-centered curriculum.
Realism	Theory of Aspiring Man: The child a seeker of wisdom with a natural appetite for learning.	Coherence Theory of Truth: Content is as vast as the universe—all knowledge is worthy of inclusion in the curriculum.	Field Theory: Emphasis on seeing relationships which exist between fields of knowledge.	Integrative View of School and Society: Teacher as learning scholar. Separate subjects curriculum with modification to provide for interrelationships.

From *Philosophical Foundations of the Curriculum*, by Tom C. Venable, Rand McNally & Co. Inc., Publishers, Chicago, 1967. Reprinted by permission of the author.

made this possible.[3] One couple persuaded a college to hire them both for a single professorial appointment, permitting them both to continue their careers while taking turns caring for their children at home. Although these examples are exceptional, there is a growing resistance to sex-determined roles.

What about the children? How do they show the effects of modern ideas and movements? It depends on many things. For example, consider Gilberto, a handsome, large, well-coordinated, hearty child, the eldest of three in a Puerto Rican family. At age four, enrolled in a public school pre-kindergarten, Gilberto speaks Spanish and understands very little English. His class of fifteen children meets in a large, well-equipped classroom with tempting materials shelved in interest centers around the room. Gilberto is pulled by one set of materials after another. Everything here is new to him—the materials, equipment, the language, and the children. The teacher and Mrs. Garcia, the teacher aide, try to plan together for Gilberto's socialization. Gilberto relates to Mrs. Garcia because she speaks Spanish, but he soon finds her constraints unbearable. Gilberto moves like the wind, leaving piles of materials behind him. Mrs. Garcia orders him to stay put, to clean up, to shelve toys, to listen to the teacher at group time, or to sit quietly. Gilberto increasingly rebels, evading Mrs. Garcia, and hiding where she cannot reach him. In this setting Gilberto is neither learning to function in a group, nor is he developing any social, physical, or intellectual skills. In this half-day program, the child is expected to do all the adjusting.

Now consider Victor, of similar parentage and culture but placed in a day care center where a young male assistant teacher, Domingo, can relate to the child. Here, Domingo receives suggestions from the head teacher and the director for adjusting the requirements to Victor's capabilities, with a plan for gradual teaching of English as a second language, and increasing requirements for the child's self-control. Victor, who spoke very little at first, begins to chatter rapidly in Spanish to the two guinea pigs in cages at the back of the room. Domingo includes English-speaking children in games with Victor, as he begins second-language teaching, but he initially uses Spanish as the major communication channel. Slowly the child makes friends, lengthens his attention span for block building, and is soon using more English in his play activities. Here, the science side of teaching

3. *New York Times*, July 9, 1975, p. 43.

is well integrated with the art side, where warmth, personalization, and relationships are stressed.

Children learn well when the art and science of teaching are well coordinated. This is shown in an example of an upper middle-class white suburban kindergarten. There are twenty-nine well-scrubbed children and one teacher in a large room equipped with many "extras" which are gifts of the parents. There is an electric chord organ, many recordings to play on the phonograph, individual filmstrip viewers, an extensive classroom library, and a generous supply of art and manipulative materials. The teacher is young, energetic, warm, and enthusiastic. While the children are mostly secure, well behaved, and highly verbal, their sheer numbers seem overwhelming. Miss Gallo copes with a very open, active program with these children through skillful classroom management and prompt attention to certain children and activities, in the midst of many choices provided for children's work. Interest centers are clearly delineated. Traffic in the centers is self-regulated by the requirement of entrance cards, color-cued to the center, and the teacher's control of the number of cards available for that center. Children trade cards to change activities. Friends help each other to tie shoelaces or aprons. Cooperation is clearly a major value in this classroom.

A delicate balance integrating the art and science of teaching promotes learning.

What is Miss Gallo doing on this early spring day with 100 percent attendance and a stream of visitors steered by the beaming principal? Miss Gallo is supervising a finger-painting activity for eight children. All aproned, she and the children are gaily trying out painting patterns and actions, with a fist, a thumb, both thumbs, some fingers, one elbow, and one nose. Hilarity rocks the room. Now two girls sway rhythmically, painting with their noses. Miss Gallo is too busy to attend to the visitors, but she waves them a bright welcome and then ignores them. She offers new colors of finger paint, she directs the children to place paintings on the drying rack, and she coordinates the clean-up procedures.

How can Miss Gallo stay absorbed in finger painting? What's happening to the other twenty-one children? It is true that the two children most likely to be disruptive are finger painting close to Miss Gallo. Another child, a very musical but emotionally immature little girl, is working hard at the chord organ. This child is following a pattern of number notations written on a sheet of construction paper. Apparently, only the pitch of the melody is notated. Suddenly, the child seems to recognize the song; she plays it again, rhythmically, so that the melody can be recognized as "Mary Had a Little Lamb." Other children are grouped in dramatic play—in an imaginatively equipped housekeeping area, in block play, in chess and checkers games, in book browsing, or in listening through headsets to a phonograph recording. One child waters plants and a few sit at a table chatting while they sew with large needles and bright yarn on white cloth. The visitors are amazed to see so much self-regulation among young children. One boy approaches the visitors for help to sound out a word in his storybook but quickly tells himself the correct sounds and returns to lie on his stomach on the rug in the library corner. Here too, the science and art of teaching are well-integrated.

It is surely a pleasure to teach children who, for the most part, enter the group setting with well-developed social and linguistic skills. When children come to school without prior experiences in group settings, or with fewer skills of self-control and independence, a certain amount of storminess is to be expected. Lack of social learning is, however, not impossible to remedy, but takes skill, knowledge, patience, optimistic expectations, and enjoyment of teaching the young. Professionalism requires a helping posture while valuing and championing those helped with knowledge and practical skill.

RAPID SOCIAL CHANGES

In order for students to develop a working understanding of the effects of rapid social change on early schooling, it is helpful to review some of the major trends underway:[4]

1. The increasing proportion of working women with young children.
2. The declining birth rate.
3. The rising divorce rate.
4. The changing life-styles of women and the growing women's liberation movement.
5. The use of television in the home.
6. Changing family structures and values.
7. The growing resistance to stereotyping of groups by sex, race, or ethnicity.

4. Leonard Golubchick and Barry Persky, eds., *Urban, Social and Educational Issues* (Dubuque, Iowa: Kendall/Hunt, 1974); Arnold M. Rose and Caroline B. Rose, *Minority Problems: A Textbook of Readings in Intergroup Relations* (New York: Harper, 1965).

8. Awareness of rising prices due to energy, food supplies, and raw materials.
9. The antipollution, conservation, and ecological movements.
10. The efforts of minority groups to move closer to their political and social aspirations.
11. Resistance to complacency about political corruption on national, state, and local levels.
12. The gap between facilities and the need for early childhood education.
13. Rising educational levels increasing the proportion of parents who are college graduates.
14. The flight to and from the cities, with the problems of inner-city housing, deprivation, and crime.

Changing social attitudes have a direct effect on early schooling.

The need for child care facilities, and the preference for early education by working mothers, is exerting strong pressures emphasizing the inadequate supply of existing facilities. Private, profit-making schools, which attempt to fill the need for more affluent families, find that high tuition costs are necessary. The costs are usually even higher for publicly supported day care for children of the poor or of the marginally employed, because of the high proportion of medical, psychological, and economic problems of the community. There is no magic cure for the costliness of good early childhood education. Failing to meet the needs for early education facilities may be a false economy. The funds saved are likely to be considerably overbalanced by public expenditures for coping with crime, delinquency, and emotional disturbance.

It may be less costly to pay young mothers to stay home and rear their own children. Many, in fact, do just this on welfare income —surviving at a subsistence level which breeds great dissatisfaction, rebellion, and antisocial attitudes for the children as well as the adults. Many women prefer to work but find the expense of child care prohibitive. Independence through earning one's own living improves one's self-concept, though exhaustion may also be a hazard for the woman who holds a full-time job in addition to her home responsibilities. Yet women who feel competent and valued because of their earning capacity provide better role models for their children.

"Consciousness raising," a by-product of the women's liberation movement, is spurring more women to pursue interrupted or missed educational opportunities for better jobs and for personal fulfillment. Parents who seek to enhance their earning capacity by furthering their education also view themselves as better parents, capable of providing more economic and intellectual nourishment for their children.

The declining birth rate is associated with more insistent demands that better services be provided for proportionately fewer children. From an economic point of view, better care and services can be provided for a smaller number of children. All-day kindergartens, public school classes for three- and four-year-olds and younger children, for all families desiring such early education are realistic goals in many communities.

The desire for personal fulfillment may be one of the major explanations of the rising divorce rate. As social and sexual inhibitions have lessened, freedom to initiate a family or to dissolve a marriage has increased. There is also less patience with remote rewards and greater demand for immediate satisfaction. Is the social good being eroded in the name of instant gratification, or is renewed emphasis on individualism bound to lead us to a more complex concept of what is socially desirable?

Television is opening homes to diverse influences, but parents are often too busy to note the quantity and quality of children's televiewing. Children view endless mediocre programs and only occasional good ones. They can sometimes sing commercial jingles when they cannot sing anything else, and they repeat some of what they hear, frequently without comprehension. Ask them about their favorite programs and find out how they interpret what they see and hear. A grandmother said to her bright, five-year-old granddaughter, "I'm going to put some pajamas in the mail for you." The child's laughter was a surprise; she was enormously amused. It soon became clear that she was visualizing a pair of pajamas wending its way in the air like a magic carpet. Detailed explanation followed, about wrapping the pajamas in a package with paper and string, taking it to the post office, and paying for stamps. How often are children's misunderstandings recognized and how much can the child understand of the complicated explanations adults offer?

The growing concern for protection of the environment is building and may well affect the present wide-spread littering, use of enormous quantities of throw-aways, and disregard for conservation of energy. A great potential lies in the attitudes developed in early childhood regarding the hazards of destruction of our natural resources. The teachers of young children have the responsibility to educate the future generation to respect the environment and help reverse the habits of pollution.

It can no longer be assumed that all Americans of black, Indian, Chinese, Puerto Rican, Mexican, or other ancestry wish to be transformed into replicas of middle-class whites. Minority groups in the United States are achieving progress toward equality in education. In the areas of employment and housing, far less progress has been made, but it is hoped that discrimination in housing and employment will diminish with the rising educational achievements of these groups. Racial and ethnic pride are helping to restore realistic ideas of cultural pluralism. American society is the richer for the multiplicity of cultural models; racial and ethnic groups are strong and proud of their own unique characteristics, history, and traditions. Early education is responsible for the inclusion of cultural diversity in languages, foods, traditions, and, in some cases, of values.

Moral education in the public schools is controversial. In a broad sense, moral education will always include a substantial measure of teaching one's values, because it constitutes an important component of the socialization of the child. The present approach to moral education, growing from the theory and research of Piaget and Kohlberg, stresses the development of intellectual capacities in a framework of universal values such as the golden rule.[5] Public dismay at political corruption supports the need for more early education and development in the sphere of values. The role of the teacher is not to "tell" children what moral values they should hold, but instead to help them to use their growing intellectual capacity to reason and to make logical choices. This kind of educational goal is congruent with contemporary active forms of learning and doing. Since better educated parents no longer hold teachers in awe, their natural collaborative bents should increasingly produce agreement about the importance of early education in the young child's moral development. On the other hand, schools no longer hold parents at arm's length but actively seek to involve them in the processes of choosing goals and determining the means to reach them. Involvement in the child's education has always been better established in settings for younger children. Perhaps, at earlier levels, there is more optimism and expectation for success.

A knowledge of moral conduct is necessary but not sufficient to

5. Jean Piaget, *Moral Judgment of the Child* (New York: Harcourt, 1932); and Lawrence J. Kohlberg, "Development of Moral Character and Ideology," in *Review of Child Development Research*, vol. I (New York: Russell Sage Foundation, 1964), pp. 383–431.

produce moral behavior. Courage and conviction, and surely tradition, are also required. It is in the affective area of feelings and desires that children need more unified support from family, community, and school if children are to internalize moral conduct.

Despite the extreme level of urbanization we have reached in the United States, a reverse trend is also under way. New towns are being created in rural areas. Small villages are experiencing nightmare speeds of expansion without adequate planning. As more people seek to live in smaller communities, to have access to "nature," and more face-to-face interchanges with friends and neighbors, density is building up at the perimeter of the big cities to match the inner-city population bunching. As small villages grow, they rapidly take on the very characteristics from which newer residents fled—heavy traffic, namelessness, facelessness, and mass experiences.

In the short run, population exchanges make considerable difference to the people who move. In the long run, the ills of the big city follow the trend to suburb and exurb. In the diffusion of problems may lie their solution. The more widely distributed societal ills become, the more unity can be expected in support of social change which seeks to remedy or improve the fabric of people's lives.

While the foregoing discussion has stressed societal ills and conflicts and their impact on early childhood education, candidates for teaching need not feel pessimistic. Every period in history has had its own problems. With instant diffusion of news and developments, especially on television, we are more quickly informed, and in greater detail, than any previous population. We are sometimes misinformed over the short run and in the heat of political contests, but our system seems to have the resilience to detect and correct error. Being well-informed and attempting to understand modern developments reported in much detail, we have to deal with information overload and rapid means of processing the great flow of data that reaches us.

We know that much information reaches us incomplete, out of context, or distorted in some way. It is possible to recognize that while constrictions occur to bar much of what we consider essential to good early childhood education, constriction is not prevention. Inadequate budgets, staff, supportive services, and materials are often strong barriers to good educational development. Most young children are now in inadequate programs, some of which are actually harmful.[6] Yet, people have always found ways to transcend obstacles. Because par-

6. M. Keyserling, *Windows on Day Care* (New York: National Council of Jewish Women, 1972).

ents are teachers' natural allies in finding optimum ways to assure children's development, the long-term prognosis is excellent for improving and developing quality educational programs for young children.

UNIVERSAL NEEDS OF YOUNG CHILDREN

The young child's basic needs continue to be universal and predictable no matter how rapidly social arrangements change. How to rear children so that they can adapt to swift changes in family life-styles and in ways of behaving challenges expert and parent alike. We know that different cultures have found many different ways to nurture

their young, and we can surely expect that our own ways will change in some respects.

All young children need warm, loving adults to help develop stable and continuous relationships. They need unconditional love from adults—not only love when they are pretty, or good, or clean, or bright. They need to experience being valued for themselves alone, not for their achievements or their promise of precocity or accomplishment. They need to experience the maturity of parental or adult love, that which accepts the growing, developing child, with his delightfulness as well as his problems, in sickness and in health, in good times and bad, as well as in tragedy. During World War II, English parents found that their children withstood the dreadful bombing of the cities when remaining with the family better than they did in the tranquility of country areas but without the family. It was thought that the safety of the countryside would be more important than physical closeness to family.[7] For short periods, safety might be temporarily more important than family relationships but apparently not for extended periods.

In our culture we stress individualism, with much less attention to group welfare. Other cultures stress the group and suppress the individual. Yet, with one extreme or the other, each culture has elaborate ways of meeting the child's basic needs for love, nurturance, and for the enduring relationships in a primary group, usually a family. In group settings, the child still needs to feel that someone knows and cares about him. He needs to have his person respected as one among other valued persons. He needs a balanced day, so that activity and rest are well provided for without overemphasis on either extreme. While children eat less than adults, they need more frequent replenishment of their energy sources. Many varied diets offer children their daily intake of the food components their bodies need, not only for replenishment but also for growth. Current practices avoid overfeeding children, and they teach early eating practices which stress nutrition, moderate eating habits, and avoidance of "empty" calories. Independence in feeding and in self-care are goals which are pursued in different ways. In a Montessori-type school, children learn to do much more in self-care and meal preparation than in other types of schools, especially where meal preparation is the prerogative of the cooks who do not care to share their duties with young children. Less

7. Anna Freud and Dorothy Burlingham, *War and Children* (New York: Foster Parents' Plan for War Children, 1944).

emphasis upon efficiency and more emphasis upon learning experiences may be one of many changes in the future of education.

Play is a necessary learning experience for all children.

Children need active experiences to use their growing muscles and to strengthen their growing concepts. It is action basically, not sitting and looking, or talking about something, which helps children to make intellectual progress. It is action which stimulates imaginative play. Play is one of the most important ways that children learn without being taught. In play, everything grows—mind, muscles, fantasy construction, and, usually, social skills as well. Stimulating activity usually requires materials and equipment. Even very simple things can be remarkably stimulating. Our sophisticated, television-fed children sometimes need novelty, change, surprise, and excitement so that they can go back to the really great simple things, where repetition seldom palls.

Children need to experience the people and the ideas of their time; educating is not isolating but, rather, is integrating and living fully. It is the child who is his own best integrator. No one else really has access to the child's mind or to the ways in which he makes patterns and meanings out of his encounters with people and things. But everything feeds this growth—sight and sounds, tactile and visual experiences, kinesthetic and taste experiences and, of course, people.

Children also need space—physical and emotional space. Crowding them is detrimental to good growth. Time is also essential; much will be resolved with growth and experience. While the child lives in the present and finds it difficult to conceptualize the past or the future, time can only take on meaning through time. By experiencing the repetition of seasons, days, and actions, the child begins to develop a sense of "before," or "later," or "tomorrow," and of patterns of occurrences.

Children also need challenge in order to grow, and the need to try different activities or behaviors, different ways of relating to other children and adults and to ideas and meanings. The challenge should not be a goad but rather the excitement of anticipation, the sparkle of seizing upon a problem. Above all, the child needs to be understood and accepted. Sometimes challenge is unbearable. Sometimes social considerations must be subordinated to personal considerations. It is necessary for the adult to understand the relative instability of early emotional development.

Students who like to be with young children, who enjoy a child's characteristic ways of behaving, are likely to be good candidates for learning to teach them. With such motivation and interest, learning to teach young children can open a lifetime of excitement and service in a demanding but very satisfying profession.

The early childhood educator has received specialized training to offer appropriate educational experiences to young children. Yet the child's early schooling cannot be separated from the life of the community, the nation, and the times in which the child lives. The child's educational experiences mirror in many ways the complex social life of which they are a part. The community, through the parents and the schools, seeks to adapt the children to the culture. But the nature of this socialization process emerges from the crosscurrents and conflicts of the times. No culture survives without the flexibility to meet new and unpredictable challenges and crises. The extent of adaptation to one's culture and preparation for the future are always very difficult decisions, interpreted in different ways by different groups.

Teachers must be familiar with their own communities and the conflicting values which exist. Teachers also need an awareness of the possible alternatives for adapting to changing social needs within the community. The acquisition and artful application of knowledge are the major part of any truly professional preparation.

This is a particularly exciting period in early childhood education. Teaching and learning are being studied in productive new ways, and there are many indications that breakthroughs are in the offing. There are indications that teaching is on the verge of substantial change in positive ways.

CHOOSING THE TEACHING PROFESSION

Some children grow up with unwavering certainty of their professional goals, and often the preferred goal is a teaching career, girls, especially, being encouraged to choose teaching. They also encounter so many women teachers that, liking many of them, they seek to emulate their selected models. Young girls often "play school" with each other and with their dolls. They just *know* that teaching will be their life goal. In other cases candidates are motivated by family pressures to select the teaching profession for security. Some students find their way accidentally or by default when they cannot decide on any other occupation.

Sex stereotypes of female teachers are gradually being replaced with more realistic models for young children. Men and women are needed as role models for children. We are moving away from the stipulation that one sex must project specific characteristics which are the opposite of those projected by the other sex. Characteristics of role models are personal and unique, not fashioned to fit people's patterns. A representational variety is now valued in staff composition. Often this requires a search for linguistic differences as well as age, race, ethnicity, and specific talents and skills.

It is often thought that teaching young children is easier than teaching older elementary children, because younger pupils are easier to manage and are not so intellectually challenging as older pupils. Yet teaching younger children may be more exhausting physically as well as emotionally and more challenging because of the necessity to keep up with the flood of research and new ideas in the field of early childhood education. Primary grade teachers know what a formidable task initial reading instruction can be. Instructional activities must be supported by adequate diagnosis, planning, and evaluation. Early childhood teachers must work in collaboration with staff and parents and are responsible for a good deal of screening and identification of possible learning disabilities. Since younger children are generally more vulnerable to the consequences of unskilled or inept teaching, needs for sensitivity in healthy nurturance are basic.

It has been said that a school should offer all children what a good and wise parent would want for his own child. Words come readily to mind. Parents want their children in school to be joyful, creative, friendly, enthusiastic, eager to go to school and regretful to leave, persisting effortlessly and tirelessly in their desire to learn. They want their children to experience sensitive, personal attention from teachers without becoming overly dependent. In fact, growing independence in self-care, in play, and in cooperative activities in the classroom

Professional expertise in teaching requires a multitude of characteristics.

sounds ideal to many parents. Parents also want the teacher to be fair, kind, and totally interested in their children's welfare. They want teachers to value each child for his own individual virtues, talents, and achievement, and for himself as a person. Does anyone embody all these ideal characteristics? Can teacher candidates learn to become so talented and skillful?

Of course, teachers are human beings just like parents, but parents look for professional expertise in teaching and for knowledge and skills that are not just intuitive and universal but which distinguish the profession of teaching. There is no doubt, however, that it takes a great deal of energy to spend one's days teaching young children. Flexibility, sensitivity, openness, and desire for continuous learning are also required. In addition, you cannot expect to be successful in early childhood classrooms if you really do not enjoy young children or are uncomfortable with them. Enough maturity to provide security and emotional support to the young, growing child is essential. You are unlikely to continue in early childhood education if the following apply to you:

Prefer quiet, sedentary occupations
Become rattled when several things are asked of you at the same time
Are uncomfortable when a room becomes messy and disordered
Cannot abide noise
Tire easily
Thrive on unvarying routines

To look on the positive side, you may be an excellent candidate for early childhood classrooms if the following apply to you:

Possess a good sense of humor
Enjoy challenge and problem solving
Prefer spontaneous to imitative behavior
Can juggle several activities without losing control
Do not feel threatened by immature behavior and needs
Can see progress even when it is minimal

Another consideration for determining whether teaching young children is your preferred age level is the requirement for helping children manage their physical needs at the table, in the bathroom, and in many other ways. For some candidates, this consideration is a deciding factor, since they prefer to work with children whose self-care is more mature. Other candidates, who see children's needs as varied and understandable, are ready to guide and teach immature youngsters in every way necessary.

Supervisors and administrators who hire day care teachers look for such characteristics as warmth, nonauthoritarian attitudes, flexibility, empathy for children, lack of prejudice, understanding and consideration for parents, intelligence, mature functioning as an adult with

Exposure to young children in groups can be helpful in the choice of a career in early childhood education.

outside interests, and capacity for further growth as a person.[8] Other preferred characteristics are the ability to encourage children's independence, responsibility, pleasant personality, and maturity.

How can you tell whether you are choosing this professional specialization wisely? Talk to teachers of young children, and be sure to discuss your questions about your career choice with a college advisor in the field of early childhood education. Most important, arrange for some field experiences in a day care center, a nursery school, a public school kindergarten, a children's playroom in a pediatric clinic, or the public library's children's room. Work with young children. Find out how you feel when a child hugs you, defies you, ignores you, or baffles you. Then go back and talk to your college advisor again. Discuss your feelings, your hopes, and your disappointments. Once you decide that you really enjoy working with young children and that you chiefly need to learn how and why, you are on your way.

SUMMARY   *The effects of rapid social change challenge early childhood education to assume new responsibilities and to adapt flexibly to changing social needs. Societal conflicts are inevitably reflected in values, procedures, and content of early education. With the expectation of a vast increase in educational facilities for young children in the near future, these social challenges offer teacher candidates the exciting prospect of moving with the times and helping to create high-quality programs to meet the needs which are being identified.*

Day care and other educational facilities for young children are expected to continue to meet the universal needs of young children while adapting in creative ways to contemporary thinking and values. Students who are attracted to the profession of early childhood education can view these current and prospective changes as guarantees that their work will be meaningful and responsive to social needs. The excitement and usefulness of this profession, however, should not obscure the teacher candidate's need to consider teaching requirements for physical stamina, enjoyment of young children's companionship, and the personal resources required to respond to the needs of immature, developing youngsters. Students are urged to discuss their interest in becoming early childhood teachers with college instructors, practitioners, and others and to seek some initial experience with young children in groups before making career choices.

8. G. S. Chambers, "Staff Selection and Training." In Edith Grotberg, ed., *Day Care: Resources for Decisions* (Washington, D.C.: U.S. Department of Health, Education and Welfare, 1971), p. 407.

✼ EXERCISES FOR STUDENTS ✼✼✼✼✼✼✼✼✼✼✼✼✼✼✼✼✼✼✼

1. Arrange a field placement on a regular basis for at least one morning or afternoon weekly, in a group setting for young children such as a day care center or a children's playroom in a pediatric clinic, a Head Start Center, or a public school kindergarten.

a. Keep a diary, and jot down after each visit to your field placement a brief summary of *what you did,* such as helping children to put blocks away, reading a story to a child, or helping children wash hands.

b. Keep a separate list of *problems* you encountered with children, such as how to handle a child's refusal to rest, to dress to go out to play, or aggression or conflict situations.

c. At the close of your field placement, write a succinct summary of your experiences for your college supervisor including:

(1) The kinds of activities you were permitted or encouraged to do

(2) The kinds of activities you were *not* permitted or were discouraged from doing

(3) Problems encountered with children

(4) Your *feelings* about your experiences, such as increased or decreased motivation to pursue early childhood education as a career, and your *reactions* to working with children

2. Read several of the articles in the bibliography on sex stereotyping in early childhood education. Write a brief report on your readings stressing *your own* reactions, agreements, disagreements, and reasons for your conclusions.

3. Write a very brief statement of your own philosophy concerning early childhood education stressing your views of its major goals and how children should be taught. This should be no more than a one-page statement.

a. Discuss your paper in a group seminar with your fellow students and determine which students seem to agree in their philosophic views. Committees might be formed to reflect each major view.

b. Either as a member of a committee or by yourself, read two of the articles in the bibliography on philosophy, such as Venable and any other title. Restate your philosophic position, as you understand it after your reading, especially concerning your *view of the child and of teaching.*

c. Discuss committee or individual reports in a group seminar with your college instructor.

✸ EXERCISES FOR TEACHERS ✸✸✸✸✸✸✸✸✸✸✸✸✸✸✸✸✸✸✸

1. Make a study of possible sex stereotyping in your classroom, list features in need of change, and list changes you wish to make.

a. Examine the children's literature you use.

(1) Are boys more often the central character?

(2) Are girls chiefly represented as interested in dolls and housekeeping, with boys as the active doers and heroes?

(3) What stories can girls identify with who are interested in sports, science, or space travel?

(4) What stories can boys identify with who are interested in cooking, art, and helping others?

(5) Do you need to add or borrow literature with less stereotyping of sex?

2. On the next occasion of parent conferences or an individual meeting with parents, plan to ask questions to elicit parents' values and priorities in goals of early childhood education. Communicate your sincere desire to elicit parent goals in order to insure that such goals receive adequate consideration. Tape record such conversation if parents consent, in order to analyze them further for identifying the following:

a. Apparent value conflicts

b. Variety in priorities of goals

c. Ways to include parents in discussions of articles, films, or other material on values and priorities in early childhood goals in order to broaden the information base common to home and school and to facilitate cooperative planning for school values and goals

d. Contrasts between your own philosophy and the views of some parents, and planning ways to further mutual accommodation

BIBLIOGRAPHY

Eiduson, Bernice T. "Looking at Children in Emergent Family Styles." *Children Today* (July-August 1974), pp. 2–6.

Frasher, R., and Walker, A. "Sex Roles in Early Reading Textbooks." *The Reading Teacher* 25 (1972), pp. 741–749.

Frazier, Nancy, and Sadker, Myra. *Sexism in School and Society.* New York: Harper, 1973.

Freud, Anna, and Burlingham, Dorothy. *War and Children.* New York: Foster Parents' Plan for War Children, 1944.

Golubchick, Leonard, and Persky, Barry, eds. *Urban, Social and Educational Issues.* Dubuque, Iowa: Kendall/Hunt, 1974.

Greenleaf, Phyllis Taube. *Liberating Young Children from Sex Roles: Experiences in Day Care Centers, Play Groups, and Free Schools.* Boston, Mass.: New England Free Press, 1972.

Grotberg, Edith, ed. *Day Care: Resources for Decisions.* Washington, D.C.: U.S. Department of Health, Education and Welfare, 1971.

Henry, Jules. *Culture against Man.* New York: Random, 1963.

Hillson, Marie, et al. *Education and the Urban Community.* New York: American Book, 1969.

Keyserling, M. *Windows on Day Care.* New York: National Council of Jewish Women, 1972.

Kimbrough, Ralph B. *Political Power and Educational Decision-Making.* Chicago: Rand-McNally, 1964.

Kohlberg, Lawrence J. "Development of Moral Character and Ideology." In *Review of Child Development Research.* New York: Russell Sage Foundation, I (1964), pp. 383–431.

Mead, Margaret, and Wolfenstein, Martha. *Childhood in Contemporary Cultures.* Chicago: University of Chicago Press, 1954.

Mitchell, Edna. "The Learning of Sex Roles through Toys and Books." *Young Children* 27 (1973), pp. 226–231.

Park, Joe, eds. *Readings in the Philosophy of Education.* New York: Macmillan, 1968.

Peters, R. S., ed. *The Philosophy of Education.* London: Oxford University Press, 1973.

Piaget, Jean. *Moral Judgment of the Child.* New York: Harcourt, 1932.

Rausher, Shirley R., and Young, Teresa, eds. "Sexism: Teachers and Young Children." New York: Early Childhood Council of New York City, 1974. (Pamphlet.)

Rose, Arnold M., and Rose, Caroline B. *Minority Problems: A Textbook of Readings in Intergroup Relations.* New York: Harper, 1965.

Saario, Terry N., et al. "Sex Role Stereotyping in the Public Schools." *Harvard Educational Review* 43, (August 1973): pp. 386–416.

Venable, Tom C. *Philosophical Foundations of the Curriculum.* Chicago: Rand McNally, 1967.

Weitzman, Lenore J., et al. "Sex Role Socialization in Picture Books for Preschool Children." *American Journal of Sociology* 77, (May 1972), pp. 1125–1150.

Whiting, Beatrice, ed. *Six Cultures.* New York: Wiley, 1963.

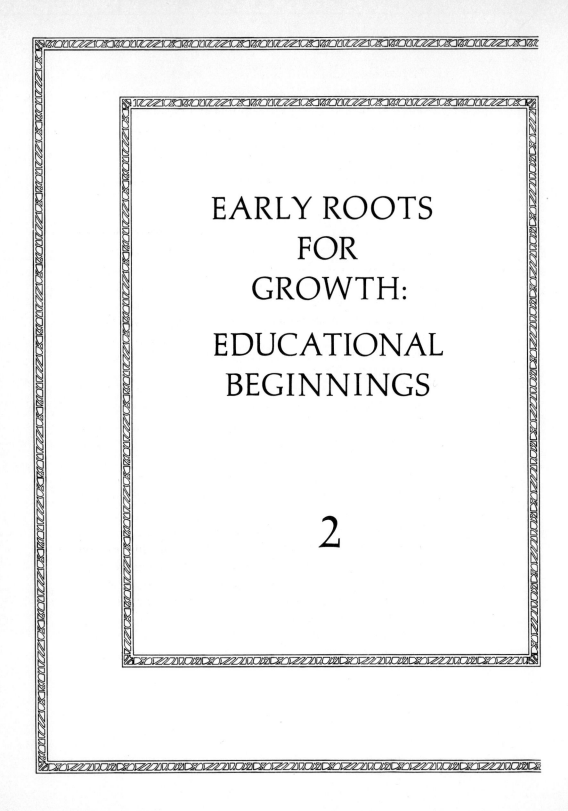

EARLY ROOTS
FOR
GROWTH:

EDUCATIONAL
BEGINNINGS

2

Parents are usually the only ones who really see the beginnings of their children's development. Except for the youngest of infants, teachers see children whose development is already in the process of becoming. Early roots for growth are stimulated as soon as the baby is born, and his educational beginnings occur mostly in his crib at home. When the child enters a group setting, the teacher perceives (usually) an attractive youngster who is appealingly immature and dependent upon adults.

For students planning to teach young children, the most important truth about a child's early development is that there is unknown but positive potential for learning and growth; no one ever uses his full potential. Starting from this basic principle, teachers of young children must learn to accentuate every possibility for progress toward maturity. At the same time, areas of weakness—slow development or deficit—can be identified for strengthening, amelioration, or bypass.

The most visible characteristics of the young child are physical features such as height, body shape and size, coloring, facial expressions and body gestures. When the child is in motion, additional perceptions of him are based on his style and pace of locomotion. When he speaks, a further dimension emerges, revealing his linguistic skills and uses of language. When he plays with objects or with children, some of his social skills, characteristic social approaches, and play interests and fantasy development can be noted. Should he be confronted with a problem, and his reaction observed, we see a partial indication of his cognitive skills and his response to problems. If we follow him to the art media or to musical activities, we see some samples of his expressive work. Yet these are all behaviors of the same child, and the more we see how he functions, the more unity we perceive of his development and personality.

EARLY CHILDHOOD DEVELOPMENT

Child development, it has been pointed out, includes both a visible and an invisible type of growth. Visible growth is seen as an "increase in the body size and change in its shape and proportions."[1] Invisible growth processes are usually assumed or inferred. Yet there is a large subjective element to our perceptions of the child, over and above the more physical. We respond to the child, we catch his moods and feelings, and we become involved with him in countless ways. We soon know much more about any child than just his physical manifestations of behavior.

Many children suffer from growth-retarding factors such as inadequate nutrition, diseases, or various kinds of physiological malfunctioning or psychosomatic problems. Good preventive medicine for children and their families would include very early screening for every possible type of physical and psychological problem and any environmental deterrents to growth. Should such screening occur early enough, therapies could begin sooner or approaches could be identified to ameliorate, cure, or bypass growth-retardant conditions. However, the lack of such early screening is closely related to the maldistribution of services in our society, and in the world at large.

One of the most growth-retardant conditions extant in the world today is poverty. If children's care, physically, medically, nutritionally, and psychologically, is primarily a factor of parental income, it is not surprising that a disproportionate share of the world's child ills is concentrated in poorer segments of any community.

Poverty is a primary factor affecting child development and achievement in school.

At a recent national conference on preventive medicine, Dr. Lawrence E. Hinkle, Jr., of Cornell University Medical College, reported that poverty and illness were associated with high rates of infectious diseases, environmental chemical hazards, and mental illness. In fact, according to the *New York Times* story on this conference. "Children born and raised in poverty were likely to be smaller, slower to develop, and lower in achievement in school."[2] Poorly educated parents were considered as less likely to provide the stimulating environments most conducive to intellectual growth than parents who are better educated.

1. I. G. Macy and H. J. Kelly, "Chemical and Physiologic Growth," in Paul Henry Mussen, *Handbook of Research Methods in Child Development* (New York: John Wiley, 1960), p. 252.
2. *New York Times*, June 10, 1975, p. 48.

The effects of environment, as well as internal physical processes, upon children's development have been well-documented.[3] Studies have shown, for example, that early experiences, which children have at home, of being read to by their parents contribute to success in development of reading skills at school.[4] Hess and Shipman showed that middle-class black mothers were far more effective teachers of their own children than black mothers from poor families.[5] Poorer mothers tended to issue commands rather than give reasons and to use verbal cues very little. Thus, there are many ways in which children's home experiences, before and during their school attendance, affect their motivation, interests, and linguistic and cognitive achievement at school.

In addition to understanding the differentiated effects of genetic and environmental history on children's school progress, there is a more universal effect on children's ability to learn, which is generally termed *developmental*. This term refers to the qualitative changes in children's growth and capabilities as they mature and their abilities and characteristic functioning approach that of adults. Development is biological in that children are born with genetic possibilities. However, it has been well-demonstrated that biological development is always a product of the environment and its interaction with natural endowment. For the most part, development can only be determined by what actually happens, not by what might have occurred. Students need to understand and perceive developmental processes well enough to plan environments and teaching strategies for the various children in their groups that are neither too simple and unchallenging nor too confusing and complex.

Developmental sequences have been studied regarding many aspects of perception, including part-whole distinctions, closure for incomplete forms, perceptual constancy of size, shape, and color, and perception of movement, of quantity, and of other features of objects. Generally, researchers find that young children are often subject to illusions which decline with age, or they can make few differentiations where older children and adults can make many, or that the

---

3. *Developmental Psychology Today*, 2d ed. (New York: Random, 1975), pp. 52–6.
4. Dolores Durkin, *Children Who Read Early* (New York: Teachers College, 1966), pp. 93–103.
5. R. D. Hess and Virginia Shipman, "Early Experience and the Socialization of Cognitive Modes in Children," *Child Development* vol. 36 (Chicago: Aldine, 1965), pp. 869–886; and R. D. Hess and Virginia L. Shipman. "Maternal Influences upon Early Learning: The Cognitive Environments of Urban Pre-School Children," in R. D. Hess and R. M. Bear, *Early Education* (Chicago: Aldine, 1968), pp. 91–103.

young child has difficulty perceiving incomplete forms whereas older children and adults readily do so.[6] There seem to be a myriad of ways in which experience, maturation, and the interaction of these two forces account for the great differences in functioning between young children and more mature persons. Yet students might be aware of the fact that research findings change to some extent as a result of more sophisticated technology and research methods. Despite changes in any specific details on how young children differ in functioning from adults, the differences are very real and noticeable. When teachers forget these substantial differences, young children's reactions to incorrect assumptions of their capabilities serve as reminders.

Realizing that young children are qualitatively different from older children and adults alerts teachers to expect young musculature to demand more activity. Their language development will require tremendous verbal usage. So also, their emotional instability will demand considerable support from loving adults to stay within bounds and, gradually, to fluctuate with fewer extremes.

Optimistic attitudes of teachers stimulate growth.

Optimistic attitudes of teachers are functional, since these attitudes are conveyed in so many ways to children. Realizing that children will attempt to meet teacher expectations, which may become self-fulfilling, teachers of the young must make a moral commitment to optimism. Upon reflection, it should be evident that such a commitment is realistic. Most children grow up and turn out well despite depressing and unstimulating environments and even when their early development seems turbulent and unpromising. As for the children who will not turn out well, no one can predict with any certainty which children will overcome environmental and developmental problems. Helen Keller reached unpredictable heights of achievement, despite her afflictions of blindness, deafness, and dumbness. Many of our great men and women overcame early deprivation, sensory deficits, and many other types of affliction. Therefore, teachers of young children must be realistically optimistic toward the possibility that time, experience, and perhaps new resources yet to be discovered will help most children to realize good growth and development.

A change in one aspect of functioning is bound to affect functioning as a whole. Fit a hard-of-hearing child with a hearing instrument and

6. Eleanor J. Gibson and Vivian Olum, "Experimental Methods of Studying Perception in Children," in Henry Paul Mussen, *Handbook of Research Methods in Child Development* (New York: John Wiley, 1960), pp. 311–373.

changes occur in speech, activity, interests, and social and cognitive skills. Gently help a fearful child separate from his mother and he is free to make friends and become joyful in his play and creative in his use of materials.

INDIVIDUAL DIFFERENCES

In addition to optimistic expectations of children's development, another major principle of importance to teachers of young children is the uniqueness of each child and the great range of individual differences within the "normal" areas of functioning as well as beyond normality. While children will usually be in groups, classes, or units of some kind, mass teaching of young children is usually unproductive. There is so much variation in interests, attention spans, and experience that every group situation must adapt in some way to the individual children who comprise the group. If students report on their classroom visitations that they observe a great deal of mass teaching which seems to be delivered to a group as a whole, they should also identify unmet needs and negative effects.

As a teacher candidate, you enter happily into your field placements to observe children, to participate in various classroom activities, and gradually to practice teaching under the supervision of a classroom teacher. At first, the sheer joy of acting in professional ways as a developing teacher casts a rosy glow on the children. They are so small, so attractive, and so lovable. They nuzzle and play and seem to be totally involved in continuous action.

Each child is a complex person with a unique personality.
Soon the "class" of children dissolves into distinct individuals. Some children are "stars"; everyone wants their friendship. Others seem to be rejects. One child defines himself by demanding incessant attention from adults. Another leaves a trail of tears and howls wherever he goes. Usually, there is at least one child who seems to be in a world of his own. Every field experience emphasizes the differences among children. The need to teach children as individuals becomes increasingly clear, though the means may be somewhat obscure. You find yourself automatically labelling children as very bright, verbal, creative, or dull. Your intuitive assessment may or may not be accurate. The young child is a complex person with a history of development and experience and a recognizable personality.

It is difficult to avoid prejudging young children. It is easy to endow a physically attractive child with every virtue and to shower so much encouragement upon that child that he seems to take on every desirable characteristic. It is not dangerous to make a child feel greatly valued; it is dangerous to make a child feel valueless. Considerable damage results from unconscious discouragement or direct messages that tell a child he really is not valued.

At the start of a school year, some student teachers feel very uncomfortable with undisciplined young children and blame the teacher for poor skills in behavior control. Such feelings usually change dramatically within a few weeks, because the children seem to adjust quickly. In a very short time, group relationships become apparent, where there seemed to be no relationships before except for positions of conflict. After several years of teaching, you can meet a class of children in September and shortly after have a fairly accurate picture of what they will be like in June, with far more self-discipline, skill, and sophistication.

Early observations of children help to chart their individual differences so that the teacher will feel more secure in efforts to challenge some children, to reassure others, and to sustain certain kinds of behavior while modelling and encouraging different ways of classroom interaction. Various aspects of child development are discussed in the next section as a basis of teacher observations of children.

APPLICATION OF KNOWLEDGE OF CHILD DEVELOPMENT

Child development theory and research are the sources of most of our understandings and expectations about children's potential and their sequence of development. Knowledge of natural growth and developmental sequences and stages helps teachers to use coherent ways to pattern expectations for children's functioning. This knowledge also helps the teacher to identify levels of functioning so she may make tentative diagnoses about potential needs. These diagnoses are extremely important to efforts to match appropriate forms of teaching and environmental designing to children's probable learning needs.

Knowledge of developmental stages is important for identification of a child's needs.

Teachers, however, have many different ways of teaching and organizing learning activities. Many suggestions are detailed in the succeeding chapters of this book. This chapter includes a summary of major aspects of child development knowledge which early childhood education emphasizes in the patterns fashioned for learning in group settings. Teachers apply this knowledge to identify and encourage strong roots for growth, to assure optimum ways to nurture and stimulate each child, and to keep long-term goals in mind in their day-to-day planning and teaching.

Play

Children's play and its important functions in child development, detailed in Chapter 3, is explored here for its signals and messages to teachers for child needs. Murphy notes that the disturbed child's play is similar in content to that of normal children but that it differs in structure, style, and cohesion.[7] Teachers are not expected to diagnose emotional disturbance, since this is the function of specialized personnel. But teachers invariably note children who do not seem to play at all, who play much less than other children, or whose play seems to be very different, disorganized, or otherwise deviant.

Gifted children seem to include more intellectual than physical activities in their play; their play is more like that of older children, and they often prefer older playmates.[8] Children with higher intelligence also seem to spend more time in concentrated play.

Imaginary playmates are common for children under six, although mothers are more likely to know about these than teachers, since many children prefer to discuss them only with trusted adults. To a sensitive, unobtrusive teacher, a child might wish to explain who his imaginary playmates are and how they behave. One four-year-old had a set of three imaginary chipmunks who accompanied him almost everywhere for a short time. His teacher had to learn to inquire where they were, in time to prevent his raging anger that someone was sitting on one of his pet chipmunks. Suddenly, he lost all interest in them and refused to say anything about them. Some teachers fear that encouraging such imaginary play will deflect the child from a desirable reality orientation, but such fears are groundless except for an occasional child who has severe emotional problems. For most children, the use of fantasy is generally considered one of the necessary steps in development, since fantasy play is one of the ways in which children test and investigate reality, sometimes with consider-

Fantasy is considered a necessary step in development.

---

7. L. B. Murphy, *Methods for the Study of Personality in Young Children* (New York: Basic, 1957), p. 245.
8. Susanna Millar, *The Psychology of Play* (New York: Basic, 1968), pp. 140–200.

able distortion. Piaget calls this phase of development *assimilation,* or the investing of oneself in self-interpretative ways in trying to comprehend reality.[9] *Accommodation,* the opposite phase, according to Piaget, is the attempt to pour one's ideas into molds that conform more to reality. Both assimilation and accommodation are considered as two sides of the same coin leading to *adaptation.* He indicates that a balancing occurs and recurs continuously, between the child's fantasy and idiosyncratic ideas of what the world is like and reality-oriented reshapings of such ideas. It takes time, experience, and the effects of social interactions, which bring other people's ideas forcefully to the child's attention, to work out these continuing balances and imbalances.[10]

Millar points out that anthropological studies have indicated that children's play chiefly reflects the richness of the cultural heritage, as shown in the cultural levels of adults, with variations often dependent upon climate, diet, health, and characteristic activities of the culture.[11] However, the child's play also reflects the confusions, misunderstandings, unorganized bits of information, and immaturity of conceptions which are usual in the young. Hence, children's play is not only a major child learning and functional form of behavior, it is also enormously informative to the teacher. It points to possible teaching and learning needs of various kinds such as lack of specific experiences, immature perceptions of others' feelings and thoughts, and problems of aggression and of cognitive and socioemotional development.

Children's play goes through recognizable sequences, usually, from solitary forms of manipulative and often very repetitive play with objects to beginnings of play adjacent to, if not with, other children. This is called "parallel" play. It is as though children enjoy being near other children but do not have the interest or social skills to combine efforts with others. Soon more social forms of play develop, even among three-year-olds. More organized and better-sustained forms of social play can be seen among four-year-olds, and fives are quite enterprising in planning and carrying out multicharacter dramatization or play with objects of various kinds. Before social play becomes well-established, children sometimes seem to be playing together, although each child appears to be following a separate script

9. Jean Piaget, *Play, Dreams and Imitation in Childhood* (New York: Norton, 1952), p. 274.

10. Piaget, op. cit., p. 215–244.

11. Millar, op. cit., pp. 248–249.

without any give-and-take or coordination of character or plot. With experience and guidance, sociodramatic play develops, often in long sustained sequences and with a sizable cast of characters. A great deal of this dramatic play seems quite imitative of the adult world as seen by young children. Also, television's impact is especially strong on young avid televiewers.

Some children seem to remain "onlookers" for a long time, unwilling or unable to join in associative or cooperative forms of play. Onlookers are often secret participants who seem to experience the play vicariously even though they play only an audience role. But children learn a great deal in such a role and usually take courage sooner or later to participate actively. Teachers sense when there is a desire to become more actively involved, and often they help by bridging a way into other children's cooperative play. One group of older three's had been playing a "boat" game for weeks with the same cast of characters. They played they were a family that lived on a boat. They trooped on and off the boat and, while on the boat, they chiefly went through eating and sleeping motions with occasional attention to steering the boat. A small onlooker had begun to look wistful and was making tentative approaches to the boat players, but the latter were too absorbed in their play to notice him. The teacher approached the boat players, trying to find some peripheral role for the onlooker to play to help him connect with the sociodramatic play. She held the hand of the onlooker, reassuringly and protectively, while she gently probed the play situation. The teacher inquired whether this family lived on the boat all the time or whether they had a house in which to sleep. The players insisted they lived on the boat all the time except when they went swimming. "Who delivers your mail?" asked the teacher. The children were interested in this question but had no response. "Here is a mailman who can come to your houseboat every day and deliver your mail," the teacher said. The boat players accepted this suggestion matter-of-factly, and the onlooker became their link with the shore, delivering mail on a very frequent schedule. His role gradually changed to a less peripheral one.

Physical development

Since children develop from the head down, hands and legs follow development of the upper part of the body. Development is always in the same direction but very individual as to pace. Pace of development may be rapid for one child during the third year and relatively sluggish during the fourth. Three- to five-year-olds are usually experiencing a great deal of large-muscle development, especially in the arms and legs, and daily vigorous forms of exercise are indicated by this growth. Six- and seven-year-olds usually show a height and weight spurt as well as notable fine-muscle skills.

Program schedules must take into account the way children grow and develop, keeping sedentary periods brief and few and furnishing as many opportunities as possible for exercise of growing muscles and physical skills. Small muscles develop later than the large ones, indicating later capabilities for writing and small-muscle control. Development is a continuous process, although it sometimes appears as though the child is growing in fits and starts. Actually, skills are constantly growing and becoming better organized and more complex, although the process may not be obvious until the child starts to do something new and different. According to Bernard, development is most rapid, for the most part, during the early years.[12] This rapid development, which takes place so early in the child's life, is another reason for maintaining stable support during rapid change, and for expectancy of behavior improvement.

Physical growth includes increasing height, weight, speed of movement, and coordination.

Another major principle of physical growth includes direction of growth from the center outward. For example, during the baby's first year, control of the leg precedes control over movements of the foot. In addition, a child's physical skills become more differentiated, that is, he can do more things. Not only can a child do more things, he can also combine or integrate physical skills into more complex skills, for example, riding a bicycle. During the early childhood years, physical growth includes increasing height, weight, strength, speed of movement, and coordination.[13] The child is capable of more sustained physical activity, with more stable respiration and physical growth in the direction of more adult proportions. While physical growth patterns are considered as primarily hereditary, physical growth is also affected by various environmental influences, especially by nutrition and health. Immunization from childhood diseases which formerly crippled or killed many children can now insure a much healthier childhood for all children. However, children from poorer families sometimes do not complete immunization sequences

12. Harold W. Bernard, *Human Development in Western Culture,* 4th ed. (Boston: Allyn and Bacon, 1975), p. 65.
13. *Developmental Psychology Today,* pp. 187–190.

or miss them entirely because of parental preoccupation with survival at low income levels.

Physical skill development plays an important role in children's feelings of competence and it affects their social development. The child who is clumsy and slower than others in the group is likely to feel helpless and inadequate. He may be rejected in his efforts to form friendships or to enter play situations. Teachers can help such children make progress in their physical skills by sensitive teaching and praise for every bit of progress. Encouraging such children in forms of skill practice such as running, throwing a ball, or using a pair of scissors effectively, with gentle guidance and considerable repetitive practice, can result in positive total development.

Sex determines the rate of children's physical development, and, on the average, girls are smaller and lighter than boys. However, by age six, girls normally are further developed cognitively than boys. As a result, they often outperform boys in reading instruction and tend to be favored in the largely feminine world of the primary grades in school.

In group settings, where teachers plan for individual children and assess their progress on a continuing basis, there is no place for favoritism for girls over boys, brighter over slower children, or healthier over children with physical problems. Each child must be viewed as a distinct person, and the child who has greater needs offers a greater challenge to the skills and expertise of the teacher.

The vast majority of people in the world are right-handed—approximately 5 percent of any population are left-handed. Some children are ambidextrous, choosing the right hand for some skills and *Teachers need* the left for others. The prevailing principle is to allow the child to use *to be alert to* whichever hand he wishes to use for any skills, without correction or *problems of a* interference. Teachers, however, need to be alert to problems en- *left-handed* countered in this right-handed world by left-handed children. Small *child in a right-* scissors can be ordered in left-handed versions, and these are usually *handed world.* made with a distinctive colored handle to distinguish them at a glance from right-handed scissors. Left-handed children are more comfortable at meals if they have a corner seat that leaves them free to use their left hands without bumping other children's right hands. Teaching children various skills such as shoelace tying or writing must be adjusted to handedness. It may help right-handed teachers to consult left-handed staff members for some suggestions for teaching manual skills to left-handed children.

Stages of development

Erikson and Piaget have developed helpful but different theories of children's growth through a succession of stages. Piaget's stages relate primarily to cognitive development, while Erikson's are chiefly concerned with personality and psychosocial development.

Piaget's theories of growth relate to cognitive development; Erikson's theories relate to psychosocial development.

Erikson divides man's lifespan into eight stages from birth to death. In the baby's first year, the first stage is described as one in which trust versus mistrust is the essential struggle. If this stage is well-resolved, it leads the baby to trust people and to feel secure and cared for. In the two- to three-year period, according to Erikson, autonomy versus doubt must be resolved. The notorious "no" period around two-and-a-half years of age is regarded as a clear example of the toddler's struggles to do things himself and to feel in control of his body and his environment. Teachers working with two-year-olds are faced with fine points of decision as to how far to let a toddler proceed before intervening. Erikson's next stage, ages four to five, revolves around initiative versus guilt. At this stage of development, it is necessary to provide many choices of activities for the child. Successful attempts on the child's part lead to a good sense of initiative rather than a sense of guilt, a result of poor resolution. The child who feels free to act in constructive ways and who gets involved in many kinds of active learning is seen as one whose family has handled this stage successfully. The fourth stage, industry versus inferiority, occurs from ages six to eleven and covers the grades where so much industry and energy is invested in producing things and in completing tasks. Later stages have to do with identity, intimacy, generativity, and, in old age, integrity.[14]

The Erikson Theory is an attempt to explain personality patterns and psychosocial development based primarily on how families respond to children's successive growth stages. Each stage, he points out, has its own major features and requires its own unique guidance. These stage-developmental theories, however, are just as helpful to teachers as to parents and psychotherapists. They suggest the goals of each stage and describe the desirable outcomes of sensitive, nurturant management.

Erikson's analysis helps the teacher to understand and articulate such desirable features of programs for young children as exclusion

14. Erik Erikson, *Childhood and Society*, 2d ed. rev. (New York: Norton, 1963).

of formal modes of instruction, which undermine the sense of initiative of younger children and their conviction of autonomy. Providing choices for young children in group settings and honoring their selection of activities is another feature of desirable programming that Erikson supports through his emphasis on the children's "freedom" to engage in activities. Erikson's emphasis is upon guiding and nurturing behaviors of the young child which are most adaptive for eventual successful development in personality and in interpersonal relationships. Therefore, his theory constitutes a major support for teachers who are learning how early childhood programs can support optimum development for young children.

PROBLEMS OF AGGRESSION

Early childhood classrooms have various problems of aggression to deal with. There are problems concerning children's immature perceptions of others' thoughts and feelings, the violent content of much sociodramatic play, conflict situations, and lack of social experiences.

Immature perceptions of others' thoughts and feelings

Flapan's study on how children perceive and infer other people's thoughts, feelings, and intentions showed that a definite shift took place around age nine.[15] Six-year-olds, the youngest children studied, seemed to be chiefly aware of gross, overt actions and to remember and note "opening and dramatic incidents" more than the detailed sequences. The nine-year-olds, by contrast, used more causal explanations and more interpretations and inferences of the nuances of people's feelings and intentions. Teachers of young children are reminded, from such studies as Flapan's and numerous others, how much can *not* be taken for granted in what children perceive, understand, or infer in their social relationships. Additional research has clearly established the great difficulty that young children experience in trying to take another person's point of view. Piaget calls this "egocentricity," or the child's self-centeredness, which precludes his ability to perceive how others think or feel. This self-centeredness begins to decline as the child approaches age six but, as Flapan has shown, most children in their social relationships are unable to perceive much that is not explicit before age nine.

Flapan's research indicates the limitations in young children's perceptions in social relationships.

In helping children to live amicably in groups in the classroom, teachers apply their knowledge of children's social development and perceptions of others by making demands on children that do not overshoot their capabilities. The younger the children, the less one asks them to share, to take turns, or to understand how a friend feels when he is hurt. Prevention is more effective than punishment or instruction at the earlier ages.

As children's friendship efforts bear fruit and they begin to enjoy group activities without too much conflict, simple rules for behavior become possible to follow, though more for some children than others.

15. Dorothy Flapan, *Children's Understanding of Social Interaction* (New York: Teachers College, 1968), p. 65.

Positive suggestions or directions are more beneficial than negative ones. Even hitting is more easily reduced or eliminated when children are helped to acquire alternative means of expressing anger or frustration. It helps to give children acceptable objects to hit. It also helps to role play with children (but not before age four) to teach them to use more verbal and less physical ways to express their feelings. Social behavior is especially affected by modeling or imitating of the behavior of others.

Bandura points out six mechanisms which alter behavior by indirect reinforcement.

Bandura's research indicates that the teacher's own behavior, or the behavior of another child who is praised or rewarded for desirable behavior, has a potent effect on the children whose own behavior is not directly challenged. He points out that, according to social learning theory, there are six ways in which vicarious reinforcement helps to change behaviors. These six mechanisms are informational, environmental discrimination, incentive motivational effects, vicarious conditioning, modification of model status, and valuation of reinforcing agents.[16] The informational mechanism helps the child figure out which behaviors are likely to be condoned or rewarded and which are not. The environmental discrimination feature helps the child to understand that the same behavior may not be appropriate in all situations, so that what is permissable, where, and when becomes clearer. The incentive mechanism reflects the child's desire to be rewarded in the same way that he sees others rewarded; if he imitates the behavior of others, he too may be rewarded. Vicarious conditioning refers to the indirect way in which the child avoids adverse consequences by adopting the behavior of the rewarded models. Rewarded models take on higher status, so the child may be adopting the rewarded behavior in order to improve his own status or to partake of the higher status of the rewarded model. Valuation of reinforcing agents refers to children's perceptions of the actions of adults, or others who are reinforcing agents, as fair or unfair. Children are more likely to value the fair reinforcer and to be positively influenced to improve their behavior.

Teacher candidates learning to handle problems of aggression in early childhood groups can try to observe classrooms where social learning techniques are used well so as to learn many positive ways of encouraging young children to develop more desirable ways of behaving, without shaming, punishment, or tension.

16. Alfred Bandura, ed., *Psychological Modeling* (New York: Aldine-Atherton, 1971), pp. 1–62, especially pp. 49–51.

Aggression is not always a negative factor in child development. Storr points out, "It is easy to accept the idea that the achievement of dominance, the overcoming of obstacles, and the mastery of the external world, for all of which aggression is necessary, are as much innate human needs as sex or hunger."[17] Viewing the role of aggression in personality development as a positive force to help a child have courage, persistence, and drive, teachers can learn to accept these positive consequences, while guiding children to eliminate the negative features of too much physical conflict and infringement upon the rights of others.

It is not unusual for teachers to observe a very shy, dependent child suddenly become transformed into a very aggressive one. If the teacher handles it well, this usually can be seen as progress, as a change of behavior which ultimately leads to more maturity and self-control. It is positive for the child to take initiative and to feel confident to move into situations where he can interact with others. If the nature of this initial interaction is negative, the intention and the effort can be encouraged while the child is guided to more acceptable forms of interaction.

Violent content of play

Many teachers are repelled by the violent content of much children's play, even though it is "make-believe" violence and the dramatic play is well within the classroom bounds. According to many developmental psychologists, it seems reasonable to conclude, however, that such content is chiefly a function of the constraints imposed on young children from the time they approach school age. If the children organize their play with mutually agreeable roles the same child is not always playing the same role, there will be rotation of role playing and variety in each child's experience. Sometimes teachers can help children distribute roles more equitably so that role-taking decisions themselves do not become constant points of conflict. In the process of playing a "good guys against the bad guys" theme, the children are likely to discharge a great deal of emotional and physical energy without any violence other than the content. However, in the interest of stimulation and guidance, teachers may wish to introduce

17. Anthony Storr, *Human Aggression* (New York: Atheneum, 1968), p. 19.

other material for children's consideration so that the sociodramatic play may develop further and serve varied purposes.

It must be recognized that our culture has been oversupplied with themes of violence on television. Since children's dramatic play tends to mirror the content and themes of the culture in which it is embedded, it can be seen that it is no small matter to moderate the violence in children's play content. Despite the large push children experience from the culture at large toward such themes of violence, the classroom can usually introduce such interesting and involving material, through experiences and trips, that the violence in the play content subsides and sometimes disappears entirely.

Conflict situations

Some children are aggressive in play to an undesirable extent because they have not previously had much social experience or because the kinds of play they have previously experienced may have lacked adult guidance. Lack of experience in play situations with other children is easily remedied by exposure to the group setting, since this is one of its strongest features. When children are playing together, the teacher plays a moderating role to insure that more fearful or shyer children are not dominated entirely by the aggressive ones. A small boy in a public school prekindergarten program refused to remove his hat for the first week of school, and he was quick to hit any child who as much as tried to touch his hat. Eventually, it was discovered that he came from a neighborhood where even a four-year-old knew that any property not well-secured was likely to disappear. He was not taking any chances with the new hat his mother had charged him to protect against theft. This child soon felt sufficient trust in his teacher and in the group to be persuaded to hang his hat in his new cubbie where he was always welcome to find it and wear it. Too fervent self-protection, protection of one's property, or action to prevent deprivation of preferred toys often reflect the child's previous experiences. Some children may fear that they will be overlooked or forgotten, as they may have been in the past, unless they act aggressively to claim their rights. The teacher learns to "read" the child's forms of aggression and the context in which they occur, and she will confer with parents to understand the behaviors properly. Some behaviors may reflect sibling rivalries at home.

Some male observers in early childhood classrooms say that women teachers of young children tend to "feminize" the boys by prohibiting "puppy play" and forcing boys to behave in more feminine ways. If this seems to be a sexist view of child behavior, it is surely an attempt to skew the sexism in the opposite direction from the usual one. Male points of view should be helpful to female teachers, because these are more likely to spot the one-sidedness of behavior fostered by women. If puppy play is acceptable in the classroom as a playful way of fighting, should it not be acceptable for all children, not just for boys? Should the girls be encouraged more in physical forms of self-defense? What about physical forms of aggression? What is socially desirable?

It is no longer acceptable to stress "ladylike" behavior when this means false and insincere ways of behaving. Neither can we accept a need for boys to be quick in physical self-defense as compared with girls. If self-defense is a desirable community goal, all children can undoubtedly improve their skills in this respect. In regard to offensive behavior, it is generally agreed that whether they are male or female all children can learn to discipline and decrease it.

Natural and spontaneous forms of behavior, not harmful to the child or to his playmates, need not be discouraged. We can feature the child's uniqueness by muting needs for conformity except where an important purpose is served such as health or safety.

Controlling aggression

Overaggressive behavior can be controlled by the teacher through use of a number of devices, among them the following:

Size of the group
Personal attention and focus of the teacher
Adequacy of space and materials
Extent of choices of activities
Wise grouping of children to separate aggressive children from each other
Interage grouping where the older children exert pressure for, and model, more mature forms of behavior
Plentiful opportunities for self-expression and discussion of feelings
Experiences of empathy from the teacher
Deflection or diversion from undesirable behaviors
Teacher modelling of desirable behavior

The small group enables the teacher to give each child a great deal of personal attention, to hear his requests and comments, and to respond in very personal, relevant ways. When the group is large, attention usually goes, not to the conforming children who are exercising self-restraint with great success, but to the nonconformists who are not. It does not take an overly bright child to see that if he wants attention in a large group, the best way to get it is to "act up" or misbehave. A few teachers know how to reward conformists, and they ignore nonconformists in a large group to raise the conformity quotient. But most teachers find it difficult to ignore the nonconformists, thus giving them the attention they want while berating them for misbehavior or meting out punishment. Some children would rather be noticed and punished than not noticed.

There are many reliable methods for controlling aggressive behavior.

Therefore, a fairly reliable way to decrease misbehavior, especially conflict situations and aggressive behavior, is to cut down the size of the group in which the child is placed. When a large group must be assembled, to prepare for a walk in the neighborhood and to review rules for crossing streets, the teacher's personal attention to potentially difficult children often prevents open aggression. The teacher learns to place herself near children who need more continuous guidance, because her mere presence is often enough to maintain peace.

Adequate space and materials help to avoid conflicts. If a child encroaches on another's territory in play situations, there is likely to be an uproar from both sides. Blockbuilders often lack adequate space for large horizontal structures or for the exciting dramatic play that accompanies or follows the construction activity. Scarce materials or equipment often become a focus of conflict if turns are too long or infrequent or if the equipment is so desirable that young children cannot bear waiting for turns. When such equipment is newly introduced, turns can be very brief to avoid conflicts for possession of the prized objects. Thereafter, turns must follow a procedure children understand and consider fair. There will continue to be children who cannot bear to wait. One remedy to reduce the pressure on highly prized scarce material is to introduce additional desirable objects. If this remedy fails, it may be best to withdraw scarce items until the children develop more interests and can manage the turn taking required.

The more that children choose their own play activities in the area they find of most interest, the less conflict there is likely to be. However, sometimes a group of aggressive children converge on the block corner regularly and create frequent conflicts. In such cases interage groupings are very helpful in that older children can demonstrate more approved behavior and help younger children to be more controlled and to follow approved procedures. If the possibility of integrating younger and older children is not feasible, the teacher needs to stay very close to such a volatile area and exert controls, and cue children in expected behaviors. An alternative to reduce a group's volatility is to control the actual composition of such a group—so that children are assigned to a specific group for block play or other popular activity to prevent conflicts from developing.

Teacher modelling of desirable behavior requires a cool presence in the midst of heated action by the children. Talking quietly and slowly, the teacher verbalizes the actions, demonstrates approved forms of interaction, praises children's moves in the desired direction, and helps everyone maintain an even temperament. It is important to avoid blame or punishment so that children will feel more virtuous and will gradually behave better.

Another strategy is to discuss problems immediately after they occur. This requires accepting all expressions of feeling while pointing out why some ways of acting are dangerous, unfriendly, or undesirable. "You really were angry back there, Steve," the teacher might say. "Why were you so angry?" This gives Steve a chance to explode verbally, especially helpful if he had been prevented from physical expression of his anger during the preceding incident. The teacher makes it clear that everyone's feelings are legitimate, but feelings are contrasted with actions. The teacher might suggest an exercise in "how else can we let a friend know we're angry" if the children are neither too young nor excited. This also deflects angry feelings and conducts them into more verbal outlets.

With some children, diversion is the best strategy. Knowing that Donald is not easily deflected from angry actions, the teacher diverts him from the center of activity. The diversion is likely to be more successful if it is real, such as an unexpected need to go next door to borrow a stapler or to send the office a message on the intercom, something most children love to do. When Donald returns from his prestigious errand or chore, he is likely to be proud and happy and his anger forgotten.

The aggressive child frequently learns to moderate his aggression when he finds that it is either unnecessary or not functional. In fact, most teachers find that it is not the overaggressive children whose behaviors are the most difficult to change, but the fearful, withdrawn ones who draw very little attention to themselves consciously. These are the children most in need of being sought out and helped.

COGNITIVE DEVELOPMENT

The sequential, orderly growth in the child's intellectual functioning is invariant, as Piaget has so clearly demonstrated.[18] The developmental psychologists agree that "there is a developmental shift in judgment activity from dependence upon sensory-perceptual properties of tasks or stimuli toward reliance upon inferential or conceptual manipulation."[19] This shift generally seems to occur around ages six or seven.

Piaget's analysis shows how much the young child is bound by his senses and is unable to reject the appearance of things through the use of logical thinking. When water is poured from a tall, thin jar *Before age six,* into a low, wider one, the child says there is less to drink because that *children gen-* is how it appears. Actually, as Piaget points out, the child is only *erally have* looking at one of the two dimensions involved, only the height, not *difficulty* the width. If he were able to coordinate the height with the width, *making infer-* he would soon be able to perceive that, in fact, there is no change in *ences based on* the amount of water. But perceptions are less reliable and more sub- *logic when* ject to numerous forms of distortion than is logic. With logic, the *these contradict* child would be able to ignore the ambiguity of the change, "Does the *perceptions.* width really compensate for the height?" by *reasoning* that there must be the same quanitity, no matter how it looks, because no water was added or taken away.[20]

Almost every object in the early childhood classroom provides the child with opportunities to test his perceptual notions, to discover gradually where these lead him astray, and to develop the reasoning ability he needs, for reliable, logical thought. More testing and reasoning is likely to occur when the teacher understands her role in stimu-

18. Jean Piaget, *The Origins of Intelligence in Children* (New York: International University Press), 1952, passim.
19. Eugene S. Gollin, "A Developmental Approach to Learning and Cognition," in Lewis P. Lipsett and Charles C. Spiker, eds., *Advances in Child Development and Behavior,* vol. 2 (New York: Academy, 1965), p. 172.
20. Jean Piaget, *The Child's Conception of Number* (London: Routledge and Kegan Paul, 1952), pp. 1–17.

lating it, designing an environment which features such intellectual activity, and guiding children to organize their ideas into more coherent patterns and forms through appropriate activities.

Before age six, young children's perceptions are in many ways "unschooled." They find it difficult or impossible to identify familiar forms when these are represented incompletely or partially. Learning to read pictures and symbols is a prime goal in early childhood classrooms; and is more urgent in neighborhoods where families are not knowledgeable about this cognitive need and neglect it. Not only do young children lack previous experiences to draw upon, they also have difficulty making inferences on logical grounds. They move in slow progression from intuitive and less stable forms of reasoning to more logical reasoning in concrete situations by about ages six or seven on the average.

Many researchers emphasize playful, exploratory activities as particularly rich in opportunities for cognitive growth. Play, being voluntary and highly involving, provides unmatched motivation. Explorations with objects helps to dispel the "magical" causes children tend to rely upon. If the nail "doesn't want to go in straight," the child gradually learns, as his own skill and control grow, that the nail has no independent will. "Animistic" thinking of this type, that is, attributing personal qualities to objects and forces, also declines as children explore, try out, argue, contest each others' ideas and, little by little, give up the more infantile varieties.

Teachers provide activities and opportunities for children to discuss their findings. Without telling children what they should think, teachers help children to figure out what happened and to find their own ways to verbalize their understandings. Often, these teacher-led discussions provide children with an opportunity for a new experience —to put their ideas into such shape that they can talk about them, ask questions, and answer them. Chapters 7 and 10 offer many teaching suggestions for children that stimulate cognitive growth.

SOCIOEMOTIONAL DEVELOPMENT

The child's characteristic ways of feeling and reacting to his experiences and to other people constitute his emotional structure. How the child relates to people is considered the area of social interaction. Since in group situations the child's customary forms of social behavior reflect his emotional concerns and structures, emotional development is often viewed in the social or group setting of the school.

Preschool children are usually learning just as much about *feelings* as they are about thinking and doing. Emotional development follows a widening course, with the children acquiring more differentiated emotions and learning to associate them, with some flexibility, with various kinds of events and people. School is new to the young child. He often comes with a "wait and see" attitude: "If I don't like it, I won't stay." Usually, he quickly learns to like school because he can play with playmates in a pleasant, safe but stimulating environment. Sometimes, he brings a negative attitude, based on previous unhappy experiences in separating from home and mother. Some children, perfectly capable of separating from their mothers, are held so close by the mother that separation is balked. School is usually the child's first away-from-home experience on a regular basis. Here, he has to learn a new set of behaviors with a new group of people.

Some children learned at home to cling to anger and temper tantrums to get their own way. At school, these behaviors soon become nonfunctional. The child begins to learn to contain some anger, to forego temper tantrums, and to try to win playmates. The child learns to care whether or not his best friend is in school or stayed home because of an illness. He learns that other children sometimes do not choose to play with him unless he fits into the play activities they have already developed. The more the child learns to enjoy playing with other children, the more motivation he acquires to act in ways that are acceptable to them. The child develops a more flexible mode of working with others as they demand more of him in adaptability. Compassion grows very slowly but it is helped by teacher modelling. Children learn to like more people and to express their feelings in ways that are increasingly acceptable in social groups.

In all aspects of social development in the group setting, the teacher's modes of creating rich environments for learning are decisive for guiding children toward more mature, friendly, and peaceful forms of coexistence and cooperation. Teachers who establish and maintain an ambience of friendliness and mutual helpfulness rarely complain that children in their classes are difficult and quarrelsome. The teacher's sensitive guidance helps the children to a more stable level of emotions. Sascasm, irony, and teasing are notably absent from settings where good socioemotional development is observed. Sincerity prevails in such settings, but so does empathy. The teacher might say

Teacher model-ling plays an important role in socio-emotional development.

to a child, "I know you are angry. I know you wanted to punch Eddie because you didn't like what he did." The teacher does not deny real feelings. Neither does she say, "Big boys don't cry." A crying child is not in need of further shaming. He needs a way to stop and to do something more effectual. He may need to learn how to verbalize his feelings, to discharge them in ways that are not harmful to others. Teachers learn to be matter-of-fact and to make firm but friendly statements. The child achieves great relief when he is prevented from hurting others by a teacher who is mature enough to restrain him without punishing him.

Teachers learn to control the schedule at its most vulnerable points —during transitional periods, when children are most likely to go out of bounds because their own energy levels are declining and they are becoming less reasonable, and because the expectations become more ambiguous. When a child returns to school after an illness or an extended absence, social learnings have to be renewed, with some support from the teacher, until the routines and group procedures become reestablished.

Fears must also be accepted as real. By accepting children's feelings, teachers can plan ways to help children outgrow and discard irrational fears. Many children have a fear of the dark or of being injured, or they fear animals or imaginary creatures.[21] Children learn to overcome some of their fears in the school setting. Regular, happy experiences with animals, for example, tend to purge fears of animals. Books and stories help many children to anticipate strange and frightening events by becoming familiar with details and picturing what is likely to happen. Discussions of common experiences such as fear of the darkness help children to face their worries, to name them, and to learn that other children also share these fears. Similarly, children learn to anticipate such common needs as having injections, visiting the dentist, and, sometimes, preparing for hospitalization and surgery. Discussions and readings are straightforward, realistic, and detailed. Nightmares shrink in size when children fashion verbal keys to exorcize them. Children's own experiences in school help make the unfamiliar more familiar in countless ways. It is then possible to face more of the unknown with some confidence.

When children's fears do not yield to familiarization procedures, parent conferences sometimes reveal the probable cause. Children

21. D. Bruce Gardner, *Development in Early Childhood. The Preschool Years* (New York: Harper, 1964), pp. 235–241.

often imitate parental expressions of fear of thunder and lightning, of medical visits, and of other events. Parents are often eager to learn how to avoid infecting children with their fears. Teachers and parents can help a child acquire some useful way to handle their own or others' fears. In some cases, children are encouraged to live with moderate fears in a variety of ways: learning that other children share this fear, talking about it, singing a special song when the fear is evoked, or taking a specific action such as clapping one's hands, tapping on an object, or making jokes about it—which may be the most potent method of all. "Whistling in the dark" happens to be a way of handling one's fear of the dark. One pretends not to be afraid by whistling. One teacher developed a "thunder chant" for her four-year-old class that proved very helpful during thunder-storms because the children had to accompany the chant with a simple Indian dance having strong accents, thus making it difficult to concentrate on the thunder and lightning.

Social gains in the group depend on program components. Some programs encourage and teach social skills to a greater extent than others. Culture, child personality, and teacher modelling are all important features of the social development goals and potential progress. The group setting is capable of stimulating a great deal of socioemotional growth if initial demands are equal to children's capabilities and growth is paced to developmental realities.

Some parents are satisfied if their children learn to say "please" and "thank you." Most teachers in contemporary programs stress children's learning the emotion and the action rather than stressing verbalization of kind words. The words are too easily acquired and the emotions are not. Real gains in social skills reflect some maturation and learning, some ability to identify with a group, and constraint for relatively short periods. Social skills are enhanced by declining egocentricity, out of some sense of other peoples' feelings and some beginnings of empathy with and sympathy for others.

GOALS FOR LEARNING

Some teachers like to make lists of child progress goals, to be approached with all of the activities and plans for learning during the school year. Some types of goals are specified in this chapter and are categorized as affective, physical, language, cognitive, and social goals.

Affective goals

Separate successfully from parents for the daily school session.

Enter freely into activities chosen from among those offered in the classroom.

Express needs and find ways to meet them.

Behave with reasonable emotional balance.

Relate to adults without extreme dependency.

Accept, offer, and seek help that is needed.

Cooperate with the group, for group purposes.

Offer and reciprocate offers of friendship.

Accept differences among children and adults as natural without affecting anyone's dignity and value as a human being.

Express ideas and feelings freely, verbally, and in socially acceptable ways.

Accept reasonable limits on behavior, for safety and for respecting the rights of others.

Use problem-solving procedures to find solutions to the many problems met in daily classroom living.

Physical goals

Be independent in toileting, eating, dressing, and undressing.

Tie shoelaces, and zip, button, buckle, or take care of other clothing needs.

Take reasonable care of one's clothing and outer garments.

Wash hands before eating.

Control art, writing materials, and other small-muscle equipment at reasonable levels.

Gently handle books and materials to reduce wear and tear.

Safely use large-muscle equipment such as climbing apparatus, bicycles, and blocks.

Independently use swings, including "pumping," and use walking boards and sand and water materials without help.

Pour juice and serve oneself without mess or spills.

Join in games, dances, walks, trips, and group activities with adequate physical skill, stamina, and control.

Throw and catch a ball.

Hop on both feet and on one foot.

Skip and run.

Walk a designated path forwards and backwards.

Do a somersault.

Jump over objects of various heights and widths.

Walk sidewise (shuffle and crossover steps).

Toss a bean bag to hit a large target at a reasonable distance.

Place pegs on a pegboard in some patterned way.

Clap rhythmically.

Language goals

Speak spontaneously and freely.

Speak fluently in one's first language.

Understand and speak English fluently.

Use adequate vocabulary to express ideas and feelings.

Use adequate vocabularly to name colors, shapes, and quantitative concepts.

Speak without immaturities in articulation or word use.

Verbally express relations of quantity, space, and time.

Use language to express fantasy and imaginative ideas.

Use standard English syntax when it is appropriate.

Follow oral directions.

Recognize and write one's full name.

Identify, discriminate, and write letters of the alphabet, both lower and upper case.

Read some selected words in a sight-word vocabulary.

Use selected phonic word attack skills.

Use picture, configuration, and context clues to story reading.

Enjoy listening to stories, retell and dramatize stories.

Succeed in beginning reading tasks, and in continuing reading skill development.

Cognitive goals

Become task oriented and persist at tasks for reasonable periods.

Complete puzzles of reasonable complexity.

Create, copy, and complete patterns of various kinds with pegs, blocks, beads, and many other materials.

Complete tasks requiring use of quantitative, spatial, or other relationships.

Sort and classify objects and seriate objects at reasonable levels of complexity.

Match objects on a one-to-one basis.

Seek cause-and-effect relationship experiences with concrete objects.

Differentiate and identify common geometric shapes.

Compare and contrast objects, symbols, and events on specified or selected attributes.

Use numerals and quantitative concepts to refer to objects and operations.

Social goals

Take turns and share.

Cooperate in small- or large-group activities of reasonable duration.

Maintain silence for brief periods when necessary.

Volunteer to initiate or complete group activities or follow a leader.

Follow rules reasonably well.

Request exemption from rules when necessary.

Contribute to group planning.

Interact courteously with others.

Use socially approved forms of expressing anger, hostility, and other emotions.

Make friends among the children and relate to the adults in reasonable acceptable ways.

If you make lists, remember that these goals are flexible; they represent only a specification of the kinds of skills and learnings most children can grow toward in school settings. Lists provide a framework for observing children in the classroom, on the playground, or on arrival or departure. The major purpose of any usable list is to help identify the level children have reached in relation to the goals of any program. Lists may vary from the suggestions made above; goals are universal in some respects but particular in others. Some groups stress individual achievement over social skills or literacy over cognitive development. The community plays an important role in goal or value emphasis, as indicated in Chapter 1. Other important variables in addition to community values are the ages of the children, their previous experiences, and the facilities of the school. The younger the children, the more likely that the stress will be on health, safety, nutrition, and physical and social development.

The fact that all forms of teaching and learning have multiple effects upon young children is well-established. However, in any particular setting, some factors may be emphasized more than others.

A professional attitude toward children's potential for learning is essential. It is similar to the attitudes of other helping professions such as medicine and social work. The major purpose of a helping profession is to improve functioning in any way possible, while maintaining the child's good feelings about himself, or helping him to a better self-concept as he learns and grows.

Teachers can strengthen childrens' early growth toward life-long learning and self-actualization by effectively applying professional skills to identify children's levels when they enter school and to stimulate progress toward more mature forms of behavior.

SUMMARY *Teachers can view young children in group settings as already involved in the process of learning and growing, with unknown but positive potential. A positive view of each child's possibilities requires accentuating and supporting early roots for growth. It is equally important to identify possible areas of weakness, for strengthening, amelioration, or bypass.*

Children's progress is easily seen in its physical manifestations, but motivation, interests, linguistic and cognitive skills are less apparent without detailed knowledge of children's functioning. Poverty is one of the most growth-retardant conditions in the world today. Yet developmental and environmental possibilities support optimistic attitudes that most children can turn out well.

In addition to optimistic expectations of children's development, early childhood teachers accept the uniqueness of each child and the great range of individual differences within the wide area of "normality." Learning the sequences of child development helps the teacher to accept each child at his current level and to anticipate probable growth and learning with appropriately supportive and educative procedures. Children's play is stressed as a major function of child development in cognitive, emotional, and physical areas and provides clues to teachers about child progress and needs.

Children's physical development patterns must be appropriately accommodated in order to support natural growth needs. Piaget's theory of cognitive development and Erikson's theory of psychosocial development both help teachers to understand and nourish early growth needs. Problems of aggression and social development can be moderated or solved in many ways in the group setting. Specifying goals for children's learning helps the teacher plan, observe, and evaluate children's progress.

❦ EXERCISES FOR STUDENTS   ❦❦❦❦❦❦❦❦❦❦❦❦❦❦❦❦❦❦❦

1. Read Erikson on developmental stages.

    a. For the first four stages, write in your own words two examples of successful and unsuccessful outcomes in family settings.

    b. For each successful outcome example in (a) above describe a school learning setting which is likely to support successful outcomes.

2. From the developmental descriptions in this chapter, and their applications to teaching, select ten specific features of early child development that teachers must take into account in planning their programs. For each feature, give an example of productive application in teaching.

3. Read one of the Piaget references on cognitive development.

    a. In your own words, write a brief description of the process of intellectual development, in Piaget's theory, especially defining such terms as assimilation, accommodation, adaptation, stage, schema, and perception-bound.

    b. Based on your statement of Piaget's theory of intellectual or cognitive development, list at least five "do's" and five "don'ts" for teaching strategies.

4. View at least three children's television programs.

    a. describe the content of each program.

    b. List "magical," supernatural, "animistic," or other features contrary to natural occurrences.

    c. List "fear-inducing" features noted.

    d. List the incidence of violent acts in each program or other material you regard as undersirable.

    e. Write a brief summary of your observations; include suggestions for improving each program.

✿ EXERCISES FOR TEACHERS   ✿✿✿✿✿✿✿✿✿✿✿✿✿✿✿✿✿✿

1. Compare Piaget's theory on cognitive development, as described in one of the bibliographic items, with your own practices in dealing with cognitive development.

a. Plan brief but similar interviews (of a Piaget clinical type) with at least five children in your class on a topic such as:

(1) What's "alive," what isn't, and how can we tell?

(2) Could we call a table by another name, and if so, what, and why? (Consult the Piaget titles in the bibliography.)

3. Tape these interviews if possible. If not, jot down, as precisely as possible, children's responses to your prepared questions. Don't hestitate to probe with further questions, for example, "How can you tell?" or "Why?"

b. Analyze these interviews and summarize *what* children seem to understand and *how* they reason.

c. Based on your analysis, identify any teaching plans you are using which are based on assumptions contrary to your findings, and plan to change these in appropriate ways.

2. Make a list of items from this chapter that indicate children's developmental needs which teaching must take into account, and identify one or two of these needs which you think require more attention in your own teaching. Jot down a list of ways these selected items can be featured in your teaching.

3. Select a television program popular with the children you teach, try to view it once or twice and then elicit from at least five children their attitudes, understandings, and reactions to this program. Prepare a checklist for your interviews with children, with such items as:

a. What is it about?

b. Tell me the names of some of the characters.

c. Is it scary? Why?

d. Is it funny? Why?

If possible, discuss this project with parents of the children and develop a collaborative plan to study children's televiewing habits and any effects that can be identified by parents such as nightmares or related fears.

BIBLIOGRAPHY

Bandura, Alfred, ed. *Psychological Modeling.* New York: Aldine-Atherton, 1971.

Bernard, Harold W. *Child Development and Learning.* Boston: Allyn and Bacon, 1973.

Bernard, Harold W. *Human Development in Western Culture.* Boston: Allyn and Bacon, 1975.

Biehler, Robert F. *Psychology Applied to Teaching.* 2d ed. Boston: Houghton Mifflin, 1974.

Brearly, Molly, and Hitchfield, Elizabeth. *A Guide to Reading Piaget.* New York: Schocken, 1966.

Comer, James P., and Poussaint, Alvin F. *Black Child Care.* New York: Simon and Schuster, 1975.

Developmental Psychology Today. 2d ed. New York: CRM/Random House, 1975.

Erikson, Erik H. *Childhood and Society:* 2d rev. ed. New York: Norton, 1963.

Flapan, Dorothy. *Children's Understanding of Social Interaction.* New York: Teachers College Press, 1968.

Flinchum, Betty M. *Motor Development in Early Childhood.* Saint Louis: Mosby, 1975.

Furth, Hans G. *Piaget and Knowledge.* Englewood Cliffs, N.J.: Prentice-Hall, 1969.

Gardner, D. Bruce. *Development in Early Childhood. The Preschool Years.* New York: Harper, 1964.

Gelfand, D. M., ed. *Social Learning in Childhood: Readings in Theory and Application.* Belmont, Cal.: Wadsworth, 1969.

Gibson, Eleanor J., and Olum, Vivian. "Experimental Methods of Studying Perception in Children." In Mussen, Henry Paul. *Handbook of Research Methods in Child-Development.* New York: Wiley, 1960.

Gollin, Eugene S. "A Developmental Approach to Learning and Cognition." In Lipsett, Lewis P., and Spiker, Charles C., eds. *Advances in Child Development and Behavior.* New York: Academy, 2 (1965).

Inhelder, Barbel, and Piaget, Jean. *The Early Growth of Logic in the Child.* New York: Harper, 1964.

Kohlberg, Lawrence, and Mayer, Rochelle. "Development as the Aim of Education." *Harvard Educational Review* 42, (November 1972), pp. 449–496.

Lynn, David B. *The Father: His Role in Child Development.* Monterrey, Cal.: Brooks/Cole (Wadsworth), 1974.

Hess, R. D., and Shipman, Virginia. "Early Experience and the Socialization of Cognitive Modes in Children." *Child Development* 36 (1965),: pp. 869–886.

Mussen, Paul Henry. *Handbook of Research Methods in Child Development.* New York: Wiley, 1960.

Mussen, Paul Henry. *The Psychological Development of the Child.* 2d ed. Englewood Cliffs, N.J.: Prentice-Hall, 1973.

Piaget, Jean. *The Child's Conception of Number.* London: Routledge and Kegan Paul, 1952a, pp. 1–17.

Piaget, Jean. *The Origins of Intelligence in Children.* New York: International University Press, 1952b.

Piaget, Jean. *Play, Dreams and Imitation in Childhood.* New York: Norton, 1952c.

Storr, Anthony. *Human Aggression.* New York: Atheneum, 1968.

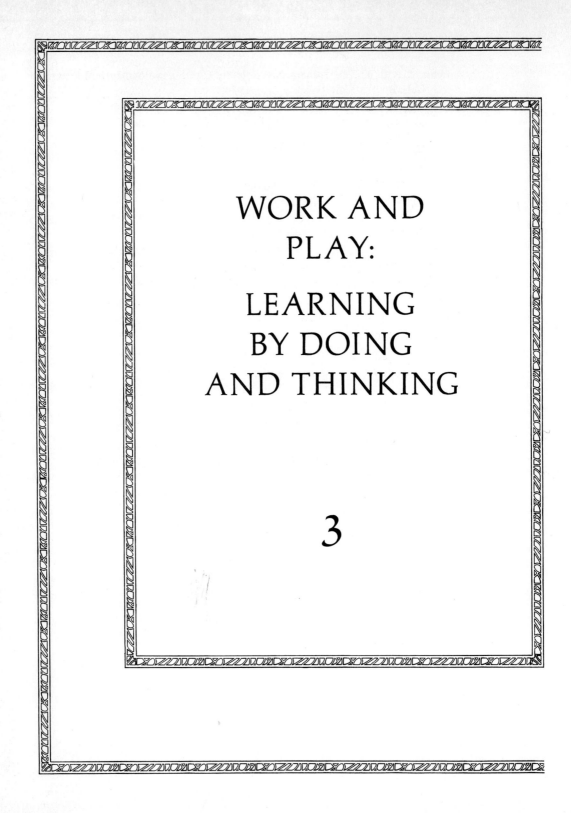

WORK AND PLAY:

LEARNING BY DOING AND THINKING

3

Children play as naturally as they breathe. Anything can be a toy. Babies delight in banging spoons on cooking pots. Young children "make believe" they are adults, heroes, princesses, bad guys, or sometimes puppies. A stick can be an airplane and a stone can be a delicious dinner. Play is children's work.

Four-year-old Sabrina enters her prekindergarten public school classroom, goes directly to the chalkboard and writes, almost legibly, "Mississippi" and "houses." Sonia enters the same classroom and runs to the housekeeping corner to dress up in "mommy" clothes and to "cook" dinner at the toy stove. Is Sabrina's activity *work* and Sonia's *play?* Is one more important than the other? Why should children play in school, when they can do so at home? These are major considerations in early childhood education today and are likely to continue to stir research, discussion, and controversy for some time to come.

Students who are preparing to teach young children will find it very useful to have clear understandings of the values and functions of children's play. These understandings are basic to planning good activities and programs for young children and for explaining and illustrating these functions and values to parents, supervisors, and visitors. Some examples are in order, first, to help sketch the dimensions of play, and the nature of skillful teaching roles in guiding play.

DIMENSIONS OF PLAY

Since dramatic play and block play are among the least structural types of children's play in school—often with the maximum of non-intervention and minimum of obvious teacher direction—play in these areas offers good illustrations of the range of child play activities and of effective teaching roles in children's play.

Dramatic play

Dramatic play, or sociodramatic play (with more than one child), is a form of improvisation which young children use to a very great extent. It is distinguished from creative dramatization or from the more common forms of dramatization in that there is no script and the children invent the dramatization as they go along. *Dramatizations* usually require enacting roles already defined, usually in writing, with actors' lines predetermined. Plays are the usual form of dramatization. A *creative dramatization* is usually done without a script, but is based on one, and is very freely enacted, with the actors recreating the action and the lines in their own words but within the meaning of the original.

Dramatic play is a form of learning by spontaneous role playing.

The *dramatic play* of young children does not require lines, scripts, scenes, or properties. One child, by himself, may sometimes be observed in dramatic play, enacting some sort of make-believe sequence or activity. However, as soon as young children in American groups begin to move beyond parallel play (where they play side-by-side but not with one another), some sort of social dramatic forms of play emerge. Some three-year-olds begin to play together in this way although, unless they are good friends and have played together a great deal, the dramatic play may quickly disintegrate because of a lack of ability to keep the give-and-take going in mutually satisfactory ways. Three-year-olds are often unable to adapt to each other's ideas sufficiently to interact in role playing or make-believe actions or representations for any sustained forms of dramatic play. But they repeatedly attempt to develop such abilities. Fours and fives usually manifest considerable skill in dramatic play.

By the time young children have developed the social and cognitive skills to act out roles, they also find anything handy useful for make-believe properties, costumes, and scene furnishings. Most schools for young children encourage this form of social dramatic play by providing a housekeeping area which suggests the kinds of experiences most familiar to the children—the varied activities of a family at home. With more imaginative teaching, additional familiar areas of child experience are suggested or recreated in the classroom, new experiences broaden the children's knowledge about life experiences, and children are stimulated and guided to use their abilities in more complex and original ways.

Examples of dramatic play.   In a kindergarten in central Harlem in New York City, five boys playing in the block corner made a construction that covered half the floor space. They had used every block of a large collection to make a floor and two walls, to enclose a space inside of which they had placed rows of small chairs. The boys, sitting on some of the chairs inside the enclosed space, at first pretended they were in an airplane. They used blocks as microphones to send messages. Suddenly, almost without warning, the play changed completely and the structure became a police bus. Instead of airplane noises, the boys now made piercing siren noises. Two girls came along, noted the police play, and joined it by playing "dead." The boys pulled them into the "bus." They used blocks as guns, making loud sounds of guns shooting. While the boys argued about whether the girls were sick or dead, the girls tired of their passive roles and left the block area.

The teacher can augment dramatic play by taking several constructive steps.

In this dramatic play sample, the children were enacting some familiar material, derived from television, with a great deal of physical action but not much conversation. What can a teacher do with such play material? In this case, the teaching strategies included the following:

Observation—looking and listening carefully.

Participation—intervening by taking some role consonant with the children's play material.

Open-ended questioning—asking questions which suggest further possibilities to children.

Planning—planning for further field and classroom experiences such as a trip to the local police precinct, a visit to the classroom by a policeman, and the use of books, films, or filmstrips concerning police work.

Materials collection and construction—helping children develop and objectify their ideas by finding or making additional props.

Having observed the play episode in the block corner involving the "police bus," and watching it soon run out of steam, Miss Brown joined the play, role playing a citizen in need of assistance. She addressed the group as "officers," said she had lost her little boy who had gone out to play, and asked for assistance to find him. The block corner was instantly galvanized into action. The children were immediately joined by others, attracted by the teacher involvement as well as the action. As the children pretended to search on shelves, in corners, and under tables, the teacher began to ask open-ended questions: "Is there any way you can let a lot of people know we're looking for my little boy?" "If you find a little boy, how will you know it's my boy?" "Who else can help us?" "Do you have any special machines or equipment that might help us?" The questions were well-spaced and in no sense constituted a bombardment. They did stimulate a great deal of conversation among the children, between the teacher and individual children, and from children in the block area to others in other play areas. They also stimulated much more "acting." One boy used a block as a bullhorn to bellow, "A little boy got lost! Miss Brown's boy is lost!" One boy used a block as a microphone, "transmitting a message": "Calling all cars! Calling all cars." When Miss Brown inquired what that message meant, the child was confused and unable to explain. Here was a clue pointing to a need for clarification.

As the physical activity subsided, Miss Brown led a discussion with the blockbuilders about the work of policemen, eliciting from them their understandings and experiences. She took notes as they talked about the questions they phrased, the confusions they demonstrated, and the nature of information to be pursued. She made plans with the group to visit the local precinct, to invite a local policeman to visit the classroom, to find books, written material, film and filmstrips about the work of policemen. They also talked about policemen's uniforms, chiefly caps, badges, belts, and holsters, and planned to collect and make some uniforms.

The teacher planned an assessment of this project because she was curious to find out what it might produce in the way of revealing *attitudes* toward policemen, *knowledge* about police work, and *vocabulary* in a group which largely used rich vernacular dialect. She constructed an instrument, chiefly using quickly drawn stick figures, to elicit favorable or unfavorable attitudes, connections (by drawing lines) to various kinds of work, and naming of pictures, mostly magazine cutouts. Only the latter required individual questioning, while the first two parts were completed with small groups of children.

It is not suggested that all block or dramatic play episodes involving so much time, attention, and detail be pursued by the teacher. However, some dramatic play can be developed, with predictable effects on children's subsequent development of action, characterization, play development, use of known information, and search for new information.

Note that the dramatic play described above happened to occur in the block corner, although it could just as well have occurred anywhere else in the classroom where there was sufficient space for dramatic play, chairs, and a few props. The blocks were minimally used for construction possibilities, and the teacher responded, in this case, to the dramatic play opportunities, not to the further development of block construction. In this instance, the teacher might just as easily have responded to the block play in preference to the dramatic play. These two kinds of play usually influence each other, although a great deal of dramatic play goes on without any block play at all. On the other hand, it is unusual for blockbuilders to explore only the constructional aspects of block play, without some dramatization involving the block structure.

Examples of block play. A block play episode was recorded in a prekindergarten group of four-year-olds fairly early in the school year. A boy was sitting on the floor in the block corner, pushing a small miniature car back and forth and making car noises but making no attempt to build with blocks. The teacher strategies used in this play area included the usual *observation*, to note what the child was doing and what direction his play seemed to be taking, some *specific suggestions*, some teacher *modelling*, and *open-ended questioning*.

In this case, the teacher joined the child and sat on the floor next to him, saying, "Oh, you're playing with a car. Would you like to make a road for your car with the blocks?" The child nodded assent but made no move to build, apparently unfamiliar with blocks for play construction. The teacher put two blocks down, end-to-end and then asked the child to hand her any blocks he thought would make a good road. After he had selected three blocks, the teacher suggested they change places so she could hand blocks to him, if he would indicate which blocks he wanted. The child very quickly became involved in the block construction and needed no further help in selecting blocks and in placing them on his developing road.

Once deep involvement had occurred and before leaving the child to work out his own ideas, the teacher injected a few open-ended questions to guide him, such as "How big a road will you make?" and "Where does this road go?" The teacher checked back now and then, to continue to project her interest to the child in his construction and to find out whether she might add any further stimulation to the activity. She refrained from further intervention, however, having succeeded in her goal—to involve the child in block construction so that he would explore its many fascinating possibilities and become skilled in some initial forms of construction. Teacher intervention is not always welcome or wise. It helps to get children *started*, to *redirect* children who sometimes use blocks in unsafe or undesirable ways, or to *stimulate* further development when play is becoming so repetitive that the children become bored with the materials. Other occasions for teacher intervention in the block area include the *management* of behavior problems there, *helping* children who are not customary blockbuilders to play when they wish to and *suggesting* block construction when it seems an effective way for children to realize some growing conceptions such as those involving spatial relationships.

Various teaching roles guide play activities to serve the child's developmental needs.

In a parent cooperative nursery school where a mother, Mrs. White, was "participating" (assisting the teacher), she was directed to work with the blockbuilders—four boys arranging an elaborate construction of walls, towers, and roads. "Just tell me how I can help," Mrs. White told the blockbuilders, among them her son Jim. The strategies that Mrs. White used, which she had often observed the teacher use, included *observation* of the children's play, asking *open-ended questions*, making relevant *suggestions*, and *participating* in carrying out those suggestions the children accepted.

Jim, an experienced blockbuilder at home and at school, quickly told his mother, "We need some signs. Will you make them?" Her response was, "What kind of signs? How should they look?" The four boys stopped to consider this question of road signs. After some discussion, they decided to tape the road signs to quadlong blocks, which they placed vertically to create "intersections," and to make some signs at the carpentry bench for entrances into the limited-access roads they were building. With the help of the tools and wood at the carpentry bench, the boys constructed these signposts, and Mrs. White helped to write road names with a felt-tipped pen, and one of the boys decided to copy and use them. The tape dispenser was located by one boy, and all signs were soon securely fastened to some sort of signpost.

Sensing the great involvement and interest of the children in this project, Mrs. White felt secure in asking further questions, in effect, making *suggestions:* "Are there any traffic lights on these roads?" When told there were none, she added, "How about toll booths? Do drivers have to pay tolls?" The boys were delighted with the idea of toll booths, well within their own experiences of suburban living, driving over bridges, and paying bridge or road tolls. They promptly started to construct toll booths. They asked Mrs. White to help them make "tickets" for the toll booths. After they decided the toll was a quarter, two of the boys stopped to help cut tickets and write numerals. The teacher came by at this point, admired the construction, and suggested that the boys, who had been developing these ideas over a three-day period, might like to have it photographed while it was still intact. This was obviously a well-received suggestion, and several photographs were immediately taken, with and without the boys within their structure. Mrs. White stayed with the construction until clean-up time put at an end to the play, but she asked the teacher's permission to let the boys stay long enough to dictate to her the story about their structure, which they had been verbalizing about so freely all morning. She tape recorded their story to be sure to get all the details and transcribed it on a large piece of newsprint while the children went out to play on the playground. Upon their return, they immediately ran to the block corner, where they were pleased to see their structures still intact and the photographs and the large story taped to the wall behind the construction. They insisted upon having it read to them immediately by Mrs. White.

VALUES OF PLAY

Observation of play can lead to selection of teaching strategies to enhance children's learning opportunities.

Notice that the play episodes described above all included teaching strategies of various kinds *based* on the children's play. In many cases, the play is observed unobtrusively, and the teacher deliberately refrains from intervening if it seems better to let the children work out their own play ideas. Sometimes, the teacher guidance occurs before the playing, sometimes afterwards. Once the child is involved in constructive play activities, the teacher can form some hypotheses about the child's needs and interests. Plans for the child's progress can follow.

There are several powerful reasons for encouraging children to play

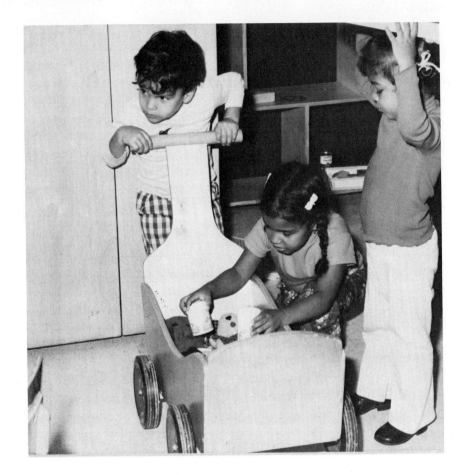

in school situations and to build learning experiences on such play activities:

1. *Play is usually natural and spontaneous.* It is not necessary to motivate healthy children to play. Neither is it usually necessary to teach a child patterns of behavior that are foreign to him. He has been playing since he was a baby, and school opportunities to play are the least threatening and most familiar ways for the child to behave in group settings, just as it is at home.

2. Since play is so natural and is thoroughly absorbing to children, *learning activities which flow from play are inherently interesting,* enjoyable, self-sustaining, and of long duration. Children at play tend to have long attention spans and they resist distractions.

3. Through play activities, *children acquire a great deal of information, improve their social skills, and make progress in their conceptual growth.* The more that children learn through play, the less teachers have to teach them. Children exchange ideas through play and often teach each other. They also develop their conceptions of time, space, and quantity as they play with objects and with each other.

4. *Through active play, children exercise their growing muscles and gain physical skills and coordination.* It would be impossible to give children as much exercise and as much repetitive activity as they need for their growing bodies and restless muscles if play were not readily available to young children for substantial periods in group settings.

5. In play, *children practice skills which may be motoric, social, intellectual, or a combination of all three.* When a child plays ball, jumps rope, or uses marbles or blocks with other children, there are always social skills involved through learning how to get along with each other, to share equipment, to take turns, and to interact in socially acceptable ways. Many of these play activities yield considerable payoff in all kinds of cognitive development and come naturally with little effort.

6. Emotionally, play *helps children to express their feelings, overcome anxiety, and work out conflicts and traumatic experiences.* Children who reduce their tensions and contain their fears, or discharge their aggressive impulses in playful activities, are better able to attend to learning situations demanding more self-discipline.

7. In play, *children often apply what they have learned to new situations.* Learning which is not anchored only in the original context in which it was mastered is personally meaningful learning which can gradually be generalized and stabilized for long-term use. This is necessary for long-term memory storage.

8. Children's *make-believe play activities develop into more complex representations and symbolic forms and become increasingly abstract.*

9. Play contributes to the *growth of the child's logical thinking because it requires some planning, imagination, and selection from different options available.* Except for the simplest forms of children's

play, planning, deciding, sequencing, changing plans, and adapting to other children's plans are regularly required to keep the play going.

10. *Play is an important life function, as is love and work.* Play activities lead to adult games, hobbies, and various kinds of recreational activities. Schools can encourage children to develop such life-long play interests as chess or checkers, sports, or dramatization.

While children's play is capable of producing all these valuable results, there is no guarantee that any child's playing will, in fact, be so productive. This is surely an important reason for teachers to observe children at play whenever possible to find out what the child is getting out of his play, whether more productive types of play could be encouraged, and some clues as to the nature of such guidance or intervention.

A kindergarten teacher found herself with an extremely volatile class. This was her second year of teaching and her skills were not yet sufficiently advanced to cope with so much turmoil. There were seven boys who were hyperactive and who seemed to have developed few skills, whether in social interaction, in independent self-sustaining work, or in any of the more sedentary activities available in the room. Observations of the class confirmed the abnormally high level of motoric activity of the group as a whole and of these seven boys in particular. The guidance counselor offered to remove a few of these very active boys to another class to help reduce the size and dimensions of the problem. However, Miss Brown refused to give up any of the children, no doubt as a matter of pride, and determined to learn how to manage the situation better. But the situation did not improve. Play periods became even more unbearable, with the active boys walking on table tops, jumping over chairs, crawling under tables, and generally refusing to involve themselves in anything other than physical activities of their own choosing. In fact, the teacher spent so much time trying to manage these boys that the rest of the class suffered from lack of teacher attention to the many other activities in progress. In despair, the teacher became punitive. One day, an observer visiting the room found the seven boys, quiet but looking extremely sullen and angry, sitting at a table with hands folded, idle and very restless. The children were being punished for their earlier uncontrollable behavior. But it was perfectly apparent that a power struggle was underway which Miss Brown was bound to lose. Those seven boys were very bright and very fast, and she could not possibly restrain all of them at once.

Since social skills were not well-developed in the boys, it seemed possible to guide some very structured forms of play which might help to advance the needed skills. Miss Brown was asked to involve the boys in any kind of well-structured game requiring some clear type of desirable social behavior and to use massive forms of praise for reinforcement purposes. A Lotto game, with a caller, and turns to be caller, was suggested. Miss Brown was desperate enough to try anything, so she set out a Lotto game. Immediately, the largest, most aggressive boy said sourly, "I ain't gonna play." He edged his chair over to the jigsaw puzzle rack, took out a puzzle and started to work it. However, a social activity was needed at this point, not individual projects. It was suggested that this child be the first caller, and he gladly accepted this role and put the puzzle away.

To Miss Brown's surprise, the Lotto game went very well as she kept modelling the desirable social forms and poured unaccustomed praise on the children who had not heard a word of praise that semester. After fifteen minutes, one boy won the game and the activity ended. The teacher, relieved at having experienced one constructive social play situation with the boys, decided not to interfere when the boys fanned out to different centers in the room. Miss Brown described this incident at an after-school meeting of teachers, adding that when it was clean-up time shortly thereafter, she was amazed to see this group go voluntarily into the block corner and do a good job of shelving the blocks. This was contrary to the usually destructive roles they played during the transitional clean-up period. She thought that her massive doses of praise in a tightly held play situation had helped to restore their own good opinions of themselves, that they felt good enough to be helpful instead of being disruptive.

This kindergarten incident illustrates a variety of teacher strategies and the great range of play activities which can be used in numerous ways to help children at whatever level of need can be established. If Miss Brown had been more inventive than punitive at an earlier stage in teaching these boys social skills and greater ability to fit into the group setting, she probably could have avoided the power struggles she generated with this group. She needed to develop a program encompassing more motoric activity so the children would not have to do all the adjusting to Miss Brown's tolerances. There are many constructive play activities which use a great deal of physical energy.

When children seem to need far more physical activity than the teacher plans, a joint accommodation may occur. The teacher can plan more action, then alternate with some less active experiences, and gradually find a more agreeable balance of motoric activities.

It is obvious that functions of play are not automatically served. The teacher's role is to help augment the benefits children realize in play so that more functions of play can be realized. In a 1967 experimental kindergarten study, teacher-child conversations about common dramatic-play topics substantially increased the frequency of dramatic play among children.[1]

When teachers observe children's spontaneous play, they look for many different possible clues to the child's development, interests, strengths, and problems. One researcher, studying young children's personalities, developed a seven-point scale to assess these characteristics of "spontaneous behavior":[2]

Tempo or speed of movement and energy level

Area of movement and ground covered

Degree of response to people

Self-enjoyment

Introversion versus extroversion

Another researcher suggests additional measures by which to note children's fantasy play: imaginativeness, creativity, divergence, ideational fluency, closeness to child's life situation, concentration, emotional response, overt aggression, and content.[3] A psychiatrist suggests that the apparent absence of fantasy in play may be a sign of the child's internal distress, of inadequately developed sense of self, or of excessive internal recourse to fantasy.[4] While teachers do not usually diagnose children's emotional problems, they are among the most acute observers of unusual behavior patterns which indicate some further needs for referral to appropriate agencies and specialists.

1. H. Marshall and S. C. Hahn, "Experimental Modification of Dramatic Play," *Journal of Personality and Social Psychology*, 5 (1967), pp. 119–122.

2. L. Murphy, *Methods for the Study of Personality in Young Children* (New York: Basic Books, 1956), p. 32.

3. J. L. Singer, *The Child's World of Make-Believe: Experimental Studies of Children's Imaginative Play* (New York: Academic, 1973), pp. 32–61.

4. Rosalind Gould, *Child Studies through Fantasy* (New York: Quadrangle, 1972), p. 264.

WHAT IS PLAY?

Huizinga, a historian of culture, defines play as requiring these elements: order, tension, movement, change, solemnity, rhythm, rapture.[5] He notes that both animal and child play have these elements and in ancient societies adult play did also. He says that "the function of play in the higher forms which concern us here can largely be derived from the two basic aspects under which we meet it: as a contest *for* something or a representation *of* something, with these uniting in different ways."[6] Other characteristics Huizinga sees in play are voluntarism or freedom, disinterestedness (satisfying in itself), limitedness (as to time and place), it creates order, it is tense in its element of chance (there is no way of knowing how it will come out), it is rule governed, it is different (either in its secrecy or dressing-up), and it wholly absorbes the player.[7]

The behavior of children at play is well-captured by Huizinga's play elements. Certainly, the child plays because he wants to. There are few things a child would rather do. Play is clearly its own reward. More intrinsic satisfactions are hard to find. The limitedness of play is seen in its beginnings and endings. The child starts to play—alone or with others—generally in a play area or someplace where play is permitted. Playgrounds, playrooms, or play corners may be designated as the place to play. In addition to the place, children usually discover there is a time to play. Partly, the time is of the child's choosing. He feels like playing and there is nothing against it. No one is requiring him to do something else, especially at school when it is "play time." Sometimes this is not true, and adults show annoyance that children "play around" when it is no longer appropriate or when play time is supposed to be over. The playing usually ends at a definite time—it may fall apart or it may be required to end. Perhaps the child has concluded his play and is ready for a different type of activity.

The order that children create in play may be quite different from adult notions of order. It is more likely to be a pretend or make-believe kind of order. The act of pretending establishes characters, relationships, and actions, and there may be outcries if the order so established by the playing children is violated by other children or adults.

5. Johan Huizinga, *Homo Ludens* (Boston: Bacon, 1950), p. 17.
6. Ibid., p. 13.
7. Ibid., pp. 7–13.

Children create many different characters in their play, frequently confronting strong characters with weak ones, sometimes strong characters with other strong ones, often centering the play on a horror theme with a monster of some kind. Television tends to influence the content of children's play. Some children are clearly acting as satellites and are content to play the baby, the cat, or the dog to a more dominant character. Alone, a child often plays wordlessly, but with rich gestures and actions, as he *becomes* a plane, car or horse or the hero rescuing the weak members of his cast. Pretending to be frightened can be fun, but a child who suddenly bursts into tears and evidences discomfort may be associating the play with real-life frightening experiences.

Make-believe play offers therapeutic as well as cognitive values.

Erikson enumerates therapeutic play values for children that include replaying an unsatisfactory scene, playing a role that is powerful or dominant, counteracting feelings of helplessness or control by others, or otherwise discharging tension, rage, or unhappiness through the make-believe play activities.[8] Piaget stresses the cognitive values of play, while he notes the emotional functions of tension-discharge or ego-recuperation. For Piaget, play offers the child many opportunities to symbolize by making objects stand for other objects, by pretending there are objects when there are none, and by gradually using words and increasingly abstract symbols to stand for ideas or concepts.[9] In addition, Piaget notes the cognitive values of social play, when children's egocentric notions are challenged by other children and glimmerings of more universally accepted ideas begin to be constructed.

Dewey pointed out: "Only by watching the child and seeing the attitudes that he assumes toward suggestions can we tell whether they are operating as factors in furthering the child's growth, or whether they are external, arbitrary impositions interfering with normal growth."[10]

One recent study of issues in play concluded that young children's play helps children in these ways:

To transform inner strivings into meaningful dramatic play episodes.

To master anxiety and at the same time to advance their cognitive understandings.

8. Erik H. Erikson, *Childhood and Society* (New York: Norton, 1950), pp. 182–218.
9. Jean Piaget, *Play, Dreams and Imitation in Childhood* (New York: Norton, 1962), pp. 162–68.
10. John Dewey, *The School and Society* (Chicago: University of Chicago Press, 1899), pp. 129–130.

To advance to self-realization, to realize and value one's own experiences.

To master developmental stress, as in separation from the mother for periods of time in school.

To understand and be able to cope with their environment.[11]

An interesting further conclusion of this study was that there probably are "developmental sequences of play which are probably biologically determined but which must be nurtured, patterned and elicited by the child's family and cultural milieu in order to function."[12] This conclusion indicates the important role that teachers can play in school and in collaborating with parents to develop a common understanding of the functions and values of play and of approaches to its encouragement and development.

An important function of play is increased motor development.

Other researchers have stressed the importance of motor development, a result of the intense activity that play can generate.[13] Any close observer of young children is bound to note the child's sheer delight in bodily movement, in repetitive forms of physical motion, and in sheer manipulation of physical objects. Piaget points out how much satisfaction young children derive from the control of their own bodies or of objects they cause to move. He calls this satisfaction "the joy of being the cause." Playful physical actions, therefore, serve bodily growth needs and continue through life to be necessary for good muscle tone and positive feelings or of well-being.

Ellis offers three main reasons for play—play as arousal seeking, play as learning, and play as meeting the developmental needs of children. He indicates that all three tend to be integrated in any play activity. Since children's interest in play relates to its stimulating quality, uncertainty as to outcomes, and increasing complexity with age and experience, Ellis suggests that better playthings are those that can provide novelty, stimulate investigation and exploration, and are manipulative.[14]

Fantasy play not only serves therapeutically to maintain the child's emotional health but also to give meaning to children's experiences in very much the same way that art experiences do. This major func-

---

11. Nancy E. Curry, "Consideration of Current Basic Issues on Play," in *Play: The Child Strives toward Self-Realization* (Washington, D.C.: National Association for the Education of Young Children, 1971), pp. 52–53.

12. Curry, *Play*, p. 53.

13. Charlotte Bühler, *From Birth to Maturity* (London: Kegan Paul, 1935).

14. M. J. Ellis, *Why People Play* (Englewood Cliffs, N.J.: Prentice-Hall, 1973), pp. 119, 135.

tion of child play has been noted repeatedly by psychologists, thera-
pists, and anthropologists. By reenacting experiences, realistically or in
distorted forms, the child comes to have a clearer notion of what
happened and how he feels about such happenings. For young children who are still somewhat inarticulate about their feelings and
thoughts and who often lack consciousness of them or the vocabulary
by which to express them, acting is the natural channel available for
producing some coherence and shape to otherwise vague notions.

Play is often described as an important preparation for life. Since
every form of development that enhances a child's maturation and
growth prepares him for later life, play activities are necessarily functional in this respect. Through play, children seem to identify with
adult roles, try them on for size, and build a bridge that gradually
spans the developmental stages to adult levels of behaving and
thinking.

It is possible to see more vividly the vital life-enhancing properties
of play by observing the pathology often symptomized by an absence
of the play capacity. Children's play connotes dynamic energy, the
ego strength to express oneself playfully, and the positive views of
oneself and one's environment to feel safe in playing spontaneously.
To be able to play is to keep anxieties and fears under enough control
to move without undue inhibitions and to have no need to repress
one's natural inclinations. Children who do not, or cannot, play can
be instantly observed as different from healthy children.

To contrast the healthy, playing child with the nonplaying child
is to measure the distance between health and illness in children. But
even healthy children exhibit their confusions, problems, and developmental difficulties in their play. Close observations of a child's play
situations, over a period of time, are helpful in furthering an understanding of the child's feelings and immediate needs.

PLAY IN EARLY CHILDHOOD PROGRAMS

If you were to examine teachers' schedules for preschool classes, you
will often find separate entries for "work periods" and "play periods."
It really makes very little difference whether children's self-chosen
activities are called work or play. But it matters greatly that parents,

supervisors, and visitors understand the role of play in young children's educational progress. It is important that teachers be able to point to the play values in their programs and not assume that everyone understands what these are.

To extol the virtues of play is not to approve common misunderstandings of teacher roles in children's play. Children's growth needs require flexible adaptations by the teacher based upon reliable observational and, in some cases, diagnostic information.

It is safe to say that no program for young children can be assessed as appropriate by contemporary standards unless it includes substantial play opportunities for children. While there is no theoretical reason why teachers need to distinguish children's activities either as "work" or "play," they sometimes do so for the spurious reasons that parents will value the work more or that the children themselves will give it more serious attention. Children benefit from variety and balance in their daily activities. If the program includes both wide variety of children's choices in activities and in degrees of structure, it seems likely that children, as well as their parents, will value all of the different program elements.

Teaching roles for play stimulation, as specified earlier in this chapter, can be seen as fundamentally the same as teaching roles for most early childhood educational activities. These roles can be specified or listed in various ways. Hildebrand lists ten ways to foster dramatic play alone, among them, the provision of materials, helping children acquire more information about roles to play, observation, and unobtrusive guidance for solving problems of social learning.[15] Similar suggestions appear in most texts designed to help new teachers stimulate productive play in early childhood classrooms.[16] Combs, in his "perceptual view of teacher preparation", stressed that the effective teacher is "a unique human being who has learned to use himself effectively and efficiently to carry out his own and society's purposes in the education of others".[17] He stresses the "helping relationship" as central to teaching—as it is to psychotherapy—although he also sees the need for the teacher to be well-informed, in addition to being effective as a person or, perhaps, in order to be effective as a person.

15. Verna Hildebrand, *Guiding Young Children* (New York: Macmillan, 1975), p. 258.
16. Helen F. Robison and Bernard Spodek, *New Direction in the Kindergarten* (New York: Teachers College Press, 1965).
17. Arthur W. Combs, *The Professional Education of Teachers: A Perceptual View of Teacher Preparation* (Boston: Allyn and Bacon, 1965), p. 9.

Major teaching roles for stimulating play

A summary follows of major teaching roles or strategies that are especially useful in stimulating productive play in group settings for children. Most of the strategies are equally effective in guiding many other activities in early childhood classrooms:

Observation of child behavior.   Observation should be more than just looking—it should be systematic. You should know what you are looking at and what you are looking for. The Cartwrights have excellent suggestions to help teachers develop or improve their observational methods.[18] Checklists and time sampling procedures can greatly improve the order of specification of what you see, remember, and can use in basing any teaching plans on observation of children. Some forms of systematic observations can be continuous for all children. More complex or demanding types of information gathering should be reserved for one or two children whose behavior is sufficiently challenging or deviant to merit the time and effort required for assembling much data.

Selection of materials and equipment.   This requires a knowledge of availability, and how to borrow, order, or otherwise improve the selection currently in the classroom. Teachers involved in the purchasing process can say with satisfaction that their classrooms reflect their own requirements for materials.

Arrangement and rearrangement of materials.   A room too crowded with materials is a much less effective environment for play than one that has organization, orderliness, dramatic impact of some kind, and clear suggestions of what is permissible in the way of play. Rearranging, in order to keep up with children's stages of growth, interests, and information, is equally important. The more the children respond and initiate their own activities, the greater the need to change the room to reflect these changing levels of experience and activity.

Planning.   Planning is necessary for guiding activities, trips, clarifying types of experiences, or explaining new uses of materials.

18. Carol A. Cartwright and Philip G. Cartwright, *Developing Observation Skills* (New York: McGraw-Hill, 1974).

Assessing.   Continual assessment of the classroom situation is recommended. How could play be more productive? Is it sufficiently differentiated? Does it serve all the children in sufficiently rewarding ways? What are the most pressing needs right now? What long-term goals are being neglected? What suggestions are made by parents, supervisors, and fellow teachers to add spice, challenge, or better data for planning purposes?

Modelling.   The teacher's behavior serves as a pattern for the kinds of behaviors children are supposed to learn, especially in the realm of social interactions and in language development in areas of vocabulary, syntax, and use of language for expressive purposes. Are children learning kindness, concern for others, the importance of hearing others out, respectful approaches to each other, and valuing each other for their human and personal qualities? Is the teacher modelling these qualities clearly and consistently so the children may acquire these social learnings? The teacher who shouts for silence is likely to receive only momentary silence. Teachers model attitudes that include curiosity, tentativeness in reaching conclusions when insufficient information is available, trust, and expectations for healthy development and progress toward maturity.

Application of child development knowledge.   This includes determining a child's readiness to accept appropriate suggestions for use of materials.

Presenting additional sources of information to children.   Young children's immaturity and lack of experience necessitates considerable teacher effort to provide additional sources of information to children, to include new and different experiences, and to help them discover personal meaningfulness through their play activities.

Guiding and monitoring children's play activities.   Guidance serves to minimize disruptive behavior and to maximize unique play experiences and individualized development.

Helping children to achieve positive self-concepts.   This encompasses helping a child to eliminate disruptive or unproductive behaviors, to acquire an ability to listen, and to develop improved play behaviors.

Sensitive interaction with children.   This includes listening carefully to children, empathizing with them and trying to understand their feelings and desires, and responding to them in personally oriented ways without stereotyping. It is important to maintain personally mature behaviors while helping immature children to control their behavior. Sensitive interaction includes acceptance of children as they are, for their basic humanity, and acceptance of their feelings. This does not mean acceptance of all the forms children may use to *express* those feelings. Hurting oneself or others is not acceptable, although the feelings which underlie such actions must be accepted because they exist. Awareness of the emotions of others is beneficial in deflecting undesirable behaviors to more socially desirable behaviors.

Acquiring new information and ideas.   In such a rapidly developing field as early childhood education, the teacher who does not grow becomes obsolete. Keeping up to date on new thinking, research, and information is essential to keep skills fresh and current. Professional journals, newspapers, professional conferences, and journals of contemporary opinion and criticism are sources for professional growth and development.

Many more specific teacher roles (or competencies) could be specified. A scan of the list above suggests that there are really very few skills that are specific to one kind of teaching in early childhood classes. Since there is no empirical or research base by which to validate any specific forms of teaching as more effective than others, experienced practitioners tend to stress variety of roles to master, then sensitivity, through experience of the various roles in practice.

SUGGESTIONS FOR PLAY OPPORTUNITIES

Teachers or teacher candidates interested in new and exciting teaching possibilities are constantly seeking ideas to stimulate play in the classroom. If children are bored, what should the teacher do to renew their interest? An easy answer is to expose them to anything they don't know or haven't yet experienced. A more helpful answer might be to try some of the following options, especially for stimulation of dramatic play:

1. Retrace a previous experience—a walk, trip, or other activity. The children will notice and understand more the second time, and there are bound to be new and unpredictable insights about material previously encountered.

2. Develop a different experience with the same material. If the children have been playing supermarket, plan with them to make or cook something real to sell. Invite other classes, parents, or community people, and let children experience different aspects of store activity more intensively and realistically.

3. Invite parents or community representatives to visit the class and demonstrate or discuss their occupations. In addition to the usual community helpers, do not overlook a beautician, barber, cobbler, tailor, clothes cleaner, baker, auto repairer, waiter or waitress, or factory operators. If parents or invited guests are too busy earning a living to accept the invitation, perhaps they can send photographs, descriptive material from their place of work, or sample products.

4. Plan to visit local establishments that may be sources of new information and ideas to the children. Arrangements can often be made to visit such places at a time when children's presence and their questions won't be unduly disruptive. Local construction activity is often in progress, and it is always fascinating to children.

Innumerable possibilities exist for introducing ideas for new play experiences.

The careers of the children's parents or the work of local businesses can provide interesting ideas for later classroom play activities, include, among innumerable others:

1. *Beauty shop and barber occupations*

    Props: Wooden make-believe shaver, plastic aprons, empty shampoo bottles, plastic basins. Avoid combs or sharp utensils, for sanitary and safety reasons.

2. *Medical professions*

    Props: Doctor and nurse kits, or stethoscopes, doctor's bag, nurse's uniform, bandages, Bandaids, and a small bed.

3. *Car repair shops*

    Props: Miniature vehicles, overalls, caps, tools, tool kit, and piece of hose (to fill gasoline tank).

4. *Restaurant*

    Props: Small table and chairs, tablecloth, napkins, dishes, utensils, pads of paper and pencils, cash register, toy money, and trays.

5. *Transportation occupations*

    Props: Steering wheels mounted on a board, paper and pencils for tickets, uniforms (chiefly hats), and miniature vehicles.

6. *Dressmaking and tailoring shop*

Props: Table, crepe paper, newsprint and construction paper, old sheets and fabric remnants, scissors, staplers, glue, needles, thread, and yarn. Dolls, to be fitted, as well as fellow pupils.

7. *Television station*

Props: Pretend cameras, television receivers, microphone, telephones, paper, crayons and art media, miniature animals, puppets.

8. *Farming*

Props: Miniature garden tools, plants, water, seeds, pots, and miniature animals.

9. *Furniture manufacture*

Props: Carpentry bench, wood, tools, nails, sandpaper, hand drills, brushes, paint, and various kinds of rulers.

10. *Telephone repair work*

Props: Wire, insulating material of different colors, telephones, tools, work clothing, hard hats, flashlights, small table, and step ladder.

OUTDOOR PLAY

Fortunately, many teachers view outdoor play as an ideal way to burn up excess energy, discharge noise and tension, and loosen whatever constraints children find difficult indoors. Outdoor play should certainly permit children to find the most unstructured and individual ways to express themselves and to relate to others.

Outdoor play provides an unstructured means of using up excess energy and releasing tension.

In areas with a moderate climate, the outdoors must necessarily share with indoor space many of the values and activities that are more structured than free physical activities. Sometimes the program is chiefly outdoors, except for intermittent rest periods or relaxing experiences to balance the more tense, energetic ones.

In the North and Midwest, where weather conditions are less benign, far more planning is required to use outdoor time wisely. When children come to school heavily dressed in mid-winter, teachers do not decide to take children outdoors on an impulse—it takes too long to dress and undress. When children arrive in the morning, it may be too cold or windy to schedule outdoor play as the first activity. If children are dressed to go out at mid-day or at dismissal time in mid-afternoon, it may be advantageous to play outdoors before going home. Weather conditions, however, seem to control some teachers or group settings more than others. Teachers who dress comfortably and seasonally usually spend more time with their classes in outdoor play than others. Most children would choose to go outdoors to play in any weather.

Outdoor play equipment

Day care centers, nursery schools, Head Start centers, and other school settings for young children only, usually are better equipped for outdoor play than the public schools are for older children. In many public schools, outdoor play is either undervalued and underfunded, or the competition for materials and equipment is too strong to yield much for the young children.

A bare playground is not necessarily an impossible site for outdoor play, but it does require more ingenuity and leadership by the teacher. The group can collect jump ropes, various kinds of balls, chalk to establish boundaries for games, and an assortment of simple materials. If there are concrete walks, clean paint brushes with small cans of water for water painting engage many children. They are interested in the way the "painted" areas dry on a windy day. Kites and pinwheels can be used on the playground—especially ones constructed by the children—or crepe paper streamers to detect wind directions. Children can make shadows or copy each other's shadows.

Without playground equipment, more structured activities may be alternated with unstructured types of play, for example, circle games with songs or chants, team or relay races, or dances or movement activities. Even a rhythm band can be developed with a box of small instruments. A marching band might be satisfactory for the lower temperatures when mittens must be worn.

Some playgrounds have only park-type equipment such as slides, swings, and seesaws. This equipment is satisfactory for many children, although one might question the values of daily swinging for children who never venture to try anything else. Climbing apparatus is very useful for the courageous, though the timid will need a great deal of physical and emotional support to conquer the succeeding rungs.

If, in addition to the above, the children also have access to a sandbox or other digging area, to grassy areas where there are also trees, shrubs, and birds, and to an assortment of boards, pegs, outdoor blocks, ladders, and vehicles to ride, the playground is very well-equipped indeed.[19] Fenced areas are great safety aids to the teachers, especially in areas of heavy traffic. However, where space is more generously available, trusted children enjoy exercising their independence and judgment in less closely supervised play, although the teachers insist upon their maintaining visibility.

New York City has some most imaginatively arranged rooftop playground space for day care centers and for prestigious and high-tuition private schools. One day care center in an old East Side slum is housed in an excellent building, formerly a theatre, with a large fenced roof where water play is offered with hoses and small plastic pools, shaded areas for hot summer days, generous equipment closets, and space for tricycles, sandboxes, outdoor blocks, and many boards, kegs, and other pieces of equipment for construction activities. Equipment storage close to the play area is especially helpful, so young children can take out and store much of the equipment without assistance.

A suburban cooperative nursery school developed a unique collection of outdoor equipment by transforming donated materials. With the help of parents, strange-looking combinations were formed, for example, a small ladder was attached to a large keg that lead to a climbing wall with several challenging rungs, at the top of which several boards were attached to form a platform which in turn lead to additional successive challenges. In this way, pieces of damaged equipment were salvaged, combined with other units, and new and unexpectedly exciting outdoor equipment was created.

A British leader in the informal infant school movement, visiting American schools for young children, found them mostly routine and unimaginative until she viewed playgrounds furnished with makeshift or combined products resulting from salvage operations. She

19. Jeannette G. Stone, *Play and Playgrounds* (Washington, D.C.: National Association for the Education of Young Children, 1970); and Ivalee H. McCord, "A Creative Playground," *Young Children* 26, August 1971), pp. 342–47.

20. M. P. Friedberg, *Playgrounds for City Children* (Washington, D.C.: ACEI, 1969).

found these more familiar and interesting, since British equipment budgets apparently are small. Community, parent, and volunteer input usually injects unique and interesting ideas for children's playground equipment.

Play opportunities outdoors can parallel indoor activities of almost every kind, with the exception of restful or quiet types of experiences, though it is possible to seat children on the grass or to encourage them to lie down on mats placed outdoors for restful stories or refreshing naps. In noisy, distracting big city schools, indoor spaces tend to offer quicker restfulness.

Teaching roles outdoors, similar to indoor play possibilities, nevertheless require some emphasis on monitoring, head counting, redirecting undesirable use of outdoor equipment, and nurturing and supporting the timid or fearful, who are often insecure in larger, looser areas. Teachers need to concentrate on the heedless, the overadventurous, the overstimulated, and the fearful children in an outdoor play environment. If the outdoor play period is substantial (approaching an hour or more), the same balancing needs apply as indoors, for change of pace and possible change of activity. More games or structured activities might be planned for use toward the concluding portion of the period.

Safety requirements are important considerations for outdoor play areas and activities.

Safety requirements are very important outdoors, where children feel freer and tend to move more rapidly with less heed to possible obstructions. Appropriate clothing also deserves regular scrutiny. If parents are asked to cooperate by sending extra sweaters, boots, mittens, and the like, especially clothing outgrown by slightly older siblings, the classroom supply is likely to be adequate to any emergency need.

Depending upon weather, facilities, and program goals, outdoor play may substitute for indoor play, supplement it in many ways, or serve chiefly as an outlet for exuberant spirits. Outdoor play should not be viewed as unproductive and therefore expendable. For some children, the indoor program is endured for the sake of the release outdoors. While some children feel insecure and less protected in an open space, most feel less restricted and more spontaneous. Much of the joy and the social excitement of programs is for many young children heightened in outdoor play. If it seems to be unproductive and a breeder of discipline problems, the outdoor play period can usually be vastly improved with planning, boundary rules, portable pieces of play equipment, and structured games or dances.

SUMMARY *Play has many values and functions for healthy child development. Dramatic play and block play are two major forms of learning in group settings. Values of play include:*

1. *Spontaneity and the lack of any need for motivation.*
2. *Inherent interest in learning which flows from play activities.*
3. *Acquisition of information, and social and conceptual skill development.*
4. *Physical skill development and coordination.*
5. *Practice in motoric, social, and intellectual skills.*
6. *Emotional values in expressing feelings, overcoming anxiety, and working out conflicts and traumatic experiences.*
7. *Application of learning to new situations.*
8. *Make-believe play develops into more complex representations and symbolic forms, which become increasingly abstract.*
9. *Logical thinking development, in requiring planning, imagination, and selection of options.*
10. *Recreational benefits.*

Children's play characteristics can be observed by teachers and applied to augment play values. Play is characterized in many ways, with stress usually on its voluntarism, intrinsic rewards, limitedness as to time and space, and requirements for order, sequence, and rules.

In addition to observation, teacher roles to support and augment play values include:

1. *Selecting materials and equipment.*
2. *Arranging and rearranging materials.*
3. *Planning for learning experiences.*
4. *Assessing process and results.*
5. *Modelling desired behaviors, especially social interactions.*
6. *Applying child development knowledge in stage-appropriate ways.*
7. *Opening additional sources of information to children.*
8. *Guiding and monitoring play activities.*
9. *Fostering positive self-concepts through improved play behaviors.*
10. *Increasing sensitive interaction with children, especially listening and personalizing or individualizing responses.*
11. *Acquiring new ideas and information for professional self-improvement.*

Outdoor play, in addition to offering values similar to indoor play, also permits the most physical, unstructured, spontaneous, loosening forms of activities. Teacher roles outdoors are similar to roles for indoor play, but usually stress nurturance and safety.

✻ EXERCISES FOR STUDENTS ✻✻✻✻✻✻✻✻✻✻✻✻✻✻✻✻✻✻✻

1. Observe children's play in a group setting, where the children are familiar with your presence, and will not be distracted by your unobtrusive note-taking, if possible.

a. Take notes, for a five-to-ten minute period, of two different kinds of play occurring in the classroom, for example, dramatic play and block play, or block play and table games.

b. Summarize your notes including:

(1) A narrative of the play activities.

(2) A list of the children involved, with brief descriptions of the more obvious features of each child's personality and appearance.

(3) A checklist of play features, based on the material in this chapter, checked off for each child in each of the two types of play.

(4) An analysis of your checklist and narrative material, noting any distinctions between the two types of play, and, individually, among the children; and your hypotheses about which play values were being served for which children.

2. With the permission of a classroom teacher, participate in an outdoor play period with an early childhood class. Keep a small notebook and pencil handy, and jot down the various teaching roles you play. Based on your notes of your own participation, sketch some further development of these roles you might implement on another occasion, or additional roles you could play to balance children's activities or to make their play period more productive.

3. Using the Index for the ERIC Clearinghouse on Early Childhood Education, or the Education Index, or Psychological Abstracts, or any two of these sources, read two articles on *Play*. Write a brief summary

of your perceptions of the major points of these two articles, and conclude with a summary statement of how these perceptions might add to your understandings of how to enhance children's educational experiences through play.

✿ EXERCISES FOR TEACHERS ✿✿✿✿✿✿✿✿✿✿✿✿✿✿✿✿✿✿

1. Place a tape recorder unobstrusively in an area where dramatic play usually occurs.

a. Tape record, at least fifteen minutes of dramatic play conversations, daily for at least three days, noting for each recording which children are present.

b. Analyze your tape recordings for each day, considering such features as:

(1) Number of children, number of boys and girls.

(2) Number of children recorded only on one day, or who returned on two days, or three.

(3) Theme or themes, each day.

(4) Characters represented each day.

(5) Repeated characterizations or themes.

(6) Most frequent characters and themes represented.

(7) Instances of make-believe, in addition to characters.

(8) Instances of confusion, misunderstanding or lack of information.

(9) Conflicts about the dramatic play—nature, frequency, extent.

(10) Ways in which the play was interrupted or terminated.

c. Based on your analysis, plan to support and extend *one* of the types of dramatic play you recorded through materials to be added, teacher roles to be implemented, and any other features you decide to change or control, such as *place* for dramatic play, *period* of play, protection from interference from other children, or the like.

d. Tape record the play session in which you implement your plans and evaluate your own input (too much, just right, not enough, too soon, too late, for example) and effects upon the dramatic play, such as: persistence, expansion of actions or ideas, use of new ideas, less conflict, more conversation, more make-believe, or more laughter.

2. Observe the block play area daily for at least three days. Make a list of plans for augmenting the play, including:

a. Teacher roles to use.

b. New materials to offer.

c. Change of rules for block play, such as area available, rights of block builders for protection from accidents or intrusions.

d. Identification of children in need of teacher guidance in block play.

e. Ways to communicate valuing of block play, such as photographing constructions or inviting block builders to show and describe their constructions to others.

f. Behaviors in need of modeling, such as sharing block resources. Implement your *plans* for several days, even if briefly, then revert to observation for several days, to assess effects. Determine whether to continue or to change your plans.

3. Take an inventory of the accessories available in your classroom for physical forms of indoor and outdoor play.

a. List items which might enhance indoor play further, especially in bad weather, such as wheel toys, rubber mats for somersaults, climbing equipment, and the like. Plan with your supervisor for ways to acquire needed items and space in which to use them.

b. List possible items of equipment which could make outdoor play more rewarding, such as large outdoor blocks, boards and kegs, water play materials, sand and climbing or construction materials. Plan with your supervisor for ways to acquire some needed equipment and for necessary storage and maintenance. Don't overlook parent or community volunteers, in looking for donations of equipment or materials or labor. Sometimes, high school classes and teachers can help to construct or to repair equipment.

BIBLIOGRAPHY

Cartwright, Carol A., and Cartwright, Philip G. *Developing Observation Skills.* New York: McGraw-Hill, 1974.

Combs, Arthur W. *The Professional Education of Teachers, A Perceptual View of Teacher Preparation.* Boston: Allyn and Bacon, 1965.

Dewey, John. *The School and Society.* Chicago: The University of Chicago Press, 1899.

Ellis, M. J. *Why People Play.* Englewood Cliffs, N.J.: Prentice-Hall, 1973.

Erikson, Eric H. *Childhood and Society.* New York: Norton, 1950.

Found Spaces and Equipment for Children's Centers. New York: Educational Facilities Laboratory, 1972.

Friedberg, M. P. *Playgrounds for City Children.* Washington, D.C.: ACEI, 1969.

Gould, Rosalind. *Child Studies Through Fantasy.* New York: Quadrangle Books, 1972.

Hildebrand, Verna. *Guiding Young Children.* New York: Macmillan, 1975.

Huizinga, Johan. *Homo Ludens.* Boston: Beacon, 1950.

Isaacs, Susan. *The Nursery Years.* New York: Schocken, 1968.

Kritchevsky, Sybil; Prescott, Elizabeth; and Walling, Lee. *Planning Environments for Young Children: Physical Space.* Washington, D.C.: NAEYC, 1969.

Matterson, E. M. *Play with a Purpose for Under-Sevens.* New York: Penguin, 1965.

McClellan, J. *The Question of Play.* New York: Pergamon, 1972.

Millar, Sussana. *The Psychology of Play.* Baltimore: Penguin, 1968.

Murphy, L. *Methods for the Study of Personality in Young Children.* New York: Basic, 1956.

National Association for the Education of Young Children. *Let's Play Outdoors.* No. 101, Washington, D.C.; National Association for the Education of Young Children, undated.

Piaget, Jean. *Play, Dreams and Imitation in Childhood.* New York: Norton, 1962.

Play: The Child Strives toward Self-Realization. Washington, D.C.: National Association for the Education of Young Children, 1971.

Pratt, C. *I Learn From Children—An Adventure in Progressive Education.* New York: Simon & Schuster, 1948.

Robison, Helen F. "The Decline of Play in Urban Kindergartens." *Young Children,* 26 (1971): 333–341.

Singer, J. L. *The Child's World of Make-Believe, Experimental Studies of Imaginative Play.* New York: Academic Press, 1973.

Smilansky, Sarah. *The Effects of Sociodramatic Play on Disadvantaged Preschool Children.* New York: Wiley, 1968.

Stone, Jeanette G. *Play and Playgrounds.* Washington, D.C.: NAEYC, 1970.

Van Camp, Sarah S. "How Free Is Free Play?" *Young Children*, 27 (1972): 205–208.

Winawer, Aaron D., and Winawer, Bonnie P. *Child's Play, A Creative Approach to Play Spaces for Today's Children*. New York: Harper, 1965.

SELF-ESTEEM:

I
CAN
DO IT!

4

What makes a child secure, self-confident, and willing to tackle new tasks with eager anticipation of success? Why are some children crippled with anxiety and the fear of failure? How can teachers assure that their relationships with children will support self-valuing and expectations for success? These are among the most important questions teachers face as soon as they start to work with children. The effect of teaching on children's self-concepts is of prime importance. Since the youngest children come to school with feelings about themselves already formed by their experiences at home, teacher candidates must learn to recognize children's feelings, as well as to teach in ways that support and enhance the child's feelings of worthiness.

A child is obviously not born with a self-concept. How parents act toward a child, how they identify him/her and show their love are the major ways in which the young learn a sense of "self," as independent of mother, family, and others. This sense of self includes one's name, nicknames and terms of endearment, body image, sense of physical control and skills, and feelings of close relationships with parents and brothers and sisters. The child's possessions, especially clothing, blankets, eating utensils, and toys, contribute concrete evidence of his unique self, since these objects are designated as his and are associated with his day-to-day functioning. The child's idea of himself, of his capabilities and his expectations for future achievement is called a self-concept.[1] The extent to which the child evaluates himself with approval or disapproval, as worthy or unworthy, important or insignificant, is called self-esteem or self-valuing.[2]

Self-esteem is the child's own judgment of how worthy he is. There are infinite ways the child communicates this

1. Harold W. Bernard, *Child Development and Learning* (Boston: Allyn & Bacon, 1973), p. 190.
2. Stanley Coopersmith, *The Antecedents of Self-Esteem* (San Francisco: W. H. Freeman & Co., 1967), pp. 4–5.

sense of self-worth to others—by overt behavior, language, body language, and all the ways the child approaches or responds to people or objects. The child's self-esteem tends to mirror the values of the people with whom he lives.[3] A hyperactive child who lives with a family which values passive, quiet behavior is bound to feel unworthy, if he receives the varied messages which tell him he is a nuisance to his family. In school, hyperactive children are among the least-valued by school staffs because they drain so much adult energy.

Genetic endowment of temperament, physical appearance, and rate or pace of maturation, affect the child's personality and self-esteem.[4] Notions about physical beauty, masculinity–femininity, and freedom from affliction with physical disabilities, all have important effects on the child's self-esteem. Yet genetic endowment, as Piaget has so clearly stated, is chiefly potential—it indicates the possible, but not the inevitable.[5] No matter how superbly endowed a baby might be, he might encounter depressing experiences, while a handicapped child might be reared to maximize his possibilities and to have a high sense of his own importance. The early maturer tends to be praised more than the slower grower. The pace of maturation may have good or bad consequences, depending upon how families and teachers react to it and what requirements they make of young children.

A variety of features contribute to a child's self-esteem.

Cultural differences, often misread as inferiority, contribute to children's self-devaluing in significant ways. A child who does not understand the language spoken in school may feel inferior because of the communication barrier. American Indian, Mexican, Cuban, Puerto Rican, and American black families are helping schools to become aware of cultural conflicts of values which confuse children. Zuni Indian children, for example, are taught at home to value cooperation and to avoid personal acclaim or achievement. These values actively conflict with the traditional American white culture, with its emphases on competition, independence, and personal achievement. Children caught in such cultural conflict may reject their own culture and devalue themselves, or reject the major culture, often with unresolved confusion about their own values and their posture toward the values of others.

3. G. H. Mead, *Mind, Self and Society* (Chicago: University of Chicago Press, 1934), pp. 200–208.

4. Paul Mussen, *The Psychological Development of the Child,* 2d ed. (Englewood Cliffs, New Jersey: Prentice-Hall, 1973), pp. 47–51.

5. Jean Piaget, *The Origins of Intelligence in Children* (New York: International Universities Press), 1952.

In addition to cultural effects on self-esteem, there is often substantial impact by social class or ethnic or religious affiliation of the child's family. A common observation of children from poor American families is that, compared with more affluent groups, they have less sense of mastery over their lives, in that they see external events controlling them. This sense of powerlessness has been noted by sociologists in many research studies. It is the "You can't fight City Hall" response, the resignation to unseen authorities. It either dampens initiative and supports resigned submission, or it stimulates illegal behavior in rebellion against unresponsive authority.

HOW SELF-CONCEPTS DEVELOP

There is general agreement that the child develops a concept of self gradually as he notices he is the object of his parents' attention, that they respond to him, and that they take care of him. The child learns his name because his family uses it to identify him, to signify him, and to communicate with him. Up to about age five, it is chiefly parents who affect the child's self-concept and self-esteem, as they give him possessions and react joyfully to his growing skills and independence in eating, toileting, dressing, and other forms of control. Coopersmith stresses that the child values himself as he is valued by the important people in his family and his life.[6] Success gives the child status and importance. As he develops skills and controls, he is able to keep his self-esteem even when he encounters adverse experiences. Self-esteem, according to Coopersmith, is based on parental approval of the child and respect for the child's independence and individuality, within clear, well-enforced limits.

Parents are chiefly instrumental in developing a child's initial self-concept.

Children with high self-esteem tend to have parents with loving hands who communicate their interest, attention, and affection in many ways. Freudian psychiatrists tend to stress the dangers to children's self-esteem from poor handling of toileting problems, since this is likely to be the first major arena of conflict between the child and his parents.[7] The child's history of success or failure at home carries over to school, so that the child who is regarded as a failure at

6. Coopersmith, *Self-Esteem*, 1967, p. 37.
7. Stephen M. Johnson et al., "How Deviant Is the Normal Child? A Behavioral Analysis of the Preschool Child and His Family" (Paper presented at the Fifth Annual Meeting of the Association of the Advancement of Behavior Theory, Washington, D.C., 1971).

home expects to fail at school. However, it is possible that a child with a fairly good sense of worthiness may encounter failure experiences at school that scale down his self-esteem to accord with school valuing or grading, or the reverse may occur.

Young children's very active physical involvement with the world brings them into frequent conflict with adult authority. A study of young children, four to six years of age, in middle-class white families, found that 96 percent of the average child's behavior was nondeviant, and that the most deviant child in the sample showed 88 percent appropriate behavior. Yet, in this study, it was found that the average child's behavior was regarded by parents as deviant once every 3.17 minutes, that is, that the child failed to obey about one in four parent commands. If the parents thought three approved behaviors out of four was a good record, chalking up deviance to immaturity and inexperience, their children were likely to gain a sense of success and satisfaction from their parents, resulting in good feelings about themselves. Overemphasis upon the deviance and impatience for a child to grow up are ways some of these parents may have communicated low valuing.

It is important to note that it is often *not* the child's behavior which is regarded as universally good or bad, but the varied ways adults respond to the child. Many children are never satisfied with their work, no matter how good it is, and their best work gives them no joy. Impossible standards set by parents or by teachers may lead to such perfectionist attitudes. Or a child may be babied too long at home. He may come to feel too small and dependent to accept even moderate challenges, or he may feel comfortable no matter how poor his work is, because he is not accustomed to responsibility and independence.

Children with high self-esteem are not as vulnerable to illness or maliciousness as children who value themselves less.[8] When the child's self-esteem is low, he may accept adversity as his due, or agree with other people's criticism of him, even when it is unwarranted. Self-concepts and self-esteem seem to be very difficult to change once they have been clearly established. This is why teachers of young children must work with great sensitivity for the effect they have on the self-esteem of the children they teach. This is also why home and school must work together to maintain and improve the young child's sense of his own worth and capability.

8. Coopersmith, *Self-Esteem*, 1967, pp. 217–18.

TEACHING TO ENHANCE SELF-ESTEEM

Teachers of young children have so many ways to maintain and enhance the self-esteem of their pupils that it is impossible to cover all of them. Major techniques include the use of child study skills, classroom and behavior management systems, individualization of teaching, use of positive feedback, child acceptance, well-designed teaching plans, self-analysis of teaching, and the support of and collaboration with other professionals and parents. Self-analysis of teaching is detailed in Chapter 13. Collaboration with parents, treated briefly in this chapter, is more fully covered in Chapter 14. The other major teaching strategies to enhance the child's self-esteem are described in this chapter, that is, child study skills, classroom and behavior management, use of positive feedback and child acceptance, and lesson plans.

Even at a tender age, the child enters the classroom as a distinct in-

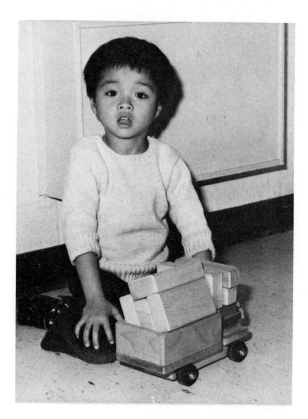

dividual, with a personality already formed and noticeable. Young children are generally attractive in their small size, dependence upon adults, need for love and support, and vulnerability to adverse conditions and people. But one boy swaggers while another slinks. One child sparkles while another languishes. Each child, even in a brief encounter, communicates clues to his personality and feelings. How can a busy teacher capture all those significant signals, while managing a classroom and handling problems? Even more difficult is separating the transient, momentary, uncharacteristic signals from the more substantial patterns that define a child's functioning.

One six-year-old girl was observed for most of a school day by a student teacher; she recorded the fact that the child uttered not a single word in school. Approaching the child the following morning, the student teacher said, "You didn't talk much in school yesterday, did you?" "No, I didn't," the child replied, with an engaging smile, revealing a tooth gap. "I had a loose tooth and I was afraid it would come out if I talked. But it fell out when I got home, so I don't have to worry about it anymore." Describing such a child as nonverbal, based on an unusual day's behavior, would be erroneous, to say the least.

CHILD STUDY

Child study, case study, or observational study, are terms used interchangeably to mean gathering data about how a child functions in school, assessing his strengths, problems, and needs. Based on such a study, the teacher has the confidence and the specifications needed to make long-term plans, for this child's benefit and to fit short-term and day-to-day activities into the long-term plans.

The time-consuming procedures required for child study have to be fitted in somewhere, simply because of their importance. Most teachers, without such studies, are unable to support their own handling of children with problems or their recommendations for referral for special treatment or placement. When teachers compile data on a child's behavior, the methods of data gathering should give the teacher, parent, and supervisor, confidence that the singular, unusual events can be delineated from the regularly recurring patterns or features of the child's functioning in school.

Methods of data collection

Teachers are urged to study only one child at a time, in order to collect the detailed data required for diagnosis and prescription of learning activities for that child. Time is required—at least a month should be spent collecting the data. Obviously, teachers must choose only the most challenging children in the group for such detailed study. One study of children's self-esteem by inner-city teachers used a "success-analysis" of the child to reveal his strengths and interests, in order to help him build a positive self-concept.[9] A set of six questions guided teacher assessment of children's self-esteem, relating to such features as his self-direction, self-acceptance and goal-orientation. While this is a global form of inferencing, it has the virtue of focusing on the child's positive characteristics. Checklists of questions of this type could be especially useful in identifying those children who seem to need more detailed study.

The first task, then, is to try to identify the children requiring the most help. A checklist might be devised with polar items, such as:

happy–sad
friendly–alone
secure–fearful
high-impulsive–reflective
active–passive
outgoing–withdrawn
independent–dependent
cooperative–resistant
persevering–flitting
appropriate affect–inappropriate affect

Such a polar checklist helps to flag the children who are at the extremes, those who have problems for which they need help. For example, a child who is checked off as sad, alone, fearful, reflective, passive, withdrawn, dependent, and inappropriate affectivity, would be an obvious candidate for further observational study. Inappropriate affectivity refers to responses which are out of order, such as failure to cry when one is truly hurt, or laughing when anger is the appro-

9. Kenneth R. Washington, "Self-Concept Development: An Affective Educational Experience for Inner-City Teachers," *Young Children* 29 (July 1974), pp. 305–310.

priate response. If this item is checked, it should be looked at in greater detail, to insure that it is not the result of misunderstanding, if for example, the child does not speak English in an English-speaking class.

Murphy suggests rating such child behaviors as tempo or speed of movement (fast-slow), energy level (high-low), area of movement (wide, narrow, stays in one place), self-enjoyment, and introversion-extroversion.[10] Singer adds, in addition to items listed above, such behaviors as imaginativeness, concentration, elation, shame, contempt, fatigue, aggression.[11]

Any child may have a moderate to serious problem to which a teacher must respond in some helpful way. These occasional problems do not require the detailed preparation of a child study, since they chiefly call for alertness to changes in children's more usual ways of behaving, sympathetic interest in causes of such changes, and readiness to listen and respond in ways that alleviate temporary or unexpected trauma or discontent. Unhappiness over a dangling tooth, or a parent's illness, or the loss of a pet, must all be taken in stride. Events which upset young children, or which uncover a hitherto suppressed or unobserved personality trait, can occur at any time. Sometimes, events precipitate drastic behavior change in a child, which indicate the need for further study. Death of a parent, break-up of a marriage, or major economic stress in the family, usually have discernible effects on children's behavior. Teacher alertness brings more information sooner about the causes of such behavior changes. Even where the teacher is powerless to minimize or alleviate the child's unhappiness, at least the teacher can refrain from compounding it, or from punishing a child for events he can neither control nor ignore.

Developmental problems indicate growth and development lags or discontinuities.

A checklist completed early in the school year helps the teacher note the children who will most challenge her skills and knowledge. As the school year progresses, some of these children will miraculously seem to have solved their problems. This is what is meant by developmental problems, the kinds of problems which do not indicate serious personality problems but primarily growth and development lags or discontinuities. For example, an only child who enters kindergarten is accustomed to having his own way most of the time and might

10. Lois Murphy, *Methods for the Study of Personality in Young Children* (New York: Basic Books, 1956), p. 32.
11. Jerome L. Singer, *The Child's World of Make-Believe* (New York: Academic Press, 1973), pp. 32–61.

react with considerable aggression and outright resistance to class-room needs for sharing or taking turns. Eventually he adjusts to the fact that at school, the fun of playing with children requires his willingness to share and take turns. Another child shows separation anxiety, and finds it difficult to part from his mother. If the teacher handles the separation well, supporting and helping the mother and the child, while keeping everyone's self-esteem as high as possible, such a child may soon become an amiable and easy-going pupil.

Child study then concentrates on a child with extreme behavior of some kind—very aggressive, withdrawn, or dependent. One such study in a public school prekindergarten revealed a major physical problem. A little girl with a serious heart condition had severe limitations on her activity. This admittedly difficult situation was well-handled by quiet attention to the limitations and strong encouragement outside of the limitations. Other studies, also summarized below, turned up problems of foster children placed outside of the family by court order, or for other reasons. A girl in a kindergarten class was found to lie about herself and her family, but after a case study, she was perceived as fantasying her wishes for a mother very different from her foster mother. One child, very passive and uninvolved in his school work, had lost his mother shortly after he entered school in the first grade, but his daydreaming and failure to learn had not been associated with his motherlessness until after a child study included data from his permanent record file.

Sensitive teachers are sometimes fearful that their child studies will reveal child misery in situations they cannot change. Better not to know than to feel helpless and distressed, some teachers say. Generally, this is a self-defeating attitude, which leads to blaming the child for his misfortune. Teachers will not be able to solve all the problems of their pupils. But they will be able to solve some of them, to diminish others, to find other professionals who can help, and to support and encourage a child even when he is most unhappy and unattractive.

Child study includes systematic observation, gathering other school and out-of-school information, and analyzing the data. Why bother to study a child, some teachers ask, when I can see for myself that he is lazy, or he steals, or he lacks motivation to learn? Yet studies often result in analyses which are very different from the teacher's spontaneous or intuitive perceptions. One four-year-old in a public school prekindergarten was labelled very aggressive and was seen as "always hitting others." A study of his behavior showed that this child was a scapegoat, who was hitting *back* but not initiating the aggression. In this case, the child had retarded speech development and immature behavior, and the young children in the group provoked him when he tried to make friends and could not be understood. In a second-grade class, the teacher was concerned about a boy who was stealing, whose mother failed to respond to requests to come to school for a conference with her. A study of this child showed his stealing was confined to taking food snacks from other children's desks. He was one of nine children in a single-parent family on welfare, and poverty accounted for his own failure to bring snacks. Since the analysis in this situation indicated that a hungry child was taking food, the teacher solved this problem very simply by supplying snacks to this child, noticing how bright and charming he really was, warmly supporting his advanced learning needs, and discovering suddenly that this dire problem had been solved. Every school in a big city must have some children who either cannot or do not bring snacks, for whom donations by the PTA or individual parents can be arranged. Classes for younger children usually supply all children with snacks, from school or parent sources. After kindergarten, the snack problem may be just as acute, with less teacher attention.

Isolated incidents should be given little weight in analysis of patterns of a child's behavior.

If the teacher notes only extreme incidents which require her intervention, she can mislabel children and treat them in ways that are inconsistent with their real needs. The teacher needs to know how frequently an "aggressive" child commits aggression, or with whom —perhaps there is just one child who provokes it. Or there may be one specific type of situation which a child finds unbearable. The goal is to avoid becoming unsympathetic to a child, and failing to see why he behaves as he does.

Time sampling methods, supplemented by anecdotal recordings, can develop a data base which will provide the information needed to analyze a child's behavior. These methods are easier to use when there is more than one adult in the classroom, such as an assistant teacher, a student teacher, or a paraprofessional. In some cases, a supervisor, guidance counsellor, or other staff member who is not classroom-based, can take on the extra task of securing the data in systematic ways. The time sampling techniques assure a way of observing a child's functioning regularly, not only when he is in trouble. The time sampled may be hourly, half-hourly, every five minutes, or any other time frequency which seems appropriate and feasible. The time sampling should not be limited to one day, or week, since the more data that is compiled, the more confidence teachers and others will have that the data is reliable and valid.[12] The anecdotal recordings can supplement the samplings by describing both typical and unusual behaviors observed. The detail is helpful to others who may not know the child and who may not be easily convinced that action may be needed to help the child.

Before starting to observe a child on a time sampling schedule, it is a good idea to decide how to record the data which will be observed. A form of some kind is helpful. Recording may be on audio-cassette, but this is not usually feasible unless the room sound level is low, or the recorder is close enough to the child to record his verbalizations audibly. More accessible would be a checklist, graph, form with blanks to fill in briefly, or with space for summary descriptions. Cartwright and Cartwright, referred to above, give excellent suggestions for simple recording forms which can be prepared in advance. It should be noted, however, that once a child is closely enough observed to identify specific aspects of behavior which need changing, the checklist, graph or form may also have to be changed, to narrow the focus and increase the data collection on such specific aspects of behavior. For example, if a child who never seems to stay with a task, is observed making many trips to the bathroom, the bathroom behavior needs to be observed, to find out whether there is in fact a physical problem or if the behavior represents a refuge from the classroom. Medical referral might be in order in this case to avoid taking inappropriate action without assurance as to whether physical or emotional problems may be involved. In any case, a checklist or other type of form prepared for observation should specify the behavior characteristics observed, and whether frequency, duration, or other features are to be recorded.

In addition to time sampling and anecdotal recordings, other classroom observations may include: child's choices of classroom activities and friends, the quality of his work, his task completion habits, and characteristic states of happiness or unhappiness. Work samples should be collected over a period of time to analyze the direction and extent of the child's progress. Finally, the teacher may plan some conversations with the child, to elicit information not otherwise obtainable about his feelings, using such open-ended questions as, "If I had three wishes . . . . " "What I most like to do . . . . " "What I hate most . . . . "

12. Carol A. Cartwright and Philip G. Cartwright, *Developing Observation Skills* (New York: McGraw-Hill), 1974.

The age and verbal ability of the child affect the content of the questions.

Analysis of data

Analysis of data should not be undertaken before any additional information is noted which may be relevant. Such material may be obtained from the child's permanent record file, interviews with other teachers in the school who may have taught him, other teachers who may know him from specialist work in art, music, in the gymnasium or cafeteria, or in after-school programs, and from school specialists, such as the nurse, speech specialist, or guidance counsellor. If the child's file indicates previous referrals to a child guidance clinic, speech clinic, or other special facility, it may be possible to secure further information from such sources, with the assistance of the school guidance counsellor or supervisor.

Parents are major sources of information, but teacher candidates must learn to approach them in objective information-seeking postures, avoiding closure about the child's problems and conveying sympathetic interest as a helping professional. Parents respond cooperatively, in the vast majority of cases, when they sense sincere sympathy and interest, without any indication that teachers are seeking to "blame" them for any of their children's problems, or that there is any adversary relationship. Sometimes, a paraprofessional may be requested to see the parents, if there is a problem about communicating in English, or for any other reason. At this point, the parents' knowledge of the child's history and behavior is sought, to illuminate his present behavior.

One mother who came in for a conference with the kindergarten teacher, about her rather "prickly" son, described his infant problems as a "celiac," a baby unable to digest starch, whose early months were characterized by continual crying and pain, until his dietary problems were solved. The mother showed considerable insight as she recalled her own restlessness and irritability, in caring for this child with a difficult digestive problem. She thought she had handled the child since his infancy as though his digestive difficulty had not been cured, and she was most eager to work out with the teacher common ways of handling him at home and at school, to help him work with more patience and tolerance for others. Not every mother is so insightful and ready to change her own rearing techniques to correct an acknowledged mistake. Nor are most cases so clear-cut as to causes.

A review of child development theory and research helps to emphasize concepts needed for a thorough analysis.

Once the data has been accumulated, from as many of the sources suggested above as possible, an analysis of the data should be written, briefly and factually. If possible, this analysis and the supporting data should be reviewed by someone else, such as a fellow-teacher, supervisor, guidance counsellor, or principal, to eliminate subjective bias and to add further insight to the data analysis. The data itself will be less subjective if more than one person helped to compile it. The data analysis might be accompanied by a review of child development theory and research, for such understandings as:[13]

1. Behavior is caused. Causes of behavior may not be immediately apparent, however.
2. Children and adults are often unaware of the real reasons for their feelings. They may think they are not angry when they are, or ascribe their anger to trivial causes, rather than to the real ones.
3. Any change in a context—teacher, classroom, children, content, activities, or materials—causes some change in all other features of that context. Sometimes, a seemingly difficult child can function better in a different activity, a different class, or with a different teacher.
4. Physical, social, emotional, and cognitive development are interrelated. A sick, hungry, or angry child may appear slow intellectually when he is not.
5. Everyone has characteristic patterns of behavior, which are not always superficially evident. Teachers are urged to gather data through systematic procedures, to reveal regular patterns and to distinguish them from chance or accidental behaviors.
6. Everyone exhibits abnormal behavior sometimes, in response to environmental or internal causes, or both. An overtired, feverish child will usually indicate his condition by unexpected, uncharacteristic behavior, such as whining, crying, or refusing his usual activities.
7. Perceptions of reality are often influenced by internal or environmental factors. A nearsighted or color-blind child perceives the world differently from other children. A child who does not understand the teacher's language may find school a cold and unfriendly place.

13. Mussen, *Psychological Development*, 1973.

8. When information is secured from several different sources, there is likely to be more objectivity than when all the information comes from one person or one source.

9. Children tend to learn better with teachers who convey good expectations for learning.

10. Economic and social conditions which are restrictive do not prevent learning when instructional strategies and plans are matched to children's needs.

11. Handicapped children "mainstreamed," that is, integrated in classes with normal children, can make good progress if the teacher understands the nature of the child's handicap and has the skills to match instructional strategies to his capacities.

Reviewing developmental theory and psychological research helps the teacher to gain perspective on the child who is being studied. Teacher candidates and new teachers are reminded that it is very rarely true that "nothing will help." An experienced teacher who has taken several successive groups through the school year can probably remember when she also thought that there were no effective ways to help children with difficult problems. With experience, she learned that some problems which loom very large at first, soon disappear, while others gradually emerge. The experienced teacher also learned how much her own attitude distorted the problem and her notions about how to handle it. She learned how responsive young children are to love and acceptance. Now, she also knows that the child senses a new teacher's insecurity and sometimes becomes anxious and defensive for this reason.

One student teacher submitted a detailed report on a case study of a child in a second-grade classroom, whose teacher regarded him as incorrigibly difficult, resistant, and insubordinate. The student teacher's conclusion was that this child's personality characteristics could not be changed and that there was little hope for him in school. Yet only a few weeks later this student reported a sequel to her study. Apparently her own interest in this child kindled the attention of the supervisor, who decided to transfer this child to another second-grade class. After two weeks, his new teacher reported the child was functioning well, since he seemed able to get along with her much better than with his original teacher. Children's problems may not always be resolved by a change of teacher, but some of them undoubtedly are better handled in this way than in any other. Five case studies follow, which were developed by student teachers in various big city schools.

CASE STUDY ONE

The kindergarten is in a school with middle- to upper-class white population. Lara is a tiny, fragile little girl. She is pretty, but much smaller than any other child in the class. She has had five open heart operations since she was born and will have another one when she is free of sinus infection. She was most recently hospitalized for pneumonia. Her nose runs constantly and she always seems to have a cold. The teacher was asked to keep her from running, jumping, or climbing. She may not walk more than two flights of stairs. Since the classroom is on the first floor and we often go up to the third floor, Lara has to be carried part of the way. She is not allowed to join in the music activities because of the running, skipping, and hopping that usually goes on there.

Lara's fine-motor control seems immature, compared with the other children. She uses scissors clumsily, she cannot zip or button her clothes, and she finds it difficult to manipulate pieces of a jigsaw puzzle. Her verbalization is difficult to understand. While she pronounces words satisfactorily, her sentences sound like jumbles of words, without clear thoughts. Here's a typical sentence: "My mommy said that, after school do you know my grandpa, last week-end we went, and you do you know what?" She rambles on at a rapid pace, making very little sense. When I tried to keep her on one topic, asking, "What did your mommy say?" she replied, "I don't know", rambling on again. For Show and Tell, she brought in something one day and said "This is my doll, and do you know what my mommy said, oh you know, the other day, my dog . . ." and so on. She never seems to complete a thought. According to her mother, Lara's long hospital stays, keeping her isolated from family and friends, may have caused her to run on like this, without trying to communicate clearly.

Lara rarely plays with any child. She mostly sits by herself. She sometimes stays with other children, but only when the teacher or I am close by. She frequently asks for adult help when it is not needed. Recently, Lara's mother came to school, to find out why the child had begun to refuse to come to school. There was no evidence that other children were bothering her in any way. The teacher and I told Lara's mother we thought she was unhappy whenever she didn't get adult attention, and that she had to learn she can't have adult attention all the time. It was agreed that the school would try to help Lara become less dependent, gradually. This has actually begun to happen, and Lara has begun to play with other children and to be less demanding of the teachers. For example, I arrived in the classroom to see Lara working a puzzle with another girl. As soon as I went over to say that I liked the way they were working together, Lara asked me for help. I said that they were doing such good work that I wanted them to finish, and I would return later, to see the finished puzzle. Five minutes later, the teacher called for "clean-up time." I asked the teacher to let these two finish the last few puzzle pieces. Soon, the two girls came over to show me their finished work, very pleased with themselves, especially Lara. But the next day, Lara was wandering around by herself again, going from one thing to another without getting involved in anything. Two days later, Lara was working by herself, crayonning, busy and persistent. I praised her good work, and asked her if she would make a picture for me and she happily agreed to do so.

What struck me most about this situation was that once Lara's mother, the teacher, and I agreed on Lara's need to learn to be more independent, and to play with other children, we knew how to help Lara make progress. I also learned that progres is not a straight line, and I don't need to be discouraged if there's a step backward now and then—as long as the general direction is forward.

Parent-teacher agreement on a child's needs usually leads to child progress in learning.

CASE STUDY TWO

This kindergarten is in a depressed area, where most of the families are black or Hispanic and have fairly low incomes. There was no question about which child to study—it had to be William! He had been removed from his parents' jurisdiction at age three, by court order, because of child abuse. With an older sister, he had been placed with foster parents who had three older boys. This semester, he has begun visiting his own parents on weekends and holidays, with the expectation that his parents will soon be considered able to resume full-time child-rearing responsibilities.

William entered this school in the prekindergarten. The prekindergarten teacher sought the guidance counsellor's help because William had frequent temper tantrums and outbursts. At a conference held at the school because of his behavior in the prekindergarten, the agency social worker agreed that the child needed psychiatric therapy, and undertook to follow through on this but apparently never did. At conferences with the foster mother, the assistant principal, and the guidance counsellor, the records show that the child was regarded as an "angel" at home, where he gave no trouble. It was the view of the assistant principal that William desired punishment for some reason and misbehaved at school in order to be punished.

In prekindergarten, William had pinched children and provoked fights. He seemed to dislike girls especially. The prekindergarten teacher reported trying out forms of positive reinforcement for desirable behavior and ignoring undesirable behavior, which "didn't work." No record of the teacher's methods was available. Group situations remained very difficult for this child.

Over a two-week period in the kindergarten, fifteen incidents of unacceptable behavior were recorded, such as:

1. *He pushed a child, then scolded this child, "Leave me alone," as though the victim was the aggressor.*
2. *He stood up and made regurgitating noises during a group time, refused to sit down, and left the group.*
3. *He angrily tore up his own art work and shoved it in the children's faces.*
4. *He stabbed at a child's head with a pencil, hurting the child.*
5. *He slapped and pulled the hair of a quiet child.*

I found William defiant of adult authority and unresponsive to commands or instructions. Often he was scarcastic, resistant, and insulting, to children and to teachers. His outbursts of physical or verbal aggression usually appeared unprovoked. The children feared him because he abused them physically and verbally and he is a large, strong child. Sometimes his anger sounds like an adult's, other times, he utters childish sounds.

In the class, William was restless, unfocused, and had a very short attention span. When he began to visit his natural family on weekends, he became increasingly aggressive, hostile, and uncontrollable. The kindergarten teacher thinks William should be removed from the class, for his own and the other children's benefit. Despite the foster mother's disclaimer of trouble at home, there were indications that William recently tried to burn his foster brother's bed. William's tension seems to have become unbearable for him, because of the confusion and anxiety generated by his bouncing from his foster home to his parents' home and back again.

This student teacher described an exceptionally difficult situation, with which no classroom teacher is likely to cope successfully without considerable help. The lack of psychological support for the child, at a time when his whole world seemed chaotic and unstable, and the lack of collaboration in any meaningful way among the school, home, and social agency, all served to compound the child's difficulties. As he grew increasingly abusive and punitive, his unattractive performance and behavior masked his great emotional upheaval and need for love, continuity, and trust. All the school adults, understandably, tended to respond negatively to William's unacceptable behavior, but no one seemed able to respond to the unexpressed needs of this greatly deprived five-year-old. Freudian psychoanalytical theory supports the assistant principal's hypothesis that William was seeking punishment, probably because of his sense of shame and guilt.[14] He seemed to feel

14. Rosalind Gould, *Child Studies Through Fantasy* (New York: Quadrangle Books, 1972), p. 254.

unloving, as well as unloved, and he seemed to need to deserve the punishment he was accustomed to receiving.

The student teacher noted that William arrived at school seething with hatred. He needed, she thought, an acceptable and effective release of his hostilities and aggressions, a physical outlet to prevent him from inflicting pain on children. However, she concluded that it was impossible to meet his constant demands for attention in the classroom because they were so overwhelming.

An interesting note, reported by the student teacher, concerns her efforts to work with this child. She wrote, "I have tried giving William an important function in the classroom. However, he sometimes abuses the responsibility. Often, he becomes extremely bossy and cruel to the children. This only reinforces their fear of him and affirms the tremendous power he wields."

To summarize this study: a child abused at an early age by his own parents was placed with foster parents who, from all the indications, were unable to cope with him. He apparently became a bully (as he was bullied earlier?) and never met with sufficient adult's love, acceptance, or reflection of self-worth. There is a self-fulfilling prophecy at work here. A child convinced of his own worthlessness behaves in ways that always make adults confirm their negative assessment. At age five, is he a hopeless case? Is there no way to slow this child's rush toward self-destruction?

Several points should be made about this observation. It typifies a record of "extreme" behavior, concentrating only on negative, emotionally charged events. Is William *only* an abusive, aggressive, unlikable child? If he is large and powerful, there must be physical skills at which he can or does excel. He may have the potential for good athletic skills which could become the needed alternative by which he can win attention, admiration, and esteem of others. It is understandable that, once a child annoys a teacher, it is hard for her to see any good in him. Was he always "bad," or only at certain times, and in certain situations? There is a clue that he found group times especially difficult, which is not uncommon for restless boys or girls.

Another consideration is that behavior change takes time, does not occur all at once, and cannot be expected to be stable without regression, as indicated above. When the student teacher reported the futility of giving the child some responsibility, she may have given up too soon. Giving responsibility to a child who "sometimes" abuses it, may be an important teaching step in the right direction. Once the

If supportive services are adequate, teachers can help emotionally disturbed children make good progress in school.

child accepts the responsibility, it is possible to value his appropriate exercise of it, to note his inappropriate exercise of it, and to accentuate the behavior which is desired. This is known, in reinforcement theory, as successive approximation to the objective, hopefully getting closer and closer to the behavior desired. A classroom climate which includes trust of children and well-established ways of interacting with kindness and consideration would offer model behavior for constant observation and imitation by a child like William. However, it must be stressed that, because of William's early abuse by his parents, the classroom teacher's efforts would have to be supported by expert psychiatric treatment, to undo severe psychic damage and to stimulate healthy development. More difficult children than William have been helped in normal classroom situations, but usually with the supportive treatment and help from therapist and from school supervisor.

CASE STUDY THREE

A student teacher who is herself an immigrant from Puerto Rico writes sympathetically of others in the same situation, in studying a four-year-old in a public school prekindergarten class, in an inner-city school, as follows:

Life is not very easy for those who leave their land to come to a strange city in search of new horizons. The new horizons have turned into sad agony. Cristina came from Mayaquez, Puerto Rico, when she was twelve months old, with her mother, father, and older brother. The mother speaks little English. Shortly after they arrived, the father left the family. Now the mother and two children are living in a five-room public housing project, on welfare, with five other people. There is another man in the house who comes and goes as he wishes.

Cristina is a little girl whose eyes seem very sad. Her height and weight are normal. She has a very light complexion and long hair. She speaks very little. She doesn't seem to know her first and last names. She doesn't attend school regularly. Most of the time she is isolated from the group and doesn't make friends. When looking for Cristina, one should look in a very small corner. Cristina would be either daydreaming or in a daze.

On the playground, Cristina moves quietly to an activity or plays by herself. She seems livelier on the slides. If she wants a teacher's attention, she pulls the teacher's hand. I wondered whether Cristina has a speech or a language problem. I tried to find this out by speaking to her in the language she knows best—Spanish. This is what happened:

8:30 I asked Cristina in Spanish to help out with the breakfast. She nodded her head postively, and did.

9:00   *I sat next to Cristina at breakfast, asking her to pass the juice, the milk, etc. I also noticed that when Cristina wanted something at the table, she addressed me in Spanish. The child has no speech problems, since she can speak Spanish. Her problem seems to be that she doesn't know English.*

9:30   *For the first time, Cristina helped me clear the table.*

10.00 *Cristina and I made puppets out of paper bags, chatting quietly in Spanish. I wanted to establish a one-to-one relationship with her. We made the puppets talk. Amazingly, Cristina said that her puppet's name was Cristina, and her favorite color was yellow. There is such a big smile on her face that I became the happiest person you can imagine. When another child approached, Cristina stopped talking. I told Cristina that Betsy wanted to play too, but she just put her puppet down and said, "Yo no quiero jugar más." (I don't want to play anymore.)*

10:30 *During the group story time, Cristina became the dreamer again. She held onto her puppet and asked me if she could take it home. She sat quietly and seemed totally uninterested in the story, which I read in English.*

When I had a chance, I read Cristina a story in English and translated it into Spanish. While her attention span is short, this seems to be true of the other children as well.

The next day, as I was putting paints on the easel, Cristina came over to me with cylinders of different heights. She said, "Quiero jugar." (I want to play.) We sat at an empty table and worked together. I let her manipulate the cylinders. I did not say one word, waiting for her to talk about them. Here are her exact words, after manipulating the cylinders for a few minutes: "Mira este (pointing to one cylinder) es más grande y este (another cylinder) es más pequeno." She was comparing the two cylinders, saying that one was taller than the other. I still kept quiet. Then she started to count the cylinders, singing, "Uno. Dos. Tres." She talked about her favorite color (yellow), while putting the cylinders away. Then she began to talk about her big brother and her "marshmallow" shoes.

After our chat, Cristina went happily to a new activity. She even went to share a puzzle with another child, without words. As I continued to observe Cristina, one day I saw her working with playdough with a group of children. She had a rolling pin and a cookie cutter. When one of the other children asked for her rolling pin, I heard a loud, "No! Es mio." (It is mine.) The boy tried to explain that he would return the rolling pin to her, but she clenched her mouth and became sullen, refusing to lend him the rolling pin. I moved in and began to play with the playdough, talking about how nice it is to play with the playdough, talking about how nice it is to share things with children, talking alternately in English and Spanish. The children began to list some of the things they could share. As we talked, I saw Cristina give one child her cookie cutter. She did not talk but I could see that she understood about sharing.

As time goes by, continuing to observe Cristina, I can see changes in her behavior. She smiles with the children. She helps other children zip their coats because she does this well. I have been able to talk to Cristina's mother, presumably because I am close to her age and speak her language. She has discussed home problems with me. She says Cristina is the same at home as she is in school—shy—but that doesn't bother her as long as Cristina behaves and does what she is supposed to do.

Bilingual teachers can ease the transition of non-English-speaking children into English-speaking American schools.

This insightful and sensitive study pinpoints the problem sharply —a Spanish-speaking four-year-old, on the shy side, in an English-speaking world. Involving Cristina with other children who speak English will surely motivate her to learn this second language, and probably go a long way to accomplishing it. Cristina is still young enough to engage her tremendous language-learning ability, to conquer a second language. Supportive English lessons, in playful contexts, would probably help to speed the second-language learning. Note also the context of the study, in a classroom where children are not punished for their immaturity but are helped to learn to play together in cooperation, sharing scarce materials. The mother apparently also needs to learn English as a second language, and if she could be helped to begin systematic study, would probably improve her own potential, for work and fuller use of the facilities and resources of the strange city which is now her home.

CASE STUDY FOUR

A black student teacher, who had worked for several years as a paraprofessional in a very low-income all-black school, wrote about a child she had observed over a four-year period, from prekindergarten through the second grade, as follows:

In the prekindergarten, Denis seemed lonely, shy, quiet, withdrawn, but very sweet. He did not seem to know where he belonged. Often, he sat in a corner, staring. At other times he played alone and sometimes laughed aloud. While he never played with other children, sometimes he knocked down their block constructions. The teacher labelled him a discipline problem, as did his later teachers.

I did not see Denis as a discipline problem. His behavior took me back to my own unhappiness when I first entered school at the age of eight in a southern rural community. My teachers did not understand me, nor did I understand them. The teacher seemed to take it for granted that I should be adjusted to school just because I was there. I was quiet, shy, nervous, and fearful of the teacher for the first few months.

I identified with Denis. Like Denis, I did not always have proper clothing to wear to school. Parents of other children in my class could afford to buy them new shoes or pants for each day of the week. This made me feel inferior to the other children. These children seemed to know how to accomplish what they wanted. Denis seemed just the opposite.

The prekindergarten teacher mostly ignored Denis. In fact, he went on to kindergarten, first and second grade, becoming more and more of a "discipline" problem, until he hurt a child badly. At this point, the teacher went to the guidance counsellor and the principal for help. By this time, at age seven, Denis was doing very poor work in school, lying excessively and daydreaming most of the time. His behavior was immature, he had few social contacts, was rather effeminate, and often laughed and cried inappropriately. Psychological testing showed that the child had average intelligence but he was diagnosed as schizophrenic with some paranoid features.

Denis was the younger of two children living with his mother, grandmother, and twelve-year-old sister. His parents had separated when he was two. His mother sheltered and overprotected him in several ways:

> *She met him at school each day to watch him eat lunch.*
> *She walked him to and from school daily, only a half block.*
> *She brushed his teeth and washed his face.*
> *She kept him indoors after school, afraid children would "pick on him."*

The mother's own poor self-concept and insecurity were evidenced by some of her statements, to the effect that she was an unfit mother, "unable to give her children what they need"; "she didn't know what to do as a mother because everything she did turned out wrong"; "everything she touched had crumbled, withered, and died." At this interview with the mother, she cried, saying she was very concerned about her son's becoming a homosexual, because he always acted like a girl. The mother was on public welfare, and the grandmother was receiving social security payments, she reported. The sister was reported to be doing average to above-average work at junior high school, apparently with no school problems. The mother indicated she had tried to get psychiatric help for Denis in the past, but she was vague about what efforts she had made.

Denis was given supportive therapy, with a male psychiatric social worker, since he was regarded as in need of a male figure with whom to identify. Denis remained in his regular classroom. Meanwhile his mother was enrolled in a guidance and counseling program for parents, in which she had weekly meetings with a psychologist.

After one year of these psychological supports for mother and son, Denis was observed as still using infantile behavior at times, but in general exercising more control over his actions, and no longer fearful. His stronger male identification was shown by his making friends with boys in the class. At home, his relationships seemed better and he lied less. Denis' therapy with the male social worker continues. The mother is no longer on welfare, and is now working in a school as a paraprofessional.

Empathy for children despite unattractive behavior, with school-home-social services collaboration, offers hope for good child progress.

In this case study, a hopeful note emerges as the result of a remarkable collaboration among school, home, and social agency, supporting change and growth for mother and son. The student teacher's sympathy and empathy for the child are also notable, since Denis, like William in Case study two, must have been difficult to see objectively, when his behavior was so unattractive.

CASE STUDY FIVE

This white student teacher, placed in a second-grade class in a low-income community, where the families were mostly Hispanic or black, chose to study a child who seemed to have a poor self-concept, was temperamental and immature. Her report follows:

Domingo speaks English well, although his mother "refuses" to learn English. His father, who speaks English to some extent, and is employed as a cleaner in an office building, checks his homework, comes to school when the teacher requests him to, and is generally cooperative. An older brother, who was in the class the year before, is regarded as much brighter and more mature. The children are well cared-for, although the mother seldom comes to school to pick them up, or for any other reason.

Domingo's first-grade teacher reported he was quite immature, threw temper tantrums when he didn't get his way, ran around the room, stomped his feet, cried and sulked often. This teacher said she ignored the immature behavior and it subsided by the end of the year.

In this class, Domingo cries when he is unable to do some school work, or to get his work entirely correct. He reads fairly well, according to the teacher, on grade level, but needs help with math. The teacher said Domingo tunes out when she gives instructions to a group, and must be shown how to do every exercise, no matter how familiar it is. He seems unable to be creative or imaginative, or to do anything unless he is told how to do it, step by step.

I noticed Domingo is generally very quiet but he cries and sulks when reprimanded. He also seems very ill-at-ease with the children, especially in his reading group of eight children. Other children often call him, "cry baby", and he shouts at them when they do. He is also very reserved with the teacher, never showing feelings of pleasure. If he is reprimanded for not following instructions, he clenches his fists, looks down, and frowns fiercely, as if he is trying to control his rage.

Working with Domingo's reading group, I noted that he had to be told two or three times to do something; that in doing workbook exercises he was most reluctant to write down an answer, for fear it might be wrong; and that, while he had no trouble reading directly from the reader, he can't tell me anything about the story, except who the characters are. He might have a comprehension problem, but there is no evidence of this.

The teacher thought Domingo was very competitive with his older, brighter brother, had unrealistically high self-expectations and when these were not met, he became very angry with himself for his failure.

I selected two goals for Domingo, that is, more self-confidence and ability to be successful in his school work and more social skills, to be less of a loner and more acceptable in play activities. To improve his self-confidence and self-esteem, I worked with him individually, gave him a great deal of attention and praised him for every possible bit of work completed or attempted independently. I tried to emphasize the value of effort more than the end-product, to de-emphasize the fear of failure. To help him become more acceptable to the children, Domingo is receiving warm approbation for sharing materials, for initiating social interchanges and for helping others. I know that these goals will not be reached overnight."

Helping a child with a negative self-concept to value himself more requires genuine teacher acceptance and individualized teaching.

Several points should be noted about this study. The same teacher who is angry with the mother who "refuses" to learn English, also "refuses" to learn Spanish—hence her ability to communicate with parents such as Domingo's mother is poor. However, the school has resources in paraprofessionals and other teachers who can speak Spanish, so there is really no great barrier to parent communication, if the teacher really wants to work with the mother or father. The second point seems obvious. A child who is tuning out instructions does not need reprimands, from which he learns nothing except that the teacher probably dislikes him. He needs some feelings of success and self-esteem. Omitting reprimands would, by itself, lessen a child's fear of failure. But teacher behavior must change, to signal a real acceptance of this child, with as much emphasis as possible on his own talents, skills, and achievements, compared only with his own history of progress. The student teacher seems to be working in the right direction, individualizing instruction, on a one-to-one basis so that there is no competition, and much less motivation to tune out. A further step would be to vary his work so that he cannot compare it with other children's answers, rewarding effort and helping him to make as much progress as his talents and efforts permit.

CLASSROOM AND BEHAVIOR MANAGEMENT

Classroom management chiefly deals with the distribution and uses of materials, transitions from one activity to another, giving time, space, and shape to the curriculum. The management of behavior, frequently called discipline, deals with setting limits and rules, and following rule enforcement procedures. Both of these are important means of affecting children's feelings of what they can do, and how worthy they are.

Arrangement of classroom materials contributes to constructive use of time and space.

Management of the classroom itself requires skills which can vastly diminish behavior problems.[15] Orderly arrangement of materials prevents frustration when teacher and children can find things when they want them. Dependency on teacher help can be reduced by child-level shelves, placement of materials in the activity centers where they are to be used, provision of newspapers, sponges, brooms, and wastebaskets for cleanups where needed, and placement of learning centers so they do not interfere with each other. The teacher's choices of materials and their placement all contribute to constructive use of the time and space available.

Good classroom management is evident in clear room arrangements, easily understood procedures, and consistent teacher guidance. Children assume much more independence and responsibility than novice teachers expect, if there is a gradual and step-by-step approach to where things go and what happens next. Cueing children helps, until they say, "You don't have to tell me. I know!" Reminding children gently helps. When children forget, a friendly acceptance of human error with confident expectations often assures better performance next time. If teacher candidates assume that young children do the best they can, it is obvious that reprimands and scolding are out of order. Better teaching is called for, not punishment, when children seem to flout the teacher's wishes for order in classroom arrangements. When drastic change seems to be needed, the change must be in the teaching, and in the arrangements, rather than the children.

15. Helen F. Robison and Sydney L. Schwartz. *Learning at an Early Age*, vol. 1 (New York: Appleton-Century-Crofts, 1972), p. 254.

Humanistic forms of behavior management are required for constructive teacher-child relationships. With young children, the setting and enforcement of clear and reasonable limits helps to make them feel worthy. Clear limit-setting has these advantages:

It tells the child clearly what is safe or desirable and what is not. The goals are clearly stated. The child knows what is expected. For example, in the block area, the teacher might say, "You may build only as high as your head, so the blocks cannot fall on your head."

The child has a specific idea of how the goal is to be attained, and how to judge whether he has reached the goal. In the block example, the teacher might add, "If you build too high, stop and remove any blocks that are taller than you are."

The child is helped to understand the reasons for the rules. "If you build too high, you might get hurt."

The child is given some independence, since he knows when he has gone too far, and he can enforce the rule himself. Here, he is encouraged to internalize the rules, not to depend on the teacher as monitor.

The child's self-concept grows as he perceives himself as one who knows rules and is trusted to enforce them himself.

The child's skill in self-control grows, because his rule-enforcing ability tends to generalize to other situations.

Clear limits, with flexibility inside the limits, supports self-esteem of children.

The setting of limits, however, needs to be tempered with flexibility inside of those limits, in order that the child is not made to feel over-controlled and unable to express himself. For example, a group of block builders wanted to find ways to make a tall tower. Accustomed to reasonable limit-setting by the teacher, they consulted her for help. Further clarity on safety requirements emerged as they discussed the reasons for the height limit, and when one boy suggested building a tower on a table, the teacher approved the idea with further safety precautions. Flexibility in rule enforcement is needed, because children often distort an idea while they are trying to understand it. To punish a child who misunderstood the rule or understood it imperfectly is to miss the substance of teaching. Instead, teachers can approve of whatever is acceptable, to support self-esteem and to clarify ideas without diminishing the child.

Rules are not learned once and for all, nor can the teacher assume everyone will remember to follow them all the time. The teacher gives reasons for the rules, which help children to remember them. It is important to listen respectfully to the child's reasons for resistance, to accept the child's right to question and to receive rational answers, and to persevere in appropriate rule setting. The child who is treated respectfully, even when he is emotional in his resistance, perceives this respect and feels worthy even though denied.

It takes time to reason with a child, to hear him out, to respond appropriately, and sometimes to make a counter-proposal to preserve his self-respect. An angry child may not be able to exercise control immediately and may need a transition, especially one which permits him to release his anger safely. Sometimes the teacher can help children understand the need for limits better if she enlists their help in constructing the rules. Gould notes that when a child's experiences are more positive than negative, he not only feels like "a good person" but is motivated to follow the rules of his caretakers.[16] Gould uses such descriptive terms, for positive affect, as "wish-to-please," "sense of entitlement," and "pride."

When Head Start classes were first formed within public schools, some teachers experienced continuing conflict over inappropriate rules in big city schools. Often, three and four-year-olds were expected to wait in lines outside the school building until the opening bell rang, and then to enter in perfect order and quiet through school corridors. Sensible procedures appropriate for young children usually won out against traditional rigidities. Parents were permitted to deliver a child directly to his classroom, and to visit briefly or at length, depending upon the situation.

In one prekindergarten, the teachers complained that they were unable to separate a four-year-old from his mother. It was school policy to require the child to take leave of his mother at the classroom door. Before this child was "expelled" from school, a conference was held with teachers, principal, the mother, and the early childhood consultant. The result of this conference was an agreement to give this mother and child more time to make the adjustment to school. The mother agreed to come daily and take cues from the teachers about her behavior and availability to the child. However, the mother insisted that she would be more relaxed at ten o'clock than at nine, with some household chores completed. The school permitted the mother to bring her three-year-old with her, to avoid baby-sitter expenses. With frequent on-the-spot discussion with the teachers and observation of the teachers' positive handling of the child during this adjustment period, the mother learned to wait patiently for the child

16. Gould, *op. cit.*, p. 219.

to get involved with materials and other children, without scolding or threatening him, and without sneaking home. It took eight days before William arrived at school and dismissed his mother. His self-esteem was high as he entered the classroom with the knowledge that he had no need of his mother for the few hours in school.

Teachers often ask whether behaviorist techniques work better than humanist procedures. Sometimes they note that when they rely exclusively on reward systems, they work sometimes, or for awhile but not indefinitely. These realistic observations of experienced teachers emphasize the desirability of good relationships with children as the highest priority. Reward systems are powerful tools for changing or influencing behavior, but they are more effective when the basic relationship with a child is good, than if this is not the case. There is the problem of training in, and use of, reward systems, which require more consistency and continuity for success in behavior management than other methods. It is this writer's view that, with basically good relationships with children, teachers may be flexible in selecting the use of reinforcement systems in specific situations, with certain children, at selected periods. If the goal is the child's own internal satisfactions with his work and his interactions with others, it may be that this goal may be advanced with some children with more external rewards until they are amenable or able to internalize needed controls. This would be especially applicable to children whose previous experiences have been sufficiently negative to make the school situation traumatic for child and teacher.

Good teacher-child relationships are required for successful behavior management.

A general problem in reinforcement systems, for children with troubled histories, is to find a sufficiently motivating reward. Behaviorist research suggests the value of observing a child in a spontaneous activity, to see what he does when he is playing, or doing naturally what he wants to do. If he is pushing chairs around, this may be the reward that worked for him. Of course, if his natural activity is negative or harmful, the child's repertoire of constructive activities may first have to be increased.

Reward systems often fail in classrooms because of inconsistent teaching. If teachers are unable to follow a plan for rewards with some regularity, its impact is likely to be weak. If the school procedures are too disparate from home-rearing techniques, the child may be too confused about expectations. It is the school's responsibility to bring about as much harmony between school and home procedures as possible, and to convey as much realistic optimism as possible.

Reward systems may also fail because the child recognizes the teacher's negative feelings about him and responds to such messages, rather than to the reward system offered. However, if a reward system leaves a child with a good feeling about himself, more has been gained than lost.

Individualization of teaching

It seems self-evident that teaching must match the child's present level of learning, that it should be neither too far above nor below the achieved capacity. Despite this long-held belief, many teachers seem able to teach children only in large groups, or entire classes. The trend has increasingly been to "open" the classroom, to individualize learning activities, and to find out where children are before confronting them with preplanned lessons which may be right for only a few. Yet, too many children in early childhood classes are being treated to such large-group or total-class instruction, particularly in reading. "It works!" school supervisors say, about such overstructured and mass-oriented teaching, pointing to reading scores in first grade which they find attractive. But if the visitor persists, to find out what happens to the children in such classes, the more candid school supervisors explain the high drop-out rate from such classes, the need to find alternatives and less-pressured programs, or more individualized or remedial programs. It usually turns out that the success figures relate only to the survivors, ignoring the drop-outs from the program.

A teaching system that recognizes individuality and supports high self-esteem is recommended.

It often happens that the children who can survive in very structured, mass teaching situations are those with enough strength to survive any system. The cost to these children of survival is seldom assessed. If they could learn in almost any system, why not a more humane one? Why not a system which recognizes their individuality and encourages high self-esteem through valuing and emphasizing individual talents, interests, and pace?

Individualized procedures may vary from true differentiation for all children throughout the school day, and the school year, to selected areas for individualization, or at certain times, or for certain children. Often, teachers are willing to experiment and to individualize the program for the slower children, but not for the rest. Characterizing children as "slower," even without voicing it but only in treatment and programming, may dilute the effect of the teaching, because of the feeling the children get that they are not worth much anyway.

For those children for whom a child study has been completed, the needs and possibilities for individualization are derived from the diagnosis based on the data. In the case studies summarized in this chapter, the relationships between diagnosis and individual prescriptions or plans for teaching were detailed. But teachers need not reserve individualization procedures for deviant children only.

The easiest way to achieve instant individualization is to offer children choices of learning activities and to note who chooses what. A simple tally system, which either teacher or children keep, to show who chose what, and how often, and on which days, results in a record of choices which is often a first basis for matching learning activities to children's needs and interests. When children tally their own choices, this is accomplished, if children can recognize either their own names, or photographs, or decals or other symbols, by placing a tally sheet daily at child eye-level in each center of learning and reminding children to make tally marks every time they play or work in that center. Based on these tally sheets, teachers learn children's spontaneous choices, and can plan to encourage, challenge or otherwise further their functioning in areas of high interest.

When children work with high motivation, in activities they choose, the teacher is free to vary her teaching methods and activities as she selects children and content for indicated teaching possibilities. There is no barrier to teacher planning to broaden children's interests and activities, as she learns the particular strengths and current capacities of each child. Sometimes the same kind of activity can be the basis for individualization of learning plans. Some children who are willing to crayon a picture about a just-completed trip are satisfied with the picture, while others want to or can be asked to dictate a story about either the trip or the picture. In addition, some children will want to write their own stories, or to copy the teacher's writing of the story they dictated, and others will insist upon reading the story they wrote or dictated. Instead of a requirement that all children do the same thing, the learning activities can be as varied as the children.

Additional ways to individualize children's learning are the following:

1. Giving children different materials for science activities, for instance, for discovery lessons, so that children cannot make invidious comparisons with each other about who is further ahead, and

so that the instructional techniques can be adapted to the materials each child is using.

2. Giving children flexibility in scheduling their required activities, so that those who become responsible and independent can enjoy the good feeling that they are successful in planning the order and timing of their work. Children have to practice scheduling their time, to stretch their independence and skills of self-management. But this means that the teacher is willing to give children time to accomplish this, and accept errors in judgment along the way.

3. Using the technology to gear the work to the pace and level of the child. Headsets with recorded audio-cassettes, for various kinds of content frees the child from mass pacing, and permits the teacher and child to choose the content which suits the needs and interests of a particular child. More expensive technology, rarely available to teachers, can generally be ignored in favor of simple, controllable materials within the budget of the school.

4. Accepting team teaching members, so that more adults are available to respond to and to initiate more individual activities for children. Older children within the classroom, in a vertically grouped school, can help by taking some responsibility for younger children, for certain activities. Parent or grandparent volunteers, senior citizens interested in making meaningful contributions to children's education, can all help. Assistant teachers, teacher aides, or student teachers may be the most helpful, because of their training, continuity over periods of time, and professional educational goals. A team of teachers of young children, working and planning together, even without additional help, can plan their programs to free each other for more individual work with children, while engaging the larger groups in constructive work.

5. Scheduling time for individual work or conferences with children, for fifteen-minute periods when classroom coverage can be handled by other staff members, such as music or art specialists.

POSITIVE FEEDBACK

In an emergency, to avoid danger, the teacher is justified in the use of extraordinary means to restrain a child. It may require bodily removal, if the teacher is close to the child's position, or a loud, screaming warning, if the teacher is too far away to use physical restraint. A real emergency means a child is likely to be hurt or to inflict damage on another child or on valuable equipment. An emergency signal has only one goal: to stop dangerous behavior. Short of danger, teachers can learn to use positive forms of feedback to children, which may be either neutral or complimentary.

Objective or neutral feedback is factual. The teacher makes a statement which carries no value judgment, such as, "Your painting has two colors, red and green," where there are no requirements as to how many or how few colors should be used. To be a truly neutral statement, the tone of voice must not carry the value judgment omitted from the words, nor must the teacher's gestures or body language do so. Objective feedback sometimes serves to remind children of their obligations, despite the teacher's refraining from such explicitness. Does it come to the same thing? Not to the child. The teacher may be serving as timekeeper, when different children have selected different times for their snack, or for some work in the listening center. Letting the child take even one small step toward independent self-control is worth the risk that he will forget, or that he will change his mind. It also encourages children to take initiative in other cases, such as sharing scarce equipment or helping a child who cannot find some materials he needs. Without these small steps toward independence, the children will never be able to take the big leaps expected of them.

Simple reminders often bring surprising results. One child who was adamant about refusing to give up her turn on the swing to other children, was charmed with the teacher's suggestion of counting slowly to ten, to time each turn. The teacher moved far away from this activity, as the child gladly counted out other children's turns until her own turn came around again. This teacher, returning when the counting was well-established, used positive feedback, when she said, "Janey got off the swing after she counted ten." It is not manipulative of children to set standards without direct control, and to give them time to assert or try out their own controls. Not only do self-controls grow, but self-esteem rises in proportion to self-control.

Complimentary feedback includes various forms of approving some or all of a child's behavior. Consider the situation in some of the case studies described, where a child seldom, if ever, did anything for which he received any complimentary feedback. Compliments cannot be bestowed without cause, or the child will sense their artificiality. But situations can be structured in which a seldom-praised child can be expected to act in praiseworthy ways. To say to a child, in warm approving tones, "I saw you give Henry his turn on the bike," is to make his day a rosier one. Or, after clean-up time, if a teacher inspects the cleaning and praises the good work, without mentioning the sloppy work, much better cleaning is likely to ensue.

The angry, aggressive or acting-out child is usually the most difficult to support in this way. In order to be able to make such complimentary statements, and to give them weight in the child's perception of how the teacher values him, there must already be a time sampling plan by which to observe such a child. Otherwise, the teacher is only likely to be aware of this child's disruptions or aggressions, without any idea of behavior which is, in fact, unexceptionable. Following these suggestions, by assiduous time sampling on a regular basis, the teacher can begin to verbalize ordinary nonaggressive behavior, so that the child comes to value its supportiveness and indication of acceptance. For example, a child who frequently hit other children, with little provocation, was engaged in plucking a rubber band he had stretched taut over a box—a neutral, harmless, if noisy activity. The teacher observed this activity with some relief, noting it on the time-sampling record as an approved action. She wondered how to communicate approval to the child. She certainly preferred aggression against objects to pushing children. She took this as her cue—she would voice approval when this child was involved in a harmless action that was not hurting anyone. Time-sampling uncovered many such actions by this child, much more than the teacher had expected. Voicing approval of actions which were not harmful to others preceded a plan which gradually unfolded to accept this child in verbal and gestural ways when he was engaging in constructive kinds of play or work.

CHILD ACCEPTANCE

It is interesting to note how pervasive the teacher techniques are for influencing child behavior. The children are often seen imitating the the teacher's speech, remarks, tones of voice, and attitudes toward specific children. Acceptance, when consistently modelled by the teacher, is likely to be copied by the children as well, adding additionally reinforcing elements. "Friends" help "friends," when the teacher models and expects this kind of behavior. "Friends" sympathize with each other, or comfort each other when disaster strikes, as for example, when an exciting block structure collapses.

Some students preparing to teach early childhood classes have doubts about their ability to relate to and accept many different kinds of children. Others, whether or not they have questions about their own feelings and wishes, would do well to put their career choice to the test, in several different teaching situations, preferably as student or assistant or apprentice teachers, if possible.

Accepting a child means reasoning with and about him as a mature adult. It means having compassion for young children when they are most demanding and unattractive. It means responding to a child in mature ways when he is testing the limits of your patience and rules in very immature, childish ways. It means recognizing your own annoyance, or other emotional reaction to a child, without assuming, "It's the child's fault." Your own annoyance may have nothing to do with this child, since you might still be reacting to something annoying that happened at home, or in the school office, or anywhere else. It means being able to continue to communicate love and acceptance to a child even when you deny him, for good reasons, something he wants to do. It means bringing into the classroom daily clear indications that every day is a fresh start, wiping out past offenses, permitting everyone to break new ground. Most especially, it means conveying to every parent a genuine sense of caring about and understanding the unique virtues of each child.

Is there a child who has no virtues? It is not likely. When a teacher sees no virtues in a child, she needs to try to see the world from his point of view. Or she needs to try to extract virtues from a child, by placing him in new and different situations.

How can a child acquire new virtues? Mostly by doing new things he never did before, such as:

Watering the plants.

Feeding the fish.

Cleaning an animal cage.

Making a terrarium.

Blowing soap bubbles colored with vegetable coloring.

Washing classroom equipment with sponge and bubbly soap.

Pasting decals on furniture, books, and equipment.

Washing or chalking, or both, on a chalkboard.

Painting a floor, wall, or chalkboard, with brush and water.

Fanning a wet chalkboard dry with a hand or electric fan.

Painting empty cereal boxes, grocery cartons, or pieces of wood, with tempera paint.

Mixing cement with a cement-mixing kit, to make or patch some needed item.

Making ice cream, or jello, or spaghetti, or barbecuing hamburgers or frankfurters.

Making a kite or a pinwheel.

Making and playing a simple rhythm instrument, such as a drum, or maraca-type shaker.

Taking and sending messages on the classroom intercom.

Singing, dancing, or making music on xylophone, piano, or autoharp.

Playing quoits or beanbag throw.

Punching a punching bag with boxing gloves.

Wading in a wading pool.

Picking flowers and arranging them in a vase.

Planting a vegetable or flower garden, indoors or out.

Delivering mail to children in the class, such as valentines.

Constructing a birdhouse at the carpentry table.

Making simple wooden boats at the carpentry table, and floating them in a tub or basin.

Launching paper airplanes.

Playing marbles.

Playing checkers or chess, or parchesi.

Playing card games, with baseball or playing cards.

Playing assistant teacher.

Making popcorn.

Making a collage with new materials, such as sand, pebbles, shells, and feathers.

Using a balance to find equalities and inequalities.

Making paterns with pattern blocks, or pegs and a pegboard, or other material.

Any other activity new to a child.

Other ways of showing a child acceptance may include such actions as the following:

Telephoning a sick child, letting him know he is missed and valued.

Sending get-well cards to sick children.

Having a special greeting for a child who returns after an absence for any reason.

Keeping in close enough touch with parents to be able to comment appropriately in personal ways about a child and his family.

Letting parents know frequently about a child's progress.

Avoiding punitive verbal or nonverbal behavior.

Helping a child to learn rules and limits, when he seems unaware of them or forgets them.

Modelling classroom behavior which includes listening to children respectfully, addressing them kindly, making exceptions for good reason, using pleasant speaking tones, and creating a warm, friendly environment in the classroom, where everyone is considered important.

To achieve these ideal conditions in the classroom, where each child comes with eagerness and readiness to work and play, requires good planning. Open classrooms require far more planning than traditional ways of teaching, although the emphases may be different. In the open classroom, far more attention is required for classroom management and materials selection and arrangement, and for the teacher's individual work with one child, or small groups. In the more traditional type of classroom, far more attention must be paid to behavior management and the scheduling of activities.

LESSON PLANS TO PROMOTE CHILD ESTEEM

The drudgery of writing lesson plans can be justified if they help teachers to teach better. When teachers produce specific types of lesson plans, which are not useful in teaching, but meet the specified requirement, it is a dismal waste of time and energy. Advising some teachers in this situation, this writer has suggested producing such plans when there is no alternative, but adapting them to the real teaching purposes they should serve.

A lesson plan should never be an exercise in futility. It should be a vehicle by which a teacher can note the direction, cues, and signals by which she expects to navigate through a day of challenging work with young children. Where does she expect to go, with what, when, and how will she know when she has arrived? These are the kinds of questions lesson plans should help a teacher answer. It makes no difference what style one uses in writing lesson plans, as long as the content is functional. A lesson plan is a record of your thoughtful reflection and decisions for teaching. It helps you to remember to procure materials and equipment you may need, to reserve any space additional to the classroom, or to secure additional adult help if the planned activities may require it. It also helps you to build continuities for children in their learning experiences, as you construct tomorrow's plan to further the important learning activities that were going on today.

A lesson plan format this writer has used with many student teachers requires statements of:

> behavioral goals
> grouping
> learning activities
> materials
> sequence of activities
> teaching strategies
> evaluation techniques[17]

Many public school teachers are required to write lesson plans which include elements for motivation. This is supposed to inspire exciting ways to secure children's interest or attention. This seems quite needless, since children respond positively to almost any appropriate activity. If the lesson is planned to be inappropriately passive, sedentary, and static, no amount of "planned motivation" will cure its low power of instruction.

Well-developed lesson plans are required for achieving an ideal classroom atmosphere.

At first, student teachers might plan for one group of children, or for one learning center. After successful implementation of such limited plans, students will find it easier to think of juggling groups and individuals, or rather of freeing children to find their own interests in a very well-planned room.

Most of the teacher planning time initially might well be spent selecting, arranging, and coordinating materials and equipment, so that a given group of children may make optimum use of the materials, time, space, and teachers available. Exciting learning environments grow out of clear goals for children's school experiences. The goals only flag end points and directions. Plans to reach these goals should take account of how children will perceive and value themselves in these activities and learning experiences.

Lesson plans should take account of the varying paces at which young children work, and their differences in attention span, which tend to grow longer with experience in the classroom, and with maturation. Must everyone clean up at the same time? What about the child who desperately wants five more minutes to finish painting a picture? If an occasional exception is not allowed, one is actually

17. Robert F. Mager, *Preparing Instructional Objectives* (Palo Alto, California: Fearon Publishers, 1962).

saying to the child that what he is doing, in painting, is unimportant —that it does not matter whether he finishes or not. Valuing what children do, when they are most involved and unwilling to stop, must be planned for. It may be that work cannot be reasonably finished at one sitting. If so, an unfinished block structure can be protected and left for completion the next day. It is possible that a child will have to be denied when he wants to continue an absorbing activity. Deny it, but value it, and plan with that child for its eventual continuation![18]

Lesson plans need assessment for *what* they value. The first priority should be: do the plans enhance the child's self-esteem?

SUMMARY   *Teacher relationships with children must emphasize positive self-concepts. Many different features of heredity and environment contribute to the child's self-esteem, including genetic endowment, developmental pace, and cultural and socioeconomic differences.*

Self-concepts develop out of children's perceptions of the feelings about them which are communicated by the important people in their primary group, chiefly their families. Children bring their self-concepts to school, where changes may result from experiences and relationships encountered.

Major techniques early childhood teachers use to enhance child self-esteem include child study skills, classroom and behavior management systems, individualization, use of positive feedback, child acceptance, well-designed teaching plans, self-analysis of teaching, and collaboration with parents and with other professionals. Well-designed teaching plans help teachers to enhance children's self-concepts in many ways.

Child study skills may be used to screen a whole group, or to identify the few children most in need of help. For these few children, detailed case studies often reveal problems which can be solved, mitigated, or eased in some ways. Five case studies illustrate some of the range of problems and possibilities which can be identified and taken into account in developing plans for teaching. Lesson plan formats and ways to develop lesson plans to support high self-esteem of children are suggested.

18. For additional readings on lesson plans see John Herbert, *A System for Analyzing Lessons* (New York: Teachers College Press, 1967); and Robert H. Davis et al., *Learning System Design* (New York: McGraw-Hill, 1974).

❦ EXERCISES FOR STUDENTS   🌲🌲🌲🌲🌲🌲🌲🌲🌲🌲🌲🌲🌲🌲🌲🌲🌲

1. Select one withdrawn and one aggressive child, with the permission of the classroom teacher.

   a. Write an observation of each child, based on data recorded on at least five different days, using time sampling methods, combined with anecdotal recording.

   b. Append to each observation your imaginative description of the feelings of these children. Pretend to *be* each of these children and write as sympathetically as you can of what it might be like to be each of them in turn.

2. For one of the two children selected, complete the following:

   a. Obtain any additional information available from in-school sources, with the permission and assistance of your classroom teacher.

   b. Analyze your data, and write a brief summary of your analysis.

   c. Based on your analysis, write a brief diagnosis of this child's instructional needs—how should he be taught?

   d. Translate your diagnosis into a prescription for instruction of this child, and write a sample lesson plan to indicate how you would implement the prescription.

   e. Discuss your case study, upon completion of the exercises, with your college supervisor and/or your classroom teacher, focusing on the following:

      (1) Adequacy of your data base. Did you secure enough information? Is any essential type of information missing? How systematic were your observations? Do you have a picture of this child's characteristic functioning? How much confidence do you have in your data?

      (2) Logic of your analysis. Does your data support your analysis? Are you going too far beyond your data? Do you really need more data to make an adequate analysis?

      (3) Appropriateness of your prescription. How will your prescription for instruction improve this child's functioning? How does it flow from your diagnosis?

3. Write a series of five lesson plans which you think your cooperating teacher might approve for your use with some or all the children in the class.

a. Plan a consecutive series of lessons in one area, such as discovery activities in science, complete with evaluation techniques.

b. Tape record, or videotape, some or all of these lessons, if possible. If not, try to arrange for someone to observe and evaluate your performance, such as your college supervisor or your classroom teacher. Indicate to the observer that you are working to implement specific lesson plans, and furnish a copy of such plans.

c. Write a brief analysis of your actual implementation of these lesson plans, and in what respects you did or did not follow them, and why. Evaluate your own performance, stressing *affective* results —your own perception of your success in teaching for enhancing the self-esteem and good feelings of the children with whom you worked. Self-criticism should include your own suggestions for improving your work or questions addressed to your classroom teacher or college supervisor, to assist you in improving your teaching performance.

❦ EXERCISES FOR TEACHERS ❦❦❦❦❦❦❦❦❦❦❦❦❦❦❦❦❦❦❦

1. Use one of the suggestions in this chapter, or from any other source, to screen your group to identify two or three children who seem to be in most need of help.

a. Select one of these children for a detailed case study, collecting data, analyzing your material, and deriving a prescription for teaching this child, following any suggestions in this chapter you find useful, or from any of the readings in the Resources at the end of the chapter.

b. To increase your objectivity in data collection and in planning for this child's progress, enlist a colleague or supervisor to share observations or to react to your perceptions.

c. Implement your plan for this child and assess results compared with your plans or intentions.

2. Review a recent set of lesson plans you implemented.

   a. Identify points at which you could have used some of the techniques suggested in this chapter to enhance children's self-concepts.

   b. Plan your next set of lessons with strong emphasis upon enhancing children's self-esteem, including as many specific techniques as you can in your plans.

3. Arrange to record, on audio or videotape, a few five-minute segments of your interactions with children in recurring situations, such as group discussions or individual conversations.

   a. Analyze your tapes to identify any of your behaviors which one or more children might have perceived as devaluing of themselves as persons.

   b. Select alternative possibilities which could be more supportive of child self-esteem, try them out, record a few segments and determine whether you seem to be more positive and supportive.

   c. If you are uncertain whether you are sufficiently enhancing children's self-concepts, invite a colleague or supervisor to help you.

BIBLIOGRAPHY

Axline, Virginia. *Dibs.* New York: Ballantine Books, 1964.

Bandura, A., and Walters, R. H. *Social Learning and Personality Development.* New York: Holt, Rinehart and Winston, 1964.

Bernard, Harold W. *Child Development and Learning.* Boston: Allyn and Bacon, 1973.

Cartwright, Carol A. and Cartwright, Philip G. *Developing Observation Skills.* New York: McGraw-Hill, 1974.

Coller, A. R. "The Assessment of 'Self-Concept' in Early Childhood Education." Urbana, Illinois: ERIC Clearinghouse on Early Childhood Education, 1971. (ERIC ED 050–822.)

Coopersmith, Stanley. *The Antecedents of Self-Esteem.* San Francisco: W. H. Freeman & Co., 1967.

Davis, Robert H. et al. *Learning System Design.* New York: McGraw-Hill, 1974.

Erikson, E. H. *Childhood and Society.* Rev. ed. New York: W. W. Norton, 1963.

Gordon, Ira. *Studying the Child in School.* New York: John Wiley, 1968.

Gould, Rosalind. *Child Studies Through Fantasy*. New York: Quadrangle Books, 1972.

Johnson, Stephen. et al. "How Deviant Is the Normal Child? A Behavioral Analysis of the Preschool Child and His Family." Paper presented at the Fifth Annual Meeting of the Association of the Advancement of Behavior Theory, Washington, D.C., 1971.

Mager, Robert F. *Preparing Instructional Objectives*. Palo Alto, California: Fearon Publishers, 1962.

Mead, G. H. *Mind, Self and Society*. Chicago: University of Chicago Press, 1934.

Muller, Philippe. *The Tasks of Childhood*. New York: McGraw-Hill, 1969.

Murphy, Lois. *Methods for the Study of Personality in Young Children*. New York: Basic Books, 1956.

Mussen, Paul. *The Psychological Development of the Child*. 2d ed. Englewood Cliffs, N.J.: Prentice-Hall, 1973.

Piaget, Jean. *The Origins of Intelligence in Children*. New York: International Universities Press, 1952.

Rasey, Marie I., and Menge, J. W. *What We Learn from Children*. New York: Harper & Row, 1956.

Robison, Helen F., and Schwartz, Sydney L. *Learning at an Early Age*. Vol. 1. *A Programmed Text For Teachers*. Englewood Cliffs, N.J.: Prentice-Hall, 1972.

Singer, Jerome L., ed. *The Control of Aggression and Violence*. New York: Academic Press, 1971.

Washington, Kenneth R. "Self-Concept Development: An Affective Educational Experience for Inner-City Teachers," *Young Children* 29 (July 1974), pp. 305–310.

Whiting, B. B., ed. *Six Cultures: Studies of Child Rearing*. New York: Wiley, 1963.

FILMS

Boy With Glasses. 45 min. B/W. Educational Film Exchange.

Children Who Draw. 38 min. B/W. Brandon Films.

Early Recognition of Learning Disabilities. 30 min. Color. Nat'l. Institutes of Health, New York.

Four Children. 20 min. B/W. Head Start. Modern Talking Pictures, 1212 Ave. of the Americas, New York 10036.

The Hyperactive Child. 30 min. Color. CIBA Pharmaceutical Co., 500 Elizabeth Ave., Somerset, N.J.

Nursery School Child/Mother Interactions. 41 min. B/W, Head Start, New York.

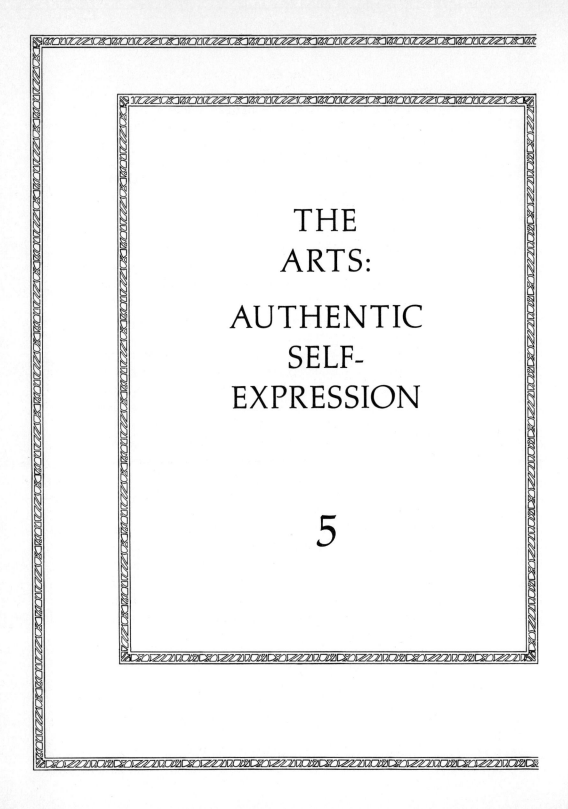

THE ARTS:

AUTHENTIC SELF-EXPRESSION

5

Maria Montessori wrote eloquently about the liberty of the child, to permit "a development of individual, spontaneous manifestations of the child's nature."[1] Montessori used the term *liberty* to mean conditions most favorable to the total development of the child. Under such favorable conditions, she said, the child's spontaneous nature would emerge and flourish. Montessori taught her teachers to respect children's natural, spontaneous movements and constructive action in the classroom. We call this *authentic self-expression*. There is great concern today for the expression of the child's own personality in a world of mass production.

Teaching children to release and develop their natural expressive and art proclivities requires subtle, sensitive strategies. Art guidance is easier if child art is understood and valued. Why not tell children what good art is and teach them to produce it?

Maria, four-and-one-half years old, is crayonning while the Head Start Center director completes an intake interview with her mother. Maria makes tree trunks and colors them purple. Her mother, embarrassed, tells her sharply that trees are not purple. "They look purple sometimes," the director comments casually, and changes the subject.

In a nursery school class, where the walls are papered with child art, children choose the four or five colors of tempera they wish to take to the easel, and show their finished products to the teacher. She receives them all respectfully, sometimes with just an appreciative nod, sometimes with an objective comment such as, "mm blues and greens. Two colors." "You made a large round shape, I see." "This is different from the paintings you did last week. You are using more colors." Notice the absence of value judgments in this teacher's comments, the absence of adult interpretations of the child's work, and the omis-

1. Maria Montessori, *The Montessori Method* (New York: Schocken, 1970), p. 28.

sion of "Would you like to tell me about it?" Notice especially the lack of negative comments, and the acceptance of all paintings with equal respect.

In a second-grade class, where most children paint recognizable shapes and figures, one child's work continues to feature vague forms. This child's work is well accepted, with teacher comments on use of color, brush work, and rhythmic features.

Many people have noted that while art cannot be taught, it can be learned. This wisdom suggests the self-teaching possibilities, the *process* or the emphasis on the *doing* rather than the products or the outcomes. There must be respect for the natural fount of each child's actions and ideas, and for his own pace of development. Especially important is the supportive and enriching environment which nourishes children's talents and challenges them to explore fully materials, tools, and media.

CHILD ART DEVELOPMENT

Child art is very different from adult art, yet there is a clear developmental line from one to the other. To the child, art is one of the many ways he uses his developing muscles and senses to explore the world, to perfect skills, to find and practice new actions and ways to use himself and materials, and to express some notions which may be neither conscious nor verbal, in his own way. Art products are far more important to adults than to children. Children quickly sense these values and catch them. The difficulty is to sort out values that teachers can teach without destroying the developing art values of the children. A more detailed examination of children's art development should suggest which values can be safely taught and which cannot or should not be taught at all.

There is little controversy about the sequencing and age levels of children's art development, but there are several very different theories about what this art development really is and what it means to the child. It is generally agreed that two-year-olds scribble whenever and wherever possible. A finger in the dust or sand, or on a steamy window, is almost as good as a pencil and paper. Scribbling is both an exercise of the muscles and a visual experience. Kellogg, a long-time student of young children's art, identified twenty different basic scribbles, from a dot to a single vertical or horizontal line, or a roving open line.[2] Kellogg's extensive studies of young children's art yield a wealth of insights about child art development and characteristic ways children draw.

Art serves as a means to express creativity.

Most teachers would agree with Kellogg and other students of child art that its major purpose is to encourage and release the child's creative capacities.[3] However, many early childhood teachers probably agree that child art does much more than this.

Children in modern Western cultures seem to experience an overload of visual stimulation from television, film, advertisements, objects, people, and all kinds of movements. The bombardment of children's senses by modern cultures seems to create urgent needs to organize this tremendous inflow, to understand it by finding ways to pattern and shape it. Children's solutions, or organization of all this sensory stimulation often puzzle adults, who see more error than pattern in child art. But the child must encounter problems in his own way, at his level of comprehension, with the best materials, experience, and guidance we can offer. We can help the child in many ways, but our first commandment must be to free the child from pressure to copy or imitate other people's inventions, or to meet an adult standard (which one?) of what is "good" in art.

How children make pictures

The art of a young child is unmistakable. Crude shapes, simple figures made of circles and more or less straight lines, any number of fingers or toes, arms attached at the head, or legs growing out of the face, characterize many drawings and paintings of young children. Younger children scribble, that is, their drawings or paintings tend to be a physical activity, the action of moving a stick, pencil, crayon, or paint brush on a surface, such as sand or paper, making an imprint. Paint or crayon or pencil is applied at first with little intention of representation.

But the hand and the eye work together, and the uncontrolled scribbles soon change to more definite shapes. Four-year-olds, after much experimentation, make shapes which look like round or oblong objects. Gradually their control of the brush or crayon grows so that intent and result begin to move closer. Children also begin to learn what they can and what they cannot represent, sometimes with frus-

2. Rhoda Kellogg, *Analyzing Children's Art* (Palo Alto, Calif.: National Press Books, 1970), pp. 14–15.
3. Ibid., p. 266.

tration. One four-year-old girl in nursery school wanted to paint a picture of a house at a corner of a garden. She painted a simple garden, finally, after several unsuccessful tries, with a prominent corner, and she put the house into her verbal description of "what you see at that corner." Her teacher must be credited for encouraging the child to find a satisfactory solution to her own composition problem without imposing an adult stereotype.

Biologically, what the eye sees is the same for all children, barring physical or neurological damage. Perception, or how the brain interprets the physical image, is clearly affected by the child's inner and outer life features, including experience, feelings, intelligence, expectations, and cultural effects. Perception, or visual thinking, as it is sometimes called, is a process which is readily affected by educational influences at home, at school, and everywhere else.

THEORIES OF CHILD ART

Various theories of child art development try to account for the unique character of children's work and the ways in which it changes.

Developmental theory

A popular theory of child art development, termed *developmental*, is chiefly associated with Lowenfeld, who identified stages in children's art as sequential.[4] This theory is in harmony with most views of child development, and was based on studies of many examples of children's art. Lowenfeld found that art development generally, although not invariably, goes through five stages, as follows:

AGE	STAGE
2 to 4	Scribbling
4 to 7	Preschematic
7 to 9	Schematic
9 to 11	Dawning realism
11 to 13	Pseudorealistic

4. Viktor Lowenfeld and W. Lambert Brittain, *Creative and Mental Growth*, 5th ed. (New York: Macmillan, 1970), pp. 91–164.

According to the developmental theory, there are five sequential stages which correspond to changes in children's growth and development.

According to this developmental theory of child art, stages succeed each other in harmony with changes in children's cognitive, affective, physical, perceptual, and creative growth. Lowenfeld tended to emphasize emotional more than other aspects of growth as having important effects on children's art work. Since the theory recognizes that there is some variability in the ages at which children move to later stages, and in the necessity to complete every stage, this theory is plausible although it does not explain why some children never seem to enter any realistic phase, or why many adults do not paint realistically.

Psychoanalytic theory

The different styles and preferences of children and adults are easier to explain in terms of psychoanalytic theory than developmental theory. Reasons for encouraging child art and ways of evaluating art development can be found in this theory.

The psychoanalytic theory attributes the development of child art to the unconscious mind.

The idea of the *unconscious* as the source of much content and form which inspires the artist and speeds his work seems to explain much ancient as well as modern art, in addition to indicating why children draw as they do.[5] Symbol making, according to this theory, is related more to feelings and universal inner images than to attempts to represent physical reality accurately. Child art is seen as a major way to give form and release to pent-up emotions and tensions, unconscious desires, or the wish to recreate reality to conform to one's real wishes. The teacher who encourages children's art work, with genuine acceptance, and absence of adult strictures, is regarded as serving a child's needs for emotional therapy or balance, as well as his need to practice and perfect his skills in art.

Psychoanalytic theory suggests that when a child paints a picture of his new baby brother as a large central figure, with the rest of the family represented as small figures, the child is not trying to represent objective reality but his feelings, as he sees the new sibling taking a place of central importance in the household, perhaps the place he regarded as rightfully his. Interpretations flow all too readily as a child paints a picture of his mother's face with an enormous open mouth, or of himself as a small pet in a cage. But feelings may not

5. Edmund Burke Feldman, *Becoming Human Through Art: Aesthetic Experiences in the School* (Englewood Cliffs, N.J.: Prentice-Hall, 1970), p. 170.

have definite shapes, and sometimes, according to this theory, end-products may chiefly be blobs of color, sometimes sombre tones of black or brown, or angry reds or cold, remote blues. Color, however, may not be a matter of the child's choice. Inevitably, the classroom supply of brighter colors runs out before the darker ones, and sometimes teachers mix tints and shades new to children, for interest and excitement..

Primary grade children tend to be tough self-evaluators, not easily satisfied that their products reflect their intentions.

Gestalt theory

Gestalt theorists, who regard perception as seeing whole images, stress the perceptual needs for continuity, structural unity, wholeness, and closure.[6] The eye is not a camera photographing what is there, and the brain is not a blank sheet on which to record the details of external

6. Kurt Koffka, *Principles of Gestalt Psychology* (New York: Harcourt Brace, 1935).

Gestalt theory stresses continuity, unity, wholeness, and closure.

reality, according to Gestaltists. Art is the child's way of making images which correspond to the structure of the *whole* that he perceives. Thus, in his early art, the child is attempting to structure and shape this whole image. Details may be omitted or changed, to fit this image, as the child produces the pattern and organizes the composition which represents this unitary vision.

The selectivity of the child's vision and the very general shapes he employs in his early art would seem to be accounted for by Gestalt theories requiring closure and unity in perception. The child seems to be giving us "the whole" picture, not its fine details.

Cognitive theory

The fourth theory which attempts to explain child art, especially its departures from reality, is called *cognitive theory*, because, simply put, it says that the child is trying to represent what he *knows*, more than what he *sees*. Kellogg, among others, has developed this theory, based on intensive study of many examples of child art.[7] If a child knows his mother is pregnant, he may draw a picture showing the baby inside his mother, according to this theory.

Cognitive theory suggests that child art represents factual knowledge.

Many pictures that children produce seem to support this theory. For example, one picture shows a figure with legs (straight lines), with a skirt added (an empty triangle), as though the skirt is a transparent fabric, with the legs showing through. Since the child knows there are legs underneath the skirt, he paints them, even though he cannot see them. Or a child paints all four legs of a table, stuck out like a paper cutout, even though the child is unable to see the table's four legs at once from that point of view. According to this theory, the child feels impelled to show all four legs of the table because he *knows* the table has four legs. The child has no conflict in representing both the inside and outside of a house in the same picture, because he knows what is inside even when he is outside.

Arnheim's theory

Arnheim suggests that the child is not painting what he *knows*, instead of what he *perceives*, but he is failing to differentiate time—sometimes he is inside the house and sometimes outside. Arnheim

7. Rhoda Kellogg, *Analyzing Children's Art* (Palo Alto, Calif.: National Press Books), 1970.

tends to synthesize the various theories of child art, with a more Piagetian notion of the child's development, his own strong Gestalt views, and his own detailed study of growth of complexity of form within the art medium.[8] For example, he indicates how the child does not deal with problems of overlapping figures or obliqueness in form, until he comes to the point of dissatisfaction with his previous representations. There is a parallel development here of complexity in art forms and of the child's growing ability to perceive and understand such increasingly complex problems in art as differentiation of time and space. The child who is drawing a house that he knows well may be a long way from conceptualizing which particular view of the house he chooses to show—he can show it from several views at the same time without seeing any problems. Once he starts to perceive and conceive of problems, he also has to be able to conceive of possible solutions. In addition, he must be able to realize such solutions by sufficient control of his art medium. The richness and detail of Arnheim's analyses of child art development, in relation to adult art, should be studied by all candidates for teaching young children. Decisions about teaching art to young children are best based upon understanding and respect for its development.

Arnheim's theory is based on a combination of the various theories of child art development.

Basically, Arnheim says, the child, and the adult as well, tries to represent "a structural equivalent of the object in terms of its medium," not a camera image of reality.[9] Pictorial growth has its own rules, from simpler to more complex patterns, according to this view. Early development shows the simpler forms of representation, as well as the personal and cultural perceptions of the child.

All of the theories help us understand child art better and to decide what teacher roles and activities seem most in harmony with child development. None of the theories dictate specific kinds of teaching, although they all indicate that child art has its own validity, value, and place in development. The theories tend to support encouragement of children's natural work, rather than demands for specific content and form. The theoretical frameworks are in harmony with teacher programming of experiences for children, teacher selection and guidance in the use of materials, encouragement and respect for child art, and stimulation of reflective self-evaluation of their work by children. Finally, there is no quarrel between theories and

8. Rudolf Arnheim, *Art and Visual Perception: A Psychology of the Creative Eye* (Berkeley, Calif.: University of California Press, 1969), pp. 187–203.
9. Ibid., p. 199.

practice in emphasizing *process* rather than *products* in child art. However, a great deal of child art is breathtakingly exciting, original, and inventive. Artists often envy, and seek to emulate, the use of intuitive inner sources that seem to stamp so much child art as uniquely authentic and nonimitative.

All children benefit from art activities. But all children are not equally talented in art. A child may not be interested in art activity all the time, or at those times that teachers designate as art periods. Some children may prefer other forms of self-expression, notably physical movement, dance, singing, playing rhythms, telling stories, improvising chants, poems, or songs, or constructing block patterns or working at carpentry. Children express what they think, feel, or want. In almost any form of self-expressive activity, children tend to play with and practice forms of adult expression, developing in skill and in understanding. All of these activities help to enrich, expand, and develop children's interests, which may become life-long hobbies, vocations, or avocations.

Feldman suggests that art promotes "discourse and the exchange of feelings among the citizens of a free society."[10] He stresses *process* in school art, as a humanizing mode in a world which has become increasingly mechanized and depersonalized.[11] Feldman interprets process to mean solving problems which promote understanding and valuing. A large part of the early childhood curriculum can be justified on this basis, and we can see how in many ways, art and expressive activities can and should dominate the curriculum for young children.

DECIDING HOW TO TEACH ART

Theory of development is complex and its relationship to teaching is often puzzling. Is the best teacher of child art one who does not interfere? Is this right for some children but not all? For which ones? Is this right for all children some of the time? How do you recognize the "right" time?

Early scribbling is mostly physical activity, although the children enjoy the imprints they make. A great deal of this is necessary, if the child is to become more skillful and controlled in his eye-hand-arm

10. Feldman, op. cit., pp. 171–72.
11. Ibid., p. 174.

motions, and if he is to gain experience in more deliberate shaping of the imprints. As forms emerge, the inventiveness of the child and his discoveries and constructions become visible. This is *not* an imitative process. The child copies no one. He makes and builds and varies and tries out, first this, then that. Yet there are universals in the child's early art work.

A list of understandings about child art development, as a basis for decisions about teaching, might include the following:

1. Initial art activities are primarily physical, for the joy of action. This is scribbling.
2. Children develop increasing control as they begin to shape their work deliberately.
3. Young children use the simplest shapes, such as the circle, dot, the mandala or sunburst effect, oblongs, upright cross, diagonal cross, rectangle, single horizontal and vertical lines, and ovals.[12] The shapes become clearer with more muscular control.
4. Differentiation comes gradually. At first, a child uses a few shapes repetitively, to represent everything. Then he includes more shapes. The child's practice efforts look very much the same—he seems to enjoy doing the same sort of thing over and over.
5. Early art work is unconcerned with flatness, perspective, three-dimensionality, or figure-ground relationships.
6. Early work seems to show objects or figures floating in space, with relationships quite ambiguous. The adult eye finds difficulty with proper perspective.
7. Shapes are usually outlined. Children are generally "hard-edge" artists. This changes later as they begin to identify specific relationships, and deliberate selection of color, detail, sharpness, masses, and other art values.
8. Children *see* far more than they represent, but what they represent is not a mirror image of what they see. The picture is a filtered end-product.
9. Young children's work in representation is predictable, because visual and motor development control the general shapes they see and are able to construct. Culture affects this early development very little, except for the materials children are given to use, and the responses adults make to their work.
10. Cultural effects determine the nature of the child's experiences, and how these affect his natural development.
11. The child's own personality, talents, interests, and total developmental pattern, also have important effects on his art work. His

12. Kellogg, op. cit., p. 14; Arnheim, op. cit., 1969a, pp. 165–198.

creativity, persistence, and skill are related to his artistic development and achievement.

12. Time is a prime ingredient of art development. As a personal, expressive medium, an art form requires exploration, discovery, trial-and-error, self-evaluation, practice and problem-solving experience. As children become dissatisfied with simplicity and repetition, they seek more complex problems to penetrate and solve.

13. Art is a major form of children's work in "identifying, understanding, and defining things, investigating relationships, and creating order of increasing complexity."[13]

14. The young child's art experiences, according to Horn, lead him to communicate with the values and media of art, to perceive the world and the structure of objects more acutely, in addition to increases in sensitivity, art appreciation, and self-confidence.[14] The very active process of making sense and creating order, of expressing one's understandings of the world, is nowhere more pervasive than in art.[15]

GUIDING CHILD ART

Teaching, or knowing when and how to guide a child, is always improved by knowledge of the subject, interest in the activity, and valuing the child's central position in his own development. Teachers who were somehow discouraged in their own art development, and who regard child art as necessary, might try to rediscover the joys of creative work and their own capacities.

Teacher candidates still in school are urged to take an art course, preferably in a medium new to them, where old feelings of failure will not intrude. If courses are not feasible, many books and art materials are available. Friends might be asked to share their interests in art work, to help you get started on your own creative work. The world is full of untutored artists whose work gives them and others much pleasure. The important thing about art is to do it, for personal enjoyment and understanding of the process.

A teacher's knowledge of art is not to be directly communicated to children. Artistic sophistication, however, should help teachers to know *when* to get out of a child's way, because he is solving *his* prob-

---

13. Arnheim, *Art and Visual Perception*, 1969, p. 200.
14. George F. Horn, *Experiencing Art in Kindergarten* (Dallas, Texas: Hendrick-Long, 1971), p. 6.
15. Rudolf Arnheim, *Visual Thinking* (Berkeley, Calif.: University of California Press, 1969a), p. 257.

lems to the best of his current ability, and when to help a child who needs some guidance to get off dead center, or to help him to find some possible ways to resolve his problems. Understandings of *children* are just as vital as understanding values in art, to make well-based decisions concerning extent of guidance, encouragement, suggestion, feedback, or approval required.

Two invariable rules to guide the teacher in art work with young children are: *never dictate an art project and never do the child's art-work for him.* Art must be voluntary. Art must be one of several choices which are almost always available. While the child should be encouraged to choose his art medium, the teacher can veto one which she is unable to supervise, usually with the expectation of fitting it in another more convenient time. Teachers can share their reasons with children for making some art media available only on certain days and not others, or for featuring specific media on occasion. As long as the child has the privilege of refusal, teacher decisions about the when and what of art media are not likely to inhibit child art development.

A teaching approach is suggested which helps the child achieve creative expression.

If a child is unwilling or unable to do an art project, it is clearly the wrong activity for him at that time. Sometimes, children's irritation with their work can be traced to parental misunderstanding of their capacity or of art development. The problem is not really the child's, but his parents', and the teacher needs to collaborate with them, to help the child enjoy his art activity and products.

Forcing children to imitate the work of other children or adults is likely to inhibit natural development and undermine self-confidence. Requiring children to copy art work constitutes dangerous interference with the child's own construction and integration of form and content out of his own activities and understandings, which is the real work of artists. The child's authentic self-expression cannot be expected to take the form of another person's work.

The conception of teaching or guiding children's art work which follows is mainly one of helping the child to collect observations and experiences, to integrate them and to find the form and content to represent them in some genuine way in art or other expressive media. It should be noted that the teacher is mainly a close observer, resource person, guide, and nurturing adult, who tries to put the child in touch with resources at the right time.

The major types of teaching include: selection and planning of experiences, environmental structuring, selection and use of materials, individualized experiences, sharing sessions, and individual responses to children's specific problems.

There are countless experiences which spin off content, feelings, and action, which children draw upon for their art work. Most of these experiences occur at home or outside of school. Families include children in such frequent experiences as marketing or shopping in stores, walking, playing at home or in recreational areas, riding in cars, buses, subways, trains, or planes, and caring for pets. In some families, or for some children, experiences are richer or more varied or more pleasant or frequent than in others. Television viewing, a second-hand but potent source of visual stimulation, has become practically a universal experience for young children. Schools can multiply these experiences, or vary them, or change the tone and feeling in which they occur. For some children schools can fill in certain gaps in their experiences.

Geography and climate have much to do with the kind of experiences families or schools can offer. Place of residence determines the extent of one's experience with extremes of weather, except for those families who travel widely. Urban children probably have greater variety of experience with people and objects, though the experiences may be more casual or shallow. Rural and suburban children are likely to have greater variety of experiences based on land, animals, and agriculture. First-hand experiencing may, however, be more limited by opportunity than by geography.

A class group experience is always different from a family activity. Even a simple experience as familiar as marketing takes on importance and new emphasis when a child is part of class on a trip.[16] Children alert each other to new perceptions. They compare their views, on the spot, and in recollection. They verbalize their experiences, and they may help each other to anchor their visual perceptions. The teacher is likely to indicate some sources of understanding the child had not noticed before, since the trip was probably selected for a purpose.

Parents can help teachers to plan new experiences, to stress new perceptions of familiar terrain and objects, or new places, people, and things. One nursery school teacher featured group home visits, during the spring semester, to her own home nearby, and by arrangement to

16. Helen F. Robison and Bernard Spodek. *New Directions in the Kindergarten* (New York: Teachers College Press, 1965).

the homes of children in the class. These brief visits were undertaken with great enthusiasm by the children, and child host and guests seemed to gain more vivid perceptions of each other.

Outside experiences

To find good out-of-school possibilities for children's experiences, teachers can take a walk within the vicinity of the school, talk with other teachers, school staff, parents, and members of the community. Municipal publications, local maps and guidebooks may contain additional suggestions. Here is one list of possible trips and experiences, out of school:

> Walks in the school vicinity, or bus or car rides, to such places of interest as a bakery, fish store, pet shop, supermarket, police station, post office, firehouse, radio or television station.
>
> Rides to a local museum of art, or history or natural history or any other appropriate kind of museum.
>
> Visits to children's homes by prearrangement.
>
> Visits to an official governmental residence or office, such as a town hall or city hall.
>
> Visits to centers of commerce, such as a downtown shopping center or an industrial center.
>
> Visits to interesting shops and factories, such as a cobbler, an arts and crafts shop, a noodle or bread factory.
>
> Picnics at a park or beach or in someone's backyard.
>
> Attendance at a school musical presentation.
>
> Attendance at a suitable local movie, theater, musical or dance presentation, or puppet show.
>
> Attendance at an open-air art show.
>
> Visits to construction sites.

This list is just a beginning. Every community has its own resources and attractions, natural and man-made, and every group of parents has suggestions of their own. One optometrist father of a child in a cooperative nursery school invited his child's class to visit his office and he tested their vision during the visit. A dentist father similarly arranged to make brief dental examinations for a nursery school class, in a very relaxed, happy atmosphere, in his office. Some parents may contribute good ideas or helpful materials, when they can. Other parents who have introduced young children to their vocational spaces and activities include sculptors, painters, ceramicists, printers, lawyers, store owners of various kinds, electronic repairmen, piano tuners, salesmen of various products, farmers, dairymen, and many others.

In-school experiences

The school itself is a microcosm of the outside community, with buildings to be maintained and repaired, a hierarchical staff, classrooms, communally used space, mail and packages coming in and going out, office and many other kinds of machines, public occasions and presentations, and visitors and parents to be guided and entertained. Children's interest in expressive activity may grow from any of their experiences in the school itself.

If the nursery school or day care center is a small, separate building, its resources may soon be exhausted for a lively group of children. In a large urban school, new experiences are available almost at any time within the building. In addition, of course, the teacher plans for selected in-classroom experiences which may stimulate children in various ways to organize and represent their perceptions. Notice how quickly children respond to an activity which they perceive as adult work, such as washing the blocks and block cabinets, or the easels and painting aprons. An offhand list of in-class experiences might include some or all of the following:

Cooking on a hot plate, waffle iron, electric fry pan or stew pot.
Making ice cream in a hand-operated freezer.
Preparing fresh fruits or vegetables for a tasting party.
Making a mural as a group activity.
Looking at objects through magnifying glasses or microscopes.
Blowing soap bubbles.
Caring for a classroom pet.
Planting a terrarium.
Preparing an aquarium.
Rigging up tin-can telephones.
Listening to live or recorded music.
Tumbling on a gym mat.
Dancing with a filmy scarf, a big balloon, or a beach ball.

Observing a visiting artist at work in the classroom.

Typing on a typewriter.

Taking an old clock or radio apart.

Serving a snack to visitors.

Playing at the sand table.

Working at the carpentry bench.

Floating simple boats or objects in water.

Making a kite.

Making faces in a mirror.

Making and wearing a paper mask.

Role playing in dress-up clothes.

Watching raindrops or snowflakes on the window.

Children need to develop art expression at their own pace.

To summarize this section on selecting and offering children experiences, a great variety of in-class activity contributes to children's perceptual thinking, to conceptual processes, to feelings, to social understandings, and to desires for self-expressive activities. Children also need time to integrate their perceptions and conceptions, and sometimes to avoid overstimulation or to withdraw from perceptual overloads. Rest periods, the provision of a quiet corner, permission to sit out activities, and attention to individual needs and capacities are all helpful.

ENVIRONMENTAL STRUCTURING

Montessori called environmental structuring the "prepared environment." She meant the orderly, well-selected arrangement of equipment and materials, which in itself, suggests to the child what there is to do and how he should behave. It includes the overall ambience —its warmth and friendliness—and the specific messages the child receives from the objects and their placement in the room.[17] If several chairs are placed at a round table in the housekeeping center, the message is that this is a good place to play with friends.

Here are a few examples of environmental structuring which may encourage or suggest various kinds of children's arts or other expressive activities:

17. Helen F. Robison and Sydney L. Schwartz, *Learning at an Early Age*, Vol. I *A Programmed Text for Teachers* (New York: Appleton-Century-Crofts, 1972), pp. 19–34.

1. Clear a large floor space of all equipment, put newspapers on this surface to catch drips and spills, place trays of small containers of tempera paint and brushes and large sheets of newsprint on this space, and accept all comers.

2. Push small tables together in a circular or semicircular arrangement, and place newspapers on the floor. Place clayboards, clay balls and water containers on the tables. Add a large assortment of manipulative equipment, such as a rolling pin, spoons, forks, a pie crimper, cookie cutters, and dull knives.

3. Arrange tables, as in number two, but feature collage materials instead, such as: cement, glue, paste, torn or cut paper, hole puncher, construction paper, scissors, crayons, paints, pastels, chalk, feathers, shells, seeds, nuts, buttons, sequins, small beads, thread, yarn, ribbon, cord, small hardware, such as nails and screws, fabric bits, straws, egg boxes, cardboard, plastic containers and packing materials, corks and bottle caps, and wallpaper sample books.

4. Place a small stepladder in one corner of the room for "bird's eye viewing."

5: Drape one long wall with "found" or "donated" fabric or paper. Offer this space for an art exhibit.

6. Create a fence with chairs in a long row, and offer this space for sharing art products.

7. Build a house out of heavy cardboard, or discarded cardboard delivery containers, with children in the central role in construction. Cover openings with cloth, and place a flashlight inside the house, for experiencing darkness in the daytime and creating interesting effects with the flashlight.

8. Clear most of the classroom floor space and play lively, rhythmic music on the piano or phonograph.

9. With very long sheets of butcher paper, lay new paths on the floor leading to the main learning centers. Let children figure out or invent uses of these paths.

10. Make a large, colorful rug by fastening together small rug samples or donated mats, and place this rug next to an art exhibit area.

11. Fasten some fireproof rosy-colored shades to the light fixtures and play very quiet music on the record player.

Classroom structuring need not be dramatic to convey intended messages to children. Easels equipped with paper, brushes, aprons, and paints speak eloquently, unless a "don't touch" message counteracts it. If materials are attractively arranged in good work spaces, children are likely to use them.

ART MATERIALS

Newsprint, tempera paint, construction paper and crayons are available to most children in early childhood classrooms. With good brushes of various thicknesses, pencils and various kinds of paper, it is easy to interest children in many art activities.

Collecting donations for collage work offers a pleasant way to involve parents and community in children's educational experiences and in understanding child art growth. Parents and other visitors are likely to value end-products to which they have contributed, when teachers explain the purposes of the activities. Sending out requests for donations often results in unexpected benefits. Many families have materials of some kind, "too good to throw away," but not clearly useful, which can be treasures for collage work.

Supplying a variety of materials may motivate children to explore new possibilities for art expression.

Variety in materials and equipment can serve important purposes. For example, some children shun the more frequent art activities available, but are attracted to novel and unexpected ones. For motivation, or renewing interest, variety is often the obvious solution. New media or materials may also inspire children to explore. One day a kindergarten teacher offered the children a pile of small slates the custodian had just discovered in storage, and she added fresh unbroken white chalk. Children chalked, erased, and washed their slates with joyful abandon. One boy, who had never painted or done any other art work before, made his first picture in white chalk, with great self-satisfaction. First-graders love to try a new medium, such as pastels, paper mosaics, or potato printing.

Some children need a different approach to art work because of emotional inhibitions of various kinds. Children may fear failure to meet unrealistic adult standards. Because the end-products are independent of the child's skill or motor control, rubbings will sometimes be useful. Rubbing is a simple activity, usually involving rubbing a crayon over a paper placed on an uneven surface. Adults make rubbings of brass or other metal art forms. Children can construct the uneven surface by collecting and arranging three-dimensional objects and covering them with a paper. Rubbing over the paper with one or more colors of crayon makes an impression or art product. Leaves, twigs, shells, seeds, string, or other collage materials contribute to good arrangements for rubbing. A string rubbing can be a very interesting composition.[18] Objects with sharp edges should be avoided, since they

18. Peter H. Gooch, *Ideas for Art Teachers* (New York: Van Nostrand Reinhold, 1972), p. 98.

are likely to cut through the paper.

Similarly, printmaking satisfies some children's needs for form and composition better than their paintings or drawings. Prints can be made out of almost anything. Children may select small dishes or containers of tempera paint, or ink, in addition to such "print" materials as:

> potato, carrot, or other vegetable cuts
> leaves, feathers, bark, shells
> corrugated cardboard
> wire netting
> hardware
> crumpled paper
> old combs or toothbrushes
> erasers, whole or carved
> cookie cutters
> wooden dowels
> styrofoam
> and other "found" items for dipping into ink or paint and applying to paper

Prints can be used to make wrapping paper for gifts, or to decorate cloth for curtains or tablecloths.

Sproul emphasizes using simple materials, such as sand, earth, water, clay, leaves, plants, or flowers.[19] Her suggestions for suspending a paper pendulum, that is, a paper cone filled with sand, over a table, to make swirling patterns as the sand drips, is one which the younger children will surely enjoy. When such sand swirls drip on a paper surface previously brushed with glue, the child's actions receive more permanent form. Similarly, when children finger paint vigorously on a smooth table surface, and then "print" a pattern by pressing the paper on the painted table, there is no interference with the action and exploratory pattern-making that finger painting provides in such abundance.

Why bother to make a print? Children like to have an end-product, even though their attention and interest is chiefly in the action. In addition, the patterns are often visually interesting to the child.

Paper folding (origami) offers fascinating activities and products for young artists. Tearing, cutting, arranging, and composing paper of different textures, thicknesses, color, and shape provides delightful

---

19. Adelaide Sproul, *Teaching Art: Sources and Resources* (New York: Van Nostrand Reinhold, 1971), p. 22

explorations in artistic possibilities. Children can be challenged to find out how many different ways there are to manipulate paper, such as stretching it, curling, folding, bending, and pleating it.[20] Crepe paper, construction, tissue, newsprint, and shiny colored paper can all be used. Paper sculpture gradually develops, by combining paper pieces in various ways, with glue, or paste or by stapling.

Papier-mâché is another absorbing art form for young children. It is messy enough to be appealing to most young children but it is not difficult for the teacher to contain the mess. With newspapers on floor and table, and sponge and mop handy, the activity need not get out of control. Anything goes in this medium, from the crudest squeezing of lumps of torn soaked paper, to the most patient layering of thin strips of paper. Children enjoy mixing the water and flour paste to a thin cream consistency, tearing newspaper or paper toweling, and soaking the paper in the liquid. Initially, the papier-mâché may be applied to cover a small juice can, or a wad of dry newspaper or a wire bent to any shape, as a core. A balloon can also serve as a core, but a good supply is recommended, to replace those that burst. This project may be especially useful for children who need to increase their span of attention, to persist in an activity, and to continue a project over a period of days. Papier-mâché must be allowed to dry thoroughly. Additional layers may be added for a succession of days. Or, the children may wish to paint the first layer as soon as it is dry. It is easy to make interesting shapes with papier-mâché, and to make sculptured objects or free forms.

Work with clay is not as common as paint and crayons in many early childhood classrooms. Some teachers dislike clay because it is messy, while others complain that they have so little clay, it is impossible to use it regularly for any one period of time. Yet this material has many beneficial qualities, not only in art development, but also in emotional and social development, that teacher candidates are urged to know this medium well and to use it in many ways. Children need water to keep clay pliable and they can learn how to use it properly. Children can be taught to do most of the clay cleanup, and they enjoy the cleaning almost as much as the modelling.

Kinesthetically, clay is a very satisfying medium for young children. A beautiful demonstration of unusual work with clay outdoors, with a first-grade class in a low-income community in Japan, is shown in a

20. Jenean Romberg and Miriam Rutz, *Classroom Activities for the Elementary School Year* (West Nyack, N. Y.: Parker, 1972), p. 26.

fine film.[21] Scenes of exceedingly creative work show the teacher and his large class in old clothes and bare feet, modelling from a huge mound of clay.

Socially, clay is a great integrative medium. A few children, seated together with clayboards, clay, and water, use their hands freely to mold and shape and their conversations flow just as freely, as they work and talk. Clay helps different children to relate to others, to find their way into the group, to reveal their interesting ideas, and to forget their inhibitions and fears. Personal satisfaction and lowered tension are invariable results of children's work with clay. It is likely that teachers will stress process over product in clay because they usually hoard their small supplies of clay for reuse. Without pressure for results or end products, this medium is a healing, outgoing form of activity for young children.

Variety in materials selection, as indicated above, need not involve expensive investments. The collections and caches with which teachers clog their closets all contribute to exciting art work for children.

Materials in which children can find stimulation for creating art forms include plaster of paris, sand, milk cartons, "edible" art in shaping cookies, bread or cake, and countless materials for sculpture, including wood, fibers, paper plates, paper bags, fabrics, corncobs, spools —or what have you.[22]

TEACHING SKILLS FOR ART WORK

Art values are usually not taught to children directly. Nevertheless, there are many ways in which teachers skillfully help children with their art work. Personalization, sharing activities, and responses to individual problems are among the most important ways teachers guide child art growth.

Personalization

A personalized or individualized experience may simply be a one-to-one relationship with a child on a project designed for that child. Such personalized experiences may be planned for a child when he is under-

21. *Children Who Draw* (New York: Brandon Films). 38 min., B/W with color segments.
22. Barbara Herberholz, *Early Childhood Art* (Dubuque, Iowa: Brown, 1974), especially Chapters 6–11.

going unusual stress, either in initial separation from his mother upon entrance into a day care center or nursery school or kindergarten, or when he has other emotional problems. Thus, a very personal and individual art activity may be planned for a child, with close teacher interaction, at times when the child needs to solve an emotional problem. It may not be the nature of the art activity, as much as the close teacher relationship, which is important here. Personalized projects are greatly needed in first and second grades, where individual interests become evident.

An individualized art experience planned for a specific child may provide a release for anxiety.

Because expressive art readily absorbs children's attention and so much energy and feeling can be represented and discharged through such activity, art work is one of the most important activities available to alleviate the troubles of young children under stress. Some children need to be as energetic as possible in the art activity they undertake. They need to slap clay, to throw it, to squish and punch it and to force it to change shape.

Individual attention and personalized projects give a child great reassurance that his teacher is interested in him and can respond to the needs he is unable to express directly. Jonathan, for example, arrived in the nursery school looking sour one morning, because his mother had been too busy with the new baby to pay much attention to him. But the teacher, who had heard from his mother what the problem was, greeted him joyfully, as though she could not wait for his arrival. She told Jonathan that she had a special project she thought he would enjoy. He looked half-interested and consented to be shown, without committing himself to the project. The teacher offered Jonathan, at a small table, cone-shaped plastic dispensers, a bowl and spoon, flour, salt, and water, vegetable food colors, and a pile of shirt cardboards, on which he was to swirl tinted, thin playdough, squeezed through the plastic dispensers. Jonathan got his apron, rolled up his sleeves, and accepted the teacher's invitation to work with her. He spent most of the morning, working on his own after awhile, and produced a large assortment of swirled designs. This personal, individual experience, with much energetic mixing and squeezing, seemed to turn Jonathan back into his usual sunny self. While he still had to come to terms with the changes the new baby had caused at home, Jonathan returned home in a more peaceful and satisfied mood than when he had left.

Heightening observation

Individual attention usually leads to possible solutions of problems with art work, in addition to alleviating emotional distress. A four-year-old boy in a day care center drew a tall building on his crayon picture, and then asked the teacher to draw some cars for him on his "street." The teacher sought to heighten the child's observational skills, instead of doing his art work for him. She suggested that they try to work out this composition in the block corner, to see how it would look. Together, they constructed a tall building and a street, and the child put miniature cars on the long flat blocks which represented the street. The child was then offered a stepladder to climb, to view his construction from the "top of the building." He discovered that the little cars looked like little boxes, and proceeded to adapt this notion to his crayoning ability, adding more detail, to satisfy his eye that they were in fact cars. (Was he drawing what he *knew*, what he saw, or both?) The child's handling and manipulation of the cars, along with his viewing from an unusual height, apparently were sufficient to give him some idea of how to draw a car from this perspective.

Sometimes, teachers can refer children to a picture in a book, a dictionary or encyclopedia, or to the object itself. One child became so interested in the books about dinosaurs that it took him a long time to get back to his drawing, but when he did, he found he could make some simple shapes that satisfied him.

Sharing

Sharing may be a show-and-tell session, but hopefully not. Young children can bore each other trying to verbalize unconscious concepts which have been properly presented in their art work. Sharing can mean that children hang their finished work or display it in a particular place, if they want to. Children's work should be accepted and displayed without favoritism. Children can sometimes be encouraged to look at the display, to view other children's work, without making value judgments or invidious comparisons. The teacher sets the tone by describing objective features of each picture, and treats them all with equal respect.

Children can be persuaded to leave their work at school for sufficient time to see changes in their own artistic development, physical control of the medium, and variety of content and form. If every product goes home every day, it loses importance, and is not available where teacher and child can note increasing maturity in use of the medium. Some teachers insist it is impossible to send a child home without his art work. Those teachers who regularly keep children's work at school know that it can be done. It helps to let parents know that selections of children's work will be sent home at intervals.

Sometimes children are very clear about the characters or the narrative their work represents, and they may have strong interests in communicating this to others. If this is the case, teachers encourage such communication in a small interested group, rather than requiring the whole class to listen. A voluntary audience, with some give and take, on an informal basis, satisfies the child artist without boring those children who prefer to do something else. Of course, the teacher can always constitute herself an audience when other children decline to listen.

Value of originality

Children may sometimes scorn the work of a very immature child or a child with physical or other problems. These are the occasions on which art values can be taught, especially concepts of originality and personal expressiveness. One child's view need not be another's. A very different composition may be given status just because it is so different. The teaching may simply consist of using the weight of teacher authority to accept and value the work of every child. It may extend to verbalizing this value. If it seems appropriate, the teacher may stress the personal meanings which each child puts into his work, which are not usually visible to anyone else.

When children begin to quibble about whose work is better, the teacher might post some prints of the work of prominent but very different artists, such as Rembrandt, Miro, and Jackson Pollack, to stress individuality of style, form, and content, and the limitless range of original work.

Indirect teaching of art values

Helping children select their own work for display gives the teacher many possibilities for indirect teaching of art values. Objective statements about children's work may suggest directions for further practice.[23] For example, when a kindergarten teacher looked at a collection of a child's work, to select two examples for display, the teacher said, "You used to make very small paintings on these big sheets of newsprint, like these. Look at the last picture you made—it's somewhat bigger." Pictures need to be dated, in order to make such comparisons.

The teacher might comment upon increasing use of variety in color or shape, or on objects represented, or in details included, or any relationships indicated, as to size, volume, time, space, or other values represented in some visual way. Occasionally, a young child seems to discover how to represent motion and actions, which is bound to be an exciting observation for the teacher. If the teacher comments, without too much fuss, "The boy in this picture looks as though he is running," other children may become interested in this idea of representing motion and may experiment with this difficult concept in their own work, if they feel ready to tackle this problem.

Indirect teaching, through objective teacher comments about a work to the child artist, and his friends if they choose to listen, tends to heighten the group's awareness of their work and of what other children are doing. Gradually, the teacher may create a workshop ambience of interesting problems to solve and the excitement of trying out any personal notions about how to resolve a problem.

Persistence is a value that can be stressed indirectly when the teacher comments to a child about his longer stay at the easel or about the value of resuming a work previously begun, instead of discarding it. It should be noted that, if the teacher refrains from pressing the child to explain his work or his intentions, voluntary communications from the child can be encouraged without pressure.

Discussions with individual children, in indirect teaching, help to develop a vocabulary for talking about one's art work. The tremendous range of names of color tints and shades can be introduced in context, as well as names of shapes.

Art vocabulary

The reader is referred to some of the titles in the resources for this chapter, for art vocabulary development. Teacher candidates can prepare to acquire skills in art language, through reading, art courses, art exhibits, art brochures, and lectures on art.

23. Herberholz, op. cit.

Certain art values are more central and general than others, for all art work. Teachers might learn to think visually. They can deliberately deal with such art concepts as line, form, shape, balance, texture, color, space, composition, motion, expression, theme, light and dark, rhythm, proportion, unity, order, feeling, fantasy, and imagination. The purpose is not to require children to intellectualize and verbalize their art work, but to help them to become consciously aware, if they can, of the problems they are tackling, or seem ready to confront. As children become dissatisfied with simplicity, they are thus encouraged to work at whatever complexity they choose. However, teachers should be reassured that far less harm comes from non-intervention in children's work than in misinformed meddling. When in doubt, leave well enough alone.

In a seminar for student teachers in early childhood education, an art workshop provided students with the opportunity to create various art works, including paper sculpture, painting, and collages. Each student came to the seminar workshop with a small collection of child art borrowed from the classroom where she was student teaching. The workshop concluded with two exhibits, one of the adult student teacher work just completed, and the other of child art. The students analyzed their own and the children's work, for the various major art values, practicing the use of appropriate vocabulary descriptively, comparing and contrasting adult and child art. They looked for color use, line and form, symmetry, balance, and relationships, texture, theme, unity, use of space and shapes, rhythmic and dynamic representations, feelings, and themes. They also contrasted the different media used, for the ways in which art values were represented.

Teacher candidates should not expect to teach young children how to represent any specific art value. Learning more about art values, however, increases the teacher's confidence in her own guidance techniques, in the ways in which guidance can be individualized and personalized, where to look for indications of what children can do, and what kinds of values they appear to be working at, intuitively or otherwise.

The emphasis upon the authenticity of the child's art work is related to the well-established idea that children do not receive concepts from others, but construct them themselves. Children's sensorimotor activities generate all kinds of ideas and information that develop gradually into the most abstract conceptions. Teachers cannot be substitutes for the child's activities, offering words instead of activity and experience. But teachers can stimulate and enhance activity for the child, endow it with value, and then help the child to make some sense out of this activity, and to persevere in extracting meaning.

EVALUATION OF CHILD ART

Can you write behavioral objectives for child art? How can you evaluate creative, expressive products objectively? These two questions puzzle many students who are preparing to teach in states or localities where "objective" goals and evaluation systems are required or encouraged.

According to Mager, a behavioral objective has three components: *observable behavior* or the goal, the *conditions* under which it is observed, and the *criteria* for its evaluation.[24] In child art, observable behaviors or goals might include *frequency* of art work, *persistence* in an art project, *independence* in the project, *variety* of media used, and *changes* or *progress* toward complexity in art values demonstrated. The latter item, progress toward complexity, could be further detailed as to more complexity in line, shape, color, or relationships of size or place. These would all be *goals,* to be observed in children's art development.

There are three requirements for writing behavioral objectives.

Mager's definition of behavioral goals also requires specification of the *conditions* under which the goals are evaluated and the *criteria* or standards for evaluation. *Conditions* of evaluation might be as follows:

Given daily choice of one art activity, or—
Given choices *twice* weekly of three art media, easel painting, crayon drawing or clay modeling, or—
Given unlimited choice of art activity, for all media found or brought into the classroom, or—
Given two art periods weekly in the art room with the art specialist teacher, or—
Any other conditions which actually prevail in classroom art work.

Criteria for some of the behavioral goals are fairly obvious. *Frequency,* for example, could be translated into a three-level scale of "always, sometimes, or never," for the criteria. It was suggested early in this chapter that the "always" criterion might not be appropriate for art work, since expressive activities are not necessarily elicited on demand. Criteria for persistence might be scaled from "completes all

24. Robert F. Mager, *Preparing Instructional Objectives,* (Palo Alto, Calif.: Fearon, 1962).

projects" to "completes no projects." Criteria for progress toward complexity might, for example, be scaled from "firmer, clearer, more varied shapes," for the desired goal, to "repetitive scribbling." Cautions are urgently needed here. Lack of progress over a few days or weeks would be a meaningless observation. Over several months, a semester or a school year, these evaluative observations could help teachers to select appropriately stimulating materials, activities, experiences, and individual guidance, to help a child make progress which is developmentally satisfactory for him.

Other goals, than those listed above, might be appropriate for all children or for a selected child. Such goals might be *demonstrating enjoyment*, by gesture, sound, and words, *clean-up competence, art vocabulary*, or *resourcefulness* in combining materials.[25]

Eisner suggests that there are three areas of child art which can be evaluated, that is, the degree of technical skill, or how well he controls his materials, secondly, his esthetic and expressive skill, or what art values he has demonstrated, and thirdly, his imagination and creativity.[26] For younger children, more important goals might well be joy in art work, frequent choice of art media and perseverance with the task selected. These goals have high valence as general goals for all school activities.

SUMMARY *Releasing children's authentic self-expression in the arts requires understanding of child art development, theories of child art, and of subtle, sensitive teaching strategies.*

The sequence of child art development is generally accepted, as well as its unique qualities. Biological processes determine initial stages but environment and culture soon show strong impact on how children make pictures. Theories of child art development include Lowenfeld's developmental theory, which stresses affective features; psychoanalytic theory which uses Freudian concepts of the unconscious and symbolization; gestalt theory which stresses unity, wholeness, and closure; cognitive theory which explains some childlike art techniques as reflecting what a child knows rather than what he sees. Arnheim's complex theory, Piagetian in its view of child cognitive development, synthesizes the various theories with his studies of growth of complexity of form in art media. All of the theories are helpful in

25. Herberholz, op. cit.
26. Elliot W. Eisner, *Educating Artistic Vision* (New York: Macmillan, 1972), pp. 212–16.

explaining child art development, and all emphasize process in this development. Teaching techniques do not derive directly from any of the theories, but are likely to grow out of teacher interest in art and in art media, and of child development, and from creative teaching designs.

A teaching approach is suggested which helps the child perceive in more complex ways, to integrate his experiences, and to find the form and content for authentic expression.

Major forms of teaching suggested are selection and planning of experiences, environmental structuring, selection and use of materials, individualized experiences, sharing sessions, and individual responses to children's specific problems. Emphasis is on helping a child solve his own problems and on developing art values gradually by identifying those that occur.

EXERCISES FOR STUDENTS

1. Participate in a visit to a local art museum, gallery, or exhibit, with a group of fellow students. Concentrate on two paintings which are very dissimilar for example, an abstract or nonrepresentational work and a representational or impressionist work. As a group, contrast the two works in every way you can and jot down your analyses of the way each incorporates the major art values.

2. Arrange for an illustrated lecture on the major art values through your college art department or local art society or any other means available.

3. Participate in an art workshop, arranged by your education or art department, and include a self-evaluation and group sharing session, to compare your intentions with your product and to learn how each of your fellow students conceptualized, realized, and analyzed his/her own work.

4. Collect a few samples of art works for each of six children, with the permission of the teacher and child. (Children may lend their products more readily sometimes, than make outright gifts.) Write a brief analysis of the work of each child, showing how the samples for each child are similar, or noting any differences, and how the style of each child differs from the others. Identify especially, how the children use

shape and color, what recognizable forms they use, and what content you can identify. Share your analyses with your fellow student teachers. Discuss your various contributions and have someone list briefly those items about which there appeared to be agreement in the group. Have this list duplicated to share it with the group.

✦ EXERCISES FOR TEACHERS   ✦✦✦✦✦✦✦✦✦✦✦✦✦✦✦✦✦✦✦

1. Collect samples of art work for each child in the group, dating each one, for at least one month.

   a. Analyze these samples for such features as:

   (1) Characteristic ways of using the medium. If you cover the children's names, can you identify the artist by style and technique?

   (2) Progress during the month. Note developmental changes for each child in his art work.

   (3) Clear examples of specific art values, such as rhythm, motion, and balance.

   b. Plan to review these samples individually with each child in positive ways, emphasizing any art values and progress in development.

2. Plan an art experience using a familiar medium, such as tempera paint, with the addition of some new tools or materials, such as different-sized brushes, use of crayons with paint, or any other new and stimulating materials.

   a. Stress individual and unexpected results, clearly valuing any ideas children express in the art work.

   b. Note the children's reactions and the effects on their art work.

3. Plan a group mural, with tempera paint, to record an exciting trip, such as a trip to a waterfront.

   a. Make some simple ground rules for children's collaboration, with their input.

   b. Encourage the children to make plans together for this collaborative effort and to help each other in the execution of the project.

c. When the mural is completed, help the group to discuss it, to remember their plans, and to evaluate the results. Model positive ways to communicate, so that children understand there is no need for adverse criticism, only objective ways to plan for future projects. Example: Teacher might say, "Is it big enough? Did you have enough paper? Or is it too big?" Positive statements may encourage reflections about the size of objects, and of the mural.

BIBLIOGRAPHY

Arnheim, Rudolf. *Art and Visual Perception: A Psychology of the Creative Eye*. Berkeley, Calif.: University of California Press, 1969a.

Arnheim, Rudolf. *Visual Thinking*. Berkeley, Calif.: University of California Press, 1969b.

Eisner, Elliott, W. *Educating Artistic Vision*. New York: Macmillan, 1972.

Feldman, Edmund Burke. *Becoming Human Through Art: Aesthetic Experience in the School*. Englewood Cliffs, N.J.: Prentice-Hall, 1970.

Gooch, Peter H. *Ideas for Art Teachers*. New York: Van Nostrand Reinhold, 1972.

Herberholz, Barbara. *Early Childhood Art*. Dubuque, Iowa: Brown, 1974.

Horn, George F. *Experiencing Art in Kindergarten*. Dallas, Texas: Hendrick-Long, 1971.

Kellogg, Rhoda. *Analyzing Children's Art*. Palo Alto, Calif.: National Press Books, 1970.

Koffka, Kurt. *Principles of Gestalt Psychology*. New York: Hartcourt Brace, 1935.

Lowenfeld, Viktor. *Your Child and His Art: A Guide For Parents*. New York: Macmillan, 1954.

Lowenfeld, Viktor, Brittain, W. Lambert. *Creative and Mental Growth*. 5th ed. New York: Macmillan, 1970.

Mager, Robert F. *Preparing Instructional Objectives*. Palo Alto, Calif.: Fearon, 1962.

Montessori, Maria. *The Montessori Method*. New York: Schocken, 1970.

Robison, Helen F., and Schwartz, Sydney L. *Learning at an Early Age*. Vol. 1. *A Programmed Text For Teachers*. Englewood Cliffs, N.J.: Prentice-Hall, 1972.

Robison, Helen F., and Spodek, Bernard. *New Directions in the Kindergarten*. New York: Teachers College Press, 1965.

Romberg, Jenean, and Rutz, Miriam. *Classroom Activities for the Elementary School Year*. West Nyack, N.Y.: Parker, 1972.

Sproul, Adelaide. *Teaching Art: Sources and Resources*. New York: Van Nostrand Reinhold, 1971.

MUSIC:

JOY IS SONG, DANCE, AND MUSIC

6

In a nation of blaring radios and television sets, young children's musical needs are seldom well served. Since the mass media fail to serve them, children have the right to expect schools to nourish and develop their music skills. Sometimes this right is superbly honored. Where children experience a fine music curriculum, there are usually some trained musician-educators at hand to help the many teachers who happen to be music-shy. All teachers can develop musical activities with young children that are enjoyable and rich in musical content, though access to a music specialist is clearly a great asset for teaching.

Music activities include singing, listening, dancing and creative movement, instrumental playing, developing musical concepts, and learning notation. Teachers without musical training, who love music and children, can do no harm and much good in acquainting children with music and encouraging musical activities. Teachers with musical training, of course, can accomplish more. Suggestions in this chapter are for both types of teachers. A major caution for teaching—in musical activities—is to avoid doing too little. Another caution is to develop musicality for its own sake, not just as an aid to reading or math or social studies. A final caution, musical activities *must* be enjoyable, otherwise, do something else.

A school for young children without music is unthinkable. The program demands music in so many ways. Young children sometimes arrive singing, and the song often turns out to be a television commercial. Teachers greet children with welcoming songs and children are caught up in the singing fun. Sometimes children enter the classroom to the dancing sounds from the record player, and they respond with free rhythmic movement. In some classrooms, record players with headsets are available at any time to a child listener. In the music corner, lucky children find a piano and are even luckier if, one at a time, they are permitted to explore the keys and to experiment with musical sounds.

Or perhaps there is an electric chord organ to explore and large oaktag sheets to read, containing numeral or line notations for well-known songs children may play.

A shelf of rhythm instruments, when it is made available to children, offers the sheer delight of practicing drum beats, or triangle, cymbal, wood block or other sound and rhythm instruments. Musical treasures other children may find are music on audiotape cassettes, pitch pipes, resonator bells, xylophones, stepwise bells, Orff musical instruments, string instruments, string instruments with bows, autoharps, or a Montessori matched music bell set.

In some early childhood classrooms, a "music mother" visits regularly, to lead musical activities. In others, a musically trained teacher works with each class for specified periods, relieving the classroom teacher for a preparation period or for other special duties. Sometimes, the PTA offers a free concert to the children in the school auditorium. Primary grade children may prepare an informal program of songs and dances for other classes or for their parents.

Always, there is the record player, but it is a mixed blessing. Often the school lacks money or volunteers to keep record players in good repair. Too often the record players make scratchy, unmusical sounds. If children are permitted to play phonographs without adequate supervision, records may be irreparably scratched and the needle badly worn.

It is far better to discard inferior or damaged musical equipment than to continue to use it because it's there. "But what can I do if I really can't sing a note and I'm terrified the children will find out?" one student teacher asked. Phonographs, tape recorders, television, and radio music programs may all help, in addition to rhythm instruments, a piano, or autoharp. The children themselves can often be more helpful to the unmusical teacher than are other people or equipment. The student teacher might take note of the many suggestions in this chapter which do not require musical training or performance by the teacher.

Detailed musical activities, for teachers with and without training, follow this summary of children's developmental potential in musical growth and some of the leading approaches to young children's musical education.

MUSICAL DEVELOPMENT IN YOUNG CHILDREN

There are musical prodigies whose rapid development leaves everyone else far behind. Most children are not prodigies, but almost all physically normal children, and many with various kinds of handicaps, hear music and gradually sing, dance, listen, and create musical expressions of many kinds.

The key to musical development is enjoyable musical experience. The younger the child, the more natural, spontaneous, and unstructured the musical experiences should be. Parents are important partners in rounding out and expanding musical experiences for children. The Suzuki method, discussed below, requires very substantial parental input to create a musical climate for the baby from birth. Froebel, who developed the first kindergarten in Germany before 1850, similarly focused on "Mother Plays," the popular finger plays he taught mothers to sing to their babies, adding finger action to songs with words.

Children who sing and are sung to a great deal, and hear much music early, seem to develop faster in their ability to sing, to match given tones, and to hold their own melody lines. It is commonly thought that young children sing very high notes. They don't, although their voices generally tend to be in higher rather than lower registers. But young children tend to sing in what is the middle range on the piano, between middle C and G. According to Smith, early singing is "directional," that is, the child approximates the up-and-down directions of the notes but seldom matches any tone accurately.[1] With practice, the child gradually becomes tuneful over a narrow three- to four-note range, usually within the middle C to G fifth. The child gradually sings a tone or two lower and, very gradually, a tone or two above the G by about age eight. Clearly, song selection should be far more closely related to the child's developing singing abilities than it usually is. Smith makes excellent suggestions for specific songs and song types appropriate to the young child's vocal development including such elements as:[2]

1. *The appropriate range of the song,* as indicated above.
2. *Repetition of songs.* Children have to hear melodies many times to

1. Robert B. Smith, *Music In the Child's Education* (New York: Ronald, 1970), pp. 16–24.
2. Smith, ibid., p. 24.

match them well. When songs are selected, teachers might consider their own willingness to sing them day after day. Folk songs stand up well, while many popular songs may become tiresome.

3. *Repetition of melodic phrases within the song.* A song with repeated melodic lines is easy to learn. Many folk songs have such repetition, for example, "Who's That Tapping At My Window?" "Skip To My Lou," "Shoo Fly, Don't Bother Me," and "This Old Man." These songs are also of the limited-range variety suitable for young children's voices.

4. *Repetition of word phrases.* Children more easily remember the words of songs when word phrases are repeated than songs with many different lines and phrases. Teachers sometimes think all children know the words and melodies of songs that they frequently sing in class, but this is often not the case.

5. *Variety.* Variety includes major and minor keys, fast and slow songs, loud and soft songs, lullabies, action songs, lyrical, patriotic, and narrative songs. Important sources of variety can be found in ethnic and foreign language songs. Rhythmic variety can be introduced with blues songs, spirituals, Caribbean music and Latin American songs, African, Asiatic, and European folk songs. (See the end of this chapter for sources of such songs on recordings and in songbook collections.)

Hearing and singing, major activities of young children, are early joined with free and rhythmic movement. While hopping and skipping movements appear later, at the four- to five-year levels, three- and four-year-olds respond to walking and running rhythms. As in vocal development, children's movements do not closely match external beats or pulses, but approximate them. Young children, with *Musical activities provide many developmental possibilities for young children.* normally faster pulses than adults, walk faster, as though to their inner pulsation. Children can hasten or slow their walking and running movements and they love to gallop when they acquire the uneven rhythm required. Other movements that young children can manage early include crawling, sliding, and skating motions, jumping, and stamping feet. Twirling comes later, along with hopping and skipping, as physical coordination matures. Children easily develop many body, arm, and hand movements, especially if they are encouraged to try out new and different ways to move their bodies.

Instrumental music requires more physical coordination than most young children have before ages seven to eight. Rhythm instruments make fewer demands for coordination and, in fact, may help children to develop physical coordination as they match or invent rhythms or accompany songs or dances.

Listening skills are very closely related to experience and to the quality of that experience.

Experience in musical homes indicates that musical development can be very rapid where there is valuing, interest, opportunity, and much musical activity. One four-year-old girl in a cooperative nursery school liked to sit at the piano and explore the keys. Other children came to watch and listen. One child asked the piano player to play "Jingle Bells." After some wrong notes, Betsy picked out the melody with one finger, and her audience, excited, shouted, "Do it again." Betsy did, but forgetting which notes she had played before, picked out the melody in a different key. It turned out that Betsy, the daughter of a musician, had perfect pitch, could match tones, and could reliably pick out a simple melody in any key or range on the piano. No other child in the nursery school at that time could duplicate her very advanced musical skills, but Betsy's performance inspired other children to try. Following the classroom rules about piano playing—clean hands, one child at a time, no tools, and firm but gentle finger and hand action—other children imitated Betsy in trying to "play" songs. The result was heightened interest in melody lines, increasing success in matching tones, and new knowledge about range, pitch, rhythm, and melody lines, as children discovered they were playing in ranges too high or low, or failing to reproduce the rhythm or the exact succession of pitch levels of the desired melody.

The developmental possibilities illustrated above were well understood by John Dewey who described the value of children's unstructured activities as offering the teacher clear indications of their capabilities and current skills. In 1902 he said to the teacher, in effect, "Now see to it that day by day the conditions are such that *their own activities* move inevitably in this direction, toward such culmination of themselves."[3] But he added that if the teacher had no knowledge of the subject, the teacher could neither know what the child's present skills were nor how to help the child realize the gradual development of more mature capacity in that subject area. In the above illustration, a trained musician might have offered the guidance and feedback which could have encouraged enjoyable and satisfying musical exploration and experience to the children choosing to work with the piano. Teachers without musical training still can:

3. John Dewey, *The Child and the Curriculum* (Chicago: University of Chicago Press, 1902), p. 10.

1. Value the musical explorations and activities.
2. Encourage the children to help each other.
3. Surround the musical activities with good management rules in order to prevent noise and disturbance to other children and activities.
4. Implement other musical activities such as playing records and encouraging rhythmic and free movement and singing.
5. Seek assistance from musically trained teachers or supervisors.

SYSTEMS OF MUSIC EDUCATION FOR CHILDREN

Suzuki, Dalcroze, Kodály, Orff, and other insightful musicians and teachers of music have developed systems for the musical training of the young. All of these systems require considerable musical proficiency and technical training in the curriculum and methods employed, but all have much to offer teachers of young children.

Suzuki

Shinichi Suzuki, who developed his Talent Education Program in Japan in 1946, involves the mothers in his work with children. Like Froebel, Suzuki encourages mothers to sing to their babies and to surround them with music from the very beginning. Mothers observe the private lessons and ensemble classes, learn to play the instrument their children are studying, practice at home with their children, and play recordings at home of selected music.[4] The Suzuki method, used *Suzuki's* chiefly in violin instruction, involves rote learning at first with music *method of* notation added after about two or three years. Older children help *music instruc-* younger children in large group classes. Tone, rhythm, and structure *tion emphasizes* are the focus of the early years of instruction. Children enter Suzuki's *parental in-* classes as young as two years of age. Yet the method, active playing *volvement and* on the instrument by rote in concert with others both younger and *rote learning.* older, apparently leaves the whole group with a satisfying sense of making music and doesn't single out "slower" or "faster" children. The deep parental involvement of self-selected parents is surely an important key to the general success of Suzuki's methods.

Suzuki writes that his method "is based on the assumption that

---

4. *Music Educators Journal,* "A Photo-Essay on Talent Education after Twenty-five Years: Faces of Suzuki" 58 (March 1972), pp. 54–57, p. 54.

humans are born with a very high potential for developing themselves" and that he is not concerned with prodigies but with "total
human education."[5] His method seems very close to Piaget's theory of
child development—that no one can tell how able a person is until
development occurs. Suzuki requires that children be helped to develop an ear for music and to succeeed in a step-by-step progression in
skill learning.[6] Ear training is simple—children repetitively listen to
records and tape recordings of music they will subsequently learn to
play, and they thus become increasingly alert in discriminating their
own tone production from the recorded models. Skill development,
while stressed, also acknowledges individual pacing capacity. Thus,
in addition to continuous exposure to a musical environment from
birth, ear training in listening, and then playing, with step-by-step
precise skill learning, Suzuki also teaches children to become self-
directive and to take responsibility for their own practice and skill
learning.

Teachers of young American children may find creativity a missing
ingredient in the Suzuki method, since there is so much focus on
instrumental performance, ear training, and skill development. Suzuki
considers creativity served, in his method, by the encouragement of
self-direction—"to assist every child to make his own adjustment in
as rich and creative a way as possible."[7]

American teachers who may not agree with the Suzuki priority
scale of values may nevertheless wish to borrow some pertinent features from his method, especially parent involvement, self-direction,
and ear training through repeated listening experiences.

Kodály

In Hungary, Zoltán Kodály, a major modern composer, has had great
impact on the musical development of young children in public
schools, where his methods are widely used. Some features of the
Kodály system include (1) major and early emphasis on singing (especially folk songs of one's own country), (2) the use of the pentatonic
scale (similar to the values of the five black keys on the piano), (3)
the use of hand signals to symbolize individual notes on the scale, and

5. Shinichi Suzuki et al., *The Suzuki Concept* (Berkeley, Cal.: Diablo, 1973), p. 2.
6. Suzuki, ibid., p. 12
7. Suzuki, ibid., p. 17.

*Some features
of Kodály's
system are early
emphasis on
singing folk
songs, the use of
the pentatonic
scale, and
hand signals.*

(4) the initiation of music notation fairly early in the first grade. American music educators, adapting Kodály's system, stress American song sources, such as Western, pioneer and Indian songs, and Negro and "white" spirituals.[8]

Kodály's hand signals for notes on the scale are easy for children to learn. In working with young children, some teachers may prefer to reduce hand signals to four (any signals will do) which differentiate *up, down, stay on the same note,* or *stop.* Children enjoy the feeling of mastery in "reading" and responding to hand signals of any kind.

Dalcroze

Jaques Dalcroze's system is one of the oldest of those still widely followed in many parts of the world and, while ear training by solfeggio (see page 196) is central, there is considerable ear training by movement and in response to fine differentiation of musical signals played on the piano. Beat, pitch, rhythm, dynamics, and melodic features are developed early in Dalcroze teaching, and notation is integrated with movement and song from the very beginning. A delightful short film, made in Switzerland, illustrates the teaching methods employed with very young and with older students.[9] Children are taught to associate specific kinds of movement with specific musical features such as a major versus a minor key, or a melody played in the treble versus the same melody played in a base octave on the piano. Alert listening to increasingly finer distinctions in tone, pitch, dynamics, or rhythm is immediately translated into appropriate movements. While creative rhythms are included in the Dalcroze system, it is chiefly geared to teach young children the fundamentals of music through enjoyable movement structured for the purpose.

Dalcroze developed a system to teach young children music by structured movement.

Orff

Carl Orff's methods to encourage young children's musical development build activities on the natural rhythms of their speech and movements. Through exploration with speech and body rhythms, Orff's system develops simple creative forms of playing folk-type

8. Mary Helen Richards, "The Legacy from Kodály," *Perspectives in Music Education,* Music Educators National Conference (Washington, D.C., 1966), pp. 402–407.
9. *Tuning Up For Life.* Teleproduction, Zurich, Switzerland, for the Pestalozzi Institute. Black and white, 20 minutes.

music on specially designed instruments. Young children can develop rhythmic control of body and instruments so that they can play together to make interesting musical sounds.

Orff's system of musical development features body movement and improvisation on instruments.

Gunild Keetman worked with Orff in developing the material, and Doreen Hall in Toronto wrote the English language version and manuals for teachers. Orff, an internationally recognized modern German composer whose opera, *Carmina Burana,* is in the repertoire of the world's leading opera companies, became interested in young children's music education in 1926. His collected materials were published in a five-volume work entitled *Das Schulwerk* and were translated into *Music for Children* in English editions.[10]

If a teacher follows the Orff system, worked out in detail in teachers' manuals and presented in sequentially more complex forms and content, the creative and exploratory features generate patterns, forms, and musical concepts. However, the Orff system requires musical training for independent teacher use though even without musical training—or with very little—some of Orff's ideas can be worked out rather freely with children. Teachers with musical training are referred to the teacher manuals and teaching suggestions Doreen Hall has written. All teachers might benefit from her enchanting recording which illustrates children's rhythmic speech compositions and a brief film illustrating children's musical progress. These materials are exciting demonstrations of the musical qualities of children's creative activities as they vary pitch, rhythm, tempo, and dynamics and construct exquisite musical phrases out of such material as the names of flowers, trees, or gems.

The following teaching suggestions are free adaptations of Orff's contributions to young children's musical development. Orff's most basic idea is that action and movement come first, that the intellectual process of learning musical notation and rigorous skills must wait until children's performance indicates readiness for symbolizing and conceptualizing the processes learned. As a composer and musician, however, Orff assumes the need for musical training when children's music-making experiences have established the need and the readiness for skill development. In his system, all exploratory and inventive activities are purposeful preparation for musical training.

Body movement.   Four types of body movement are featured in the Orff system: clapping, "patschen", stamping, and finger snapping.

10. Doreen Hall, *Orff-Schulwerk, Music For Children: Teachers' Manual.* (New York: Schott Music Corp., 1960).

"Patschen" here means slapping one's knees or thighs with the palms of one's hands. Most three and four-year-olds may not be able to snap fingers but all can clap, slap knees, and stomp. These movements can be separate or combined in various ways and are meant to be free and relaxed but vigorous. Teachers can add such movements as running, marching, hopping, skipping, galloping, or any others the children like to do.

Suggested body movement activities may be any of the following or any variation on these suggestions which teachers or children wish to try.

1. Children walk around the room following a "leader" who may be a child or the teacher, clapping a steady unaccented beat as they walk. The walking rhythm, at the children's pace, will establish the regular, steady pattern.

VARIATION

Speed up the walking pace.

Slow down the walking pace.

Teacher, beating the steady rhythm on a drum, changes pace to slow, fast, slower, faster, while children respond to the drum's changing-pace.

Children take the teacher role and beat the drum for other children's walking, first steady, then faster, then slower.

Change the instrument from the drum to other rhythm instruments such as the triangle, sleigh bells, cymbals and finger cymbals, wood block, claves, tambourine or gong.

Sit in a circle passing a rhythm instrument from one child to the next, each child taking turns in establishing the tempo for the group's clapping, patschen or finger snapping.

Change the dynamics, that is, vary from soft to loud.

Combine dynamic and tempo changes as with soft-fast or loud-slow.

2. Each child chants his name and claps the rhythm of the chant. Examples are: *Pau-la* (2 equal beats) and *Jon' a than* (accent on first beat, one long, two short beats).

VARIATION

The group echoes the child's chanting and clapping of the rhythm of his name.[11]

11. For variations of this activity, see Helen F. Robison and Sydney L. Schwartz, *Learning at an Early Age*, vol. II: *A Curriculum For Young Children* (Englewood Cliffs, N. J.: Prentice-Hall), pp. 33–38.

The children may choose other word categories for chanting and clapping such as names of colors, birds, flowers, fish, or trees; street names; names of teachers. Other body movements should also be used especially patschen, foot stamping, and free movement either around the room or in one designated area.

3. The teacher plays short musical selections on the piano, tape recorder, or phonograph, some in four-quarter time (four beats to a measure), some in three-quarter time. Children clap, clap and stomp, or clap and patsch in rhythm. The rhythm in which young children clap to melodic music will usually be the basic meter which is similar to a metronome's regular beat. For example, the steady beat may be four steady beats to a measure. On the other hand, the rhythm of the melody may determine the pattern for clapping. Variation results from alternating these two rhythmic patterns. As children gradually come to distinguish the rhythm of the basic beat from that of the melody, the teacher can name them as "steady beat" and "melody rhythm" and plan to alternate or combine them.

4. With increasing child control over body movements and more child experience in hearing and moving with different rhythms, gradually the teacher may suggest combining the steady beat with child-invented rhythmic variations. Here the group plays on rhythm instruments or marks the steady beat with body movements while one child at a time invents a rhythmic variation to fit the steady beat. For example, the group claps a steady four-quarter-note rhythm, then a child claps — – – — —, or one quarter note, two eighth notes, finishing with two quarter notes. (Teacher and children may hear the rhythm clearly without knowing there are quarter notes and eighth notes.) Again the variation is played or marked by one child, along with the steady beat by the rest of the group. After much practice, groups in the primary grades can probably carry three different rhythmic patterns (including the steady beat) at the same time within the same basic four-quarter measure.

For instance, the group is divided into three subgroups as follows:

Group 1 marks the steady beat by clapping:

____   ____   ____   ____

Group 2 agrees to this rhythmic pattern on wood blocks and triangles:

____   rest   rest   rest

1

(This group plays only on the first of the four beats in each measure)
Group 3 decides to mark this rhythm by stomping.

$$\underline{\hspace{1.5cm}} \quad \text{rest} \quad \underline{\hspace{1.5cm}} \quad \text{rest}$$
$$1 \qquad\qquad\qquad 3$$

(This group is marking the first and third beats and ignoring the second
and fourth beats in each measure. With this pattern, all three groups
play together only on the first beat. Groups 1 and 3 play together on
the third beat as well.)

5. The teacher helps the group make up a story with several characters and then helps the children make simple costumes for each
part. The story might be about cowboys taking cattle out on the range,
about astronauts walking on the moon, or a story about a skating
party (three-quarter time could be used here). Costumes may be paper
hats or helmets or other easy-to-cut-and-assemble items. With the story
and characters specified, the teacher helps the children find some
movements which they like and which fit into a basic rhythmic
pattern, as in a ballet. For example, the astronaut story may use a
steady four-quarter-time beat played by a large band on rhythm sticks,
wood blocks, and castanets, together with a syncopated rhythm representing the astronauts' loping, gliding walk in space. From three to
eight children can be astronauts. Obviously, each astronaut will
gradually find his own variation of the steady beat, after marking one
syncopated (uneven) rhythm in unison with the other astronauts, in
a foot-stomping or in a leaping pattern.

Instead of inventing a story, the children might enjoy dramatizing
a well-known story through movement. Rowen suggests a list of
poems and stories including "Jack and the Beanstalk" and Edward
Lear's *Complete Nonsense Book* which can be used.[12]

6. The teacher plays a steady beat in four-quarter time on a low
note in the bass register of the piano and children walk in rhythm.
Gradually the teacher adds a high note—at least two octaves higher
in the piano's treble register, playing only the first beat (or second, or
last) in each four-beat measure on this high note, to which the children clap. Thus, the children clap only on one beat of each measure
while walking steadily in rhythm with the four-quarter beat.

12. Betty Rowen, *Learning Through Movement* (New York: Teachers College Press, 1963),
pp. 66–73.

VARIATIONS

The teacher beats one measure and the children, without piano support, mark the beats on the second measure. Here, the children echo the piano patterns—but without the piano—on every other measure. Or every third or fourth measure could be used, or the children could beat two measures after the piano plays two measures.

7. The teacher sings a simple melody to the children using either one he or she invents or a well-known song such as "Mary Had a Little Lamb." The children sing with the teacher and clap the melodic rhythm.

VARIATIONS

The children sing while one child claps the melodic rhythm or the steady beat.

The children sing while one child marks either the melodic or steady beat rhythm with one rhythm instrument such as a tambourine or sleigh bells.

Each child uses a rhythmic instrument to accompany the song melody, inventing any rhythmic pattern he likes for accompaniment, while the teacher beats the steady beat.

8. The teacher encourages the children to create simple melodies to sing while marking rhythms with movement. For example, the children work together, with or without the piano, to invent a lullaby. When they are satisfied with their melody, the teacher helps to tape record it or, if he or she knows how, she notates it on a musical staff. The teacher might, instead, use lines or numerals to indicate the melodic direction and duration of notes.

The first line of "Three Blind Mice" might be indicated in the following way:

> Three

> Blind

> Mice

The lines, of equal duration, indicate equal beats and the direction of the melody is clearly descending. Instead, the teacher might use lines with numerals as:

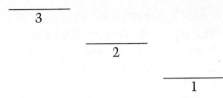

Again, the lines are descending, of equal length, but the use of numerals gives another clue to the melody, indicating it starts on the third note of a scale and descends by whole steps. The group which invented the melody teaches it to the whole group.

A variation might be for subgroups to invent harmonizing or accompanying lines—in effect, they could create parts for part singing. One group might sing a simple countermelody:

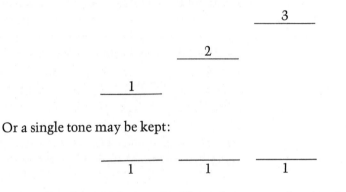

Or a single tone may be kept:

First graders might try doubling the notes, that is, singing eighth notes instead of quarter notes:

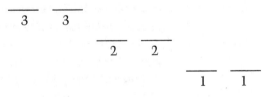

Or some six-year-olds might introduce a syncopated (uneven) phrase:

Here, the note on 3 is held a half beat longer and the note on 2 is reduced by one-half. Young children will need practice to hold one part that is different from a part other children in the group are singing.

9. Using bells, xylophone, glockenspiel or metalophones, the teacher helps children to invent simple melodies and parts on these instruments. This is the instrumental equivalent of exercise 8 above.

Orff uses an "ostinato" when children combine to play a small group of instruments together, that is, one instrument, usually in a lower register such as an alto or bass instrument, establishes a variation on a steady beat. The variation has to establish a clear pulse but it need not be a monotone or a monotonous steady beat. The ostinato may vary both tone and rhythm within a basic meter pattern. For example, instead of playing a low octave C four times as four quarter notes, the ostinato achieves the same result and establishes the meter in a more interesting phrase:

(¼)	(¼)	(⅛) (rest)	(⅛)	(¼)
C	E		G	E

This phrase follows two quarter notes, C and E, with an eighth rest, then an eighth note on G, and a fourth quarter note on E. Again, this is a syncopated, or uneven rhythm within the four-quarter meter. This notation is suggested here only as a guide for teachers, since children are not taught any notation system in the Orff method until they have had many experiences in making up rhythms and dancing to rhythmic patterns. Audiotape recordings can replace notation for teachers with little musical training.

The children, who are unlikely so far to know anything about scales and harmony, may become very frustrated trying to fit parts together if they use instruments with all tones available. The Orff-type instruments have removable note bars, are all tuned to the key of C major, and have different voices—bass, alto, soprano—and clear, ringing tones. Young children may use these instruments easily if the teacher removes sufficient note bars to leave only the notes of a pentatonic scale. Teachers unfamiliar with pentatonic scales are urged to explore melody-making—and encourage children to do the same—on a piano using only the black keys. Working with these mallet-played instruments designed by Orff, children have no problems with harmony because, in this limited range, all tone combinations sound pleasant. The tonal qualities of the instruments resemble those in a Javanese orchestra which have exquisite timbre (musical sound related to the quality of the materials of the instrument).

While Orff-type instruments are expensive, they are also well-made, durable, and useful over a wide age and ability range in the school. These are not toys, and they can be used by children who read and write music and understand some of the subtle relationships of key, voice, harmony, and ensemble playing. Tuned musical glasses (with different amounts of water in each glass to sound different tones when struck) can be used with these instruments, as well as the excellent percussion instruments that Orff designed for children, or any other rhythm instruments available.

Teachers without much musical training who are eager to try the Orff system might secure the help of a school music specialist or another teacher who has musical training. Helping children explore melody, pitch, rhythm, and timbre, teachers will themselves learn more about these musical features along with the children.

British schools, many of which use the Orff system in their open classrooms, stress the creative as well as the performing activities at all stages. Teacher roles in British classes include creating the environment, opportunities, and materials, helping children on technical points where such help is needed; developing the vocabulary of music, suggesting verbal rhythms for translation into musical rhythms, and constructive criticism of children's work.[13]

MOVEMENT AND DANCE

In musical ways, the child's naturally active forms of doing and learning can be encouraged in free and structured movement activities by all teachers. Movement can be encouraged by musical cues, teacher modelling, story dramatization, properties (or props), scene selection or development, open-ended suggestions or questions, or cues from art, poetry, or other sources.[14]

13. John Horton, *Music.* (New York: Citation, 1972), p. 21.
14. See also Robison and Schwartz, op. cit., pp. 29–52, and other titles cited in the bibliography.

Musical cues

*Recorded
music, singing,
and rhythm
instruments
stimulate
children's
movement.*

Phonograph records, tape-recorded music, singing or instrumental music, or rhythm instruments may set the tone to encourage children's movement activities. Recorded music which is strongly rhythmic is often the easiest way to suggest movement to children. Some among the many possible recordings are the following:

Aaron Copland, "Circus Music," from *The Red Pony* (Children's Suite), *Adventures in Music*, Grade 3, vol. 1, RCA Victor.

Bela Bartok, "Bear Dance," from *Hungarian Sketches*, *Adventures in Music*, Grade 3, vol. 2, RCA Victor.

Wolfgang Amadeus Mozart, "Sleigh Ride," from *German Dances:* Mercury 90438, Angel S 35948.

Ludwig van Beethoven, *German Dances*. London 6656.

Serge Prokofiev, *Lieutenant Kijé Suite*, op. 60. Columbia MS-7528 (Includes "Love for Three Oranges," March)

Franz Joseph Haydn, Symphony No. 101 in D ("Clock" Symphony) RCA LSC-2742.

Instead of recorded music, a teacher may produce rhythmic music on the piano, guitar, recorder, clarinet, or any other instrument he or she can play, or, lacking instrumental training or an instrument available for playing, the teacher may produce rhythms on such percussion instruments as the drum, rhythm sticks, or a tone block. Teachers who sing with confidence can use songs to stimulate children's movement, adding the accompaniment of clapping, patschen, finger snapping, or the conductor's hand beat.[15]

Teacher modelling

If the children for some reason fail to move freely to the musical cues, the teacher can easily stimulate such movement by his or her own modelling of movement. If the teacher begins to move about the room rhythmically and children begin to follow, the teacher could step aside and turn accompanist, spectator, occasional guide, and continuous giver of encouragement and approval. Since children are likely to imitate an adult, once the children participate actively, the teacher

---

15. Louise Kifer Meyers, *Teaching Children Music in the Elementary School* (Englewood Cliffs, N. J.: Prentice-Hall, 1961), pp. 64–66.

might challenge the children to find more spontaneous and individual actions by such questions as, "What else can you do?" "What can you do that's different?" "How else can you move your arms (or legs, or head)?" Valuing differences and individual child responses, the teacher soon finds imitation declines and children become more intent on finding their own ways of moving.

Story dramatization

Stories to dramatize may come from sophisticated recordings with clearly differentiated themes such as *Peter and the Wolf* and *Tubby the Tuba* or simpler recorded or narrated stories about The Three Pigs or Cinderella. Stories for children, such as "Ask Mr. Bear" or "Caps For Sale," can also serve this purpose. A teacher-invented story or a group-invented story may sometimes catch the children's interest more than other material. Stories may be complete with both characters and action, or children may wish to start movement explorations with characters only, finding ways in which to move that differentiate a child from an old man, perhaps, or a happy woman from a sad one.

Even simpler, shorter dramatization experiences may develop from simple teacher suggestions such as "move as though ...":

> You're hungry and you have a long way to go to get home for dinner.
>
> You're going to your best friend's birthday party and you're carrying a lovely present which is fragile; it will break if you drop it.
>
> It's raining very hard and you're wearing a raincoat and boots and carrying an umbrella.
>
> You come out of your house and find it's the coldest, frostiest day of the year, and you're wearing your warmest clothes.
>
> You're hurrying home from school to start out on a vacation trip with your family.

After the teacher has made a number of such specific suggestions, children may take turns specifying the conditions or feelings to be dramatized. Finally, children are asked to develop their own themes, move to dramatize the theme, see if other children can interpret or guess the theme, then explain each other's selection of movements in relation to the self-chosen themes. This last activity must come after the children have many experiences in movement dramatization, because it requires conscious awareness of movement selection and the ability to explain it verbally. Where verbal skills are less well developed, the activity itself may become a useful exercise in vocabulary development and in sentence structure for communication.

Use of props

Giving children objects to manipulate often helps to dissolve inhibitions and to stimulate freer, more spontaneous movement. The list of props children can use to suggest, activate, or help to vary movements is a long one. Among others, favorite props are:[16]

> Balloons, varied sizes and colors
> Balls, light and heavy, large and small
> Bean bags to throw, catch, and bounce
> Scarves, large, bright colored, of silk or nylon or rayon
> Anklets or wristlets made of cloth or elastic band, with bells or shells to ring or rattle
> Shakers, which may be maracas, or rice sealed in a small can, box, or ball of some kind
> Flashlights to be used as "pretend" candles
> Hoops of plastic
> Jump ropes
> Colored paper streamers or ribbons
> Kites on short strings, or other paper shapes on strings
> Rhythm instruments such as tambourine

The use of props should be intermittent so that children do not depend on objects for free movement. Props are especially helpful to stimulate movement, to suggest changes or variety of movement, to stimulate larger, freer movements, and to spark imaginative notions about actions, characterization, feelings, or moods.

Scene selection or development

Selecting or creating a scene is chiefly a motivating and stimulating device. See what happens when you take children into an unusually large space such as a gymnasium, or an outdoor space such as a park,

16. Edna Doll and Mary Jarman Nelson, *Rhythms Today!* (Morristown, N. J.: Silver Burdett, 1965), p. 187.

especially if there is a gentle slope for rolling or sliding. Sheehy urged use of outdoor areas whenever possible for music and movement.[17]

Scenes can be created right in the classrooms. One kindergarten group, after several trips to a nearby beach, made a large mural depicting sand, water, sun, bathers, boats, and a boardwalk. Using such a mural as a backdrop, and drawing on their recent vivid experiences at the beach, children readily produced many varied movements of wave action, swimming, and rowing boats. Besides murals, scenes can be created simply by fastening appropriate paper or cloth to room divider panels or by floating selected items from a wall or ceiling-attached object.

The weather often provides ready-made scenes, as on a dark and threatening day, a sparkling and sunny one, or when there is heavy snow or rain. Inventing movement to respond to extreme weather conditions is often very stimulating to children.

Open-ended suggestions or questions

Open-ended suggestions or questions are usually more productive after the children have had a great many movement experiences. Inventiveness increases as a child's repertoire grows. The idea is to throw the responsibility to the children to suggest a "premise" or scene possibility or to create a story to dramatize, to suggest characterization possibilities, to choose props, and, generally, to make choices and to put their growing inventiveness into practice. If children are perplexed when first asked to make suggestions, sometimes a neutral action will trigger some ideas. For example, one teacher joined the children in a circle and began to bounce in place, suggesting that they follow suit until they thought of something, then either to do it or tell it.

Cues from art, poetry, and other sources

A trip to an art museum, a school art exhibit, or a classroom exhibit of art reproductions may suggest movement possibilities. Realistic,

---

17. Emma D. Sheehy, *Children Discover Music and Dance* (New York: Henry Holt, 1959), p. 85.

impressionistic, and abstract art forms all offer different possibilities.

Children may in some cases find stimulation for movement activities in their own art work, especially finger painting, wet clay, or easel painting with large brushes on large sheets of newsprint paper. When children begin to verbalize their movement choices in relation to the art work, the teacher has a fine opportunity to work on the development of a meaningful vocabulary for art and movement. Many words are used in both art and movement contexts, such as rhythm, balance, movement, composition, mood, and color. Equating or finding the different expressive features of "color" in art and in movement can be a challenging experience for children.

Poetry has frequently been used to stimulate movement. The poetry can be simple chants children invent or works from the world's best poets. Teachers may choose poetry written for children or poetry which is adult-oriented but accessible to children.

Additional movement suggestions might come from making puppets or using commercially made ones, from social studies sources about jobs people do or about ways of living of peoples in other lands, from popular film or television programs, or from news stories of discovery, adventure, change, and heroic actions.

Important points in this section on stimulating movement are that there are many ways to do it, that variety is not only possible but desirable, and that the more children do, the more interesting, varied, and creative their movement activities will become.

LISTENING EXPERIENCES

Young children find it easier to move than to sit still. If, at first, listening is a by-product or an incidental result of moving to music, far more will be learned than is taught. Some children happen to be avid listeners, by temperament or as the result of home experiences, and insist on many repetitions of a recorded or live musical piece. But for most children, sitting still to listen is too difficult because muscles seem to move of their own volition. During brief or extended rest periods, day care centers often use recorded music extensively to help children relax and rest. Yet it would be regrettable indeed if children grew up to associate music listening only with falling asleep.

Listening experiences can build a solid auditory base for all kinds of differentiation of musical elements, as long as distaste for listening is avoided by eliminating unreasonable listening requirements. Among many possibilities listening experiences can include the following:

Associating musical themes or signals with expected responses. Familiar associations are chants for clean-up time or time to don outer clothing for dismissal, for rest time or snack time, or other recurring activities. Instead of a chant, the teacher may use one or more lines of a song melody, a theme of recorded music, a rhythm instrument signal, or a signal on a piano, chord organ, or other musical instrument

Creating movement patterns to recorded or live instrumental music. The variations in creative movement are likely to increase along with different types of music played. Listening is evidenced when children change their pace of movement when the music changes tempo, or otherwise adapt their movements to the musical development they hear.

Many opportunities for promoting a variety of beneficial listening experiences are suggested.

Exercises in producing specific types of movement to specific elements in music. For example, children may be asked to move with their arms forward when the music is loud and to fold arms when it is soft. This kind of exercise may broaden to listening for particular instruments (the violin or the oboe) and making specific movements when those instruments are heard, or pointing to pictures of them if the children have had experiences with such instruments.

Matching another child's movement with a rhythm instrument such as a drum or tambourine.

Dramatizing action when specific themes are heard in such vivid program music as *Peter and the Wolf*. Children take parts and act out the story they have come to know well by listening.

Naming a song after hearing a recording.

Timing one's activity by the duration of a song. For example, "When this song is finished on the record, start setting the table for lunch."

Listening for specific purposes:
Find the steady beat.
Beat the rhythm of the melody.
Curl up on the floor when that bassoon plays those low notes.
Jump up high when you hear that high flute.
March when you hear that marching drum.

Accompanying recorded music on rhythm instruments.

Playing games such as "Musical Chairs," where alert listening is required to stay in the game.

When listening experiences develop children's real interest in various kinds of music, insistent demands for the familiar often impede the introduction of new selections. Remembering that children are quite open to new music, although they tend to like what they know, the teacher needs to remember that the way to keep children listening to new music is to introduce it regularly and use each new piece of music to heighten or sharpen musical development. In New York City, in a kindergarten class that included quite a few children whose parents had recently arrived from different countries, a great deal of folk music was introduced with questions about which country it came from. Children were encouraged to bring recordings of folk music from home but to refrain from telling other children its origin until after they had first tried to guess. The game became very popular with the children, and their parents as well, and the children developed surprisingly sharp discrimination between rhythms of different countries, characteristic instruments, and melodic styles. Film strips, movies, and photographs could be used to help children anchor their increasing auditory skills in other aspects of foreign cultures.

With television and other mass media, American children are likely to hear some variety in music, although most of what they hear is sure to be popular contemporary music. Suggestions for musical sources and resources at the end of this chapter give a wide variety of musical selections for young children's listening, singing, and moving. Parents are a good source for additional types of music. In face-to-face meetings, in notes or class news reports, or by telephone, parents can be kept informed of musical needs and requests for the temporary loan of suitable recordings. Loans will increase if the teacher guarantees care of the recordings and returns them promptly in good condition.

Listening should come about because the child wants to hear the music, not because he has no choice. But group living requires us to observe the rights of others as well as our own. Nonlistening may be accepted where it does not interfere with others' desire to listen. Choices and reasonable alternatives can usually satisfy listeners and nonlisteners alike. Nonlisteners choosing to crayon pictures may be required to speak only in whispers when most of the group is absorbed in a listening experience.

SINGING EXPERIENCES

No materials are required for singing. Songs lift children's spirits on dull days and when the weather is good, allow them to give expression to their natural exuberance. Songs make all kinds of chores bearable, introduce variety of pace and emotional level, and bind groups together in social units. Let no day go by without a song. Children learn many songs easily if the songs are sung frequently and well led.

How do you teach a song to young children, student teachers often ask. Line by Line? All at once? Over and over? Most music educators advocate the whole-song approach. Sing the song through or play a recording. Signal children to join in at any time, but especially on the second hearing. If the children insist on another repeat, by all means accommodate them. If not, pick it up the next day and lead the children through it several times. If it is an action song such as "Skip to My Lou," "Little Red Wagon," or "The Paw-Paw Patch," the teacher will want to end the song before the children are ready to go on to another one. It seems best, when teaching songs to young children, to emphasize the action songs and alternate them with other songs, especially music which has well-marked rhythms. Children prefer fast to slow songs; they love surprises. If the children have learned a song well, they are delighted to hear the teacher then introduce some simple harmony, by voice or piano or other instrument. Nonsense syllables and words tickle young children's sense of humor. Or use unexpected dynamics—louder or much softer.

If songfests start early in the year with two or three short songs, singing sessions can gradually lengthen. Singing, of course, can be part of musical activities which include action songs, listening, group singing, movement, and rhythm instrument playing.

Teacher collections of songs are well worth the time and effort involved. Collections might differentiate between short songs in the middle register with a narrow range, such as from middle C through G on the piano, and songs which require a wider range—more intricate songs rhythmically or melodically, action songs, songs to which simple harmonies can be added, easy part songs, and simple rounds. Lists should also distinguish between records and cassette recordings and piano, autoharp, guitar, or other instrumental music. If these titles are clearly subgrouped, listed on 3 × 5 cards and kept in a suitable box, planning musical experiences takes very little time.

RHYTHM INSTRUMENTS

The usual idea of a rhythm band—with young children banging away, each doing "his own thing"—is no fun for teacher or children. It is just uncontrolled noise! Young children should have many op-

portunities to explore the individual sounds and rhythms different instruments make. Instrumental playing of any kind is a learning experience for the child. Teaching opportunities occur as children satisfy their curiosity and their sense of control over sound production. But the first lesson about rhythm instruments concerns self-control; there are times a child may play such an instrument freely and other times when he may not. There are also limits on a child's use of rhythm instruments—how they may be handled, and where.

If a music learning center is part of a well-equipped and well-arranged classroom, several rhythm instruments may safely be stored there, with frequent changes in the instruments made available for use. Here, rules are a necessity but they can be few and simple, such as, clean hands, no tools from other centers, one instrument is played at a time, and playing ceases on teacher cue when it begins to interfere with other activities. Classrooms fortunate enough to have sets of matched Montessori bells have available excellent ear-training material with built-in problem-solving tasks. Similar goals may be pursued through tuned water glasses, if the teacher tunes two sets and encourages one or two children to try to match them when they are not placed in graduated order. Or children may be interested in trying to construct a set of water glasses to match a piano octave or at least the pentatonic scale represented by the five black keys.

Group control of rhythm instruments follows from individual experiences in self-control. If the teacher conducts a rhythm band, unison playing might be only occasional, such as at the end, and otherwise one or more instruments are cued to play in succession. Before trying such a conducting session, a teacher candidate might think through and jot down the sequence, such as the following (using four-quarter time):

triangles only	three measures
drums only	three measures
cymbals (hand and finger)	one measure
rhythm sticks	three measures
cymbals	one measure
drums and rhythm sticks	three measures
all instruments together	two measures

Cues are simpler if signals and words are used together at first. If children are seated by instrument so the teacher can point to one section or another, signals can gradually be used without the verbal cue. The following ways of communicating clear messages can be used:

The teacher picks up the instrument to be played and holds it until she puts it down, signalling, "That's all now."

The teacher holds clear, simple photographs or sketches of each instrument at child-eye level and changes them when cuing instruments to stop or start.

The teacher uses words only, such as, "Triangles!" "Triangles and drums!" "Everybody!"

The teacher uses clear hand signals which indicate which instrument is next, such as a drumming pantomime for drums and pantomiming the action of each instrument in turn.

An arms-out, welcoming posture could mean, "Everybody play now."

Children find this great fun, playing in such a band or leading one. As soon as the cues are well established and some controls evidenced, children volunteer to take turns conducting. Since a child may be unwilling to relinquish the conducting role, the teacher might insure that everyone has a turn to conduct by ringing a small bell to indicate when each conductor's turn is over.

Early notation can be in the form of simple symbols on a chalkboard or flannel board to indicate a proposed orchestration:

        △   This symbol says triangles play.
      3   The numeral tells how many triangles there are.

        ▽   This symbol says drums play next.
      2   The numeral tells how many drums are being played.
           No triangles play now.

        ◯   This symbol says cymbals play next.
      1   The numeral says there is only one cymbal.
           Neither triangles nor drums play now.

  △ ▽ ◯   This symbol says all three instruments are now playing together. This is known as a "tutti" in orchestration.

This notation uses symbols suggesting the shapes of the instrument, numerals to show how many children are playing each instrument, and a symbol to indicate when all instruments play together. As children learn this form of notation, the symbols are placed horizontally, instead of vertically, to add the value of left-to-right direction as in reading words or music.

As in the Dalcroze Method of music instruction, when notation is used in association with movement, young children easily absorb the notation along with the action, and much more musical development occurs over shorter periods of time.

NOTATION

There is no teacher so unmusical that she is unable to introduce some elements of notation in appropriate activities along with action. With the help of a musical peer or the school music specialist, simple notation elements can be prepared and be ready for use at the right time.

The notation suggested above for rhythm instrument playing is an ideal first form of notation, since it is completely tied to the action of playing the instrument. It might be followed by separate oaktag cards with symbols for a whole note, half note, quarter note, eighth note, and, later, rest signs. As in the Dalcroze method, these note symbols can be just as clearly associated with action—a child chooses a card and tries to walk, walk slowly or fast, or run, to indicate understanding of its meaning. Also, a child may arrange a series of note cards on a shelf and use a rhythm instrument to match the time values of the cards selected.

With a chord organ, the teacher can paste numerals or names of notes on the keys. Notation to "read" music, using numerals or the letter names of the notes, can be prepared on oaktag cards available in the music center for simple, well-known songs. Soon the children will insist on more than pitch values; they need time values also. At this point, the notation can be offered on a large staff, with time values indicated as well as rests. Resonator bells or similar instruments can also be used in "reading" music notation. The piano is ideal for this purpose, and the music shelf can be used to hold the notated cards. It is only a small step from *playing* to singing notation on cards.

Early childhood teachers who have serious doubts about how much music young children can learn may find it instructive to study the curricula followed in other countries. Caldwell, visiting kindergartens in the People's Republic of China in late 1973, reported on the "high *Music programs* value upon achievement in music, a subject in which the children *adapted to the* seem talented. They learn to sing by the use of solfeggio and appear *level of the* to learn new songs rapidly."[18] Solfeggio is an ear-training method in *children provide* singing instruction used with children as young as three or four and *delightful* is part of the music training system designed by Dalcroze. Exercises *learning* in singing musical phrases, at first solely by ear, undoubtedly sharpen *experiences.* auditory perception and differentiation and develop good intonation even in young singers. Caldwell also noted that every school had a piano, accordian, or chord organ for musical activities.

Hefferman suggests a continuum of music-reading activities by grade level and deemphasizes technical work before grade two. In grade two, he advocates: "Much concentration on developing a strong sense of beat, emphasis on physical expression of rhythm, improvement of pitch-deficient children, development of acuity of hearing,

18. Bettye Caldwell. "The Little Apple: How China's Kindergartners Grow," *The Instructor* (June–July 1974), pp. 42–44, p. 43.

and, in general, more attention to rhythmic aspects of music than to pitch but some pitch reading with numbers should be started."[19]

Considering how much children are expected to accomplish in learning to read by the end of the first grade in school, it is apparent that musical notation should be well within the capacity and interest of most young children by age seven. In fact, the action-oriented symbolism of early music reading will surely contribute to children's facility for reading words and sentences.

Other early forms of symbolism in music notation which young children quickly grasp include such activities as:

1. Associating higher pitch with movements, such as upward-stretching and jumping, and lower pitch with movement downward such as curling up and dropping down to the floor.
2. Associating pitch changes with chalk lines on a chalkboard: upward, downward, or horizontal for no change in pitch; and, later, demonstrating this understanding on resonator bells, the piano, or the chord organ.
3. Placing oaktag "notes" on a large oaktag staff to show ascending, descending, or repeated notes which the teacher plays on the piano or other melody instrument. If the teacher places the first note on the staff, the children have only to decide the direction of the succeeding notes.
4. "Reading" notation on an oaktag or chalked staff, distinguishing whole, half, quarter, and eighth notes. Later, rest signs can be added and learned. The "reading" may follow the children's clapping the relative time values.

The development of music notation, out of movement and action, can be planned with classroom teachers by a music specialist or a musically trained teacher on the staff. Where specialist help is not available to classroom teachers, notation skills can be postponed to later grades where the assistance of a music specialist is more likely to be found.

If teacher candidates practice whatever music skills they have, as joyfully as they can, the children they teach are likely to love musical activity and be receptive to later teaching of music. The only caution to teacher candidates bears repeating: Leave the children hungry for more music.

Teacher candidates and teachers who are working in competency-

19. Charles W. Hefferman, *Teaching Children to Read Music* (New York: Appleton-Century-Crofts, 1968), p. 95.

or performance-based programs will recognize that most of the suggestions made in this chapter are easily translated into behavioral objectives for teaching and have rather obvious possibilities for criterion-referenced tests with specific conditions for mastery. Competency-based training programs for teachers, both graduate and undergraduate, are treated in detail in Chapter 13. Here, however, reference can be made to an excellent source for teachers who are looking for behavioral statements of music skills and criterion-referenced tests to assess skill development. Sidnell, who gives the expected general music skills as listening, singing, playing, and reading, in addition to movement and creating, lists very specific behavioral objectives under each title with suggested test procedures.[20] For example, under listening, one skill objective requires that the child "given an aural stimulus," identify a march, lullaby, and program or descriptive music, while another requires identifying melodic movement "as to ups and downs, high and low, same and different patterns."[21] It would not be difficult to adapt these objectives to the age-grade level or levels of the children in the group one is teaching and to design exciting and productive music programs to help the children become as keen and sensitive to musical characteristics as possible.

SUMMARY   *Music activities include singing, listening, dancing and creative movement, instrumental playing, developing musical concepts, and learning notation, all of which must be made enjoyable activities for children.*

Musical activities can be selected which are appropriate for the children's level of music development including songs with narrow note ranges, movements which are not too complex, and listening experiences which are active and involving. Teachers without musical training can provide many delightful musical experiences, although teachers with musical backgrounds can do more.

Contributions to children's musical education from systems developed by Suzuki, Dalcroze, Kodály, and Orff can be adapted to early childhood classroom practices. Many specific teaching suggestions are described, especially those derived from Orff's system, including the

20. Robert Sidnell, *Building Instructional Programs in Music Education* (Englewood Cliffs, N. J.: Prentice-Hall, 1973).
21. Ibid., pp. 44–45.

use of the musical instruments he designed which make it easy to play ensemble in the pentatonic mode. Specific teaching suggestions are made for musical concepts, movement, story dramatization, listening, singing, rhythm instruments, and musical notation.

✸ EXERCISES FOR STUDENTS ✸✸✸✸✸✸✸✸✸✸✸✸✸✸✸✸✸✸✸✸

1. Collect the words and music of ten songs appropriate for the age grouping you intend to teach.

a. List these songs on file cards. Note on each card the pitch range of the song, such as "middle C to G." Note also on each card possible movement or other activities.

b. Compare your cards with those of your peer group and add interesting titles to your own collection.

c. Participate in a workshop with your peer group and teach each other some of your songs.

2. Compile a list of twenty-five recordings of rhythmic music you can use for listening, movement, and other musical experiences with young children.

a. For each item listed, note some teaching possibilities.

b. Select one recording to play for your peer group and work out together various teaching possibilities with this music. Record your decisions and distribute duplicate copies to your group.

3. Attend a chamber music or orchestral concert.

a. Select the title on the program you liked best and, if a recording is available, secure it if you can.

b. Learn to know this music well by repeated listening.

c. Plan ways to use this music with young children.

4. Organize a musical activity group among your peers.

a. Plan attendance at concerts.

b. Plan to make music together—sing, dance, play instruments—or listen to music.

c. Advance your musical skills by enrolling in a music course, undertaking to learn to play a musical instrument, or by joining a chorus.

✸ EXERCISES FOR TEACHERS   ✸✸✸✸✸✸✸✸✸✸✸✸✸✸✸✸✸✸✸✸

1. Plan an active series of singing sessions to help children learn at least ten new songs in a four-week period.

a. Select ten songs which lie within the note ranges your children can sing. If in doubt, try it out. If a song's note-range is too wide, substitute another song. Select a group of songs with some variety, such as a few action songs, a lullaby, a foreign language folk song, a waltz, and a march. Select only songs that you like.

b. Plan singing periods so that they can be featured daily during the four-week period.

c. If possible, acquire recordings of some of the songs so that singing-listening experiences can occur during other periods as well.

d. Plan a before-and-after assessment of children's knowledge of the words and music of the songs.

e. Analyze your post-assessment.

(1) Did some children refuse to sing?

(2) Did you offer such children appropriate alternatives?

(3) Did some children learn words but not music, or the reverse?

(4) Which songs were learned best? Why?

(5) Can you plan further, based on this assessment, to help more children enjoy singing and to learn the words and music more accurately?

2. Select a musical composition with a lively story, such as *Peter and the Wolf,* and plan a musical story dramatization with the group.

a. Plan active listening experiences so that the children will learn the music and the story well.

b. Cast the characters, doubling some of them, to include as many children as possible.

c. Help the children select or make simple props or costumes which are attractive and which symbolize the characters in some ways.

d. Offer opportunities for informal dramatizations until the children develop familiarity with the action, words, and music.

e. If the children become very enthusiastic about their dramatization, suggest they invite an audience of parents or another class, but keep it low key and unpressured.

3. Plan a series of rhythm band rehearsals to develop alert listening, stable rhythms, and good ensemble.

a. Avoid uncontrolled noise by directing the band or having children take turns being conductor.

b. Model some conducting techniques—signals to start and stop, beat time, and cue in the various instruments.

c. Use audiovisual aids, such as symbols made of chalk on a blackboard, flannel on a flannelboard, simple pictures of the various instruments, or a metronome.

d. Start with very brief band sessions and gradually lengthen them as children gain more control of their instruments.

RESOURCES

Basic music series

Birchard Music Series. Kindergarten Book. Evanston, Ill.: Summay-Birchard, 1962.

Discovering Music Together. Chicago: Follett, 1968.

Exploring Music. New York: Holt, Rinehart & Winston, 1969.

Growing with Music. Englewood Cliffs, N.J.: Prentice-Hall, 1966.

The Magic of Music. Boston: Ginn, 1965.

Making Music Your Own. Morristown, N.J.: Silver Burdett, 1966.

Music For Young Americans. New York: American Book, 1966.

This is Music. Boston: Allyn and Bacon, 1965.

Music for Early Childhood. Morristown, N.J.: Silver Burdett, 1952.

Song collections

Dietz, B. W., and Parks, T. C. *Folk Songs of China, Japan, and Korea.* New York: John Day, 1964.

Echoes of Africa in Folk Songs of the Americas. New York: David McKay, 1969.

Greenberg, Noah, et. al., eds. *An Elizabethan Song Book.* New York: Doubleday, 1956.

Jenkins, Ella. *This Is Rhythm.* New York: Oak Publications, 1962.

Jewish Center Songster. New York: National Jewish Welfare Board.

Landeck, Beatrice. *Songs to Grow On.* New York: Edward B. Marks, 1950.

Landeck, Beatrice. *More Songs to Grow On.* New York: Edward B. Marks, 1954.

Landeck, Beatrice, and Crook, Elizabeth. *Wake Up and Sing.* New York: Edward B. Marks, 1969.

MacCarthey, L. Pendleton. *Songs for the Nursery School.* Cincinnati: Wills Music, 1937.

Mursell, James L., et al. *Music around the World.* Morristown, N.J.: Silver Burdett, 1962.

New Music Horizons Series: Experiences in Music for First Grade Children. Morristown, N.J.: Silver Burdett, 1952.

Nye, Robert, et. al. *Singing with Children.* Belmont, Calif.: Wadsworth, 1962.

Pitts, Lila Belle, et al. *Our Singing World Series: The Kindergarten Book.* Enlarged edition. Boston: Green, 1959.

Seeger, Ruth Crawford. *American Folk Songs for Children.* Garden City, New York: Doubleday, 1953.

Films

Music For Children. Contemporary/McGraw-Hill. 13 min.

Tuning Up For Life. Teleproduction, Zurich, Switzerland, for the Pestalozzi Institute.

Sources of instruments and equipment

George Kelischek Workshop. Atlanta, Ga.

Magnamusic-Baton, Inc. St. Louis, Mo. (Orff instruments)

Magnamusic Distributors, Inc. Sharon, Conn. (Orff instruments)

Rhythm instruments

Childcraft. New York, N. Y.
Children's Music Center, Inc. Los Angeles, Cal.
Lyons Band Instrument Co., Chicago, Ill.
Peripole, Inc., Far Rockaway, N. Y.
Rhythm Bank Inc., Fort Worth, Texas
Schirmer Music Co., New York, N. Y.
Wexler, Chicago, Ill.

RECORDINGS

Catalogs

"Phonograph Records and Filmstrips for Classroom and Library." *Educational Record Sales*, 157 Chambers St., New York City, N.Y. 10007. Recordings are classified by age and type of activity, as song stories, creative rhythms, ballet stories, folk, and square dances.

CMC Catalogue. *Children's Music Center, Inc.*, 5373 West Pico Blvd., Los Angeles, Calif.

Schwann-1, Record and Tape Guide. *Home Reference Guide to Recorded Music*, 137 Newbury St., Boston, Mass. 02116. Issued Monthly.

Companies specializing in educational records

Folkways Records, 117 W. 46th Street, New York City, N.Y.
Folkcraft, 1159 Broad Street, Newark, N.J.
Rhythms Production Records, Educational Research Associates, 13152 Grant Avenue, Downey, Calif.

Suggested records

Sioux and Navajo. Folkways Records.
Folk Songs and Dances of Puerto Rico. Folkways Records.
Exotic Dances. Folkways Records.
Folk Music of Haiti. Folkways Records.
Music of India. Shankar and Lal. Angel Records.
Azuma Kabuki Musicians. Columbia Records.

Drums of Trinidad. Cook.

Bolero, Ravel. London 6367.

Tubby the Tuba. Siegmaster.

Carnival of the Animals, Saint Saëns. Columbia M 31808.

Toy Symphony, Haydn. Angel S 35638.

Peter and the Wolf, Prokofiev. Columbia M S6193.

Symphony in D, op. 25 ("Classical"), Prokofiev. Columbia M S7159.

Candide (Overture), Bernstein. Columbia MS 6988.

Symphony No. 1 in C, Bizet. London 6208.

Carmen (selection), Bizet. RCA LSC 3341.

Appalachian Spring, Copland. MG 30071.

Billy the Kid (Ballet Suite), Copland. MG 30071.

Symphonie fantastique, op. 14, Berlioz. London 2101.

Firebird Suite, Stravinsky. Columbia, MS 6014.

Le sacre du printemps, Stravinsky. London 2308.

Marches militaires, Schubert. RCA ARL 1-0014.

Symphony No. 5 in B♭, Schubert. D. 485. Columbia MS 7295.

Symphony No. 7 in A, op. 92, Beethoven. Columbia MS 6112.

Waltzes, Chopin. Columbia MS 30063.

Children's Corner Suite, Debussy. London 6567.

Sorcerer's Apprentice, Dukas. London 6367.

Carnival Overture, Dvořák. Columbia M 31817.

Slavonic Dances, Dvorak. Columbia MS 6879.

Young Person's Guide to the Orchestra, Britten. Columbia S 31809.

Concerto in B♭ for Bassoon, Mozart. Angel S 3783.

Sinforia Concertante in E♭ K. 297b. Mozart. Angel S 36582.

Symphony No. 39 in E♭, Mozart. K. 543. Columbia MS 7029.

Pictures at an Exhibition, Mussorgsky. London 6177.

BIBLIOGRAPHY

Britten, Benjamin, and Holst, Imogen. *The Wonderful World of Music*. Rev. ed. Garden City, N. Y.: Doubleday, 1968.

Caldwell, Bettye. "The Little Apple: How China's Kindergarteners Grow". *The Instructor* (June-July 1974), pp. 42–44.

Copland, Aaron. *What to Listen for in Music*. Rev. ed. New York: McGraw-Hill, 1957.

Choksy, Lois. *The Kodály Method*. Englewood Cliffs, N.J.: Prentice-Hall, 1974.

Dewey, John. *The Child and the Curriculum.* Chicago: University of Chicago Press, 1902.

Doll, Edna, and Nelson, Mary Jarman. *Rhythms Today!* Morristown, N. J.: Silver Burdett, 1965.

Fargeon, Eleanor. *Poems for Children.* New York: J. B. Lippincott, 1938.

Flagg, Marion. "The Orff System in Today's World." *Music Educators Journal* 53: 4 (December 1966).

Hackett, Layne C., and Robert G. Jensen. *A Guide to Movement Exploration.* Palo Alto, Cal.: Peek Publication, 1961.

Hall, Doreen, adaptor, *Orff-Schulwerk, Music For Children: Teachers Manual.* New York: Schott Music, 1960.

Hall, Doreen, and Walter, Arnold, adaptors. *Music for Children.* By Carl Orff and Gunild Keetman. New York: Associated Music Publishers, 1960.

Hefferman, Charles W. *Teaching Children to Read Music.* New York: Appleton-Century-Crofts, 1968.

Horton, John. *Music.* New York: Citation, 1972.

Huntington, Harriet E. *Tune Up.* New York: Doubleday, 1942.

Myers, Louise Kifer. *Teaching Children Music in the Elementary School.* Englewood Cliffs, N. J.: Prentice-Hall, 1961.

Music Educators Journal, "A Photo-Essay on Talent Education after Twenty-five Years: Faces of Suzuki." Vol. 58, No. 1 (March 1972): 54–57.

Nash, Grace. *Music with Children.* Scottsdale, Ariz.: Swartout, 1965–67.

Richards, Mary Helen. *Threshold to Music.* Palo Alto: Fearon, 1964.

Richards, Mary Helen. "The Legacy From Kodály". *Perspectives in Music Education.* Washington, D. C.: Music Educators National Conference, 1966.

Robison, Helen F., and Schwartz, Sydney L. *Learning at an Early Age.* Vols. 1 and 2. Englewood Cliffs, N.J.: Prentice-Hall, 1972.

Rowen, Betty. *Learning through Movement.* New York: Teachers College Press, 1963.

Saffran, Rosanna. *First Book of Creative Rhythms.* New York: Holt, Rinehart & Winston, 1963.

Sheehy, Emma Dickson. *Children Discover Music and Dance.* N. Y.: Holt, Rinehart & Winston, 1959.

Sidnell, Robert. *Building Instructional Programs in Music Education.* Englewood Cliffs, N. J.: Prentice-Hall, 1973.

Smith, Robert B. *Music in The Child's Education.* N. Y.: Ronald, 1970.

Suzuki, Schinichi, et al. *The Suzuki Concept.* Berkeley, Calif.: Diablo, 1973.

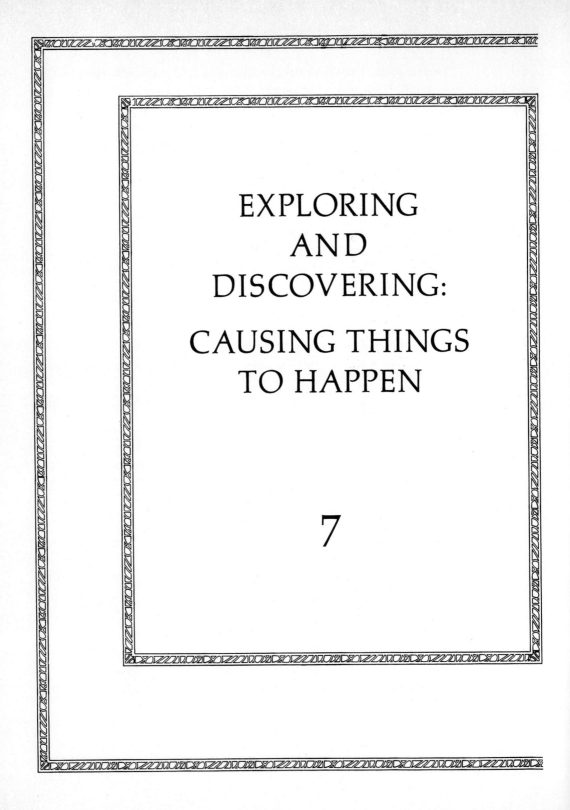

EXPLORING
AND
DISCOVERING:

CAUSING THINGS
TO HAPPEN

7

Stimulating children to participate actively in exploratory investigations of the properties of objects is to insure the kind of natural cognitive development Piaget has described in great detail. According to Piaget's theory, the child has to construct his own conceptions of the physical world, and he can only formulate them out of his motor and sensory activities.[1] Manipulation of objects and tactile and kinesthetic reactions to body movements are the fundamental sources of child understandings about the relationships that exist in time, quantity, space, and physical forces.

Sensory experiences contribute rich detail to the child's accumulating store of intuitive knowledge about the world —out of which concepts grow. The child is constantly acting on these developing concepts, and finding them mostly too gross, undependable, or incomplete. Because of his actions and the resulting sensory feedback, the child learns to modify or change his or her immature ideas for more adequate notions. If the child has been encouraged to make independent investigations, without too much adult interference other than offers of help or challenges to more precise understandings, the growing practically of his ideas gives him a good feeling of competence in his activities.

Teachers know how easy it is to teach a child to count by rote. The number words are remembered. But if this is only verbal learning, the child will be unable to use this knowledge in actuality. Ask a child for five marbles and see whether the marbles counted out are actually five. Or ask the child to pick out as many marbles as he or she has fingers on one hand to see how stable the child's conception of five is, or his notions of equivalence—that is, a marble for each finger. It is in the application of concepts to tasks and to problem solving that the concepts are tested against reality and are often found wanting. The need to find out how to change an inadequate conception becomes the most

1. Jean Piaget and Barbel Inhelder, *The Psychology of the Child* (New York: Basic Books, 1969).

powerful form of motivation, since it is internal and profound. This desire to work with objects, which tends to clarify understandings, has been given many different names by those who study child development. Whatever you choose to call it—Piaget called it "the joy of being the cause"—the use of one's body and the manipulation of objects inevitably builds a sense of independence or coping ability, even as it helps to structure one's concepts.

Hence, teachers find children capable of surprising feats of self-teaching through exploratory investigations or experimental tryouts. Verbal transmission of concepts is viewed as an impossible objective. The child builds the concepts, although it is usually the adult who gives it a conventional name. Once the child has realized the concept, it becomes portable and useful. It can be applied in unfamiliar contexts and, eventually, generalized, with exceptions identified.

CONCEPTS OF INTELLECTUAL DEVELOPMENT

Piaget—and easier-to-read writings of many Piaget interpreters—explain why learning *how* is the basic learning of young children. Some major concepts of Piaget's theory of intellectual development include the following:

> Words are not necessarily parts of young children's concepts; conceptual understandings may be non-verbal.
>
> The *order* in which children's thinking becomes more logical is fairly well fixed.
>
> The *pace* at which children develop, however, is unique to each child, although there are age expectations for most children which mark the achievement of various steps on the way to logical thought.
>
> Children do not "receive ideas from others": ideas or concepts are constructions of the child's own mind and must be fashioned by the child himself.
>
> It is through interactions between the child and objects and other children and adults that the child's idiosyncratic notions are challenged by others and he becomes aware that his ideas may not be shared with others.
>
> There are stages through which each child progresses in developing logical thinking. These stages are not voluntary. The child is unable to skip one stage just because a teacher or a mother would prefer to teach him at a more advanced stage.
>
> Each developmental stage gives the child somewhat more mature ways

of thinking than the preceding one. But each stage must reach a satisfactory level of completion before the child can go on to the next one.

From intuitive and somewhat unstable ways of reasoning before age five, for example, the child may achieve a fairly reliable mode of concrete logic concerning objects, if he has been encouraged to work his way from one stage to the next, by about age seven or eight. But a long period lies ahead of the child before stable forms of abstract logic can be expected of him. This may come in early adolescence for some children, later for others, or it may not be attained at all by some.

The preschool child may be considerably on the far side of any kind of stable logic, while the primary grade child begins to show some stability, especially with concrete objects that he can manipulate and reason about.[2]

Teachers find it difficult to let a child reason from his own experiences if the reasoning leads to a false deduction or generalization. It often seems better to give the child the "right" answer, to avoid error. For example, a child finds that when water freezes into ice cubes, the water expands. From this, a child is likely to overgeneralize that all liquids expand in freezing. A teacher might tell the child that he has overgeneralized and reached a false conclusion. But such verbal communication about physical processes is likely to become file-and-forget information. Correcting a child's reasoning might discourage further discovery activities. Worse, it undermines the child's confidence in his ability to find answers to his problems. Only adults know the right answer. Ask an adult to explain the world; don't use your own problem-solving skills.

Trying to correct children's immature concepts is frequently precluded by the current stage of the children's reasoning ability. An adult conception may require the simultaneous juggling of several variables, at a time when the child can manage only one variable at a time. Piaget's example, which has been validated by numerous researchers, concerns pouring water from a tall, narrow tumbler into a wide, flat one and asking children under six years of age whether the quantity of water remains unchanged. Young children, able to work with one variable at a time, are likely to say that there is less water, looking at the height but not the width. When an adult pours the

2. See also R. M. Beard, *An Outline of Piaget Developmental Psychology* (New York: Basic Books, 1969); J. L. Phillips, Jr., *The Origins of Intellect: Piaget's Theory* (San Francisco, Calif.: Freeman, 1969); M. A. S. Pulaski, *Understanding Piaget: An Introduction to Children's Cognitive Development* (New York: Harper, 1961).

water back into the tall, narrow tumbler, the young child is likely to say there is more water, again looking at the height but not the width of the column of water. Telling him he is wrong is unlikely to change a conviction perceptually based, that is, it seems to be either more water or less. The conviction that the shape of the container (how it looks) is irrelevant grows with increasing logical skill. It takes a firm grasp on logic to be able to say that it makes no difference whether it looks like more or less, since the quantity of water has neither been increased nor decreased and must therefore be the same.

Explorations and discoveries must, however, be confined to discoverable types of data. People's names, or the names of objects, are not discoverable. These are appropriately told when needed. Problems may be pursued, and projects fashioned, to yield much discoverable knowledge.

VALUES OF EXPLORING AND DISCOVERING

If we insist upon telling children "right" answers to problems, it is apparent that their memory may or may not be reliable and, if not, further motivation to learn more is cut off. The child who knows *how* is not dependent upon a memory of told facts—he can apply problem-solving strategies himself and discover the right answer. One excellent text by McGivack and LaSalle on teaching science to young children stresses the importance of "the investigative know-how," with content serving as the vehicle of learning.[3] According to the authors, the child functions "as an inquirer, object manipulator, idea organizer, explorer of curious phenomena, generalizer, discusser, and communicator of ideas and conclusions."[4] Notice how many active ways to learn this approach offers. Also note that *literacy* is not a requirement for meaningful discovery and exploratory learning. Children who do not yet read, or who are only beginning readers, can nevertheless observe carefully, manipulate or transform objects or systems, note changes, try to account for or control the changes, or classify and design their own patterns for shaping the information and ideas identified. Children who are literate can, of course, use written sources for information gathering as well as for communicating, but the exploratory learning experiences are fundamentally the same.

3. John J. McGavack, Jr., and Donald P. LaSalle, *Guppies, Bubbles, and Vibrating Objects* (New York: John Day, 1969), p. 16.
4. Ibid., p. 19.

*Exploring
fosters
independence,
improves self-
concepts, and
develops logical
thinking.*

Major outcomes of active participation in exploratory learning are the child's secure feelings that *he* is finding out for himself what the world is like, that he *is* discovering how things work, and that nobody knows everything so there are some things nobody knows at all. The exploratory aspect of young children's learning, in art, music and other major creative areas, contributes to the child's sense of autonomy and independence and these support his feelings of competence. A child who has such a "can do" attitude engages problems at home and at school without wasting time in false starts or attempts to escape self-testing situations.

Student teachers often report encountering considerable difficulty in a tightly structured classroom when they have tried to develop a small-group or individual learning activity of the active participation type. The principal difficulties are management of children and materials. The children, accustomed to strict external controls, promptly go out of bounds when offered free movement and manipulative opportunities. Materials are equally difficult to manage, students find, outside the framework of the typical classroom.

Clearly, the explorations of physical things cannot be well developed in unfamiliar contexts, because these create insecurity, ambiguity, and "what can I get away with" attitudes. However, teachers who wish to move gradually to a more open classroom approach could concentrate first on exploration as a program component and as a model for gradually transforming the rest of the program from overly tight to looser structure. This can be successfully accomplished with planning, positive instructional techniques to help children accept more freedom and choice without overstepping the bounds, and teacher modelling of acceptable activity levels. Children can participate in making and monitoring the few needed rules.

FEATURES OF CONSTRUCTIVE EXPLORATIONS

*Open-endedness
and continuity
are requisites
for constructive
explorations.*

In selecting materials and exploratory possibilities teachers might bear in mind that "one-shot" learning activities do not build children's competence, while open-endedness does. For example, if children plant lima beans in good soil, place the pots in a sunny window, and experience successful plant growth, the activity could end there. More open-endedness occurs when children are encouraged to try different planting techniques so as to find out which are better and what their plants' essential needs are: Do they really need water? What if we try to grow some without water? Do they really need soil? What if we try to grow some without soil? (Or we'll try some without light, or warmth, or sunshine, or in crowded or uncrowded pots.) Children might think of other possibilities such as growing horizontally instead of vertically or away rather than toward the sun.

Another important feature, for young children, is that, while the activity should not be too short or accomplished at one sitting, neither should it be too long, tax memories, and result in loss of interest. Additional constructive features of exploratory activities are:

1. That the activities be multisensory and active.
2. That the children have sufficient familiarity or interest in the materials to want to work with them at length.
3. That there be no hazards to health and safety, such as the use of open flames, frayed electrical connections, or chemicals which may cause skin damage.
4. That the children can work with the materials relatively independently.
5. That the materials can take the child manipulations expected without causing problems of high cost of replacement.
6. That the children can find some ways to pattern their observations and the results of their manipulations.[5]

In many classrooms, a science learning center or a math-science learning center is the area reserved for these exploratory activities. In others, materials may be stored in one center but need not be used only in that area. In some classrooms, a crucial problem is access to water and cleaning materials. A sink in the classroom is, of course, ideal. But many teachers use buckets of water when they have no sink. Children love to help get the water and can be trusted to do this when they work in pairs and fill the bucket only to a clear marker, thus avoiding too-heavy loads and water spills. Sometimes, upper-grade monitors may help if the water source is not close to the classroom.

However the teacher arranges the materials and the activity areas, the children must understand what is permitted and must be helped to develop self-control when involved in possibly messy activities. Aprons may sometimes be necessary to keep clothing clean and dry. If the center is a rather small physical space, the teacher must decide how to manage the children's ebb and flow and the possibility, at times

5. Helen F. Robison and Sydney L. Schwartz, *Learning at an Early Age*, vol. I: *A Programmed Test for Teachers* (Englewood Cliffs, N.J.: Prentice-Hall, 1972), pp. 113–194.

of very high general interest, of permitting all interested children to work in various parts of the classroom space. A defined center has certain advantages. Children can regularly observe what is being offered there or the progress of various activities, and the area of messy work can be delimited and managed. As long as there is flexibility to expand space when interest surges, many different classroom arrangements can serve equally well.

To be truly exploratory, the center must be a "please touch and do something with the materials" place. This should not be an area in which to arrange an exhibit for adults or to display objects under glass. Neither should there be judgments about the relative merits of the work of different children. There might be activities of both the individual variety and those which require or benefit from small-group cooperation. Regularly, the teacher will be assessing the effectiveness of the center in stimulating children's explorations, noting the ways that different children explore. If children are not drawn to the center, its lack of attraction requires analysis of the arrangements, the materials, the nature of teacher guidance, and the extent of teacher interest in the activities. Any one of these components or some combination of them may explain the lack of activity. It is also possible to have one such wildly successful center that other centers suffer from lack of interest. Occasionally, such total group involvement can be expected, as when a new small animal is introduced. Usually, however, a lack of balance in the room's attractions can be changed by dramatizing the materials or activities in the less attractive center in order to use space and equipment better.

TEACHING ROLES

Student teachers who see a great deal of "teacher center-front" in a classroom dominated by teacher talk often find it difficult to identify teaching roles for children's exploratory activities. Does the teacher do something else while she leaves children to play with materials? There must be more to such teaching than just getting out of the way, it would seem, even though there is considerably less structure than in a lecture-recitation format.

Teaching roles, sensitively selected for the child or the activity, may include nurturing, participating, information-giving, rule defining, eliciting information, challenging, probing, creating cognitive dissonance, modelling actions, receiving dictation, re-arranging materials, suggesting activities.

Nurturing

Nurturing gives emotional support to a dependent or shy child or one with great needs for personal affection. The nurturance may give a child the courage or motivation to engage in activities with materials instead of clinging to an adult or sucking one's thumb.

Participating

Participating is self-explanatory—the teacher does what the children do, in the same way or at a reduced level, or as little as possible while doing some of the activity. In nurturing, the teacher may be at hand but not participating; the encouragement, interest, and approval of activity would be the teacher's projection to the children.

Exchanging information

Information giving and receiving, eliciting information, and receiving dictation are all information exchanges. Some information giving may be required at the beginning or end of an exploratory activity, such as offering the premise that a battery which does not seem to work is probably a dead battery and needs replacement. Eliciting information from children must not be intrusive. Sometimes the children invite it or the teacher tries it out. No harm is done in trying, only in pushing for responses the children are neither willing nor able to make.[6] Receiving dictation is not likely to occur without teacher suggestion. If she asks, "Do you want me to write down what you just found out? Other children might like to read it, or want me to read it to them," she establishes the need for recording the results of one's activity, especially for the purpose of communicating it to others. The information exchange is best tied to the actions: "What do you see now?" "Did it change?" "How is it different?"

6. Mary Budd Rowe, *Teaching Science as Continuous Inquiry* (New York: McGraw-Hill, 1973), p. 337.

Defining rules

Rule defining may not be necessary if well-defined rules govern potentially messy activities and apply to explorations as well. However, some materials may require new or different rules, for example, "It is all right to dig up the seeds you planted in *your* pot but not in the pots of other children." Some materials may require some delimitation in use as by keeping bulk quantities unmixed or covering a table top with newspaper or a plastic cover. It is always more meaningful to the children if they are involved in the rule definition and can regard it as needed and fair.

Modelling

Modelling actions are often more potent than verbal rules, and they establish clear examples of possible actions or delimit the permissible. For example, whenever there are animals in the classroom, the teacher's modelling actions are usually the most potent to establish kind and safe ways of handling or caring for them. If a rabbit or guinea pig is permitted to wander about the classroom at times, it is very important that the children learn not to chase or frighten it and learn approved ways of picking it up.

Stimulating action

Challenging, probing, creating cognitive dissonance, or suggesting activities are all ways of stimulating children either to take further actions or to interpret their observations or inferences. The challenge might be: "Did it really happen?" "Can you do it again?" The probe might be: "What did you mean when you said that the bean sprouts like the sun?" Creating cognitive dissonance is a procedure which is used to confront a child with actions or information contrary to his understanding and which may require him to discard or transform his understanding. For example, the child who overgeneralizes from early explorations with magnets that "magnets stick to metal things" is given nonmagnetic metals such as copper, in addition to the magnetic metals, to transform his overgeneralization to a somewhat more specific understanding.

Children may be challenged to take new and additional actions to sharpen their observations. For instance, a child who is blowing soap bubbles might be challenged by the question: "How can you blow a larger bubble?" This would probably be premature if this is the child's first bubble-blowing experience, but, in subsequent experiences, the child might combine the pleasure of the activity with the challenge of controlling the size of the bubbles.

One important point about teaching roles is that there are many options; and student teachers have to learn these roles so their repertoire will be varied and rich. The *art* of selecting the right role for the child is one to be developed with flexibility and out of experience. Another point is that "telling" children, or expecting understanding to result from rote memorization, is a lost cause. Rowe points out that long-term memory requires a nonrote, meaningful context.[7] If you, therefore, think you can, by telling a child the answer, cut short the child's lengthy exploration with materials learning how things work, your teaching is unlikely to contribute to the child's growing conceptualizing.

The process of learning is marked by gradual changes that lead toward long-term cognitive development.

In teaching children to learn how to find out about the properties and processes of the real world, the *process* of learning is the only focus which has the possibility of long-term results. Process can be the focus whether the teacher uses a thematic, discovery, problem-solving, or cognitive skills approach.[8] Process means confronting or stimulating a child to wonder about, say, why the fish tank is low on water on Monday morning and try to think of some possible explanations as that the fish drank the water, the water spilled or leaked, or the water shrank. He or she picks a likely explanation and does some things to test it out. One test might be to find out whether a tank of water—without fish—if left over the weekend, will have the water level unchanged.

A thematic approach might be to select an area of explorations like machines or ant colonies or a physical process such as evaporation or heat conduction. In selecting a theme, the teacher identifies either the objects or the concepts to investigate, instead of leaving the content to be selected by the children or through chance occurrences. Some

7. Ibid., 527.
8. Ibid., pp. 566–579.

teachers might prefer a thematic approach because it narrows the field and makes it possible to collect adequate materials quickly. The discovery approach, which can be embedded in a thematic one, offers the child opportunities to work with materials often enough so he finds out about the exciting and interesting properties of objects, makes detailed observations, and begins to ask questions which lead to more purposeful activities.

Problem solving generates a high-interest state for organizing learning activities. Problems arise every day. Some children fortunately become very curious about some of these problems. When they don't, the teacher does—infecting the children with her curiosity. Focusing on cognitive-skill development is clearly compatible with any of the three approaches specified above. In this case, the teacher may have selected a transitional conceptualizing stage such as seriation (ordering materials, for example, as to length) or conservation of liquid quantity (understanding that liquid is not affected by size or shape of container) for children's learning opportunities. Whatever cognitive skills are involved, the teacher is likely to choose a discovery, problem-solving, or thematic approach.

"Telling" children has another disadvantage, besides its ineffectiveness in terms of retention. It is important for children's gradual development of scientific attitudes that they gradually understand that there are many unanswered questions, children must find out that many books and scientists disagree about which are the best answers to some questions, for instance, how the universe began.[9] A scientific attitude in an early childhood classroom is therefore much better exemplified by teacher questioning than teacher telling.

Constructive manipulation of materials requires that teachers should not only refrain from *telling*, but they should ask good *questions*. Rowe cites her study of helping teachers to *wait longer* after posing questions, resulting in not only reduced teacher talk, but also such benefits as children's lengthened responses, more volunteered responses, fewer failures to respond, increase in children's speculative thinking, more evidence cited by children, increased contributions from slower students, and decreased teacher disciplinary actions.[10] Just rattling off questions in rapid succession may only serve to confuse, frighten, and silence children; they must be allowed thinking time.

9. John H. Rosengren, *Outdoor Science for the Elementary Grades* (West Nynack, N.Y.: Parker, 1972), p. 19.
10. Rowe, op, cit., pp. 255–261.

TEACHING REQUIRES KNOWING

Student teachers, and teachers as well, are often urged to develop exploratory activities about which they know little and to "learn along with the children." The truth is that very few adults are comfortable in such ambiguous situations. They fear losing face with children, with being perceived as one who is ignorant or uncertain, and they fear unfavorable reactions from colleagues and supervisors. Sometimes teachers can grasp a very exciting problem about which they really know little and can turn it into a magnificent learning experience, modelling their own learning activities as well as guiding the children. It is far more likely, however, that teachers will avoid developing learning activities on topics or areas in which they feel personally inadequate. Therefore, the writer urges student teachers to read widely in the many excellent books now available in order to approach children's exploratory activities with some feeling of security. Workshops in college or school classrooms are additional sources of learning how to deal with materials and children for exciting teaching possibilities.

Suggestions follow about some very accessible kinds of explorations children can make with plants and animals, with resources in the immediate neighborhood of the school, and with the multitude of objects that surround them in their daily living.

PLANTS, ROCKS, AND ANIMALS

City children have few opportunities to observe natural processes of plant and animal growth. Yet these can be studied in the classroom or school or outdoors. Inside the classroom, planting and caring for plants are always popular activities with young scientists. Soil is a fine material to play with. If the teacher can avoid a rushed planting experience, as when trying to have seeds sprouting in time for Mother's Day presents, children can learn a great deal about plant development through different seasons and over long periods of time. The longer time periods give children the observational base and the reflective time needed to figure out explorations, try them out, and attempt to understand the results. If seeds fail to germinate, or if leaves yellow or wither, there are usually several plausible explanations, and it is not self-evident as to which one is correct. Sometimes the teacher needs time to consult some resources, i.e., a gardening encyclopedia or a knowledgeable nurseryman, or the county agent. When the children become interested in observing a plant grow, simple records, charts, and graphs can develop along with the plants. Without didactic teaching, children understand some features of symbols, as when they paste a green square on a chart for each sprout in the pot. They see the need for symbols, to designate by name which pot belongs to which child. They also enjoy dictating, copying or writing stories or love messages to go with the plant to mother. Thus, reading, writing, and learning to use simple symbols and simple counting activities, all get satisfactorily mixed with plant growth and management.

Suggestion is often more potent than requirement. If teachers let children decide how much they choose to become involved in the many activities which explorations enhance, and which enhance explorations, there is likely to be a very high proportion of involvement. Those few children who do not choose much involvement may still benefit from the reports of those who do and from the general ambience of excitement in voluntary investigations and communications. Excitement is catching, and soon everyone plays some part in the developing experiences. One small boy, who seemed rather remote from the classroom planting operations, turned out to have a large fund of information about planting from gardening activities he shared with his father. Without pressure to conform to group experiences, this child made his contributions from his past and ongoing home activities and gradually took part in classroom explorations as well.

If plant care goes on all year long in the classroom, it becomes possible to deal with longer term changes and plant needs. Questions come up naturally. Why do some plants die? Why do some plants flower while others do not? What do we do with a crowded pot? Do all plants grow from seed? How did trees get where they are now? Could we put a tree on our school playground, or do we have to plant a seed? What about fruits? If we planted apple and orange seeds in a pot on the window sill, will we grow apples and oranges in the pots? If not, what about the playground space—can we grow fruit outside?

Gardening on school or park sites is not uncommon. One kindergarten teacher worked with the parent association to beautify the school grounds, to overcome vandalism when plants were torn up, and to develop community support for the maintenance of the garden. If children have the great joy of harvesting flowers from a garden they have tended, the self-satisfactions become very great indeed.

When outdoor gardening is not feasible, walks and trips to parks, botanical garden, or even on city streets yield a surprising bounty for the sharp eyes of children. Leaves and seeds can be observed, gathered, carried into the classroom and there sorted, classified, and compared and contrasted. Trees can be closely observed and compared, named and studied in pictures and books, and watched in the different seasons to find out how they leaf and develop seeds.

Rosengren suggests developing a "key" to use for the classification of any group of objects being studied.[11] By key, he means any base for the sorting of, or differentiation among, the objects which will work for that group of objects. For example, for a tree, the key might be to differentiate evergreens from nonevergreens or to classify on the basis of whether leaves are arranged on opposite sides of a twig or are not so arranged. Similar clear classes might be used to group or differenti-

11. Rosengren, op. cit., pp. 62–63.

ate animals, insects, or birds. Such classifying efforts often lead to continuing investigations by children to find new members of the main classes identified.

Collecting, observing, and investigating plants and rocks generate a wealth of learning experiences.

On the school playground, for example, in spring and early summer as well as fall, in most geographic areas children might begin to identify and group members of such classes as trees, shrubs, wild flowers, grasses, fungi, roots, ferns, or lichens. If children have any regular access to a site that yields some variety of rocks, a great deal of enjoyable collecting, observing, and comparing can go on out of doors, followed by laboratory examinations and investigations back in the classroom. Children can think up many interesting questions about rocks, such as:

Can you break it? How? How do the broken surfaces look?
If you put it in water, what would happen?
Are all rocks heavy? Can you weigh a rock?
Are rocks different in color, shape, bumpiness?
Are there rocks you can see through?

With a simple balance or produce-type scale, an old sock—to put a rock in when breaking it with a hammer so as to avoid injury from flying bits—a small hammer, water, a bowl, and a magnifying glass would make a very absorbing center for working with rocks. After some playful work with rocks on their own, children are usually ready to share their findings with the teacher and their speculations and questions with everyone. On a fairly long-term basis, this is the kind of activity that children voluntarily return to, and one which generates a great deal of communication. Usually, children begin to tell their parents about their interesting collections of rocks at school. Before long this touches a sympathetic chord in many families, who go on rock-hunting trips on country roads, in parks, in old quarries, along streams, and in many other likely places. Soon, someone comes in with a rock that has a clear fossil imprint and this opens new avenues of speculation. Or the teacher may take the class to a lake-front or to a creek nearby where everyone hunts rocks or shells and tests them for the flatness and shape required for "skipping" stones —to sail them across the surface of the water.

Every classroom for young children should have some land or aquatic animals to observe and care for. Cages for rabbits, guinea pigs, hamsters, gerbils, and other small animals are fine projects for class-

*Children ac-
quire values of
responsibility,
respect, and
empathy by
caring for
animals in the
classroom.*

room construction. Children learn how much forethought is required for the care of an animal. Where will it live? What kind of a house does it need? What does it eat? What does it do? What do we need to do to care for this animal? What are this animal's needs for air, light, heat, or water? What other needs are there?

Care for animals helps children understand and exercise responsibility for people. Kindness and thoughtfulness are sometimes easier to understand when the "others" are small animals, dependent for their care on others. Small pet animals also work wonders for shy, lonely children or children undergoing stress. Watch the cuddling of the rabbit, the stroking of the guinea pig. Notice how the guinea pig suddenly becomes a baby in a carriage and a little mother "feeds" and soothes it. The vicarious working out of early love-hate relationships through small animals is very helpful to young children provided that the animals are adequately protected from too much acting out of emotions.

Classroom animal care often leads to trips to the pet shop and the zoo. Short trips are better than long ones, with time provided to watch a particularly interesting animal or to observe feeding time at any animal cage. Working with animals can involve value orientation as well as affective needs of children and pets. The values would relate to respect for animals and for their needs (apart from the particular ways in which animals serve us), for conservation of vanishing species, and for some glimmerings of the symbiotic roles played by plants, animals, and mankind in their joint use of planet Earth. This kind of value orientation is probably best established through teacher attitudes, through stories and books, and through interviews with knowledgeable people in the school, pet shop, zoo, or among the parents. Preferably, value orientation grows and connects with community activities and interests in the same direction, that is, ecological balance. For this kind of connectedness, teachers need a great deal of contact and close working relationships with parent and community groups. With such connections, children experience greater unity in their educational development and stronger feelings of what is universally good.

While it is not possible, in this chapter, to list all possible types of explorations with plants, rocks, and animals, student teachers might develop varied listings of possibilities as they browse through books and programs and visit other teachers' classrooms for good ideas.

OTHER RESOURCES

Take a group of children for a walk around the school block. What do they see? A firebox to send fire alarms, overhead wires, telephone poles, mailboxes, traffic lights, gullies or other water-eroded sites, perhaps some type of water (creek, lake, river, rivulet, reservoir, run-off of some kind), trees, plants, birds, insects, cats, dogs, squirrels. According to Rosengren, anything that catches the children's interest can be pursued, along with any questions children can be stimulated to raise, such as:[12] What's it for? Who takes care of it? What's happening? How long has it been here?

Some of the found objects can be brought back to the classroom for further observation and study including seeds, leaves, an animal skeleton, a hard-shelled butterfly pupa, or a snakeskin. Some of the things observed which cannot be brought back—the mailbox or firebox, for instance, can, be related to social studies and social learning activities in which the group may be engaged or in which they indicate an interest.

Air, water, wind, and sand

Investigations of air, water, wind, and sand are always in order for children, especially when they can manipulate these in any way. Making air move is fun, especially when you can see how it helps to dry a wet chalkboard. Using the force of air (as wind) is exhilarating when you want it to fly a kite or to turn a pinwheel. Sand is surely one of the most sensuous materials to play with, and it is infinitely malleable, in combination with water, for so many different possibilities. Water may lead to liquid measurement and to developing the understanding of quantitive relationships such as "more," "less," or "the same amount." Water, of course, offers endless delight as a playing medium. When playing with water, children begin to observe the processes they will later name as evaporation, condensation, and dissolution. They investigate how water interacts with other liquids— vinegar, oil, or pancake syrup, for example. They play with plastic eyedroppers, observing how water drops form on wax paper,

12. Ibid., p. 48.

paper towels, wrapping paper, foam sponges, wood surfaces, metal and plastic surfaces, and anything else that can be made available. They drop various objects in water to see what happens. Salt and sugar seem to disappear but not a pencil, crayon, or plastic chip.

The learning is in the doing and in the questions evoked by doing. Through many interesting investigations, children build a large repertoire of how things work, and, if the teaching is effective, they also develop intense curiosity about why things work as they do. They try to put their knowledge in order and give it some shape and pattern which is personally meaningful.

Vibrations

Studies of the vibrations which produce sounds are always of interest to young children.[13] They make simple rhythm instruments which can be struck, plucked, or otherwise made to vibrate and produce different kinds of sounds. Tin can telephones are fun to make and to use for communication, in play, or in games. Tuning water glasses to form a scale, or matching tuned water glasses tone for tone, provides excellent ear training as well as some practical illustrations of the ways in which pitch can be varied. Since music is always welcome, once you have a water glass scale, there ought to be some singing and tune-making fun. An everyday way to study sound vibrations is to play with the various rhythm instruments and to find out, by changing the ways in which the vibrations are produced, whether the same instruments can be made to produce different kinds of sounds. For example, how does the triangle sound when you hit it with a wooden drumstick, or how many different ways can you make the drum sound?

Contributions and flea market objects

There are endless sources of objects to investigate. Parents often contribute items found or collected on trips, from seashells to tadpoles. These often result from periodic communication to parents of the

13. McGavack & LaSalle, op. cit., pp. 132–138.

need for such contributions as well as gratitude for the use of the objects. Whenever possible, the teacher should give parents some specific examples of how the contributions were used by the children in their learning activities. Sometimes local businesses contribute small gifts which are very useful and for which there is often no budget. Communication is very helpful here, to feature the gift and the giver and the ways in which the program is enhanced by such contributions.

Junk shops, flea markets, attics, and spring cleaning activities may disgorge old clocks, waffle irons, radios, and many such small items no longer useful. These are fascinating "take apart" activities for the children who sort out the parts and sometimes use some of these, such as springs, in constructions. It is difficult to have too many materials except where storage is really inadequate. Cartons labelled for different materials and activities facilitate location of needed objects and contribute to orderly storage. Taking small machines apart often triggers machine building with the children using levers, ramps, rubber-band springs, pulleys, wedges, and other objects easily come by.

Block corner physics

Beginning activities which later lead to thoughts about energy and work can start in the block corner with levers, pulleys, or improvised contraptions. Making a ramp with long blocks and trying to move miniature vehicles up and down opens opportunities for questions about faster movement or using objects to reduce the human energy input. Many good questions arise in the block corner if the teacher is there either to hear them or to stimulate them. How can we move heavy objects or raise them? How can we make a shaky structure more stable? This is where, with enough sustained interest and effort, a delightful re-invention of the wheel can occur.

Ecology

Pollution and ecological studies leading to a focus on the physical environment and man's survival needs are unfortunately richly illustrated almost everywhere in our country. Children can begin to learn, at early ages, to live in ways that do not worsen environmental problems and, hopefully, in ways that promise improvement. Since early habits linger on, children can learn from the very beginning not to litter but to pick up and make neat as they go along so that they do not leave their area worse than it was before.

New ways for old

While many teachers grow tired of magnets, weather, time, seasons, and shadows, or of the trite old activities repeated endlessly, they might be pleasantly surprised by possibilities in these activities which are seldom explored. Shadow play is fun, for example, but also demands concentrated effort to produce interesting or hypothesized effects. Instead of simply noting the daily weather, much more excitement comes from making weather vanes, testing wind directions and velocities, using barometers, thermometers, and rain gauges, and daily charting rainfall, sunny days, smog, or several temperature readings. Simple graphs can be maintained by the children, so that instead of just hearing verbal repetition of weather conditions, they can study the rising or falling line of temperature and chart wind or sunshine. Imagine the excitement of the child whose turn it is to observe and empty the rain gauge after a particularly heavy rainfall! Recording such an observation high on the chart becomes meaningful because of the various associations and experiences with the events and the records, day after day.

Marking time

Teachers rely upon clocks too much to tell time. Timers are more useful to young children to mark off brief periods when these are personally meaningful, e.g., the length of a turn with a new piece of equipment. For brief periods, egg timers are fine. Mechanical timers which ring at set periods mark time usually in visual as well as in audible ways. Children can also make simple timers with paper or plastic cups and sand or rice.

EXAMPLES OF ACTIVITIES FOR CLASSROOM DISCOVERY

Concepts of size, weight, and number

In a kindergarten in a low-income area, the student teacher had been featuring play with a balance in the science area. She noticed that the children evidenced much confusion about size, weight, and number in their balancing activities. Mostly, they were trying to balance the two arms using small rocks. The student teacher substituted poker chips for the rocks, expecting the equal units would be easier for the children to understand. Three children showed immediate comprehension of the equal units concept and were able to predict that if three or five chips were placed on one side, the same number would be required on the other side to bring the balance into equilibrium. The other four children in the group seemed unable to make such predictions. Working individually with these four children in order to assess their number concepts, the student teacher discovered that they were not yet able to count reliably on a one-to-one basis and to match object to counting numbers. This discovery lesson alerted the student teacher to some of the steps children cannot skip in making concepts their own. The incident also suggests how much the teacher can learn about children's cognitive skills when free discovery-type explorations are available to them. In this case, the remedy was not to remove the children from the fun activities but to supplement these with planned counting experiences, matching object to number in many functional ways.

Concepts of air

Concepts of the movement of air or wind can grow through playful activities with soap bubbles. In a kindergarten experience with soap bubbles—a favorite good-weather activity for this group on the playground—children blew bubbles, tried to "chain" them together, challenged each other to make the biggest bubbles, and noticed how the breezes blew the bubbles about. One little girl started to dance lightly, saying she *was* a girl bubble and other children joined her, dancing bubbles blown by the wind.

What I hope student teachers will gather from the foregoing is that what is important in investigative activities is not only the children's ways of learning but also a lack of fine distinctions between work and play, naming and manipulating, planning to do and doing, and no fine distinctions made among math, science, reading, writing, music, and art. If the "unit" of study is wholly clear-cut and distinctive, and is not permitted to overlap other units and goals, it is probably too tidy for the *real* world of learning. It is not contradictory for student teachers to plan very specific learning activities, as long as they develop the flexibility to transform their clear designs into the ways the children respond, and to the learning interests of the children as these become visible.

A lesson plan is only a "vehicle" for starting out on a journey, a plan resulting from studying "road maps" and alternate routes. Once on the way, the teacher is no longer in sole charge. How fast, by which route, where to linger, what to skip and how far to go—only the children furnish realistic answers to these questions.

SUMMARY *Based on Piaget's theory of intellectual development, learning how, or the process of learning, is the most important aspect of cognitive progress for young children. Piaget's idea of children's active learning can be realized by encouraging children to explore the characteristics of their environment by manipulating things and reflecting upon their actions. Action-oriented problems to solve create vivid kinds of knowing which are not easily forgotten. This type of active learning also fosters children's independence in further learning.*

Teachers who wish to move gradually toward more informal learning situations find this program component, of manipulating objects and exploring the physical world, an effective vehicle for transformation of the whole program. Constructive explorations require open-endedness and continuity as opposed to "one-shot" lessons. Also needed are multisensory experiences, action, interest, safety in the use of materials and experiments, child independence in explorations, and appropriate ways for children to pattern or organize their findings.

Learning centers, well-supplied and arranged, with clear rules for use and flexible nonjudgmental responses to problems and progress should invite investigative activities. Teacher roles may include nurturing, participating, information giving, rule defining, eliciting of information, challenging, probing, creating and cognitive dissonance, modelling, receiving dictation, materials arrangement and suggesting activities. There are innumerable constructive activities for dis-

coveries about the physical world using plants, animals, all kinds of objects, and natural observations within or near the school.

✿ EXERCISES FOR STUDENTS ✿✿✿✿✿✿✿✿✿✿✿✿✿✿✿✿✿✿

1. Complete a file of 25 cards, listing on each one the possible explorations with specific types of plants, animals, or rocks for young children. Include on each card a reference source for content.

2. Select one school with which you have frequent contact and list naturally occurring resources you note on a walk around the school block and back to your starting point.

   a. Try to retrace this walk in a different season of the year and note seasonal contrasts which might be instructive to children.

   b. Include on your list such resources as trees, shrubs, grasses, flowers and other plants, birds, small animals, insects, and such man-made objects as houses, stores, mailbox, fire-alarm box, telephone booth, or other structures.

   c. Use this list, if possible, as a basis for planning frequent walks with an early childhood class or group for observation, collection, sorting and classification, and identifying questions or problems for further explorations.

3. Plan to walk to a spot nearby where the children can collect some objects—seeds, rocks, or leaves—with the help of the classroom teacher.

   a. Plan to encourage the children upon return to the classroom to select some sorting containers and to work in small groups trying to find some basis for sorting or classifying the objects.

   b. Accept all the children's work but try to ask questions or to probe their basis for sorting and their reasoning in classifying ambiguous objects or those not clearly related to the sorting base.

   c. Encourage children to work at sorting these objects again the next day, if they wish, to try to find any *different* base for sorting.

4. Plan a demonstration in your college class to show some interesting science explorations you developed with some children in a school

setting. Take notes on other students' demonstrations which you think you would like to try out, especially on materials and ways of stimulating children to ask questions and to try to find answers.

✣ EXERCISES FOR TEACHERS   ✣✣✣✣✣✣✣✣✣✣✣✣✣✣✣✣✣✣✣

1. Plan a walk, in the early fall, in mid-winter, or in the spring to a nearby park, wooded area, or other such spot where children can collect objects like seeds, rocks, or leaves. Take a small notebook along to jot down children's observations and some bags or containers for collections.

a. Along the way, stop at safe places and encourage the children to observe and identify *everything* they see and to jot down their observations. Encourage children to look up, for aircraft or birds or high wires on telephone poles or tall treetops, and to the far horizon as well as nearby to note natural as well as man-made objects.

b. Plan sorting and classifying activities in the classroom with children determining how many classes or boxes to use for sorting and re-sorting on a different base.

c. Plan with the children for a second walk to check disputed observations, to increase the collections, or to observe additional features.

d. Invite children to dictate stories about the trip or about their sorting activities.

2. Plan a series of manipulative activities with selected materials to which the children can return for experimentation over a period of time, i.e., planting activities or explorations of vibrating objects.

a. Initiate the explorations by participating and suggesting actions.

b. Revive interest, if necessary, by adding objects or further suggestions, requesting story dictation, or otherwise valuing and expressing interest in the activity.

c. Give emphasis to your valuing of the process by sending class newsletters home to parents and to the parent-teacher organization about the explorations; by photographing children in various activities; or by making duplicated booklets, with children's participation, illustrations, and suggestions about the various phases of the explorations.

3. Select an appropriate activity for your group, from one of the science programs such as SCIS or AAAS which include curriculum for young children.

a. Follow the activity instructions to the extent that they are congruent with your program generally.

b. Use your own or the program's assessment instruments to determine how much progress the children made with this activity, either immediately after, after an interval of about one week, or both.

BIBLIOGRAPHY

Audubon Aids in Natural Science. New York: National Audubon Society, 1130 Fifth Ave., New York, N. Y. 10028.

Brandwein, Paul F. *Elements in a Strategy for Teaching Science in the Elementary School.* New York: Harcourt Brace & World, 1962.

Cailliet, G., Setzer, P., and Love, M. *Everyman's Guide to Ecological Living.* New York: Macmillan, 1971.

Cantzlaar, George L. *Your Guide to the Weather.* New York: Barnes & Noble, 1964.

Davidson, Jessica. *Using the Cuisenaire Rods. A Photo/Text Guide for Teachers.* New York: Cuisenaire Co. of America, 12 Church St., New Rochelle, N. Y., 1969.

Dienes, Z. P. *An Experimental Study of Mathematics Learning.* London: Hutchinson of London, 1963.

Dienes, Z. P. *Sets, Numbers and Powers.* New York: Herder & Herder, 1966.

Dumas, Enoch. *Math Activities for Child Involvement.* Boston: Allyn and Bacon, 1971.

Farb, Peter. *The Insects.* New York: Time-Life Books, 1962.

Kohlberg, Lawrence. "Early Education: A Cognitive-Developmental View." *Child Development* 39 (1968), pp. 1013–1062.

Kohlberg, Lawrence, and Mayer, Rochelle. "Development as the Aim of Education." *Harvard Educational Review* 42:2 (November 1972), pp. 449–496.

Lorton, M. *Work Jobs: Activity-centered Learning for Early Childhood Education.* Reading, Mass.: Addison-Wesley, 1972.

McGavack, John Jr., and LaSalle, Donald P. *Guppies, Bubbles, and Vibrating Objects.* New York: John Day, 1969.

New York State Conservation Dept. *The Conservationist.* Albany, N. Y.: The Department 12201.

Robison, Helen F., and Schwartz, Sydney L. *Learning at an Early Age.* Vol. 1: *A Professional Text For Teachers.* Englewood Cliffs, N. J.: Prentice-Hall, 1972.

Rosengren, John H. *Outdoor Science for the Elementary Grades.* West Nyack, N. Y.: Parker, 1972.

Rowe, Mary Budd. *Teaching Science as Continuous Inquiry.* New York: McGraw-Hill, 1973.

Schmidt, Victor E., and Rockcastle, Verne N. *Teaching Science with Everyday Things.* New York: McGraw-Hill, 1968.

Schools Council Publications, *Early Experiences: A Line for Teachers.* London: MacDonald Educational, The Council, 1972.

Science and Children. National Science Teachers Association, 1201 Sixteenth St., Washington, D. C., 20036.

Shanks, Ann Zane. *About Garbage and Stuff.* New York: Viking, 1973.

UNESCO Source Book for Science Teaching. New York: UNESCO Publications Center, 801 Third Ave., New York, N. Y.

Unifix: Structural Math Material: Teachers Manual. Andover Hants, England: Philip and Tracey, 1962.

Walter, Marion. *Make a Bigger Puddle: Make a Smaller Worm.* New York: M. Evans, 1971.

Wetmore, Alexander. *Song and Garden Birds of North America.* Washington, D. C.: National Geographical Society, 1964.

Zim, Herbert S., and Gabrielson, Ira N. *Birds.* New York: Golden Press, 1964.

SOCIAL LEARNINGS:

PROGRAMS ABOUT PEOPLE

8

All that we take for granted in the pattern of our social lives, in our conceptions about people in the past, present, and future, here and elsewhere, children have to learn. In the first few years, the young child's preoccupation with his own needs precludes much interest in understanding about other people. By age three, and increasingly thereafter, the child defines himself by trying to clarify relationships, roles, and experiences of family members, relatives, and friends. Initial questions always focus on *me*—how do people relate to *me* or affect *me* in any way? These egocentric interests slowly give way to curiosity about other people's lives. Curiosity and growing maturity propel children into investigating social questions about their own and other people's patterns of living, an area we call social learnings.

Initially, it is the family in its primary nurturing role that exerts the predominant influence on the developing child's impressions about people and how they affect him. However, since the family responds to all the currents that reflect the neighborhood and to national and international movements, the child is also affected by contemporary happenings. Through a gradual process, the child differentiates himself from others and then constructs increasingly clearer understandings about the relationships between himself and others, and among others.

As a child develops a sense of himself as a person, he becomes aware of other people as persons, not just as fixed parts of his own life. A two-year-old can only think of his mother as a parent; he would find it impossible to think of her in other roles like wife, daughter, wage earner, trade union member, or Sunday school teacher.

Oriented firmly to the present, the young child has great difficulty understanding that there was a time before now, and that there will be a future. Gradually, the child begins to wonder whether his own parents were ever young. Where did they come from? Did they have mothers and fathers? The meaning of grandparents begins to grow. What about their lives, so very long ago? The child asks—did they have television and cars?

Relatives and friends keep telling the child, "Look how much you've grown! You'll soon have another birthday. You're growing up fast." The child wonders what she will grow up to be. Will she be a mommy like her own mother? Will she have children too? The child presses relatives to tell stories about when they were very little. Every bit of information helps the child build concepts about how people grow, change, and develop relationships and responsibilities. Overgeneralizing and misapplying ideas that are dimly understood, the child receives constant feedback from family members, so misconceptions are whittled away and are slowly replaced by more realistic understandings.

FORCES AFFECTING CHILDREN'S SOCIAL LEARNINGS

Neighborhood laboratory

The child's ideas about people and social relationships, first forming within the family, are soon tested in the local neighborhood. Are other families like mine? What foods do they eat? What do they do for fun? Children take their early fixed ideas out into the community and find an amazing variety in family composition, occupations, housing, food preferences, language, religion, types of festivities, and recreational patterns.

Families, it soon turns out, sometimes have a single parent instead of a mother and a father, and some are rather complex, as when parents bring children from previous marriages together in a new household. Some children have adoptive parents, others foster parents. Children often accompany their families on many social occasions to visit other families, restaurants, and places of worship or recreation that are ethnically different in unexpected ways. Children participate in public or community festivities for Christmas, Chanukah, Chinese New Year, and the great variety of other religious and ethnic celebrations which enrich our culture.

Children observe closely and see much that is puzzling to them or inconsistent with their developing ideas, based on experience in their own families, about the private and public ways people interact with each other. Questions are abundant, as children try to fit new information into rigid compartments. When children find this impossible, their overgeneralizations and hypotheses begin to change to accord with their changing conceptions. The most vivid experiences for the child are those in which he participates—at the supermarket, roadside produce stand, community fair, doctor's office, the beach, the church or school social, or the political club picnic. Moving out of the home and into the neighborhood, the child grasps some concepts about the restrictions the outside world imposes on behavior. But the broader arena also suggests to the child the great variability that exists in human characteristics and in social interactions.

Heterogeneity of neighborhoods.   Neighborhoods are increasingly less homogeneous than they were formerly. This insures much more variety of individual experience in terms of the variations in culture the child encounters. With high family mobility in this country, (about a fifth of all families moving somewhere at any one time), children are experiencing more than one neighborhood, in many cases, before school entrance. Some families reside abroad for extended periods or travel outside the country on vacations with children, so there is a surprising amount of first-hand experiencing by young children of foreign cultures.

Neighborhoods are less homogeneous than they used to be and offer children more variety of experience with people.

Teachers can take little for granted, even with quite young children, about their experiences before school entrance. The challenge is to try to ascertain what kinds of experiences children have had and, even more important, what meaning they have derived from such experiences.

Effects of television

Television brings the child masses of information about people close by and far away. Unfamiliar customs receive close-up scrutiny on the television screen; for instance, in a far-off icy Lapland near the North Pole people are seen also slapping mosquitoes! The danger is that children will think they know a great deal about others when their knowledge is entirely superficial. Mosquitoes may be familiar to the child but the reindeer culture is not. How far afield can the young child's intelligence really travel?

When a black American prize fighter defends his international championship in an African country, all children suddenly acquire new information about distant places and peoples via television. The instant character of the television news overwhelms children with its pictorial detail and rapidity of transmission. Unless families control children's televiewing time, children's struggles to understand and pattern vast information loads may be overlooked or misunderstood by adults.

Problems and values of television.   Television captures children's attention for periods of time that might otherwise be spent in play, exploration of materials, playing with playmates, or in more frequent contact with adults. Studies have just begun to scratch the surface so far on the effects of television upon young children's current and subsequent behavior. But teachers are concerned about children's expectations of too great novelty and sensation in activities, of their uncritical acceptance of "commercials" and bias in presentation of information, and are concerned about the possible effects on learning that spending too much time in passive televiewing may have.

However, it is possible that television provides cognitive stimulation, good language models, and challenging ideas for children whose families may be too busy trying to survive to provide these good learning conditions themselves. It is apparent that, in many cases, television is a substitute for playmates, an aid to custodial care for a sick child or an overburdened parent, and often an inducement to balance over-activity with needed quiet inactivity.

Since young children spend substantial periods of their waking time looking at television, sometimes staying up to see late programs and getting insufficient sleep at night, teachers cannot ignore either the obvious effects of sleepy or overstimulated children or the more covert problems children have in trying to digest so much information.

Cultural pluralism

Acceptance of the idea of cultural pluralism requires avoidance of comparison of cultures for the purpose of establishing which is "better" or "worse." Instead, human creativity is valued for inventing the many different ways there are of coping with man's universal needs for love, family, food, shelter, spiritual and moral values, aesthetic expression and brotherhood.

Renewal of cultural pride and the search for one's heritage and

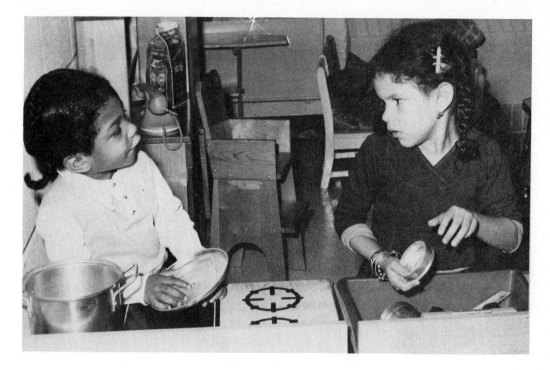

traditions have contributed to rapid growth of ethnic restaurants and food stores and interest in other people's music, dance, history, customs, and experiences. Discarding the idea of the melting pot, we seem to have reached a more sophisticated appreciation of the value of cultural pluralism—variety and difference in cultures.

Cultural pluralism fosters a sense of equality among children, according them equal value.

People bored with the invariant products of mass production search out the handicrafts and the home-made products that preserve earlier traditions of pride in workmanship and in the details that indicate the cultural source and the individual variations on the major cultural themes. At the same time, television, frozen foods, cars, and contraceptive devices travel to far corners of the world where they were previously unknown, including the South Pacific and Central Africa. Modern mass production gives peoples around the world more choices than they had before, although the struggle to sustain and preserve unique artifacts and patterns of living occurs everywhere, not only in our own country.

Cultural pluralism encourages groups to take pride in themselves and to feel equal to any other group. For children, a sense of equality in self-valuing, without the elitism of feelings of superiority or the destructiveness of feelings of inferiority, may be the most important virtue in cultural self-acceptance.

Also, cultural pluralism encompasses acceptance of wide variation in family composition and structure; families are changing rapidly here and throughout the world. One-parent and extended families of many kinds are found almost everywhere, although in this country the nuclear family continues to predominate.

Increase in materials for sound learning

New research and writing in history and the social sciences are enriching school resources to deal with cultural pluralism. American history was formerly written from the point of view of the large white majority. Now, increasingly, it is reflecting cultural changes and resulting in more complete coverage on and far greater interest in the contributions of blacks and immigrants (many of whom were neither white nor European), as well as the indigenous American Indian population.

Teachers who are looking for high-quality children's literature and other materials that reflect the values of cultural pluralism can now find them. Excellent annotated lists of books, films, and other audiovisual materials are available from various sources (see the selected bibliography at the end of this chapter). These published lists, of course, reflect the national interest in developing such material and are the publishers' response to this demand. Books for young children about other cultural groups can be found written in English but they are now also available in Spanish, Chinese, and other major languages. Similarly, filmstrips with sound are increasingly available in Spanish as well as English and, if there is sufficient demand in other languages, these will surely be forthcoming. (School systems with special language needs presently unfilled by manufacturers can consider making their own recordings and translations.)

Place of bilingual education

Here, readers may ask about bilingual education in the school and whether the use of another language in school in addition to English may interfere with children's learning English. This important question is discussed in Chapter 9 on Communication. Here, let it suffice to say that when a public or private school chooses to encourage children and adults to use languages other than English, the resources for such programs are better than ever. Some of the most expensive private schools in this country feature two languages and appear to succeed in producing fluent speakers of a second language, but this is seldom true as yet in public schools. Children could just as well study Navajo, Spanish, or Swedish in addition to English, if the school and community value it and fund it adequately so that new materials can be purchased. Clearly, these decisions belong to parents and community in the context of our American legal system.

Cultural liberation movements

Why should language, race, and ethnicity now loom so large in teaching young children about themselves, their families, their history, and about other people? The answer to this question must be sought in contemporary movements that demand respect for an individual and for differences among them. Such movements include the women's liberation groups seeking to eliminate sexism, black organizations intent on restoring pride in self and heritage, Jewish groups concerned with civil rights for themselves and others, Hispanic organizations, and numerous nationalist, ethnic, and racial groups including those of the American Indian. It is as though Americans of varied backgrounds suddenly find their voices and say: "I'm American too! Why isn't *my* history American history? Why aren't *my* values and customs part of the American fabric?" Building self-pride and feelings of equality seems to work. Children of minority groups more and more are expecting to be considered on their merits.

CURRICULAR TRENDS IN SOCIAL LEARNING

Styles change in social learning curricula in response to many social influences. Ideas for teaching young children about themselves and others reflect broad curriculum movements in education generally, social movements affecting the society at large, along with changing values and developments in psychological theory and research about how children learn. Major curricular shifts vary in their emphases on how children learn (theories of child development and learning theories), what children learn (selection of content), and the purposes of learning (objectives of education). It is a safe bet that changes will increasingly occur in ways to integrate these three major variables in the curriculum matrix, with a growing emphasis on the characteristics of the children to be taught.

Four major forms of school learning curricula have been used in the past and are still in use today.

Social learning curricula in the past have included the concentric circle base, the child development emphasis, content selection known as the structure of the disciplines design, and process objectives in either the open classroom or Piagetian-based programs. Contributing to major changes in social learning curriculum design have been such movements as child study, standardized testing and, more recently, interest in featuring cultural pluralism. Some schools have clung to older designs without too much change, while many others have had no hesitation in changing with the newest fashions in social learning curriculum. Because of the strong impact of social change on social learning curricula, this is a particularly volatile area of design change.

An incisive statement of our contemporary curriculum problems was made by Caswell when he said, "We are in a period in which values are being questioned, in which teaching practice has undergone great change, in which a vast array of new content has arisen, in which the demands upon schools have increased with each passing year, and in which goals of education are a major source of controversy."[1] Caswell's last point is especially relevant in pointing out that where major disagreements exist as to the purposes of education, there is bound to be lack of agreement on the methods and content.

CONCENTRIC CIRCLES

The concentric circles design is easily diagrammed to show the child and his family in the center, with a series of ever-widening circles taking the child out into the neighborhood or community, then into the larger municipality, and later into the state, national, and international scenes.

1. Hollis L. Caswell, "Emergence of the Curriculum as a Field of Professional Work and Study", in *Precedents and Promise in the Curriculum Field,* edited by Helen F. Robison (New York: Teachers College Press, 1966), p. 6.

Using this base, teachers directed children's attention at first to family roles and relationships, responsibilities, and functions. Teachers stressed the young child's responsibilities for self-care and for mutual helpfulness at home. Care of pets, with discussions about such care, frequently emphasized empathy for others' needs and learning to take care of others. Children practiced fulfilling responsibilities by performing helper jobs in the classroom—distributing supplies, feeding fish or watering plants, picking up litter from the floor, and washing work tables.

Kindergarten classes often explored the school to learn how it operated, visiting the custodian, viewing the heating plant, the principal's office, the food preparation area and staff, and such special resources personnel as nurses or speech specialists.

By ages five and six, the wider circle of social observation included the immediate neighborhood and its resources. Uniformed civil servants such as policemen and firemen were usually singled out for special attention because of their visibility and universality. Children visited firehouses, police stations, post offices, and libraries to note the "helper" occupations most easily found in the local community. The next step was the larger community of the village, town, or city where commercial, industrial, or governmental offices might be located. Sometimes the foray into the municipality was focused on a trip to a museum, zoo, or special holiday exhibit of some kind. State, national, and international relationships were regarded as too far away in time and conception for young children to be concerned about. For younger children, the concentric circle was bounded by the area in which the child could visit and observe.

CHILD DEVELOPMENT BASE

Along with the concentric circles design, but making increasing impact since the thirties and continuing through contemporary movements, there has been a major focus, based on psychological theories and research, generally known as the child development approach. Despite its ups and downs, children owe most of the humaneness and personal interest of teachers to this movement.

The focus on child development, growing out of American interest in Freudian psychology and especially out of American research and studies of children's emotional development, was a reaction against a prior subject-centeredness in educational settings. Colleges established laboratory schools for young children, parent cooperative nursery schools developed, psychiatrists became specialized in childhood emotional problems, and a greatly needed swing back to children's needs and resources occurred. Dewey's stress on social interaction—or group work and play as a way to socialize children into democratic living—fitted into the prevailing preoccupation with personality development and, especially, avoidance of permanent psychological trauma in children's development.[2]

The child development base subordinated content selection to meeting children's psychosocial needs.

The curriculum subsumed under the child development approach was never rigidly defined as to content, since content selection was subordinate to meeting the child's social, intellectual, emotional, and physical needs. This design stressed children's needs and gave teachers wide latitude to choose experiences and content capable of meeting such needs. Active social and manipulative forms of activities were stressed. In the social learnings category, classroom interactions featured learning to take turns and to share, to help other children when necessary, and to practice in dramatic play, not only dealing with one's emotional problems, but also the roles of adults as family members and in familiar occupations such as doctors or storekeepers. The child's social-emotional development was guided, in this design, toward greater maturity by movement toward finding socially acceptable ways of discharging tension, working out traumatic happenings, and learning acceptable forms of social interaction. Practically, the curriculum highlighted holidays with songs, dances, craft projects, and dramatizations.

Teachers using this design were concerned about the causes of children's behavior—in order to deal with such causes—rather than trying to change only the external symptoms of children's problems. This important emphasis stemmed most directly from classical Freudian psychoanalysis, where the symptom was the clue to the problem, not the problem itself. While no distinctive content can be identified as uniquely associated with this design, specific activities were generally fostered, especially dramatic play, block play, puzzles and manipulative materials of many kinds, and a great deal of art and music.

---

2. John Dewey, *The Child and the Curriculum* (Chicago: University of Chicago Press, 1902), pp. 15–16.

STRUCTURE OF THE DISCIPLINES CURRICULA

In the sixties, Bruner and others stressed a spiral approach to content that featured teaching the same broad concepts and major ways of knowing in each body of knowledge but in increasingly complex ways as children matured and could handle more abstract material.[3] This movement was an attempt to avoid feeding children endless, fragmented bits of unrelated information.[4] Instead, the basic concepts in each field, selected by scholars in the field, would be the content to be learned and conceptualized. There was hope that teachers could find ways to help children understand key concepts because the program would be developed to illuminate and develop such conceptualizations. More substantive goals, well-patterned and articulated, would provide more intellectual nourishment for children, it was thought. It was also hoped that teachers would be more effective in teaching content to children if the content could be more clearly related to fields of adult research and study and more authentic, scholarly sources of materials could develop which would clearly be worth children's learning.

This design for content selection in social learnings required a spiral approach to key concepts in the bodies of knowledge.

The effort to make patterns and to develop key concepts in each body of knowledge—economics or anthropology, for example—or in broad fields of knowledge as in the social sciences, or in broad social themes such as communication and transportation proved to be unexpectedly difficult. In the mathematics and science areas this approach was easier to follow, although there was never full agreement on the key concepts in any body of knowledge. Teaching young children "ways of knowing," as with scientific processes in the sciences or in-depth field studies as in anthropology, are not in themselves inappropriate for young children. In fact, these processes are often more successfully adapted for young children's use than the substantive content, which changes more frequently.

PROCESS OBJECTIVES

The preoccupation with content in the sixties was succeeded by concern for *process*, or *how* children learn, in the seventies.

3. Jerome Bruner, *The Process of Education* (Cambridge, Mass.: Harvard University Press, 1960).
4. Evelyn Weber, *Early Childhood Education: Perspectives on Change* (Worthington, Ohio: Charles Jones, 1970), p. 13.

Reemphasis upon development

Theories of child development, as indicated above, describe and illustrate the sequences of physical, cognitive, and emotional growth of children and how these various growth aspects relate to each other. Piaget has for a long time dominated the cognitive growth area.[5] He seems most interested in natural development, not in school learning. His chief contribution to teaching is a healthy respect for *how* children learn, not for *what* to teach. He has advised teachers everywhere to stress active learning—with manipulation of objects and physical actions—instead of "telling" children or lecturing them about concepts.

Proponents of the concentric circles base for social learnings claim that this design is based on child development theory because it is anchored in information that is familiar to the child and moves from such familiarity toward the less familiar aspects of the wider world. But Piaget has been little concerned with *what* information children have. Rather, he has conceptualized and theorized about how children *think*—what he has called the structures of intelligence. Piaget's emphasis on logical thinking has dealt with many different content areas, although they tend to fall within what schools call math and science. Piaget calls this logico-mathematical knowledge, but he has not prescribed it for teaching. His studies of children's thinking and how it develops have chiefly sought the course of natural learning, not school learning, in logico-mathematical knowledge.

The renewed emphasis upon how children learn is reflected in the many varieties of the open classroom and in Piagetian-based curricula, notably the one developed by Constance Kamii. In the programs that stress process objectives, content is not usually prescribed. Instead, teachers select content they think will help them to make the process objectives work. Both the British and American varieties of the open classroom, for example, emphasize strongly their observations of children's interests as a guide to content selection. In many cases, the content is varied in the classroom to appeal to different children. However, teachers usually do not hesitate to include their own interests in content selection, since teacher enthusiasm tends to ignite children's interest.

---

5. Jean Piaget, *The Origins of Intelligence in Children* (New York: International Universities Press, 1952).

SOCIAL MOVEMENTS AFFECTING CURRICULUM

Among the many social movements that have affected the social learning curricula for young children, two especially powerful developments occurred—standardized testing and interest in "mental hygiene," as it was called. The testing movement received great impetus from its widespread use in the American armed forces during World War I, and it rapidly transferred a major focus to the schools. The concern for mental hygiene of children, or for their healthy emotional development, emerged from the emphasis upon child study, which was the growing edge of humanistic movements in the larger society. Early in the twentieth century, the schools began to look at children more carefully, not only to ascertain how high their IQ's were, but also to note their levels of anxiety, fears, and emotional dysfunction.

Standardized testing

Humanistic concerns for children led to standardized testing and an emphasis on mental hygiene early in this century.

Standardized testing became well entrenched in the schools as early as the twenties. This movement has continued unabated since then, although with increasing controversy about the objectives and meanings of the tests. Interest in testing became so widespread that tests were developed for almost any conceivable purpose. Standardized tests most widely used have been achievement and IQ tests, although tests have been developed for personality types, interests, self-concepts, logical thinking, and many other aspects of human functioning.

Standardized tests attempt to establish "norms," or averages of various types, and are generally referred to as norm-referenced tests. These tests chiefly compare an individual's performance with others in his reference group. Such tests tend to answer questions such as, "Is this child average for his group in . . . ?" (whatever the test tests), or, "Is he above or below the average and if so, by how much?"[6]

Standardized testing came under considerable attack in the sixties

---

6. For information about norm-referenced and criterion-referenced tests, see W. Robert Houston, ed., *Exploring Competency-based Education*, Part 4 (Berkeley, Cal.: McCutchan, 1974), pp. 189–308; and James W. Popham, *Criterion Referenced Measurement: An Introduction*, ERIC ED 053 200 (Englewood Cliffs, N. J.: Educational Technology Publications, 1971).

for cultural or racial bias. Children of the poor were generally found scoring in below-average ranges. When it was found, at one time, that 75 percent of the children identified as retarded in California were children from Mexican-American families, serious questions were raised about the validity of the tests used. Were these children scoring low because of a language problem, cultural differences, or cultural bias?

The criterion-referenced test was developed to counteract possible sources of bias in norm-referenced tests. Instead of comparing one child with another, a child is tested against a criterion such as tying a shoelace, cutting with scissors on a straight line, oral identification of letters of the alphabet from flash cards, or other yes/no kinds of performance. Language and cultural differences may still interfere with successful performance of the criterion, but it is thought that teachers and testers are more likely to find out reasons for failure, especially when the criterion is specifically defined as to its requirements. If the child has to comprehend an instruction given orally in English in order to demonstrate his satisfactory performance, more attention seems necessary to the child's "entering" behavior in relation to the criterion, e.g., whether he understands English sufficiently.

Testing and assessment continue to be controversial in early childhood education, with many teachers resistant to the time, effort, and possible adverse effect on the child of low assessment scores, labeling (i.e., categorizing a child as "retarded"), or improper placement in succeeding grades in school. Diagnostic testing is often acceptable where other kinds of tests are not, since the purpose of these tests is to define areas where help can be provided the child, whether educational, medical, emotional, or other sources of support and amelioration.

Pros and cons of tests.   The use of IQ and achievement tests to track children into supposedly homogeneous groups to facilitate teaching has had articulate proponents and opponents. Since its effects appeared to heighten segregation of children by race, language, and socioeconomic level, opponents stressed negative effects on self-concepts of children relegated to slower tracks and labelled in various uncomplimentary ways. Opponents of testing often say that it is the school's most effective way to teach children to fail as early as possible. Proponents stress the informational results of tests and their potential use in facilitating more effecting teaching methods and curriculum design.

Mental hygiene

The interest in mental hygiene led to more humane school conditions.

Originally, mental hygiene was viewed as analogous to physical hygiene. Since teachers were required to stress good physical health habits such as tooth brushing and hand washing, the need for a sound mind in this healthy body seemed to require equal time. However, mental hygiene was recognized as fundamentally different, in that it was the result of good teaching methods and therefore chiefly outside of the child's control.

It was the child study movement sweeping educational circles with the novel idea that children's feelings had to be considered by teachers, as well as their minds, that fostered the mental hygiene thrust. Child study, or observing children closely, inevitably uncovered the many emotional problems that children brought to school with them or that were generated by inappropriate forms of teaching. Montessori identified child study as one of the most important features of her curriculum as early as 1905. But the interest was worldwide, resulting from major social developments.

Teachers for the first time were urged to consider the effects of their curriculum plans and methods on the mental hygiene of the children. The focus on children's emotional development remained virtually unchallenged in early childhood programs in this country until the ferment in the sixties on whether children were learning adequate content.

The challenge for racial equality

Broad social movements for racial equality have been challenging the centrality of early childhood concentration on children's emotional development. Parents of poorer children were concerned that there was so little "academic" preparation for their children in early childhood classes. Such parents pointed out that they themselves were the products of poor education and that, therefore, they were unable to provide the kind of home environment that might be most helpful to prepare their children to succeed at school. Since it was undeniable that their children were generally doing poorly in school, the issues revolved around *where* early intervention or preparation should take place—at home or at school. A further controversy developed as to the most effective types of preparation—whether cognitive or conceptual, as most educators and psychologists recommended, or chiefly concerned with literacy, as many parents insisted.[7]

VARYING EMPHASES IN SOCIAL LEARNING

The foregoing description of the major trends in social learning curricula for young children is far from exhaustive, and is chiefly meant to highlight the continuing struggle to define the appropriate types of social learning for young children. Emphases have shifted to more concern with how children feel and learn, then to what they learn, then on to the purposes of early childhood education, and back to one or another of these bases for curriculum design.

Problems of content selection

Since there is no consensus on what children should study in the social learning area, it is possible to take the position that any content will do and that there is no need to waste time on content choices—any teacher's selection is sure to be as useful as any other's. In fact, it is often thought that by deemphasizing content, the child is benefitted because the teacher must really concentrate on him, find out *his* interests and needs, meet him where he is, and help him to live as richly as he can.

This beguiling view of child-centeredness obscures the issue. Content selection, no matter how it is made or for whom, still must occur. Can a teacher who knows little, or who has spent little time exploring possible content sources, select as well or as relevantly for any specific child as a teacher who knows a great deal about content possibilities? Observe teachers who spurn content as unimportant because they are "child centered." What content *do* they select? One teacher seems to be always turning to art and woodworking activities (because this teacher happens to be skillful in these media) but not to music or dance or representational or constructional activities with blocks or other three-dimensional objects. Another teacher seems to concentrate on puppetry and dramatic play because this is what *she* knows best. It is as though one would say to an amateur cook, "Just cook the dishes

Every social learning design has to solve the problem of content selection.

7. For reading on the cognitive versus literacy goals controversy, see Carl Bereiter, *Must We Educate* (Englewood Cliffs, N.J.: Prentice-Hall, 1973), pp. 99–110 especially.

your mother taught you. Never mind about any other cooking possibilities." It is as though we assure teachers that uninformed intuition is just as good as reflective thinking and informed judgment.

Content in process-oriented programs

Process objectives have been especially stressed by open classroom advocates and by programs that attempt to build on Piaget's cognitive theories and research. It is interesting to note that Constance Kamii, who developed a very imaginative Piagetian-based program featuring cognitive processes—processes of classification and seriation, for example, as well as other processes, with content regarded as peripheral and unimportant—has redeveloped this program with a new emphasis on content selection.[8] In the revised program, the content is still in a subordinate position to process goals but is no longer irrelevant, intuitive, and random.

Philosophers differ as to what a child should learn. When the social pendulum swings to the right, an "essentialist" philosophy prevails. In this view, there are universal standards and we know what content children should learn. Learning-prescribed subject matter may not be fun, but children should know that they all have to buckle down for the serious business of acquiring the basic subject matter. When the educational and social pendulum swings way to the left, educators claim to be "child centered" (not "subject matter centered"), with process goals of "self-realization" or "learning how to learn," instead of getting ready to pass tests on knowledge and achievements. Who is right?

Updating concentric circles

It would not be difficult to update the concentric circles design, since it is undeniable that children have most frequent access to their immediate family and neighborhood groups. Also, young children are most likely to understand the primary groups with which their interactions are most frequent. Selecting content that is familiar and accessible should certainly continue to be regarded as appropriate for

8. Ellis D. Evans, *Contemporary Influences in Early Childhood Education*, 2d ed. (New York: Holt, Rinehart & Winston, 1975), pp. 233–234.

Creative and exciting social learning programs can be built around many topics.

young children. Perhaps the dilemma of content selection can be resolved by flexible choices of content that vary with local resources and the children's actual experiences. An important caution, however, is to enter selected content at some familiar points in order to open up new learning paths instead of constricting children's opportunities to explore and experience richly by drawing too tight a circle against the world of possibilities.

Studies of the work of community service personnel need not be restrictive. If teacher and children visit a post office in order to experience the mailing and receipt of letters and then set up a classroom post office, they have found active entry to familiar content. If they also find out about mail to other cities and countries, collect stamps and observe such mail services as package sorting and delivery, more aspects of the post office are noted. A study of a local post office may point up:

1. Interdependence of people and governmental service for communication purposes
2. Job differentiation or career education
3. Money costs (and math concepts and weight measurement)
4. Geographic concepts (destination and origin of mail—local, domestic, foreign)
5. Transportation vehicles (foot, truck, train, bus, boat, airplane)
6. Language arts and writing practice

No topic is thin and restricting in itself. Resourceful teachers can build substantial and exciting learning opportunities on almost any topic.

Bodies of knowledge content

The structure of the disciplines design for social learning attempts to pattern the knowledge and the ways of knowing in each major body of knowledge. This effort proved exceedingly complex and more constructive in some knowledge areas, especially in mathematics and science, than in others. In the social sciences, while some interesting programs were constructed in many areas, extraordinary difficulties in patterning knowledge dampened enthusiasm and enterprise. Much can still be done, however, to enrich programs that were lacking in substance before.

Numerous new curricula were generated by this fresh look at what and how to teach children, many sequenced from kindergarten to the twelfth grade.[9] This movement to infuse more and better organized content into school programs helped to break old molds. But to many early childhood educators, too much concern with content seemed to detract from the child-centeredness which they deemed far more important than content.[10]

Continuing effects of social movements

Social concerns continue to be addressed, for curriculum purposes, by expressions of citizens' concerns and by legislation requiring specific kinds of content. For example, state legislation may require teachers to include content concerning prevention of alcohol or drug abuse.

Citizen concerns for particular directions for curriculum may often be transmitted to the schools rather directly, through parent-teacher associations or in many other ways. If citizens, revolted by unprecedented convictions of holders of high office in the national government, demand that children receive instruction in ethics and moral values, a groundswell is discerned and curriculum bulletins and textbooks quickly reflect the new emphasis identified.

Multicultural emphases

Challenges to traditional content in social learnings are coming from many different groups who resent the lack of consideration for differences and variety of cultures. These groups are finding many channels through which to transmit messages of their dissatisfaction with content that is primarily viewed from the perspective of the white middle-class majority.

Sex stereotypes are being identified, and numerous efforts are under way to reorder previously biased views of history and social developments. The direction many groups are taking is a sharp turn away from assimilation toward recognition of differences in race, sex, na-

9. Helen F. Robison and Bernard Spodek, *New Directions in the Kindergarten* (New York: Teachers College Press, 1965).
10. Bernard Spodek, "Social Studies for Young Children: Identifying Intellectual Goals," *Social Education* 38 (January 1974), pp. 40–45.

Increasing chal-
lenges are being
heard from
groups working
to eliminate
stereotypes and
bias.

tional origin, religion and lifestyles, without value judgments. Historians are rewriting the texts on the role of indigenous Indian groups, of blacks under slavery, of the experience of oriental groups as immigrants, and of the many ethnic and racial groups who played important roles in our national history.

These growing multicultural emphases are being woven into children's literature, into television content especially planned for children, and are being integrated into the social learning content in numerous other ways.

So it seems that in schools efforts are underway to correct previous errors or biases, to create more rational perspectives, to offer more points of view, and to eliminate old prejudices. If new prejudices and biases are creeping in, time must again be counted upon for their elimination and correction.

If they can find them, students are urged to visit classrooms that illustrate philosophical extremes and to read leading advocates of contrasting positions. Philosophy and foundation courses usually feature readings that differentiate the extremes as well as the continuum of beliefs filling in the spaces between the extremes.[11] It is not unusual to find two teachers in the same school whose classrooms reflect extreme differences in philosophy. Open-mindedness is also urged upon students. Too early closure about beliefs and philosophy makes it very difficult to explore other positions in depth and to view alternatives clearly.

DESIGNING SOCIAL LEARNING CURRICULA

Curriculum selection

It seems apparent that we must stop trying to choose among psychological theory, knowledge content sources, and the requirements of contemporary society for curriculum sources. These are not distinctive choices; they are each part of a whole. Ignoring one of the three major curriculum sources always induces distortions and gaps. We have to teach children in the *way* that they are able to learn. But

---

11. Students, especially those in philosophy, might wish to browse in such readings as the following: Tom C. Venable, *Philosophic Foundations of the Curriculum* (Chicago: Rand McNally, 1967); or R. S. Peters, ed., *The Philosophy of Education* (London, England: Oxford University Press, 1973).

we have to teach them *something*. And the society around us keeps sending sharp signals that there are some things they *want* children to learn.

Logical cur-
riculum design
requires con-
sideration of
process, content,
and com-
munity's wishes.

This writer suggests that programs can only be as rich and exciting as is the *content* that teachers draw upon. The programs can only be as effective as the teaching methods are appropriate to the children's cognitive, emotional, and physical development. And, finally, we will only have community support for our teaching if, in fact, we respond constructively to the demands of that community for content.

This process of rational selection of curriculum can, therefore, become a logical process of understanding how children learn and think, assessing children's growth, selecting exciting and meaningful content from broad sources, and satisfying the community that its needs are also being met.

Using relevant content with process

This writer leans to child-centeredness without sacrificing either content or responsiveness to contemporary community needs. Granted that children may be as happy with one type of content as another, still, if carefully chosen, content will both nourish children's growth needs and supply the material they must have in order to organize their experiences in manageable understandings and processes. Children living in this contemporary society need to learn to understand and manage this world as they experience it daily.

Certain content may be universally required. For example, if school goals continue to stress the pluralistic character of our democratic society, it seems necessary for young children to experience early the different ways in which the same human needs are met.

Stress on independent learning.   A recent international workshop on education, looking to curriculum needs of the eighties, concluded that formal teaching methods will decline in importance and independent learning will become more important. It was further projected that a core curriculum would emerge, linking three broad areas—the natural sciences, the social sciences, and communication and expressive arts.[12]

12. Centre for Educational Research and Innovation, *The Nature of the Curriculum for the Eighties and Onwards* (Paris: Organisation for Economic Co-operation and Development, 1970), pp. 73–77.

Another source suggests that teachers select values of cultural diversity and pride in ethnic identity, model these values in teaching, and encourage them through classroom interactions, discussions, and research.[13] Specific suggestions from this source include designing family trees, representing family migrations on a world map, and interviewing friends and neighbors. These suggestions are likely to be more fruitful where the children represent diversity in backgrounds.

Reality orientation.   There is no hint in this approach that children will not unearth history featuring problems and unresolved inequalities in our society. The need to confront problems and to encourage solution of social problems is stressed in a recent yearbook of the National Council of Social Studies. The 1972 issue states its theme: "The social dimensions of the curriculum must focus on and teach about the immediate realities and problems facing human beings in the city. Equally important, we must do all in our power to intervene in vital aspects of our urban environment."[14]

For a long time a "precious" view of young children prevailed in early childhood classrooms, requiring children to be spared the ugliness of life. This view has yielded to the more realistic one that children are often in the position of experiencing life's ugliness without protection or understanding. Grandparents die, sometimes parents do also, or siblings fall ill or die in accidents or fires. Crime becomes visible to children in big cities when they see or hear about violence visited upon people and property. Some children get too little to eat. Others live in dreadful houses which makes them keenly aware of the seamy side of life. While no one advocates teaching children to be fearful and gloomy, children's fiction increasingly deals with realities, such as an unwed mother, discrimination in jobs or housing, or bureaucratic responses by governmental agencies that fail to respond to human needs. It is not too difficult to agree that children should be helped to understand the world of haves and have-nots and of needs often neglected.

13. Evelyn Berger and Bonnie A. Winters, *Social Studies in the Open Classroom* (New York: Teachers College Press, 1973), pp. 85–86.

14. Richard Wiesniewski, ed., *Teaching about Life in the City*, Forty-second Yearbook (Washington, D.C.: National Council for the Social Studies, 1972), p. 4.

Problems of teaching social activism

But what about teaching *intervention*? Should children be taught to *change* those features of our urban or rural environment that are currently seen as dysfunctional?

In a world of food shortages and critical shortfalls of goods and services, should American children be taught to eat little, if any, meat so that the world supply of grain will feed more people? Should our children learn to walk more, ride less, and use fewer electrical gadgets so as to help preserve the limited supplies of energy? What about pollution of the air and water, foods grown or manufactured with unneeded and possibly dangerous chemicals? Or abuses of political power? If we teach our young children they are responsible for improving the physical and moral climate of our country, how can we expect this responsibility to be manifested? Can we teach responsibilities that many adults refuse to shoulder much of the time? Do we know *how* to teach children to cope with the difficult realities of our time?

We can help children to learn what responsibility means by giving them opportunities to discharge responsibilities of which they are capable. Whether they choose to become social activists as they grow up, and for what causes, must be their own choices.

FINDING CONTENT FOR CREATIVE SOCIAL LEARNING

Teachers frequently ask for new, creative ideas for the social studies or social learning area. When they tire of the same old holiday activities and quickie units on community helpers, what other content is there to draw upon?

Fortunately, there are many challenging and exciting systems for teachers to consider for social learning content. All of them can help young children become more aware of themselves and their unique identities. Each system offers the child some strong leads to other people, opening doors to more informed views of how we relate to others. Furthermore, every one of these systems invites the child's active participation in social inquiry. Whatever the content teachers choose for curriculum planning, the major objective of a people-oriented learning experience can be central.

Seven different designs suggest content for creative social learning.

The following discussion describes seven different designs for social learning curricula, followed by examples of how some of these designs can be applied in programs for young children. The seven themes suggested for teachers' selective application include 1) broad content themes, 2) child value concepts, 3) a social action approach, 4) moral development or social values themes, 5) political socialization, 6) career education, and 7) key concepts of various kinds.

BROAD CONTENT THEMES

Having broad content themes provides the teacher with two major guides to content, a central theme or topic and a specified list of goals. Themes can be selected from contemporary concerns that affect children but that are important for everyone in the community. Examples of broad themes are such topics as energy conservation, prevention of drug abuse, or nutritious food habits. Teachers can select themes that they find of interest and that they perceive as age appropriate for the children they teach. Good themes should be sufficiently socially pervasive to tap community resources needed for substantial curricular content.

Broad content themes provide a central topic and a specified list of goals.

The second requirement of the broad content themes social learning design is the list of goals to guide the development of the curriculum. A wide range of learning experiences about people is suggested by such goals as knowing, sensitivity, creativity, social participation skill, valuing, community research, and social action.[15] Since these goals can be adapted to any age-grade level, to any community's priorities and decisions, and to any teaching-learning situation, this design is easily adapted to almost any program.

CHILD VALUE CONCEPTS

Another good source for curricular development is found in the theme of child value concepts—ideas that reflect the child's needs for both self-valuing and for feeling valued by others. Sondergaard and Moore provide a list of child value concepts that offer universal goals for

---

15. Wiesniewski, op. cit, p. 90.

curricular planning.[16] Ploghoft and Shuster also list child value concepts for program goals:[17]

Feelings of belonging, at home, school, and playground
Choices of activity—doing what one wants to do
Independent activity within established limits
Joy and laughter in day-to-day activities
Sense of being listened to by others
Awareness of new learning
Experiencing surprises and unexpected happenings
Expectation of growing up important
Some control over how one spends time, including solitude or privacy
Self-understanding and understanding others
Be respected and respect others

Ploghoft and Shuster suggest ways that teachers who wish to pursue such concepts can work with parents in collaborative efforts:[18]

Consulting parents for insights and understandings about the child
Involving parents in school or community projects affecting their own children's welfare
Eliciting from parents their values
Reinforcing parental values
Reassuring parents of the soundness of their values
Helping parents pursue their own values with their children
Suggesting to parents creative ways to guide children toward more maturity and independence
Specifying to parents how to foster values and to promote school skill projects through ordinary homelife experiences.

Basic to the Ploghoft and Shuster design is the structure of human experience, both sociological and psychological, not the structure of the subject matter. Since this design stresses the relationship of families and others in the community to children's social concerns, such as their wish to be respected, the use of this base suggests many activities and experiences that would be very meaningful for young children.

---

16. Arensa Sondergaard, "What a Child Values," *Childhood Education* 32 (February 1956), pp. 255–256; Bertha M. Moore, "Adults Look at Children's Values," *Childhood Education* 32 (February 1956), pp. 257–261.

17. Milton E. Ploghoft and Albert H. Shuster, *Social Science Education in the Elementary School* (Columbus, Ohio: Charles E. Merrill, 1971), pp. 53–54.

18. Ibid., p. 54.

Since the child value concepts central to this design all emphasize children's autonomy and welfare, presumably parent collaboration in this project would have to be in line with these concepts. Perhaps teachers can use the design to raise the consciousness of some parents about the need to be less authoritarian in their relationships with their children.

SOCIAL ACTION

Some writers suggest involving even primary grade children in efforts to improve the quality of their own lives. The social action design values an activist base for reforming society, beginning with early school experiences and centering at first on school situations with potential for reaching out to the surrounding community.

Joyce suggests that teachers work toward two affective goals, first, to develop in children a commitment to improve society by finding ways to improve school life and life in one's immediate neighborhood and, second, to help children reach out to others, to "make contact," and to try to love, understand, and grow with others.[19]

Social action begins with the school as a community.
He also suggests that teachers of primary children concentrate on the classroom as the community, for learning how to improve life in one's social group, along with such appropriate outreach activities for first graders as interviewing parents and neighbors for their suggestions for social improvement activities.

It seems likely that a social action orientation would contribute to children's self-valuing as they view themselves behaving in responsible and planned ways for good causes.

MORAL DEVELOPMENT AND SOCIAL VALUE THEMES

The work of Piaget originally, and then of Kohlberg, on the moral development of children has inspired many interesting program suggestions for helping children to reason logically about moral questions. The Shaftels suggest a focus on ethical behavior including individual integrity and group responsibility.[20]

19. Bruce R. Joyce, "Social Action for the Primary Schools", *Childhood Education* 46 (February 1970), pp. 117–122.
20. Fannie R. Shaftel and George Shaftel, *Role Playing for Social Values* (Englewood Cliffs, N.J.: Prentice-Hall, 1967).

Shaftel's focus on feelings and ethics

One of the major objectives of the Shaftel design is education for citizenship. The materials used are "problem stories that pose key dilemmas of middle childhood and early adolescence in American culture in the solution of which young people discover their own feelings, their modes of action, and their values, and learn to modify them intelligently."[21] While the social values design of the Shaftels was chiefly developed for children older than those with whom the teacher candidates who are reading this book are concerned, there are good possibilities here in relation to the needs of young children for social learning. The methods used—role playing and sociodrama— are particularly appropriate for the young child's way of exploring ideas by playing characters and improvising action, a uniquely personal way to build a concept.

Moral develop-ment themes provide ways for children to deal with ethics and with personal feelings.

According to the Shaftels, "Role playing proceeds into problem definition, deliberation of alternatives for action, exploration of the consequences of those alternatives, and decision making."[22] This approach deals with real dilemmas that confront them in day-to-day living. If a child finds a nickel on the classroom floor, for example, should he pocket it or try to find the owner? If a child sees another child take something that belongs to someone else, is there any responsibility to do anything about it? If an older child bullies a younger one into giving up his lunch money, should the younger child do anything about it? What if two children on the playground are fighting and they are very mismatched physically, do the bystanders have any responsibility to prevent an unfair fight? If a child is given money by his mother to buy a few groceries and finds some supermarket toy irresistible, what should he tell his mother?

Kohlberg's research on moral reasoning

Kohlberg's research on how children reason about moral questions is stimulating curricular development for children at all age levels. Kohlberg identified three major developmental levels in moral reasoning, and he further subdivided each level into two stages, making a total of six developmental sequences. Piaget had found that children's

21. Ibid., p. 9.
22. Ibid., p. 9.

reasoning changed—in three distinct stages—from rather primitive logic to the complex logic of adults. The early stage he called intuitive reasoning, the next concrete operations, and the third, reached at maturity, operational or abstract thinking.[23]

Similarly, Kohlberg termed his three levels of moral reasoning preconventional, conventional, and postconventional.[24] In the first or preconventional level, the two stages are called the *punishment and obedience orientation*, followed by the *instrumental relativist orientation*. These two stages occur usually before ages six or seven. Generally, at this level children regard as right whatever moral decisions are rewarding physically or otherwise, and they consider as wrong whatever brings punishment or disapproval. In other words, young children accept the superior power of those who make and enforce the rules. At stage one, the child chiefly seeks rewards and avoids punishments. Kohlberg saw in stage two some beginning ideas of fair treatment and mutual sharing but solely in relation to the child's sense of his own needs.

The conventional level, from about ages six or seven to twelve or thirteen, is characterized by *conformity* and *loyalty*. At this level, children expect to do their duty, meeting the expectations of those who make laws. Kohlberg calls stage three a "good boy-nice girl" orientation. Intention begins to be credited, although "law and order" is the prevailing mood of stage four. There is great respect for social authority.

Finally, the postconventional or principled level occurs after age twelve, with more adult forms of logic applied to moral questions. The sixth stage is one of universal ethical principles such as the golden rule, but defined more autonomously and personally, without seeking to conform to one's group.

The Kohlberg framework is not a didactic method; it does not seek to indoctrinate or teach moral values. It deals with reasoning, with how one reaches conclusions and defends them. Of course, the purpose of the concentration on the logic of one's reasons is to help children learn to spot illogical arguments and to correct their own logical errors once they recognize them. The methods used are to pose mostly theoretical but realistic types of dilemmas that can have several different solutions. Probes of weak points in the reasoning some-

23. Jean Piaget, *The Moral Judgment of the Child.* (Glencoe, Ill.: Illinois Free Press, 1948).
24. Lawrence Kohlberg, "From 'Is' to 'Ought,' " in *Cognitive Development,* edited by Theodore Mischel (New York: Academic, 1971), pp. 222–226.

times alert the child to more logical reasons. Teaching is generally aimed in the direction of the next higher stage of moral judgment than the one the child illustrates in his reasoning (if he is able to move that much).[25]

A perplexing problem in the moral judgment theme is the tendency people have to profess a stage of morality they do not in fact practice. But it seems that ethics are often specific to the situation. The moral judgment design cannot resolve this problem. It can only help children use the most logical reasoning of which they are capable and to become aware of the nature of moral dilemmas and the possible ways to resolve them.

POLITICAL SOCIALIZATION THEMES

Another interesting suggestion for political socialization comes from Hess and Torney and is based on studies of school children's socialization into the political system of the United States.[26] These authors refer to political socialization as "the process by which an individual child is prepared to become an adult member of the political community."[27]

Political socialization prepares a child for adult citizenship.

In their studies of children's conceptions of the president and of our political system, an unexpected finding was that "the school apparently plays the largest part in teaching attitudes, conceptions, and beliefs about the operation of the political system."[28] While Hess and Torney agree that the family contributes a great deal to children's basic loyalty to the United States, these basic feelings are considerably developed at school through study of selected content and concepts. A further finding of the study: "The school is particularly important for children from working-class or low socioeconomic areas. Most of what working-class children learn at school is not reinforced by home or community."[29]

In this writer's opinion, the most important reason given by Hess and Torney for featuring political socialization in poorer communi-

---

25. Nancy Porter and Nancy Taylor, *How to Assess the Moral Reasoning of Students* (Ontario, Canada: The Ontario Institute for Students in Education, 1972), p. 5.
26. Hess and Torney, op. cit., p. 212.
27. Ibid., p. 1.
28. Ibid., p. 217.
29. Ibid., p. 218.

ties is that otherwise the children would not learn this content and these concepts and attitudes. It is interesting to note, more specifically, that the family's influence here is regarded as rather indirect, chiefly relating to authority and conformity to rules. The schools also tend to overemphasize rules, conformity, and authority, it seems. More emphasis seems to be needed on the rights and obligations of citizenship, especially on *participation* in governmental endeavors and on *group action*. Some of the curricular sources identified above suggest very specific forms of group action in the classroom, school, and neighborhood and would be quite appropriate to help children conceptualize the rights and obligations of concerned citizens.

CAREER EDUCATION

It seems as though every mandated program turns out to be a K-12 curriculum. Hence, teachers of young children may find themselves saddled with a "career education" unit or project or program.[30] For young children, there is likely to emerge an over-emphasis on the work ethic, probably in the hope of counteracting the world-wide decline in adherents of this ethic. Yet there are undeniable riches to be mined from studies of jobs, how people grow our food, make our endless "goods" and help put roofs over our heads and food in our mouths. Matching content to children's ability to conceptualize, and to have access to first-hand experiencing, would surely enrich children's understandings of their lives and of the society in which they live.

A fine use of a career education theme is to broaden children's horizons about careers that are unfamiliar to them and to encourage children to dream about some careers that might seem unattainable. While career education is often thought of as a way to guide children into training programs that do not require a college education,[31] there is no reason why teachers cannot offer experiences and information that might inspire children to pursue careers they might not otherwise have known about.

30. John R. Ottina, "Career Education Is Alive and Well," *Journal of Teacher Education* 24 (Summer 1973), pp. 84–92.
31. David T. Borland and Richard Harris, "Preparing Career Education Specialists," *Journal of Teacher Education* 24 (Summer 1973), pp. 93–96.

KEY CONCEPTS THEMES

As indicated above, the structure of the disciplines design to social learnings opened new avenues to content selection from the social sciences. Structuring these bodies of knowledge was a very difficult task compared with the more exact sciences. But ideas were contributed by social scientists that were often novel or unknown to teachers. Thus, content sources for teaching could be more interesting and varied.

Concepts could be selected from one of the major social science disciplines or from a broader base that might integrate the various social sciences. Examples can be found of interesting curriculum ideas growing out of this orientation in economics, history, geography, and other related bodies of knowledge.[32]

As goals in social learning curricula, some key concepts might include self-knowing, self-valuing and group membership, in sociological content, spatial relationships, representing features of physical space with physical objects, and directionality in geographic content, and from economics, using coins and bills as money, differentiating buyers from sellers in stores, and specialized jobs within stores.[33]

APPLYING CONTENT TO SOCIAL LEARNING CURRICULA

Examples of how some of the designs described above might take shape in social learning curricula for young children follow. If teachers try out any of these suggestions, the richness and depth which good plans generate will readily become apparent. Because of teacher creativity, the same plans will develop in different ways in each classroom.

Putting new plans to work is always easier if teachers work together and support each other by sharing resources, options, and results. As a group, teachers will find more and continuing access to supervisors, parents, and community volunteers, sometimes with additional funds allocated for materials that might not be offered to a single classroom.

32. Robison and Spodek, op. cit., *New Directions in the Kindergarten.*
33. Helen F. Robison and Sydney L. Schwartz, *Learning at an Early Age: A Curriculum for Young Children,* Vol. 2 (Englewood Cliffs, N.J.: Prentice-Hall, 1972), pp. 166, 194, and 208.

USING BROAD CONTENT THEMES

Selection of broad content themes is usually the easiest step in developing this base for curricular planning. Every community is concerned about some important features of daily living. It might be children's safety in getting to and from school. In many communities, littering is a constant irritant (in addition to other forms of pollution). Energy conservation is a universal problem everywhere in the world.

Starting with the three broad content themes of reducing pollution, saving energy, and improving nutrition, Table 8.1 indicates some ways the reader might use the design, for children in the four to five age range and for primary grade children. For each of the three broad content themes, and for the two age levels, Table 8.1 indicates briefly appropriate types of activities for the seven goals of knowing, sensitivity, creativity, social participation, valuing, community research, and social action.

This design is particularly helpful to teachers in its breadth. Some groups or individual children might concentrate on some of the goals, or all children might gain experience in the activities suggested for each of the seven goals.

DEVELOPING CHILD VALUE CONCEPTS

In selecting content for the goal of developing child value concepts, the child values have to be identified first. Teachers might identify one child value, such as "sense of being listened to by others," and work with children and parents to design activities and experiences likely to approach this goal at school and at home.

Instead of teacher selection of the goal, selection might be the result of a series of discussions, dramatizations, stories, and option-selection experiences with children playing the dominant role. In some cases, the selection might offer teachers excellent means of collaboration with parents and community, thus emphasizing their input and their important roles in reinforcing school social learning.

Identifying child values precedes the development of child value concept themes.

Experiences could include such self-expressive activities as writing poems and stories, painting pictures, or creating other art, music, or dance forms to convey feelings. Dramatizing problems or feelings

TABLE 8.1 CONTENT THEMES WITH GOALS

GOALS	THEME—REDUCING POLLUTION	
AGE-GRADE LEVELS	4–5 YEARS	PRIMARY GRADES
Knowing	Hear stories and books Take trips Discuss problems with visiting specialists	Read stories Compose and write stories Library research Reports, oral and written Take trips
Sensitivity	Identify pollutants in community, e.g., gasoline fumes	Articulate pollution-reducing possibilities Identifying pollution problems in books, films, TV
Creativity	Paint, or other art forms Compose stories or poems Compose dances	Creative dramatizations Write stories or poems Make models or constructions Paint mural
Social Participation	Compose letters to parents and friends Make picture posters	Write letters to newspapers and government agencies Hold meetings in class Report to other classes
Valuing	Share stories and songs about the values of pure air, food and water	Compare values of reduced pollution with evils of pollution
Community Research	Identify in school and community varied voluntary and official efforts to reduce pollution	Interview neighbors and officials Visit sites of pollution or of pollution-reduction
Social Action	Assist in school nonlittering project	Plan and carry out a school project to reduce pollution, such as recycling cans and bottles

*List of goals reprinted with permission of the National Council for the Social Studies and authors Anna S. Ochoa and Rodney F. Allen, "Creative Teacher-Student Learning Experiences about The City," p. 90, in Richard Wiesniewski (ed.), *Teaching About Life in the City,* 42d Yearbook, 1972, National Council for the Social Studies, Washington, D.C., pp. 89–158.

Table 8.1—Continued

GOALS	THEME—SAVING ENERGY	
AGE-GRADE LEVELS	4–5 YEARS	PRIMARY GRADES
Knowing	Hear stories and books See filmstrips and films Take trips	Read books Do library research Take trips Interview specialists Report on TV programs
Sensitivity	Identify wasteful energy use such as failure to turn off unneeded lights	Report and write about personal experiences in identifying energy waste
Creativity	Develop personal energy-saving plans Paint pictures	Write energy-saving suggestions Write poems, stories, plays
Social Participation	Take notices home to parents about saving energy	Participate in committee and school efforts to advertise plans to the community
Valuing	Identify "helper" jobs to monitor energy saving such as turning off lights	Write class book about children's various energy-saving efforts
Community Research	Identify energy-saving possibilities in school and home	Take trips to find out energy-saving efforts or needs
Social Action	Assist in communicating to parents need for car-pools, or walking instead of riding in car	Participate in an energy-saving activity in the school or community

through pantomime, dramatic presentations, or puppet shows are involving ways to help children to deal with feelings constructively.

This design goes further than identifying problems. It should be especially helpful to teacher and children in creating interesting ways to solve problems. If children wish to enjoy the sense of being listened to more often, how can the classroom or program accentuate this value or feature it where it was not really operational before? Teachers, children, and their parents will have many interesting answers to this question but here are a few:

Table 8.1—Continued

GOALS	THEME—IMPROVING NUTRITION	
AGE-GRADE LEVELS	4–5 YEARS	PRIMARY GRADES
Knowing	Discuss food habits Hear stories, see films and film-strips about nutrition Identify nutritional needs	Read books and other materials on nutrition Identify food needs Make charts Read recipes and menus Write experience charts
Sensitivity	List major types of food needs Classify foods as good or bad nutritionally	Record personal food habits and identify needs for improvement
Creativity	Create a menu and help cook and eat the meal Develop puppet play	Write a class cookbook Write stories, plays Prepare dramatization of a story
Social Participation	Bring can of food for collection for hungry children	Help collect money, or earn money, to contribute for food for others
Valuing	Report on self-improvement in eating habits	Plan ideal menus to meet nutritional needs
Community Research	Take trips to food stores to identify varieties of nutritional foods	Study lunch menus in school cafeteria and children's lunches, evaluating nutritional needs
Social Action	Help compose a letter to parents on cutting down on children's sugar intake	Prepare written material for parents on need for improving children's food habits

Install a listening corner with a tape recorder

Fashion a listening house (out of heavy paper cartons, cloth or paper curtains, and some floor mats) to be used by no more than two children at a time for talking and listening.

Plan teacher listening time in the daily schedule for individual child-teacher charts.

Make and hang a mailbox into which children place notes to each other or to the teacher (especially useful in the primary grades).

Create a dramatization to contrast nonlistening and listening experiences.

Write and post some classroom rules on how to listen and how to be
listened to.

Ask children to dictate or write "I wish that . . ." kind of story on how
they would like to be listened to at school and at home.

Plan evaluation discussions with children to find out whether changes
are occurring and, if not, how to increase the pace of the project.

If the child value concepts are to be developed in any depth, they
should be featured for long enough periods of time to grow and
change as the children give them meaning through their experiences.

PUTTING SOCIAL ACTION THEMES TO WORK

Joyce's suggestion of using the classroom as a community to permit
children to practice ways of improving the conditions of their own
daily lives is well worth exploring. The various social goals that
could be selected for social action can all suggest meaningful activities, inquiries, studies, reading, writing, and creative maturing social experiences for young children.

Which social goals would be useful in a social action program for
young children? Following are suggestions for social goals and their
definitions:

The golden rule. Do unto others as you would have them do unto you.

Human rights. Where individual rights and social needs must be
integrated.

Rule making. The process, the purposes, the problems; how to make
rules that free us with the flexibility we need for creative interactions.

Responsibilities. How individuals respond to and initiate actions to
support social goals.

Creativity. Procedures and materials to encourage pursuit of creative
ideas in discussions, inquiry, projects, and products.

Social contributions. Helping others through service and contributions
of goods or money.

Social institutions. Creating or participating in the work of such social
institutions as Red Cross, citizen's environmental groups fighting
pollution and energy waste (local collections of litter, cans, paper,
and bottles) or local groups working for beautification of the community (planting trees, shrubs or flowers, picking up litter, monitoring municipal street cleaning or garbage collection).

*In putting social
action themes
into practice,
children work
to improve the
conditions of
their own daily
lives.*

Some ways to move toward these social goals are given in the outline below as activities for young children. It suggests various teaching strategies likely to enhance the meaningfulness of children's social actions. For example, under the *Golden Rule*, teaching strategies to consider are teacher modelling of desirable forms of verbal and nonverbal address, appreciating and rewarding small steps toward goals, and avoidance of punishment. Similarly, under *Responsibilities*, teaching strategies suggested include encouraging children to help each other in learning situations and stressing initiative in offering help to others or in responding to requests for help. Many other such strategies could be added.

Social action themes and activities for young children

Golden Rule

1. Stress graciousness, friendliness, and mutual helpfulness in daily interactions of children. If possible, ignore ugly remarks, gestures, or hostile actions by children. Suggest alternative and more desirable behaviors to a child engaging in less desirable activity.
2. *Model* desirable forms of address, verbal and nonverbal, *stress* them in incidental and planned ways, *identify* them when they occur, *reward* them, and *advertise* them to parents and school community.
3. *Instruct*, don't *punish*. *Appreciate* and *reward* small steps in desired direction.
4. As a teacher, avoid giving a child help that could be furnished by another child, but suggest such help where it is not spontaneously offered.
5. Keep a class log or diary in which children record (by writing or dictation) examples of experiencing golden rule effects from others or of personal initiatives.

Human Rights

1. Stress valuing of human rights as well as the social needs of the group.
2. Keep a large chart of human rights. Add to it whenever an incidental or planned activity features such rights or suggests additional ones. Rights might include:
   a. Freedom from physical attack.
   b. Security of property (specify, such as clothing, school books and materials, one's food, or personal toys).

    c. Expectation of help when needed (specify, such as finding lost articles or carrying heavy things).

    d. Exchange of kind words in interactions (specify, such as greetings, ways to request help, ways to respond to requests).

3. Keep an equally large chart of social needs. Add to it whenever an incidental or planned activity features such rights or suggests additional ones. Social needs might include:

    a. Needs for order

    b. Livable noise level

    c. Pursuing one's activity without distracting others

    d. Keeping the classroom clean, safe, and enjoyable

    e. Maintaining task orientation and goal directedness

    In children's terms, these social needs might be characterized as:

    a. Not too messy

    b. Not too loud

    c. Don't disturb others

    d. Keep room clean

    e. Keep room a healthy place

    f. Avoid accidents

    g. Work well

    h. Finish tasks

    i. Enjoy our classroom and keep it happy.

Rule making

1. Involve children in rule making, rule revision, rule monitoring, and rule evaluation.

2. Pursue with children such questions as:

    a. What's a rule for?

    b. How can we make a good rule for a specific purpose?

    c. How can we improve a rule which is not working well?

    d. How can we find out how well our rule is working?

    e. How good is this rule? How does it help us and how does it hinder us?

Responsibilities

1. Create a we-group atmosphere: We help each other and our group works well because everybody helps. Encourage children to help each other: tying shoelaces or art apron strings, zipping coats, or buttoning clothing; in learning activities by working in pairs to learn sight words, phonics, or skills, to hear each other read, to collaborate in math measurement activities; to serve on committees making studies, inquiries, or doing laboratory work.

2. Model and reward responsibilities.

3. Stress to children taking initiative to offer help to others.

4. Stress to children the need to respond to requests for help in constructive ways.

Creativity

1. Offer children continuous opportunities to do creative work.
2. Change materials available to stimulate creative work.
3. Appreciate and value creative work in prominent ways.
4. Exhibit children's creative work without value judgments or invidious comparison.
5. See chapter on teaching suggestions for art and other creative activities.

Social Contributions

1. Discuss regular collections for Red Cross or other social agency to relieve human suffering.
2. Form committees and other participatory groups to facilitate collections of money or goods.
3. Identify possibilities for children's participation through personal services, such as:
   a. Telephone calls to hospitalized relatives or friends.
   b. Cards and letters to shut-in or ill relatives, friends, classmates, and neighbors.
   c. Talks to other classes to solicit participatory help.
   d. Make posters for supermarkets or other such places to encourage community participation to meet specific social needs.
   e. Enlist in antilitter drive at school or on one's own street.

Social Institutions

1. Create a classroom committee to lead an activity to meet a social need.
   a. Create and elect classroom governance, with elected officials and rules for governing, to accomplish specified purposes.
   b. Or, a committee might be elected to spur parents, friends, and neighbors to vote in school board elections or in general political elections for local, state, and federal offices.
2. Study, through trips, books, pamphlets, filmstrips, or film, some interesting social institutions such as museums, zoos, art galleries.
   a. Participate in creating a local institution at the school, for example, a regular art gallery for children's and artists' exhibits. Work through class and school groups; confer and discuss with school staff—supervisory, administrative, and custodial—and enlist parental and specialist participation individually and through the parents' association.
   b. Help children support a newly created school social institution by making contributions (art work or money), staffing it, using it, and enlisting others to support it.

STIMULATING MORAL DEVELOPMENT

Teachers interested in finding good curricular suggestions for stimulating moral development will find that much new material is becoming available. Curriculum materials based on Kohlberg's research are being developed and will be useful with young children. This vein of curriculum is intellectually challenging and will appeal to many teachers seeking this kind of curricular resource.

Shaftel's sociodrama

If the Shaftel's methods are adapted for younger children, it is best for teachers to work with small groups to avoid overtaxing the young child's interest in dramatizing feelings. Sociodrama or role playing can be used to relieve tensions and help children give meaning and form to feelings of guilt, anger, frustration, or shame. Teacher guidance is essential to maintain a noncritical, nonjudgmental atmosphere in which to explore feelings and action possibilities. To avoid bruised egos and difficulty in objectifying the theme, audiences are best dispensed with when working with younger children.

The representational character of sociodrama helps children construct understandings about people's feelings.

Perhaps the most effective use of sociodrama and role playing for young children lies in its representational character. Physical and active representation of characters, themes, and actions, with accompanying costume and props, are advocated by many early childhood educators as a way for children to *construct* their conceptual understandings. But young children need to play "as if" situations without feeling threat from reality. The child who is asked to play a bully role should never be the one who is, in fact, a bully. The bully had better play the role of victim and "pretend" to be frightened and upset. It is as though children are enabled to "try on" roles for size and fit. Children learn to be more alert to hitherto unnoticed features of action, especially how victims or scapegoats feel.

The social goals of taking turns and sharing are highlighted for young children through sociodrama, and they begin to realize that if they enjoy a longer turn, someone else is unhappy because his turn has been deferred. Ethical questions have to be limited to the intellectual levels of the children participating. Sixes and sevens can handle some aspects of objectivity better than fours or fives. The primary grade children can also be expected to be somewhat more dependable in their logic.

FOSTERING POLITICAL SOCIALIZATION

In response to children's needs for political socialization, a curriculum was produced by the American Bar Association and was designed to teach older children about the American legal system and its government by laws. This project will surely inspire other attempts to meet the same needs, since problems and controversies will no doubt arise about such issues as the following:

> How to teach children concepts and information without indoctrinating them.
>
> How to deal with the difference between the ideals of our legal system and the realities of its enforcement.
>
> What about corruption by officials sworn to enforce the law, illegal activities of government officials and employees, and inequalities and abuses in law enforcement procedures?
>
> What about comparative studies of other governments different from ours, such as those of the People's Republic of China, the Soviet Union, or Saudi Arabia?

If teachers of young children think they won't have to deal with these issues, they reckon without television, political movements, or the children's real-life experiences at home or in their community. True, children's early political conceptions relate to personalized authority figures at home and nationally. The president is clearly conceptualized, and children relate to him as the point of contact with the national government.[34] Concepts of city, state, or nation are hazy or vague among young children. Yet Hess and Torney found that the school fostered very rapid development of political attitudes and concepts, even when information and knowledge were sparse.

Children see good guys and bad guys

Besides the president, children also have rather articulate notions about a policeman, chiefly how he protects people. Apparently, no clear conceptions are found in young children about political figures other than the policeman and the president. Children also view the world in black and white; everyone is either a good guy or a bad guy. It takes considerable time and experience for the child to perceive the

34. Hess, op. cit., p. 221.

great complexity of political figures and institutions and to acquire the information to illuminate this complexity.

Considering adults' feelings of political powerlessness found by social researchers in poorer neighborhoods, there seems to be a prevailing view in such communities that the government is not responsive to their needs and that people are unable to bring about needed social change. If children in such communities learn that our legal system does, in fact, vest power in the people to group together so as to exert pressure for desired changes, will children reject such learning because it is not in accordance with the experiences of their family and community? The indications are unclear as to what the effects of such learning might be, but it is surely challenging to try to teach more children how our system works and especially how they are needed to make it work better. As an aftermath to the enormous scandal of Watergate, more people than ever before would probably support the effort as worth an extensive trial. In fact the story of Watergate is itself an example of responsiveness of governmental agencies to the clear demands of justice; neither the president nor the vice president could flout the law with impunity.

Learning how to succeed as citizens

Children need to learn of the successful efforts of such groups as one in Oregon who insisted on a law requiring returnable bottles and another group who thwarted a freeway in Boston. Many environmental protection groups have rescued irreplaceable natural resources—swamps, bird sanctuaries, mature forests, and lakes—from bulldozers and other forms of encroachment or overdevelopment. The magnificent mountains, deserts, and other natural beauties of the western states face frequent battles for survival. In the urban centers, where people seem most powerless, children need to learn how our system works so they can participate in making it as effective as possible.

While no curriculum for young children has yet emerged from the Hess-Torney studies, it would not be difficult for interested teachers, parents, and curriculum writers to find collaborators among lawyers and political scientists to identify meaningful content and to devise school learning experiences appropriate for various developmental levels.

The youngest child in school should have a sense that he has "rights" and "obligations" and recourse to appeal procedures when he feels justice has been blindly dealt out. Wherever parents fight for the installation of a traffic light near a school, for improved school bus service, or for other local needs, children can be involved in the efforts, to gain political knowledge.

REALIZING CAREER EDUCATION

While career education is still rather new, there is considerable precedent in early childhood education for acquainting young children with the world of work and of the variety of jobs people work at to earn a living. An element of novelty can be injected into the career education experiences by helping children to overcome widespread stereotypes of the kinds of work suitable for the sexes or for ethnic and racial groups. When girls want to be air traffic controllers or head chefs, it should be the role of career education to help them realistically evaluate their personal qualifications for such jobs, without assuming that sex bias for specific occupations cannot be breached.

Young children would have great difficulty understanding the characteristics of many jobs in our society. Computer programmers, public relations personnel, and many kinds of administrative, research, and managerial staff cannot readily convey to children the kind of work they do. One little girl, knowing her father was a lawyer, visited his office one day, only to tell a friend later, with obvious disappointment, "My daddy talks on the telephone." Perhaps this is why kindergarten seems to confine its job studies to uniformed civil servants. At least, everyone knows what policemen, firemen, and mailmen do.

The world of work can offer a great many observations of occupational possibilities. Construction work is to be seen everywhere, especially road maintenance and repair. Residential and industrial construction fascinates children. So do such jobs as telephone linemen and installers, automobile repairmen, service station attendants, retail store personnel, and farmers. Some children can meet forest rangers and learn about their work. Hospital and health occupations are also easy to identify in most communities.

If the major purpose of career education for young children is to help them and their parents to keep options open and to develop an interest in learning about many career possibilities, every community offers many resources for learning.

MAKING KEY CONCEPTS MEANINGFUL

The use of key concepts from the social sciences for content selection can make for exciting learning experiences for young children. A social learning curriculum for a kindergarten illustrates some of the possibilities.

Robison and Mukerji report that when a kindergarten class of many ethnic and racial backgrounds made vegetable soup in school, they learned names of vegetables they had never seen before, they tasted raw and cooked vegetables new to them, and they created a classroom aroma and atmosphere that encouraged tasting and adventuring.[35] The teacher should note carefully that these were not just "cooking experiences" in the classroom. These cooking activities were selected and planned for precise goals.

Robison-Mukerji study

The Robison-Mukerji study was a demonstration of a kindergarten program in a very poor, ethnically mixed neighborhood and emphasized language growth, concept development, and symbolic representation. Based on child development contributions to children's developmental needs, the program emphasized an integrated social studies, math, and language curriculum pattern. In a Dewey-like approach to intellectual content, the social content goals—or key concepts—were these:[36]

1. Interdependence as a characteristic of our society
2. Specialization as a characteristic of our society
3. Cultural pluralism as a value in our democratic society
4. Map concepts

These social studies goals were integrated with a few mathematics goals (one-to-one correspondence, cardinal numbers and rational

35. Helen F. Robison and Rose Mukerji, *Concept and Language Development in a Kindergarten of Disadvantaged Children*, Cooperative Research Project S-320 (Washington, D.C.: U.S. Department of Health, Education and Welfare, Office of Education, 1966).
36. Ibid., p. 10.

counting, numerals and denominations of money); language goals (names, labelling, vocabulary); fluency of communication; language structure, sentence form; esthetic quality; expressiveness, colorfulness, and affective qualities of oral language; and symbolic representation goals of map concepts and signs and labels. These general goals were further concretized to generate curriculum activities.

Use of key concepts.   The first phase of the study chose "providing for families' food needs" as the key concept within which to pursue the goals specified above, and the second phase pursued the same goals in an "air transport" project. The latter project might seem far afield for a kindergarten class, but it was selected because many of the Hispanic children had recent flight experience to and from the Caribbean and, surprisingly, so did other children who were recent immigrants from Hong Kong, Japan, and Greece.

The Robison-Mukerji study illustrates the implementation of social content goals.

The concept of interdependence, for example, was developed out of exciting, involving experiences in the classroom and at the airport. Children learned about the jobs of air transport workers and how each job fits into a service that provides transportation to people and to objects. There was a great deal of dramatic play and creative dramatization using costumes, props, teacher involvement, block play and constructions, art work, music, and dance. In the curriculum, emphasis was also put on reading stories, writing numerals and names, making symbols, identifying symbols, making simple maps and calendars, and reading the clock. There were bus trips, followed by the viewing of slides taken on the trips and the reliving and verbalizing of observations and experiences. The broad goal of cultural pluralism was one that generated a great deal of marketing, cooking, eating, listening to ethnic music, encouraging children to speak their natural language, dancing, and involving parents in special holiday events and activities.

Teaching representation.   Representation was fostered through many play activities as children donned parent-made costumes or used teacher-made props. Children pretended to pack bags, buy tickets, pay money, enter the airplane, seat themselves and fasten seat belts, sleep on pillows, eat from small trays, fuel the plane, sell tickets, carry baggage, stow baggage in the plane, pilot the plane and sight direction, announce take-off and landing, and otherwise play parts as passengers or flight crew members, mechanics, porters, and ticket sellers. Tickets came to be understood, gradually, to represent a way to tell who paid and where people wanted to go. Play money represented real money. Everyone pretended to be grown up, except for an occasional child who was willing to play a child role. Uniforms were understood to symbolize occupations. Labels were used also, especially for "ticket clerk," "mechanic," and "passenger." Children learned to recognize and many learned to write their own names and names of classmates, as these were extensively used in air transport play. Numeral writing had high interest. Pictures were painted at the easel as the air transport theme became increasingly involving. Children learned to read and write signs such as *IN* or *OUT* and to associate clock time with meal times and school activities. Pictorial representation was pursued in many ways, after the many physical representation experiences made pictorial forms clearer. Globes and maps came to be used for representational purposes after prior playful exploration, and films offered another form of representation. In the opinion of the writer, this is the kind of program which generates genuine intellectual ferment among teachers as well as children and makes each day a challenge to find new paths to selected goals.

Integration of content and process. It should be noted that the program just described did not neglect either child development theory or children's interests and concerns. A Chinese child who had great difficulty learning English and adjusting to the school situation was given a great deal of individual attention, and she gained considerable prestige when her father brought some Chinese food for the class to taste. Her own tranquillity increased as she learned English and especially when she tried later in the school semester to help a newly arrived Japanese child who spoke no English. A Greek boy whose mother spoke no English succeeded in bringing her to visit the classroom when parents were invited for a party, and his mother was willing thereafter to share some lovely recordings of Greek songs she treasured and demonstrate some Greek dances. Spanish-speaking children, while given intensive instruction in English, were encouraged to take pride in their own language, to teach the class Spanish vocabulary and forms of greeting, and to use their Spanish freely. The very large proportion of this program which gave children activity choices, with very imaginative forms of environmental structuring, guaranteed the teacher's ability to observe children, to respond to their needs and interests, to initiate activities likely to engage one or many children, and to maintain the flexibility needed for sensitive, responsive teaching.

ADDITIONAL CONTENT POSSIBILITIES

Many of the curricular designs in use for a long time can be updated by adding fresh content from the contemporary scene or by reviving excellent material formerly used.

Dewey-Mitchell content

John Dewey, one of America's most original thinkers and contributors to educational theory, developed very exciting programs for young children that became the prototypes for progressive education. Lucy Sprague Mitchell, whose work was inspired by Dewey, made substantial contributions to ideas about what and how young children could learn.

Progressive education continues to offer constructive content for children's learning.

In the Dewey-Mitchell approach, children's concerns were well integrated with bodies of knowledge at a level of learning congruent with young children's development, that is, pitched at a first-hand experiencing, observing, manipulating, and verbalizing level. The more recent American open classroom movement is in this class, but often with much less clarity about the use of bodies of knowledge and with more centrality to the child-initiated interest. Dewey and Mitchell recognized that the child needs to find his way to the meaningfulness of adult-shaped bodies of knowledge. Dewey hoped that if young children tried to grow cotton and to harvest it manually, they would discover the problems of cotton culture and why cotton took so long in man's history to become cheap and plentiful. Thus, instead of "telling" children that Eli Whitney's invention of the cotton gin in 1791 revolutionized cotton culture by making cotton infinitely cheaper, Dewey wanted the children to find this out through their own first-hand experience.[37]

Mitchell's geographic concepts. Similarly, Mitchell's genius in finding ways to make concepts accessible to young children, was motivated by a desire similar to Dewey's—to help children under-

37. John Dewey, *The Child and the Curriculum* (Chicago: University of Chicago Press, 1902), pp. 20–23.

stand some aspects of man's knowledge. Mitchell seemed never in doubt about *what* she wanted children to learn, only about how to help them understand and conceptualize it. When she used a tangerine to show the map problems of representing a three-dimensional sphere on a flat surface, it wasn't the children's interests she was pursuing but her own view of what children needed to learn. As the tangerine was peeled vertically and the peels spread on a flat surface, she demonstrated graphically how globular shapes have to be distorted in order to be represented as a map on a flat surface.[38] Neither Mitchell nor Dewey, it seems, would have ignored children's concerns or interests, but it probably did not occur to them that immature children could identify these better than mature, informed adults. It is questionable anyway whether any two adults would perceive children's needs in the same way. Personal filters exercise powerful distorting influences.

The thrust of progressive education was originally very intellectual, but this seemed to become increasingly diluted as more schools offered rather empty programs named "progressive education," "social education." In the United States this movement died out except in the nursery schools where it flourished unchallenged until the sixties. The progressive education movement, a slogan to most people, died before it ever developed fully in this country. Fortunately, the British experience was different, and the movement was able to grow and change as its conception became clearer.

Pratt's projects.   Program ideas for this approach can be found in Caroline Pratt's delightful little book, written in 1924.[39] She was very "project oriented," as Progressive educators tended to be, and every grade in her school had a specific project for which it was responsible. All served a real function in the school, such as running the supplies store or running the school bank for children's savings. The tasks were real, the interest of the children was generally high because of the usefulness of the function, and the learning opportunities flowed directly from the project tasks and functions. Children responsible for balancing bankbooks did not have to be told why arithmetic computation was essential. The practical uses of reading were equally apparent to all.

38. Lucy Sprague Mitchell, *Young Geographers* (New York: John Day, 1934).
39. Caroline Pratt, *Experimental Practice in City and Country Schools* (New York: Dutton, 1924).

Why do contemporary schools fail to use this approach instead of complaining that lunches become "instant garbage," motivation to learn to read is lacking, and teachers are primarily disciplinarians? Imagine how interested young children would be in nutrition if they had the responsibility for planning school lunch menus, figuring costs, learning nutritional balance, and food serving. Think of the reading, writing, math needs involved. How much children could learn about each other, based on food likes and dislikes, eating habits and the like. How much social responsibility and social action could develop from children's functions in this one area alone. Food is an obvious key to the study of children in other countries—what they eat, who provides the food, how it is grown, distributed, and prepared, how it is cooked, what fuel is used, and how food is stored. They will ask where they can buy such food and learn some new food tastes. The younger children will become more food tolerant through marketing, cooking, and eating experiences.

New curriculum proposals are regularly offered as concern shifts from one to another aspect of socialization and social learning needs of young children. The only useful caution to students is to continue to study and keep in touch with new emphases as they develop.

SUMMARY *Contemporary movements demand respect for the individual and for cultural pluralism, or for the equal valuing of all cultures. Hence, language, race, and ethnicity are important aspects of children's learning about themselves as persons, about their families, about other people, and to build self-pride.*

For studies about people, curriculum sources have included the concentric circle design which radiates outward from home and family, the structure of the disciplines approach with its spiral feature, the child development approach with its important impact on humaneness in schools, and process objectives with their current flowering in informal education. In effect, curriculum sources for young children, as for older children, have been sought in theories of how children develop and learn, in bodies of knowledge, and in broad social movements. All three sources are usually required to teach children in appropriate ways, to use content which is of interest and use to children, and to accommodate social needs. Content with process and relevance are advocated.

Creative teaching suggestions for children's learning may be found in broad content themes, child value concepts, a social action approach, moral development or social values themes, political socialization, career education, process objectives, and key concepts approaches, among others. Students are urged to read widely in the literature for suggestions and new ideas.

❦ EXERCISES FOR STUDENTS ❦❦❦❦❦❦❦❦❦❦❦❦❦❦❦❦❦❦❦

1. Select an *area of social learning* suitable to a group of children with whom you are working with some regularity in a field placement. Use a title for your selection, such as "transportation," "empathy for other children," or any other title that seems appropriate to you.

a. Choose two from among the approaches described in this chapter and write a series of brief outlines for developing this area of learning.

b. Contrast the two approaches you outlined to show how the activities and outcomes would be different.

c. Ask permission from your cooperating teacher to try out one of the two approaches—the one that seems most interesting to you— over a period of at least two or three weeks and keep a log of what actually happens.

d. Summarize your log in a brief report to your college supervisor, assessing your implementation of your project and specifying its strengths and its needs for improvement.

2. Select a content theme from Table 8.1 with goals that you think you would like to try out in a student teaching or field placement. Write an outline of how you might implement this content theme, specifying materials, activities, grouping of children, types of teaching strategies, sequence of activities, and expected outcomes. Note that the outcome may be process goals, end products, or both. Finally, indicate how you would assess the project.

3. Select two titles from the bibliography to this chapter, for their relevance to your field placement needs and write a report for your college instructor, including:

a. The major theme of each book.

b. Your selection of ideas from each book which you could implement or adapt in your field or student teaching experiences and detailed suggestions on how you could use these ideas.

c. A critique of each book, noting *omissions* of material you could have used as well as *inclusions* of helpful suggestions.

✤ EXERCISES FOR TEACHERS ✲✲✲✲✲✲✲✲✲✲✲✲✲✲✲✲✲✲

1. Select some teaching suggestions from this chapter that are different from your most recent program, and plan to implement these ideas during the school year with some continuity in theme, activities, or direction.

a. Acquire any materials needed, or make them with help from parents, volunteers, or school staff.

b. Plan broadly for the sequence of activities. Be flexible and change your plan whenever it makes sense, either to be responsive to the children's interests, to take advantage of unexpected resources on film, television, or in local occurrences, or from local people.

c. Keep a log and jot down brief items daily or weekly to identify the activities in progress and to note interest, extent of participation, use of materials, and quality of experiences.

d. Design an assessment procedure or instrument to determine the effects of your project, such as extent of *concepts* explored, *ways of thinking* about relationships, interest and participation, or usefulness in math and reading interest or in social skill development.

2. Plan with parents for home-school collaboration in fostering values of cultural pluralism in such projects as:

a. Parent visitations and participation in class cooking, eating, or costume-making experiences.

b. Borrowing recordings, artifacts, photographs, or other objects for children to share in the classroom to foster cultural pluralism values.

c. Classroom trips to home or community facilities where differences in culture can be identified and valued.

3. Develop a brief questionnaire on political knowledge and concepts to administer individually to the children you teach to ascertain their notions about such political figures as the current president, those presidents whose birthdays are celebrated on holidays, the governor, the mayor, policemen, or any others you care to include. Ask questions and probe answers nonjudgmentally, such as, "Can you tell me a little more about it?" Jot down exactly what each child tells you.

a. Based on your findings and readings, determine at what level of understanding you can communicate with the children about major political figures.

b. Plan some projects to develop children's concepts further, including such activities as clipping pictures of the president or mayor from newspapers, and featuring these pictures on a bulletin board, role playing or creative dramatization, or reading or telling stories about functions of political or community figures.

BIBLIOGRAPHY

Association for Childhood Education International. *Cooking and Eating with Children.* 3615 Wisconsin Ave. N. W., Washington D.C., 20016.

Bailey, Ronald W., and Saxe, Janet C. *Teaching Black: An Evaluation of Methods and Materials.* Stanford, Calif.: Multi-Ethnic Education Resources Center of Stanford University, 1971.

Baker, August. *The Black Experience in Children's Books.* New York: New York Public Library, 1971.

Banks, James A., and Grambs, Jean D., eds. *Black Self-Concepts: Implications for Education and Social Science.* New York: McGraw-Hill, 1972.

Banks, James A. *Teaching The Black Experience: Methods and Materials.* Belmont, Calif.: Fearon, 1970.

Berger, Evelyn, and Winters, Bonnie A. *Social Studies in the Open Classroom.* New York: Teachers College Press, 1973.

Books In Pre-School, A Guide to Selecting, Purchasing, and Using Children's Books. ERIC-NAEYC Publication In Early Childhood Education. Washington, D.C.: National Association For the Education of Young Children, n.d. (Or ED019993, ERIC Document Reproduction Service, 4936 Fairmont Ave., Bethesda, Md. 20014.)

Borland, David T., and Harris, Richard. "Preparing Career Education Specialists." *Journal of Teacher Education* #24 (Summer 1973): 93–96.

Bruner, Jerome. *The Process of Education.* Cambridge, Mass.: Harvard University Press, 1966.

Centre for Educational Research and Innovation (CERI). *The Nature of the Curriculum For the Eighties and Onwards.* Paris: Organisation for Economic Co-operation and Development (OECD), Publications, 2 rue Andre-Pascale, Paris 16e-No. 29.553, 1972.

Dewey, John. *The Child and the Curriculum.* Chicago: University of Chicago Press, 1902.

Dworkin, Martin S. *Dewey on Education Selections.* New York: Teachers College Press, 1959.

Elam, Stanley (Ed.). *Education And The Structure of Knowledge.* Chicago: Rand McNally, 1964.

Evans, Ellis D. *Contemporary Influences in Early Childhood Education.* New York: Holt, Rinehart and Winston, 1971.

Glancy, Barbara Jean. *Children's Interracial Fiction:* An Unselective Bibliography. Washington, D.C.: American Federation of Teachers 1969.

Hess, Robert D., and Torney, Judith V. *The Development of Political Attitudes in Children.* Chicago: Aldine, 1967.

Joyce, Bruce R. "Social Action for the Primary Schools." *Childhood Education* 46 (February 1970): 254–258.

Kindergarten Bilingual Resource Handbook. Fort Worth, Texas: The National Consortia for Bilingual Education, 6745A Calmont St., 1971.

Maccoby, Eleanor E., and Zellner, Miriam. *Experiments in Primary Education: Aspects of Project Follow Through.* New York: Harcourt Brace Jovanovich, 1970.

Mitchell, Lucy Sprague. *Young Geographers.* New York: John Day, 1934.

Moore, Bertha. "Adults Look at Children's Values." *Childhood Education* 32 (February 1956): 257–261.

The New York Public Library. *No Crystal Stair: A Bibliography of Black Literature.* New York City: The Library, 1971.

The New York Public Library. *The Black Experience in Children's Audio-visual Materials.* New York City: The Library, 1973.

The New York Public Library. *The Black Experience in Children's Books.* New York City: The Library, 1974.

Ottina, John R. "Career Education Is Alive and Well." *Journal of Teacher Education* 24 (Summer 1973): 84–92.

Parker, Ronald C. *The Preschool in Action: Exploring Early Childhood Programs.* Boston: Allyn and Bacon, 1972.

Piaget, Jean. *The Origins of Intelligence in Children.* New York: International Universities Press, 1952.

Ploghoft, Milton E., and Shuster, Albert H. *Social Science Education in the Elementary School.* Columbus, Ohio: Merrill, 1971.

Pratt, Caroline. *Experimental Practice in City and Country Schools.* New York: Dutton, 1924.

Robison, Helen, ed. *Precedents and Promise in the Curriculum Field.* New York: Teachers College Press, 1966.

Robison, Helen F., and Mukerji, Rose. *Concept and Language Development in a Kindergarten of Disadvantaged Children.* Cooperative Research Project S-320. Washington, D.C.: U.S. Department of Health, Education and Welfare, Office of Education, 1966.

Robison, Helen F., and Schwartz, Sydney L. *Learning at An Early Age.* Vol. 1. *A Programmed Text for Teachers.* Vol. 2. *A Curriculum for Young Children.* Englewood Cliffs, N. J.: Prentice-Hall, 1972.

Robison, Helen F., and Spodek, Bernard. *New Directions in the Kindergarten.* New York: Teachers College Press, 1965.

Salkey, Andrew, ed. *Breaklight: The Poetry of the Carribbean.* Garden City, N. Y.: Anchor, 1973.

Shaftel, Fanny R., and Shaftel, George. *Role-Playing for Social Values: Decision-making in the Social Studies.* Englewood Cliffs, N. J.: Prentice-Hall, 1967; and *Words and Action: Role-Playing Photo-Problems for Young Children.* New York: Holt, Rinehart and Winston, 1967.

Sondergaard, Arensa. "What a Child Values." *Childhood Education* 32 (February 1956): 255–256.

Weber, Evelyn. *Early Childhood Education: Perspectives on Change.* Worthington, Ohio: Charles Jones, 1970.

White, Doris, comp. "Multi-ethnic Books for Head Start Children, Part I: Black and Integrated Literature." Urbana, Ill.: ERIC Clearinghouse on Early Childhood Education and National Laboratory on Early Childhood Education, 1969.

Wiesniewski, Richard, ed. *Teaching about Life in the City.* Forty-second Yearbook. Washington, D.C.: National Council for the Social Studies, 1972.

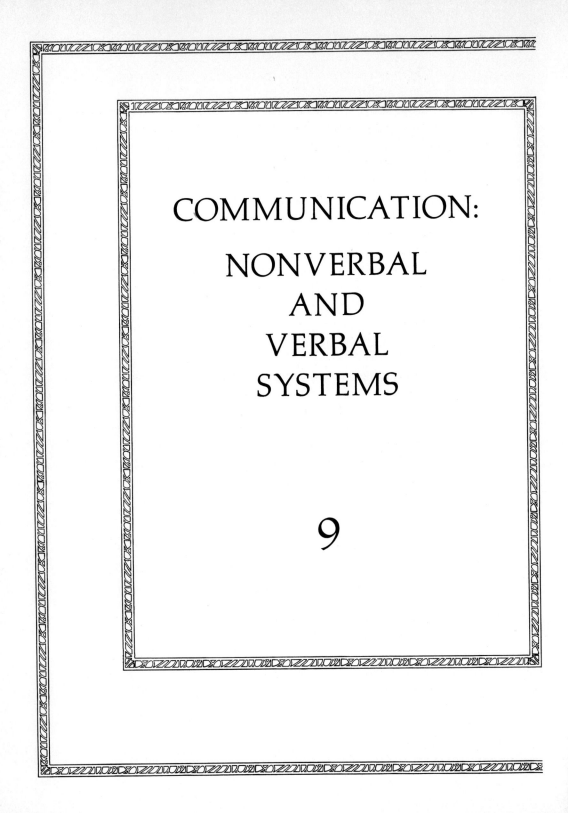

COMMUNICATION:

NONVERBAL
AND
VERBAL
SYSTEMS

9

Communication is both personal and social. The child sends and receives signals and messages. On the receiving end of communications, the child makes his own meanings out of what is perceived. When he sends out messages, the child's communications have to be understood by others or be responsive to the messages others have sent. To understand others, and to be understood, are two basic communication tasks of young children. A surprising amount of such communication occurs nonverbally. But while schools tend to constrain verbal interaction, they stress verbal achievement above all.

Two major teaching goals face the teacher of the young —guiding developmental communication patterns and identifying and planning to meet children's individual needs. A major contemporary issue which many teachers of young children have to deal with concerns when reading instruction should begin and by what means. Though not a new issue, it is an urgent one with various possible solutions.

Guiding children's progress in communication skills poses difficult dilemmas in group settings. Can children become creative and expressive on demand, yet suppress or turn these desirable traits off, also on demand? What forms of teaching are developmentally right for all children? How much deviance, in speech or language use, signals remediation needs? Should young children be required to talk in full sentences in school? Should dialect speakers learn to read in the dialects they know best? What about second-language learning in school? Who should learn "ESL" (English as a second language) or a language other than English? What are good choices from the overwhelming array of children's literature?

This chapter deals with the major teaching needs in guiding young children's communication development in group contexts. Teacher candidates should note that this is a lively field for contemporary research and that those who seem most informed are often hesitant to make prescriptions. Where the experts are in doubt, teaching seems best based on informed understandings of the questions, and knowledge of what the best contemporary practices seem to be.

NONVERBAL COMMUNICATION

Children express themselves eloquently in many nonverbal ways. Teachers who learn to read these nonverbal messages and expressions can usually relate to children with remarkable speed and appropriateness.

A child refuses to release his mother at the kindergarten door but he looks longingly at the block corner and the vehicle collection he really loves. His teacher reads his ambivalence, his straining to stay with, as well as to leave, his mother. She can say with assurance to his mother, "Stay for a few minutes. Billy will say good-bye as soon as he starts his block construction." And he does.

Another child is so tense she seems to shrink in size as she pulls her limbs and head toward her center, as though to present the smallest possible target to a hostile world. No words are needed to express the fear and anxiety shown by this tight posture. The teacher sits near her, while talking to a boy, gradually putting a protecting arm around her, gently stroking her hair and smiling reassuringly as though to say, "Just let anyone here try to hurt you!" Nonverbal messages are quickly exchanged here, and when the teacher rises to move away, she holds out her hand to the small girl who quickly grasps it and moves more confidently with her.

Physical communications—touching, gesturing, uttering sounds, moving—are more important than most teachers realize in establishing rapport and common understandings among young children. Teachers usually verbalize most messages, but they clarify meanings by pointing, acting out directions or expectations, and using facial expressions to convey feelings. Young children often convey more of their messages physically than verbally, even those children who are highly articulate. Here a child who is especially pleased with her clay product literally "jumps for joy." Another child's unhappiness streams his eyes, swells his face, reddens his skin, and jerks his muscles. Emotion is not well controlled by children but, over time, more of their feelings become verbalized. Physical cues do not disappear but are often accompanied by, and sometimes displaced by, talk. Slowly, the child reaches a more stable emotional state.

Teacher candidates can learn to identify and interpret their own "body language" by studying replays of videotapes of their physical behavior in teaching situations.[1] Such features as tone and quality of voice, pacing, extent of modulation or monotone pitch levels, as well as body and head gestures, movements and actions, facial expressions, and sounds emitted, all help to "read" the important verbal messages communicated.

Two young children were observed chatting away merrily with each other as they played with sand and water at the beachfront, and their communications seemed well received and understood until the observer discovered the children were speaking in different languages, one in French, the other in German. Their physical communications and voice usage made a common verbal language unnecessary.

One child returned from kindergarten class to report to her mother at home, "Miss Smith wore her brown dress and we all knew she was going to be mean today." This teacher would have been startled to find out how accurately her young pupils "read" her.

Projecting feelings

A group of teacher candidates were role playing brief tutoring scenes to illustrate how they worked with children. As one young man performed his role, one of his fellow students asked, "Do you always talk like that? Your voice had so little expression you used a monotone which practically *said* you weren't really interested in the child. No wonder you're complaining that nothing you do works!" The young man, somewhat annoyed, responded heatedly that he had tried many different methods before conceding failure. Another student said, "Now you sound concerned—your voice reflects feeling. Maybe you can practice as if telling this child you really do care, and maybe he will start to respond."

Great performances—without real feeling—are more likely to be witnessed on the stage than in the classroom. Young children are not

---

1. Charles Galway, "Nonverbal: The Language of Sensitivity", *Theory into Practice* 10 (October 1971). Ohio State University, College of Education, pp. 227–230; and *Teaching Is Communicating: Non-verbal Language in the Classroom*, AST Bulletin No. 29. (Washington, D.C.: Association for Student Teaching, affiliate of National Education Association, 1970).

deceived into thinking teachers care when this is not the case. But some teachers can learn to convey and project feelings of acceptance and caring better than they presently do.

LANGUAGE DEVELOPMENT IN CHILDREN

It is rare to find a nonspeaking child in a school setting, although it sometimes happens. Lack of speech is properly regarded as a danger signal. But first, the *fact* of lack of speech must be established. There are cases of delayed speech development for some very brilliant as well as some very retarded individuals. The lack of speech—a symptom— should not inevitably lead to diagnosis of retardation.

Most young children in group situations communicate capably with each other and with adults. Three-year-olds can construct simple sentences, with verbs, pronouns, adjectives, prepositions, and nouns. They don't always use whole sentences, and verb tenses and pronouns may be unreliable. They may also be confused by many words and say "tomorrow" when they mean yesterday. They can understand and act on far more speech than they can use, an observation which is true for almost any age group. That is, receptive language is always greater than productive language. Three-year-olds may be quite shy out of the home, and teachers and other nonfamily members seldom hear as much of the child's language as his family does. The family, with its secure familiarity, not only stimulates more child speech but also understands the child's imperfect and developing language better and faster than other people. Responding to the child more immediately and appropriately is one of the reasons for the family's ability to stimulate more child language production.

However, some families may respond too quickly to a child's needs thus making it unnecessary for him to verbalize them. If too many needs are anticipated, there may be too little speech production at home. In such a case, a group setting with a teacher and other children may be very beneficial in stimulating the child's speech production. Twins, who frequently find separation from each other almost unbear- able, may benefit from such separation for periods in the day when they have to communicate with others in more standard conventional language usage. Luria and la Yudovich, Soviet psychologists, described a case where a pair of twin boys, speaking only a private language in which they communicated with each other, were enrolled in a kindergarten.[2] Separating them in different classes stimulated rapid language development and, Luria adds, conceptual development as well, as evidenced in superior block building.

By age four, most children can tell a connected account of some recent experience and can carry out in sequence two simple directions.[3] Five-year-olds converse comfortably with others when they are familiar with the content and the vocabulary, and their language is usually quite understandable—barring some mispronunciations or occasional immature articulation. Verb tenses and pronoun use are often tentative or uncertain and plural forms may cause problems. Word and phrase repetition, often misdiagnosed as stuttering, is frequent as young children's thoughts seem to race ahead of their language fluency.

Expansion rather than correction

Cazden has cautioned teachers not to "correct" children's mismanagement of grammar or to "correct" dialect usage. She advocates, instead, "adding, enlarging, and refining."[4] Generally, she seems to say that children who hear a great deal of well-formed speech, with variety in sentence form and word use, have richer sources to draw upon as they develop their own language forms, and they may often correct their own immature syntax. There is still so much that is not known about children's language development that Cazden errs on the side of caution, urging teachers to avoid damaging the child's language development. For those children whose language development seems quite deviant, referral to specialists for assessment and diagnosis should certainly precede teacher planning for remediation.

Six-year-olds are expected to begin to learn to read in our schools and most of them seem to have the requisite language. Those who do not have the expected language skills too often are targeted for trau-

2. R. Luria and F. la Yudovich, *Speech and the Regulation of Mental Processes in the Child* (Baltimore, Md.: Penguin, 1971), pp. 39–72.

3. U.S. National Institute of Neurological Diseases and Stroke, National Institutes of Health, Public Health Services, U.S. Deparment of Health, Education and Welfare. *Learning to Talk* (Washington, D.C.: U.S. Government Printing Office, 1969).

4. Courtney Cazden, "Some Implications Of Research On Language Development For Pre-school Education," in *Early Education*, edited by Robert D. Hess and Roberta Meyer Bear (Chicago: Aldine, 1968), pp. 131–142, 139.

matic experiences instead of beneficial programs in language-rich settings.

Wide variation in children's vocabulary is clearly associated with their prior experiences at home and elsewhere. Television may seem to be a great instrument for vocabulary diffusion, yet its role in this respect is not yet clear.

TEACHING FOR LANGUAGE DEVELOPMENT

Vocabulary and comprehension are enriched by involving children in new experiences.

Children learn vocabulary words and meanings through experiences. The more active and involving the experiences, usually, the more meaningful the learnings become. Syntax and more complex grammatical constructions seem to develop as children hear a great deal of varied language structure. This is why selection of books for reading to children is so important, as well as children's spontaneous conversations with adults who present good language models. If children are *not* "corrected," or required to speak in full sentences, their language grows in maturity of form and content and words if they live or work in rich language atmospheres. Since a child may talk less when his speech is frequently corrected, other ways to stimulate language are preferred.

According to Chomsky, we learn language rules implicitly, and we follow these rules in our speech even though we may not be able to state them. She says that the young child is "creating his own sentences according to grammatical rules that he continually constructs and revises."[5] Viewing linguistic development as natural for the child, Chomsky suggests that, since six- to ten-year-olds are still learning complex language structures, this learning can be encouraged in school by stimulating experiences which are language rich. Interestingly, Chomsky speculates that wider reading of the more complex material to the child who cannot yet read, as well as wider reading by the child who can, might be especially useful for this linguistic development and learning.

Follow Through evaluations further support the teacher's role in improving young children's language usage through planned attention to individual needs.[6] The long-held view of the educational

5. Carol Chomsky, "Stages in Language Development and Reading Experience," *Harvard Educational Review* 42 (1972), pp. 1–33, 3.

6. Jane Stallings, "Relationships between Classroom Instructional Practices and Child Development" (paper presented to American Educational Research Association, 1975 Annual Meeting. Washington, D.C., April 1975).

importance of the teacher's role in language development is increasingly seen as a purposeful tool for achieving selected goals.

Listening experiences

Since meaningful listening experiences help children acquire more varied language, often, the best medium of instruction turns out to be good books, heard many times, in warm, close small groups. When sharing feelings and ideas about the stories heard, children often try to use newly heard forms of language. Teacher-told stories may be just as effective, providing the teacher is a good story-teller and does not oversimplify the language. Of course, the story has to be interesting to the children. Many good books suggest criteria for selection of books to read to children or to offer young readers. Some good sources are suggested in the bibliography of this chapter.

If teachers wish to *tell* stories, they are often puzzled as to what to tell stories about. Ask the children. They will tell you quickly, "Tell us about when you were little." Or, "Tell a story about me—about a little boy like me, and what he did." This simple formula will go far —tell stories about yourself and about the children. Use the children's names in the story; the younger the child, the less you need much else.

When this writer taught a three-year-old class, rest time turned out to be too turbulent to renew energies. A first remedy was to offer children cuddle toys with which to rest. Sometimes this became too active, with toy swapping, dramatic play with the toys, and active conversation. In despair one day, the story telling began. It was a bedtime story, told in such a quiet voice that the children fell silent in order to hear. The story mentioned each child by name, relating how he or she went to bed at home. The children waited breathlessly to hear their own names and listened carefully for repetitions. It was a very repetitious story about an imaginary child who, unlike all those present— they were named frequently—would not go to sleep at bedtime. The imaginary child, having been kissed good-night, called for a drink of water (unlike the list of all those present). Another drink of water. (Names again). And another drink of water. (Names again). And so on. The children obviously identified with this child who was so unwilling to say good-night and with the universal stratagems to prolong the process.

Four-year-olds would find such a simple story less absorbing. They like a little action, even some plot. They like a little danger, as long as it happens to someone else and everything comes out all right in the end (but the bad guy must get his just desserts). For fives and sixes, you need more content. Characters, locales, and story development are required. In fact, this age group would probably enjoy participating in the story development, helping to name characters and suggesting some of the appropriate action. Seven-year-olds enjoy hearing well-chosen stories and taking turns reading.

Purposeful listening.   In the classroom, occasional use of radio or television, with well-selected programs, sometimes provides just the kind of enriching language experiences desired. Student teachers should remember, however, that most children watch too much television at home. Therefore, personal language use by the teacher, in interesting, personally involving contexts where verbal and social interaction prevail, are needed to balance too much out-of-school passive listening.

Purposeful listening can be built into any areas of the curriculum.[7] Some possibilities are the following:

1. *Group-action story construction*
    a. For a group story to flow readily, it must be built on some mutual experiences. These can be a just-completed trip or a craft activity resulting in products which are made the focus of the story.
    b. The story should be quite impromptu and spontaneous, with the teacher chiefly helping the group to get the story started and to keep it flowing. The teacher might occasionally summarize the action to stimulate further narration.
    c. A tape recorder could be used to tape the entire story-telling effort. The tape itself might become a library addition for voluntary listening, where there are headsets available for children's listening choices.
    d. The teacher might analyze the tape for an assessment of the children's language use, noting syntax and vocabulary needs of some or all of the children. This assessment might be used to plan various types of practice activities.
2. *Listening for specific types of language*
    a. The teacher prepares a story to read or tape-records it for children's listening on headsets. Simple duplicated sheets, or boxes of objects, may be prepared to give children some way to demonstrate comprehension or language labels. For example, the dupli-

---

7. Harry A. Greene and Walter R. Petty, *Developing Language Skills In The Elementary School* (Boston: Allyn and Bacon, 1971), pp. 152–184; and Sam Duker, *Listening: Readings* (Metuchen, N. J.: Scarecrow, 1966).

cated sheets might have pictures of animals, with instructions to color each one a specified color. The end product offers the teacher a basis for assessing, and the child for practicing, ways to demonstrate listening results or needs.

b. Working with a collection of selected objects, for example, some items of doll furniture, a doll, and some miniature animals, the listening material might focus on terms of spatial relationship, such as "over," "under," "in front of," or "on top." The child's task, while listening to the story, is to arrange the objects in a box, following the spatial relationships described, such as, "The cat crawled *under* the bed. Please put the cat under the bed."

3. *Paper doll story action (or flannel cutouts)*

a. In this activity, the children re-create on the flannel board with flannel cutouts, or with paper dolls and paper cutouts, the action of a very repetitive narrative such as *The Gingerbread Boy*. The action of the children in manipulating the cutout figures on a board serves both to keep listening intense and to offer immediate feedback on their comprehension and language knowledge.

b. In a variation of this activity, two children work together with these materials, and they take turns making up the story and directing their partners in realizing the action. The listening in this version is likely to be very attentive as the children become completely absorbed in creating the story.

4. *Fill in the words.* Children are asked to help tell a story they have heard many times before by filling in the words that the teacher omits. This can be either live or tape recorded. If it is a taped story, it is better to ask two children to work together to help each other to remember the words.

5. *Listen before you move.* This is a game of following directions and focuses on specific language forms, such as color or number names or quantitative words (many, several, more, or less, for example), terms of spatial relationship or time sequences (first do this, then that, then that; or, before you get your coat from the cubbie, take out your rubbers or boots). The language forms may deal with the copula (forms of the verb "to be") or with irregular past tenses, such as "went" (to go) or any other selected language need. This is a particularly appropriate game to play just before dismissal or at major transition points in the program, such as clean-up time, when a great deal of action is necessarily in progress and is easily used for planned language exercises. A common focus is on color names, as when the teacher says, "All those children wearing something blue may get dressed to go out to play."

6. *Guess which object is missing.* In this game, a small group of children play, using a collection of about five or six objects. All children name the objects, together or in turn. One child turns his back and when he turns around, he has to name one object that another child has removed.

Language production

It is inherent in group situations that the children are constrained and limited in many ways, especially in keeping noise levels bearable. Hence, it is usually more effective to plan language production experiences in small groups to minimize constraints. Where informal procedures predominate, there is usually much more language production by more children.

Informal work and play experiences in small groups provide the most constructive language production experiences.

Most classrooms for young children feature insufficient language production. Considering the tremendously rapid verbal development that occurs in the early childhood years in word acquisition alone, it is obvious that much more spontaneous and natural language usage is required in order for children to try out new language and acquire fluency.

Teacher candidates might find it useful to compare different settings for young children for the purpose of estimating comparative opportunities for children's language production. Informal work and play periods provide the longest and most constructive kinds of language production experiences, because it is natural for children to talk while they interact with each other and with materials. Well-planned schedules, however, include conversational opportunities at all but a few selected points.

Speech development

Children's speech matures very rapidly during the early years, especially when group settings offer a great deal of natural conversational opportunities. The teacher's own speech is, of course, a very important model for the children.

Instead of oversimplifying their speech, teachers can speak naturally and clarify and give meaning to new words or to mature forms of syntax. Using new words or syntax in conjunction with the objects they represent, the actions they describe, or the situation or idea to which they refer are good ways to anchor them for children. For example, children learning to take care of an aquarium quickly learn "evaporation," "condensation," "female" and "male," "gravid." This is not to say that the child who identifies "condensation" correctly can also understand the process—that comes more gradually. When children in one four-year-old group complained to the teacher on a Monday morning that the fish were drinking up all the water in the tank, it was time to use the word "evaporation," and to illustrate the process more visibly by evaporating water from a chalkboard, from the children's hands, and from materials which children could manipulate directly.

Teachers generally expect to observe young children's speech development and to identify problems in this important function. Observations should seek to pinpoint lack of speech, hesitant or timorous speech, repetitive speech, speech which cannot be understood, and immaturities in articulation and in language structure. Many apparent speech problems dissolve upon closer observation. The child who never talks finally warms up to the group and becomes an incessant chatterbox. Shy children talk in one-to-one situations but not in group settings. The child who comes with baby talk that his parents cherish because it's so "cute" soon learns to use more standard speech in order to be understood by his peers. Immature speech forms gradually drop out as initial consonants become clearer and final consonants more differentiated. Telegraphic speech forms take on verbs and adjectives, and pronouns are sorted out and used more conventionally. Some children who seem to stutter as they hesitate, and repeat words, syllables, and phrases, begin to utter smoother speech with fewer tangles and explosive starts. But natural development may not cure all apparent problems.

It is often surprising to teacher candidates how very verbal young children are and how much speech they produce. While there is usually little difficulty in understanding children's communications, they sometimes take these forms:

"I don't got no milk."
"Dey knocked it down de doors 'n winders."
"I has one sister and a brudder."
"De apple no is jello."

Teachers should broaden their understanding of the uses of various dialects.

We can recognize the first and third sentences above as one of the vernacular dialects, illustrating the multiple negative in the first sentence, and the verb form typically used with the first person singular in such dialects. Teacher candidates should come to understand the nature of dialect, *not* as incorrect forms of language, but as variations or different forms of language, which is what a dialect is. If the child spoke "incorrect" English, any random mistakes are possible, as when one is speaking a poorly learned foreign language. In each dialect, the rules of syntax are uniform and well-developed but different from one dialect to another.[8]

The fourth sentence above is clearly from a child whose first language is not English, since this sentence structure does not occur in the English dialects. It was spoken by an Hispanic child who was using the Spanish placement of the negative before the verb and was pronouncing the y in yellow as it is pronounced in Puerto Rican Spanish. The second sentence is less clearly identifiable without further language samples.

Standard English, school English, and correct English are used interchangeably in this chapter to refer to the language patterns used by educated people and in books. In helping children to learn this language model, teachers must first determine how far from this objective any child's first language is—that is, whether school English is a foreign language to the child or an unfamiliar form of his native language. It is essential to refrain from denigrating a child's first language while teaching him school-preferred structures and sounds. While school English may be very different from the home or street forms the child already knows, there is a time and place for both.

Language flow of young children may sometimes be constricted by inappropriate requirements for too much silence, or "speak in complete sentences," or "speak only in English." Yet children are tremendously elastic in their responses to school situations, and most five-year-olds have very abundant language and almost-mature speech.[9] Apart from the more complex forms of syntax in English, by age six the vast majority of American children seem to be well developed in their native language. After six, children master more complex grammar while continuing to acquire new vocabulary.

But some young children have speech or language problems. Some stutter, and a few can scarcely be understood. On rare occasions, a child appears to produce no language at all.

A student teacher selected a child in her kindergarten placement, one who had not been observed to speak at all in school, for systematic observation. The child, a very active boy from a Spanish-speaking family, seemed to be fairly well accepted by the children in play and

8. William Labov, "The Non-Standard Negro Vernacular: Some Practical Suggestions," in *Position Papers from Language Education for The Disadvantaged.* Report No. 3, NDEA National Institute for Advanced Study in Teaching Disadvantaged Youth, June 1968.

9. Courtney Cazden, *Child Language Education* (New York: Holt, Rinehart & Winston, 1972).

in other situations. The student teacher tested the child informally for hearing and for comprehension of English and found, surprisingly, that neither seemed to be defective. The child responded sufficiently by gesture and in action to make clear he heard and understood various very specific verbal requests. When the child's older brother came by to pick him up one day, the student teacher asked the brother whether the child talked at home, and she received a very positive response in fluent English. When pressed to give examples of his brother's home speech, however, none could be elicited. It is far from clear why this child did not talk in school and how he got along as well as he did with his classmates without using speech. A medical or psychological workup was therefore recommended to find out whether, in fact, the child really could speak.

It happens frequently that the teacher is the first professional to have continuing opportunities to work with a child in a setting where his age-graded peers offer instant and recurrent examples of what is "normal" or "expected" for his developmental level. At home, parents tend to adjust to the unique personalities and day-to-day development of their children. On the other hand, parents, usually so close to their children that objective judgment is difficult, do have a wealth of detail to offer about their children's home behaviors. This detailed information is enormously helpful to the teacher. But a teacher is unlikely to receive such detail unless excellent relationships are maintained with home and community. A parent has to view a teacher as a mature, skillful, helping professional to feel free to discuss and share serious childhood problems. Yet many parents are glad to talk to teachers about their fears and anxieties concerning their children's development, about signs of homosexuality, retardation, sensory deficiency, or other worrisome problems.

A caution is in order about "normal" and "expected" development. The range of normality is wide. Some children carry infantile articulation through age seven or eight and without speech therapy eventually develop mature speech. Every variation is not a signal of abnormality. The more different the situations in which a teacher observes a child, the better base there is for fitting these observations together so as to view the child as a whole person who functions in his own unique ways. The new teacher should flag potential problems without assuming they are not developmental. Remediation is not usually required for developmental problems, because they signal growth in process. However, some parents prefer to seek specialist help, for their own peace of mind or because they really are perplexed about how to respond to developmental problems. Sometimes, special attention in the form of preventive or instructional efforts helps to maintain good expectations on everyone's part, warding off unnecessary anxiety.

Preventive efforts

In language development, preventive efforts are chiefly in the form of screening tests for hearing, vision, or other organic or functional problems. Teachers are often the first to notice and suggest such screening tests, to establish the nature of the problem.

In any school system where there are many children from non-English-speaking homes, the problem is usually to establish which language the young child knows best and whether he knows any English at all. Good language tests are hard to find, although given the present interest in determining children's dominant language, better tests may be available in the near future. Informal testing by the teacher is not difficult and often produces more information than formal testing by someone the child does not know.

In one kindergarten, when a student teacher found one little girl who appeared "dazed" and "tuned out," the student asked another child known to be fluent in Spanish as well as English to convey communications. This informal test quickly established that the girl was no more responsive to Spanish than to English communications. In another case, this technique worked beautifully and gave the teacher a good basis for beginning English instruction. Informal tests include unobtrusive observations of how the child communicates with other children, with which other children, and in which language. See Chapter 4 for an example of how a bilingual student teacher discovered a "nonspeaker" to be a fluent speaker of Spanish in a pre-kindergarten class, and who gradually involved the child in play and art activities with other children to advance her learning of English.

Screening tests, after the teacher's informal efforts to identify the problem, are best performed by medical and psychological specialists. Here, the school needs to be able to work in close collaboration with other institutions and professionals so that all work to the same purpose and support parent and child in every way possible.

Instructional efforts

Instructional efforts may be needed to help a child learn a second language or to develop either the first or second language, or both, to the vocabulary and syntactical level at which the child can best function. These are not properly termed remedial, since it is not a remedy the teacher can offer here, but initial, developmental forms of instruction. Teachers can plan instructional sequences for children on an individual basis, with drill-practice materials as well as informal, playful activities in which children will teach each other language at a pace that can probably not be duplicated by adults.

Some of the numerous drill-practice activities that will help the child advance his learning of standard English include the following:[10]

1. *Listening activities of many kinds.* Listening activities may be enhanced by the use of teacher-made kits of objects to be manipulated in some way and producing an end product the teacher may assess for progress. Pictures, books, flannel boards and cutouts, and many similar materials can be used. The following may also be used:
   a. Recording of songs in English; also songs in English with other first language versions.
   b. Radio and television broadcasts on appropriate content for the child.
   c. Cassettes, either commercially prepared to parallel popular trade books, such as the Weston Woods Spanish language versions of records or cassettes, or teacher-recorded, or child-recorded material.
   d. Language-master type of activities that coordinate sound, symbol, and picture symbols of various kinds.
   e. Reading to one or more children, either familiar or new stories, child-dictated stories or teacher-made stories, poetry, riddles, or nursery rhymes.
   f. Finger play songs, stories, chants, or action songs where the action illustrates the words meanings.
2. *Games*
   a. Activity cards of many kinds with picture or other cues
   b. Lotto-type games
   c. Games with playing cards or cards made by the teacher for the special language lessons planned
   d. Games with dice or spinners
   e. Many games with objects that offer vocabulary and syntax practice

10. James A. Smith, *Creative Teaching of the Language Arts in the Elementary School* (Boston: Allyn and Bacon, 1973), pp. 75–83; and Longacker, op. cit., p. 95.

3. *Action games.* These are often best because they are fun, totally involving, and require quick action responses to verbal directions, tending to speed up language learning. Examples:

a. In a small language-mixed group of children with space for movement, the group forms a circle. The teacher calls out verbal action signals such as "clap," or "jump twice." As soon as the game seems well understood, children take the lead one after another. Appropriate kinds of action might be march, skip, hop, skate, climb, swim, fly, bend, sit, fall down, chew, gallop, and stretch.

b. Similarly, terms of color, number, and other concepts can be taught in this game.

4. *Music and movement.* See Chapter 6 for additional suggestions for chant and movement possibilities.

a. Vary pitch and rhythm to distinguish sentence forms, such as positive and negative statements, contrasting, for example, "I have a cookie" with "I have no cookie" or "I don't have a cookie." Use a high monotone for one statement and a low monotone for its opposite. Divide a group into two groups with one group chanting the positive, the other the negative. Distribute cookies to those chanting the positive, and when these are eaten, switch statements after distributing cookies to the second group. Next, help the children develop more melodic chants.

b. Ask children to compose chants for action, and to teach these chants to each other with the appropriate actions.

5. *Constructions and craft projects.* Select projects which require children to ask questions and act on the answers—to follow instructions, to instruct others, or to evaluate their own products. If the children are grouped for these activities in mixed-language groups, good language progress often results. For example, to make a pinwheel or a paper basket, children might have to request the specific materials needed, choose colors of paper, and learn to verbalize the actions required in the construction in order to teach the process to others.

6. *Language labs.* Some work with language labs for fives, sixes, and sevens might speed up familiarity with some forms of English, giving the child the needed mastery over some poorly understood English forms. Where such material is available, the selection of the tapes must be closely adapted to the child's needs. Teachers can, with some assistance, produce lab-type of exercises with cassettes, adding the manipulative possibilities of flannel boards or collections of objects. This is a time-consuming effort, and teachers need assistance from other school staff or volunteers to produce these and accompanying slides and photographs when they are needed.

7. *Play.* Playful activities, either with the teacher or with English-dominant children, are often the most powerful language-learning experiences. Such forms of painless language learning may be used either with children learning standard English as a second dialect

or as a second language. It is important that these playful activities occur with great frequency and that the teacher monitor or guide them in regard to language needs. Puppet play has been found to be a delightful way to teach language. The dramatic play activities in the housekeeping area offer wide scope for selection of vocabulary needs or structures. Other playful activities include board games, block play with dramatization, and various constructive types of play.

BILINGUAL EDUCATION

Bilingual education has been controversial for a long time, both as to its usefulness and its content. English as a second language or teaching only one language, is often confused with bilingual education. Broadly speaking, it can be said that "the aim of bilingual education is to provide children with a sound opportunity to become fully literate and articulate in two languages and to impart a sensitivity to the cultures in which these languages evolved."[11] Sometimes, the term is applied to monolingual education, as when the language of instruction is not English. It is not surprising that there is so much misunderstanding and controversy about bilingual education, when you consider the enormous problems public schools have to resolve, to feature two languages equally. It is no wonder that the instructional system tends to slide over entirely to one or the other language or to treat one of the two languages as peripheral.

Many writers point out that language decisions really hinge upon whether the school philosophy is primarily assimilationist or culturally pluralist. If the school philosophy is assimilationist, its goals are clear —the child is to become a fluent English speaker and reader and the maintenance of his first language is no concern of the school.[12] This was the prevailing philosophy in American schools for a long time and is still the dominant one. However, the concept of cultural pluralism, as applied to school languages, has been developing for some time and acquiring increasing support among various groups in the community.

Kjolseth, among others, points out that most bilingual programs in the United States are assimilationist and encourage the loss of the

11. Ellis Evans, *Contemporary Influences in Early Childhood Education*, 2d ed. (New York: Holt, Rinehart & Winston, 1975), pp. 170–173.
12. Ibid, p. 171.

non-English mother tongue.[13] He, however, stresses encouragement of children to switch language usage in different settings and to maintain both languages. Problems in French-speaking Canada exemplify the great difficulties of language maintenance if one of the languages enjoys economic or cultural superiority, usually both.

It is important for teacher candidates to understand that linguistic relativity means the equal validity or value of all language and dialect systems.[14] Longacker stresses that all human groups have language; no language is any better than any other; all languages are constantly changing; and language changes are neither good nor bad—they just are![15] While each language community in the United States presents a different situation with its own history and current problems, the question of philosophy is the same for all.

There are both value and legal questions. For some groups, the question is primarily one of value—how much are the parents and the community groups willing to press for bilingualism when the children are demonstrably successful in school using English? The legal questions chiefly emerge when the non-English-speaking children are visibly unsuccessful in schools where English is used. Problems today are more noticeable for indigenous Indians and for the various Hispanic groups from Puerto Rico, Mexico, Cuba, and Latin America. But serious problems also exist for many Chinese children, for small groups of other Oriental language-speaking children and for small groups who speak French (chiefly Haitian), Greek, Portuguese, or Italian, for example.

The courts are moving toward legal interpretations which require rapid responses of school systems to the needs of children who do not speak English. In Lau vs. Nichols, the United States District Court held in 1974 that schools receiving federal funds must provide special remedial aid to their non-English-speaking children.[16] There seems to be solid ground for working on the assumption that the courts expect public schools to find ways to teach children English. Teaching chil-

13. Rolf Kjolseth, "Bilingual Education Programs in the United States: For Assimilation or Pluralism?" in *Bilingualism in the Southwest,* edited by Paul R. Turner (Tucson: Arizona Universities Press, 1973), p. 3.

14. Roger D. Abrahams and Rudolph C. Troike, eds., *Language and Cultural Diversity in American Education* (Englewood Cliffs, N. J.: Prentice-Hall, 1972), p. 93.

15. Ronald W. Longacker. "An Initial Look at Language", in *Language and Cultural Diversity in American Education,* edited by Roger D. Abrahams and Rudolph Troike, pp. 95–100, p. 95.

16. American Jewish Congress, Commission on Law and Social Action and Urban Affairs, "The Civil Rights and Civil Liberties Decisions of the United States Supreme Court for the 1973–74 Term" (New York: The Congress, undated).

dren English, however, with special forms of instruction tends to approach bilingual education. The courts clearly indicated that something more or different was required for non-English-speaking children than the methods which had apparently failed.

Pros and cons of bilingual education

Many arguments are presented advocating and opposing bilingual education in the schools.

There are positions for and against multilanguage instruction in schools. For children who live in cultural groups which are equivalent to enclaves of a foreign language, as in sections of cities such as Los Angeles, Albuquerque, San Antonio, New York City, and San Francisco, teachers find it difficult to teach English effectively in school when children do not speak English at all outside of school. Teachers claim that children lack English-speaking role models in the home and community and lack the motivation or opportunity to develop adequate English fluency. Often, teachers feel they are pitting school against home by demanding practice in speaking English and in trying to suppress the child's use of his only functional language.

Is it better for a child to learn arithmetic in Spanish than to fail to learn it because he does not understand English? How will we achieve success in teaching English as a second language if the child actually learns substantive content and reading in Spanish? How many different languages can any one school cope with efficiently from the point of view of staffing and costs? And what about the many teachers, themselves first-, second-, or third-generation members of families that emigrated to the United States, who are certain that since their families succeeded in learning English and becoming successful in an English-speaking world so can non-English-speaking groups today.

Arguments for bilingual education

In favor of bilingual-bicultural education there are such arguments as these:

1. It makes possible immediate learning to read and learning substantive content without long delays required for achieving fluency in English.
2. It establishes the success attitudes which motivate children to work and learn in school.

3. It eases the child's adjustment to the strangeness of the English-language cultural expectations.

4. It is a powerful deterrent to dropping out of school—nothing succeeds like success and the expectations of continuing success. Children who stay in school and achieve well are most likely to become productive and contributing members of our society.

5. It helps to maintain children's and families' self-valuing and feelings of competency when language barriers are removed from schools.

6. It keeps more options open for the children who, if they truly become bilingual, may have the best of both worlds by being able to function in the communities of both language groups. Since many Puerto Rican families, for example, return to the island from the mainland, when jobs decline here, bilingual-bicultural education is probably the most efficient way to help them maintain their abilities to function well in either area.

7. It embodies a view of modern society as multicultural and multilingual with the goal of preserving and valuing all language-cultural groups and of educating as many children as possible to be at least bilingual and respectful and informed about the cultural groups in the community.

8. It is based on some research which indicates that children conceptualize better in the first language and that bilingual education stimulates more flexibility in conceptualization.[17]

9. It is well established that young children have rapid language acquisition in appropriate settings and pick up second languages readily.

10. Contemporary historical research has challenged the assertions that most immigrant groups did well in school in the past.[18] Instead, the historians are finding that failure rates of non-English-speaking children have always been high.

Arguments against bilingual education

In opposition to bilingual education are such arguments as these:

1. If you teach children to read and they learn substantive content in their first language when it is not English, they will never be able, or have the opportunity, to become equally fluent in English.

17. Elizabeth Peal and Wallace E. Lambert, "The Relation of Bilingualism to Intelligence" (Washington, D.C.: The Psychological Association, 1962).
18. David K. Cohen, "Immigrants and the Schools," *Review of Educational Research* 40 (February 1970), pp. 13–29.

2. This is an English-speaking country, and our schools should teach only in English.

3. English is so superior to any other language for vocational reasons that all efforts should be directed to English learning, without wasting resources on first-language maintenance.

4. Staffing and administering bilingual education is not feasible.

5. If we want our children to learn foreign languages, they can study them in high school and college as many do now.

6. Bilingual teaching will fail to prepare children for higher education and good jobs in the United States.

The single most cogent reason for some forms of bilingual education seems to this writer to be the great failure of our schools to teach English, using only the English language, to the various non-English-speaking children in our country. The poor school performance of these groups requires willingness to change methods and to introduce some more imaginative and powerful ways to help these children succeed.

DIALECTS OF ENGLISH

Much is heard about "standards." American children, one hears, should speak correct English, yet many different dialects of English are spoken throughout our country. Are they all "incorrect" except one? The linguists are helping us to understand that everyone talks dialect, that some people know and use more dialects than others, and that the real problem is not eliminating dialects but matching the dialect to the occasion.[19] Dictionaries define dialects as varieties of language shared by groups of people who are distinctive socially or geographically. In addition, dialects are said to differ from each other in phonology, or sound patterns, as well as in grammar and vocabulary.

Think how stiff and unapproachable you would sound if you talked in the formal dialect known as standard English all of the time. This might be appropriate for an oral presentation to a learned professional society meeting, but it's hardly the way to talk on the telephone to family or close friends. On the other hand, if you only know a vernacular dialect, this would not be appropriate for the formal pre-

19. William Labov, *Language in The Inner City* (Philadelphia: University of Pennsylvania Press, 1972).

sentation suggested above. There is a time and a place for different dialects.

There is a substantial body of opinion among sociolinguists that all human feelings and ideas can be expressed in every dialect and every language. Among the dissenters are those who claim superiority for standard dialects and even the superiority of some languages for certain purposes. Eskimo, for example, is the language with the most differentiated words to describe snow in its various aspects. In the same vein, French might be regarded as a superior language for cooking and English for technological vocabulary. Yet language groups have always borrowed from each other without hesitation. Note the many English and American words that the French have introduced into their language, and the many foreign words in ours.

Need for standard English

I think that school *is* the appropriate place to model, practice, and use more of the standard dialects in order that all children become well acquainted with them. Since this is the language of literature and of textbook and scholarly writings, children who fail to learn the standard dialect have unnecessary limits on their learning potential and their vocational choices. As in bilingual education, however, the standard dialect should not be the only one the children are required to use in school. Nor should children be made to feel that their own dialects are "inferior." Instead, children can understand that various dialects have their uses for different functions.

As to "correct" English, we all know how rapidly yesterday's slang either disappears completely or becomes tomorrow's "correct" English.[20] Language is dynamic and changing because it reflects actual usage. New imagery and life experiences are inevitably reflected in new phrasing. The drug culture in the sixties contributed many popular new words and phrases such as "hippie," "turned on," "with it," "mind-blowing" and many others, language which generalized from specific drug-related experiences to wider usage unrelated to the drug culture.

The growing women's liberation movement is having a profound

20. Hallet Garth, *Wittgenstein's Definition of Meaning as Use* (New York: Fordham University Press, 1967), pp. 9–10.

effect on the English language as people become sensitive to the endless ways in which the language reflects male superiority. Whether or not one likes words such as "chairperson" or other attempts to change sex-specific to sex-neutral terminology, the language will probably never be the same. Some changes will be accepted by all and some ultimately rejected as awkward and changed in other ways. Similarly, English usage is accepting changed terminology which reflects minority groups' self-definition as it rejects older words associated with prejudice, such as the change from "colored" or "Negro" to "black people." There is nothing sacred about language. People agree on usage and ultimately people agree to change it. The only unchanged languages are dead ones such as ancient Latin or ancient Greek. Despite the changing and dynamic nature of language, at any one time there is also fair agreement on "standard" dialect because this is the form preferred by well-educated people. Yet dictionaries and experts will continue to differ on many points because language is always in the process of changing.

Arguments against writing nonstandard English

In attempting to "meet children where they are," some linguists have advocated a language experience approach to reading which starts with writing down the child's own dialect. This is based on the notion that written words represent speech, or is "talk written down." Others dispute the idea that we write as we talk. Writing—a slower, more gradually learned skill—is necessarily a clumsier, more formal, rule-governed activity which lacks several important characteristics of speech, notably pitch, rhythm, and stress. A written sentence may mean different things depending upon stress, as in the game of shifting stress across the words to change the meaning of such sentences as:

What *am I doing now?*
What am I *doing now?*
What am I *doing now?*
What am I doing now?
What am I doing now?

Speech is often couched to tease, to challenge, to carry double or ironic meanings, that is, to say the opposite or something quite different from the literal message of the words. If writing is not really speech written down but a different type of symbolic representation, does this argue for teaching writing in standard English, rather than other dialects, to facilitate reading instruction?

This writer leans to this view because if children are learning a new symbol system anyway, and they learn it in the standard form, they can readily equate it with the dialect they know since dialects tend to be far more alike than different. At the same time, they are learning writing usage as generally found in books and written material.

This procedure would seem more efficient and would have long-range benefits. Written nonstandard dialect that is *not* to be found in books has to be unlearned; this is a major argument against its use. Another problem with using the child's own dialect to teach written language forms is that many children can manage more than one dialect such as both a home and a street dialect. Which one should be used in writing? In addition, in a class with several different dialects, it seems unreasonable to expect any one teacher to be competent to handle them all well.

When speaking, one chooses dialects for functional use. There seems to be no functional use for nonstandard written English.

WHY NOT TEACH CHILDREN GRAMMAR?

"Why don't they teach grammar anymore?" is a frequent complaint of college professors outside of the English department. It is also a complaint frequently voiced by parents who deplore their children's awkward written work. It may be that effective ways of teaching graceful and communicative forms of writing with generally accepted rules of syntax and spelling will develop. Meanwhile, it has been demonstrated that teaching "grammar" directly does not necessarily result in learning and using it.

Good grammar is the result of continual exposure to good learning experiences in language.

Good grammar seems to be an end product of good language experiences. Children who read a great deal or are read to, and who hear a great deal of "educated" English speech, seem to write better than those who do not have such experiences. Good writing, on the other hand, can only develop out of frequent writing experiences.

If you were to tape-record spontaneous mother-child conversations in different socioeconomic groups, the differences in language use would be startling. The four-year-old in the economically more advantaged family is likely to be heard using remarkably complex sentence structures—as does her mother—with a large and relatively sophisticated vocabulary. Children's speech reflects that of the adults in the family and the ways they respond to the child's verbalizations, the mother particularly. According to Evans, language development can be defined, broadly, as "a progressive increase in the quantity, range, and complexity of both receptive (understandings) and expressive (producing) language."[21] On this basis, children from upper socioeconomic backgrounds seem much further advanced than their peers from poorer homes in abundance of language and in the varieties of structures and words used, especially in the standard English dialect.

Behaviorist instruction

However, there are several different points of view about language development, especially about how much the teacher can change language by training or guidance. The strong emphasis upon tightly structured language training, offered by Engelmann in the Distar program, has been very controversial among early childhood educators. The Distar program uses training procedures similar to those frequently used in teaching adults foreign languages and known as pattern drill.[22] A rote, brisk teacher and small group dialogue is completely programmed as a major teaching strategy, with teacher reciting and children echoing (but only on sharp signals from the teacher). Thoroughly behaviorist in strategy, reinforcement procedures are built in to reward both behavior and correct answers. Feedback is continually provided. Children not only know immediately whether they are giving correct answers and performing in acceptable behaviors but are also "corrected" at once. Teachers have no part in curriculum selection, construction, or adaptation in this program. Among teachers, supervisors, and community groups who advocate this approach, an important advantage cited is its specificity, in effect programming the teacher so that all instructional decisions are specified in the materials.

21. Evans, op. cit., p. 140.
22. S. Engelmann, J. Osborn, and T. Englemann, *Distar Language Program* (Chicago: Science Research Associates, 1972).

Developmental instruction

Among the pros and cons of a pattern-drill type of program behaviorally implemented, it seems most vulnerable in its antitheoretical base and its rigidity. No theory of language development supports it.

Cazden, who cautiously reminds us that little is yet known about natural language development, supports theorists who view such development not primarily as an imitative activity but more as a rule-making, hypothesis-testing procedure.[23] When a child hears much complex language, for example, he is usually unable to duplicate it. Instead, he approximates it—takes a shot at it based on a somewhat erroneous impression of what he heard. But the adult hears the child's approximation and responds to it. The adult may actually correct the child and ask the child to try to repeat it correctly. More often, adults simply restate their own utterance. This gives the child additional hearings of the new structure, much like hearing a new piece of music several times, after which the melodies begin to emerge and one can even sing them after several hearings. Thus, the child gradually compares what he says with what he hears as adults help him to do so, but the child is, after all, the one who has to be able to understand the structure enough to reconstruct it when speaking. In many ways this view is similar to Piaget's theory of cognitive development in that the child does not and cannot imitate adults but *constructs* his own conceptions, tries them out, changes them as he understands them better, and gradually refines them in a more mature mold.

Ambiguity of research on language arts

Research produces ambiguous results on most school-based samples of language arts programs because so many variables are uncontrolled. In addition, if only the "survivors" in the program are assessed, results are based only on those who succeeded. It might be an interesting assessment, in comparing different language and reading programs, to try to determine relative failure rates. Failures may be due largely to heavy absentee rates—the more sequential and rigid the program, the more difficult it can be for children whose attendance is sporadic or whose mobility is high. Many programs founder on high turnover rates among the children. But failures may also be due to boredom of

23. Cazden (1968), op. cit., pp. 134–135.

children to dull, repetitive programs or lack of teacher flexibility to meet the needs of different children in the group. Teachers who deplore rigidity of materials and approach must necessarily demonstrate skills in flexible forms of individualizing creative ways to help children make rapid progress in language development.

Strengths and problems of language experience approach

The language experience approach to language arts development is widely used with young children, both for preschool and for primary grades. This approach offers a very natural way to build on children's many expressive and cognitive activities to advance verbalization skills. Children play very active roles in personalizing meanings and finding ways to express them. Many teachers like this approach for its flexibility, creative opportunities, individualization, and open endedness. Critics tend to point to its lack of systematic development, undefined goals, and often the lack of visible end products. This approach puts a large burden on the teacher to carry out the varieties of activities which are supposed to characterize the method, to individualize activities in flexible ways, and to accommodate to the many different needs and skills in the group. Yet this approach is an important one if used expertly.

Language experience as a reading approach is favored by this writer, not only because of its flexibility and adaptability to the needs of different children, but also because it flows so naturally from language production and reception to symbols and writing and reading. The "pencil kids" like to copy words on paper, and once they have written something, they want to read it.[24] In their infectious love of writing, such children often teach their peers as well as themselves. Sylvia Ashton-Warner depended upon children's teaching each other sight words, as a major way for them to acquire an initial sight vocabulary.[25] Yet the teacher can also be the one to write all the "organic" sight words demanded by children who cannot yet control a pencil but who also wish to "own" some words.

I suggest, therefore, that new teachers collect a large repertoire of activities for the language experience approach from the many writers who have contributed to the development of this method and to be

---

24. R. Van Allen, "The Write Way To Read," *Elementary English* Vol. XIX, (May 1967), pp. 480–485, 491.
25. Sylvia Ashton-Warner, *Teacher* (New York: Bantam, 1963).

ready to match child and activity as experience and results indicate.[26] With younger children, teachers should expect to offer mostly playful, involving, and very active experiences—the kind that seem to demand communication and conversation. Caring for animals or working with water, sand, and clay are very high on the list for such involving-communicating experiences. There are countless others and many ways to build in or integrate any specific language skill needed or desired. However, since no one reading approach has yet been found superior for all children, teachers should also be able to use flexibly any features of phonic, linguistic, or sight word approaches which seem useful at any time. Phonics games well-timed, for interested children in the five to seven age range contribute to independence in word attack skills.

PROBLEMS WITH REQUIRING EARLY LITERACY

It seems to the writer that too many children are being pressured far too early to become literate. Pressuring children to learn to read is always risky. Helping them find some plausible reasons to learn to read seems more reliable, over the long pull, than pressure.

It is difficult to understand why four-year-olds should be made to sit still to learn phonics. How can such fragmented, unmotivated learning become meaningful and enjoyable to the young child? Sometimes parents or community leaders pressure the school and the teachers for early reading instruction, hoping to inoculate the children against later reading failure. They feel that the sooner the child is *instructed* in reading, the greater his chances will be to negotiate schooling successfully. Here again, research results cannot support this belief.

Teaching reading too soon

It seems essential to restore some sanity to the reading component in early childhood programs. Four-year-olds who are feeling this pressure for early literacy are the very ones who most need the language de-

26. Russell G. Stauffer, *The Language Experience Approach to Teaching Reading* (New York: Harper, 1970); and Doris Lee and R. V. Allen, *Learning to Read through Experience* (New York: Appleton-Century-Crofts, 2d ed., 1963).

velopment—in speech reception and production in systematic school contexts—in order to acquire the motivation and skills which seem to be associated with successful reading instruction. So many psychological correlates of reading instruction are inappropriate for young children that it seems inconceivable that those who insist upon such early reading instruction are not defensive or tentative in their advocacy.

Some children teach themselves to read, at three, four, or five. These are few and far between. Others may demand reading instruction from an older sibling or parent although not, of course, in any rigid and predetermined way. It cannot be argued from such exceptional cases that every child from age three must be required to be taught to read. Self-instruction or requested instruction is a far cry from *imposed* instruction. The play activities of young children have never been replaced by any other learning activity of the same power. Should children only play in school, parents ask? It does not follow that all components of the curriculum must have the same goals and outcomes. But it does follow that, when we deprive a child of his spontaneous and personal ways of learning and constructing meaningfulness, there must be justifiable reasons. It is difficult to see such justification in the requirements of early reading curricula.

Beginning reading without pressure

In school, children are likely to choose many activities which might be regarded as initial reading exercises or beginning learnings. Such activities include a great deal of story reading by the teacher, story telling by teacher and children, browsing in books and "reading" pictures, dictating stories, developing dialogues with puppets, or creative dramatizations. Other activities include playing with flannel board and flannel cutouts to reenact a story or to compose one, making calendars and booklets, and playing with alphabet letters of sandpaper, felt, paper, or wood, sometimes matching these to one's name card or other words. Also included are paper and pencil activities of the children's choice, for instance, to draw pictures or to write about them. Where no pressures are placed on children and they are free to choose among many attractive activities, the children often make surprising progress in early reading skills. But it must be remembered that these activities are not more important to the child's total development than

dramatic play, painting, dancing and singing, discovery-type of activities, and games and trips. Balance and variety and choice are the major requirements of good programming for children.

Teacher leadership on reading instruction

As befits well-prepared professionals, teachers should expect to take leadership roles in communicating to parents and with community groups the reasons for the good programs they develop and the reasons to avoid unbalanced, inappropriate types of programs. Teacher collaboration with fellow teachers, as well as with administrative and supervisory staffs and related professionals in medical, psychological, and social work fields, may help to convince parents and other community groups that their children's best interests are indeed being furthered in school.

Reading is surely among the greatest pleasures available to all. Long-range goals to produce educated people who love to read must not be defeated by early regimentation and inappropriate forms of reading instruction for the very young.

CHILDREN'S LITERATURE

A major point stressed in this chapter has been that reading good books to children, frequently in cosy, high-attention settings, is one of the most powerful techniques available to teachers and parents for children's language development. It follows that student teachers must prepare for such reading by acquiring a sound knowledge of the available children's literature, criteria for selecting books, and effective reading skills.

Skills in reading to children

Reading skills are not difficult to acquire for those who like children and books—a very happy combination! If students have access to a module on reading stories, they can quickly reach a high level of skill without much assistance. Increasingly popular, modules are written, packaged units of instruction usually containing specific behavioral goals, enabling activities—such as readings in books or screening films or filmstrips or use of other audio-visual materials—and self-evaluation procedures and sometimes using videotaped teaching samples. As a result of completing such a module on reading stories to children, one student teacher reported in her log that early in her kindergarten placement she was able to cope successfully with a large new group of children through the use of story reading. Skills featured in such modules would include eye contact with children, varied use of voice with changes in pitch, stress and rhythm, ways of involving children in the story, and coping with distractions. Successful reading performance also deals with showing the pictures so that the children can see them and you can still read the text and stimulating discussions after the story or sometimes during the reading. A videotaped self-assessment, with a checklist of skills, enables the student to identify further practice needs or to feel competent in this important teaching function.

Children's book sources

Getting to know the field of children's literature takes far more time. (An exercise at the end of this chapter suggests a way to begin.) Classes for young children usually have some book collections, though school library collections are larger. Finally, there are book stores and the public libraries, especially the latter, for comprehensive collections. Professional journals—*Young Children, Childhood Education, Instructor, Grade Teacher*—and many other periodicals carry children's book reviews regularly. Librarians' reviews are usually very helpful.

The selection of appropriate children's books is important for furthering children's learning.

To become knowledgeable about children's books, it is necessary to browse through many of them, reading them as often as possible in group settings for children. If one is fortunate enough to be a member of a family with young children, frequent reading to them out of many different books is ideal skill practice in book selection. Experience with children and books builds sure knowledge of suitability of style, vocabulary level, and content for specific children. An important outcome of this experience is usually an appreciation of the enduring values in children's literature and a firm basis for rejection of books that are badly written, talk down to children, treat serious problems falsely, or that use imagery that is too remote from young children's understandings.

Criteria for selecting children's books

How do you select books for children? Criteria are plentiful, are frequently cited, and include such features as:

    Poetic or literary language
    Characters with whom children can identify
    Action that children find either familiar or imagination stirring
    Fantasy of many kinds
    Realistic situations of many kinds
    Humor
    Informational material
    Therapeutic ("bibliotherapy")
    Nonsexist
    Nonstereotyped as to race or culture
    Featuring universal needs or emotions

Contemporary in imagery
Beauty of illustrations and pictures
Developmentally appropriate
Dramatic elements[27]

Arbuthnot suggests criteria relating to children's insights into their own lives or other lives, interest-holding, unforgettable characters, humor, and other features.[28]

Children's humor.   These criteria suggest attributes of books of various kinds. Books that are humorous are always well received by young children, but the humor must not be of a sophisticated adult variety. Children's humor is broader, more obvious, quick to seize upon what they know that the characters don't. A child dearly loves to correct an error which a character in the story makes. Incongruity can be very funny to a child, but only when he is familiar with the material. Remember how much of the world is not yet accessible or understandable to a young child; much incongruity is over his head. Irony is also difficult for the young. *Harry the Dirty Dog* is so funny to children because they know all along that the dirty dog is Harry, but his family is unable to tell who he is until they bathe him.

Memorable language.   The language of the story is surely one of its most important criteria. It should not be too simple or too mature, but it can and should be more complex than the language the children have already developed. New words, well developed in context, are quickly picked up by the avid listeners, and the complex sentence structures become targets they approach in one way or another. One child will be intrigued with the notion of "a soft grey fog," while others will roar at "millions and millions of cats." The Milne poems and Pooh stories entrance the young and old with charming characters, delightful imagery, and memorable language.

Some books remain high on the list for their literary qualities, such as Kipling's *The Elephant's Child* and *Just So Stories* and Wanda Gag's *Millions of Cats.* Kipling's "great grey green Limpopo River" rolls

27. Joan Fassler, "Children's Literature and Early Childhood Separation Experiences," *Young Children* 29 (July 1974), pp. 311–323; L. B. Jacobs et al, *Using Literature with Young Children* (New York: Teachers College Press, 1965); and Nancy Larrick, *A Teacher's Guide to Children's Books* (Columbus, Ohio: Charles E. Merrill, 1960).
28. May Hill Arbuthnot, *Children and Books*, 3rd ed (Glenview, Ill.: Scott, Foresman, 1964), p. 19.

around the tongue every time—the repetition of this phrase is eagerly awaited, and children pick it up and supply it when the teacher pauses. But new favorites come along every year. *The New York Sunday Times* prints an annual children's book review that will help to sort out some of the many new titles worth reading.

Fantasy for children.   Lucy Sprague Mitchell tried to anchor children's stories in the familiar content of their everyday lives. In her *Here and Now Story Book*, she urged families and teachers to avoid fantasy and fairy tales because she felt young children were usually struggling to understand reality and generally found it difficult to separate the real from the imagined.[29] At the time Mitchell was writing, stories for children were overwhelmingly of the fairy tale and fantasy genre. Her influence on early childhood education was so profound that, until very recently, early childhood teachers tended to avoid books that were not reality oriented.

It is interesting to see a swing at least part way to the fantasy world, as with such stories as Maurice Sendak's *In The Night Kitchen*. Many teachers are still wary of fantasies which might stimulate children's fears—of the dark, of being lost, or of losing a parent's love. Some teachers choose to read fantasy stories because they think the story helps the child to deal with his often unexpressed fears by talking about them and finding out that other children have the same or similar ones and that such fears, according to adults, are groundless. Student teachers might carefully observe how children respond to a story which seems to concretize a child's fear of the dark, as *In The Night Kitchen* does. Is there relief because the fantasy is exploded as a fantasy, or do some children still seem anxious and confused?

Nonracist treatment.   Stories which treat black children casually and deal with their feelings in insightful ways are good finds. *Peter's Chair*, *What Mary Jo Shared*, *Snowy Day*, and *Abby* are some fine choices that deal with life multiracially. Other good stories dealing with nonwhite families include *The Rice Bowl Pet*, *Good Boy, Bad Boy*, *When the Moon Is New*, and *Red Fox and His Canoe*. Fortunately, there are many others.

Nonsexist books.   Many critics are deploring the sex stereotypes that abound in children's literature. Boys have been central characters in

---

29. Lucy Sprague Mitchell, *Here and Now Story Books* (New York: E. P. Dutton, 1921).

the vast majority of books written for young children. Traditional role assignments usually make sharp distinctions between occupations, household and family responsibilities, and personal characteristics based on presumed masculine or feminine capabilities.

Glamorous, adventurous, or leadership roles are most often cast for boys. Girls are too likely to be characterized as timorous homebodies, preoccupied with domestic responsibilities in imitation of their stay-at-home mothers. Despite the large and growing proportion of mothers who are employed outside of the home, it is a rare story which depicts a working mother. However, when girls are permitted to aspire to jobs, suitable occupations are usually confined to such conventionally approved "female" vocations as teaching, nursing, or typing.

Since publishers are responding to the increasing requests of early childhood educators, librarians, and parents for children's books which avoid sexual stereotypes, it should become easier to make a more balanced collection of story books.

Informational books.   There are innumerable informational books about almost any topic the children become interested in: machines, fathers' or mothers' jobs, animals, plants, other cultures, transportation, agriculture, and many, many more. There seem to be high standards for such books, and many use well-selected vocabulary, carefully researched factual material, good illustrations, and interesting formats. Avoid encyclopedic detail in stories. Too much is too much.

Bibliotherapy.   Bibliotherapy is a term used half-humorously to identify stories which seek to help children come to terms with tragedy, loss, and problems of various kinds.[30] Death, single-parent families, displacement by a new baby and sibling jealousy, feelings of strangeness of language and customs in families newly arrived from other countries, feeling too small or clumsy, or unnoticed, anxiety about visits to the doctor, dentist, or hospital—there are books about almost any problem a child may have. Analyze such books carefully, however, before reading them to children, to be sure that the author's approach is sufficiently sensitive and age appropriate.

A list of children's books is given at the end of this chapter. It is not meant to be exhaustive but only to suggest some interesting ex-

30. Jane Webster, "Using Books to Reduce the Fears of First-Grade Children," *The Reading Teacher* 14 (1961), pp. 159–162.

amples of the many kinds of stories children enjoy hearing and from which they learn—linguistically, affectively, and cognitively.

Select well-written stories that you like, and share your love of books with children.

SUMMARY *Major teaching needs in guiding young children's communication development in group settings is an active area of contemporary research where the experts are often in doubt. Practices may change, so students will have to keep informed of research and new curriculum ideas, as in all other aspects of early childhood education.*

Skill in receiving and sending nonverbal communications is very helpful to teachers of young children, since verbal fluency is seldom sufficient to express young children's thoughts or feelings. While a remarkable proportion of language development occurs early and in predictable sequences, developmental pace and progress vary widely even for normal children. Teachers need support from specialists in cases where extreme deviance in language and speech is observed.

Language development, especially in vocabulary and comprehension, grows through active involving experiences. Telling and reading stories, especially with purposeful forms of listening, enriches the child's language. Standard English can be taught, as a second dialect or a second language, without denigrating the child's first language or dialect; both have a time and place. Early observation of children's language and speech development is essential to identification of problems, as is home-school collaboration in solving such problems and making appropriate referrals for therapy or remediation. Preventive efforts, when systematized, guarantee that a child's needs will not be overlooked. Instructional efforts include many types of activities, including purposeful listening, games, music, construction and craft projects, and language labs.

Of the arguments for and against bilingual education, a major argument in its favor is the failure of American schools to educate the non-English-speaking language communities. The dynamic nature of language as a continually changing living instrument suggests flexibility and respectfulness toward all language forms.

Behaviorist teaching methods, contrasted with the language experience approach, seem too narrow to accommodate the needs of the different individuals who compose a class group. However, the flexibility and adaptability of the language experience approach puts con-

siderable responsibility upon the teacher for realizing the benefits of individualization.

Controversy over early literacy can often be muted through sharing with parents and community the initial reading practices which are inherent parts of the many involving and meaningful activities that children pursue in early childhood classes. Reading instruction can be fostered on a personalized basis, without pressure, to build life-long pleasure for dedicated readers. Good use of selected children's literature is a major avenue toward reading progress.

✿ EXERCISES FOR STUDENTS ✿✿✿✿✿✿✿✿✿✿✿✿✿✿✿✿✿✿✿

1. a. Compile a card file of at least five annotated children's trade books (children's literature) under each of the following headings:

   (1) Nonsexist treatment of jobs for women

   (2) Nontraditional roles for men

   (3) Different cultures in American society

   (4) Different cultures in other countries

   (5) Family and child problems

   (6) Holidays and heroes

   (7) Value conflict problems

   b. Exchange titles and suggestions with other members of your class

2. a. With the permission of your cooperating teacher, record brief discussions with each of three children in a student teaching placement using some pictures or attractive objects to stimulate the conversation.

   b. Replay the recording and jot down any examples of:

   (1) Immature speech articulation such as *r* or *l* mispronunciation, lisp, or omission of syllables

   (2) Immature use of syntax such as "he go-ed away"

   (3) Inappropriate word use such as "yesterday" for "tomorrow"

(4) Dialect samples, other than the standard dialect

(5) First-language interference with English such as "he no come"

c. Write a lesson plan, based on your analysis of this language recording, to help these children develop more mature English standard speech. Include in your plan the use of audiovisual materials
such as tape recorder, hand mirror, filmstrip projector, or other
such materials. If your cooperating teacher permits you to implement this lesson plan, try to make another recording to find out
whether your teaching showed any results. (Remember that some
results take a long time to achieve.)

d. Summarize this teaching sequence in a brief written report to
your college instructor with self-evaluation of the plan and your
implementation and include your own suggestions for improving
either or both.

3. With the permission of your cooperating teacher, plan a series of
language-stimulating lessons.

a. Use puppets or creative dramatizations and simple costumes or
props.

b. Have clearly-defined language goals.

c. Employ selected materials, grouping, teaching strategies, and
assessment procedures.

d. Afterward, write a brief report to your cooperating teacher or
your college supervisor on your implementation and the results of
your assessment.

4. Construct a kit, sufficient for a group of about five children, for experiences with pictures, language, or other symbols. Examples of
such kits might be:

Individual flannel boards with flannel cutouts for children to reenact well-known stories or to make up stories.
A Lotto-type game using stick-figures or any other symbols and
varying the number of figures on a card or the color of the figures
or the size. Other symbols might be geometric shapes, numerals,
picture of objects, letters of the alphabet, or words such as *stop* or
go.

a. Plan to focus on *one clear goal*, but without eliminating related
material or children's contributions. The goal might be the use of

picture clues to order a series of pictures by time of occurrence, the identification of a sight word such as *stop*, or matching alphabet letters from an unsorted box with the letters of one's name on a name card.

b. Use the kit at least twice with two different groups of children, having no more than five children in each group.

c. Keep a checklist on each child's work with the materials in the kit.

d. Write a brief summary of the activity and your use of the kit with the children. Analyze your checklist data for such features as:

(1) Length of time the child remained with the activity.

(2) Interest in the activity. This might be scaled from reluctant to whole-hearted with a midway term of moderate.

(3) Success in use of the materials.

(4) Imitation versus initiation behavior in using the materials.

(5) Extent of verbalization during the activity (from little or none through moderate to considerable).

❦ EXERCISES FOR TEACHERS

1. Take an inventory of your classroom supply of children's literature using any criteria you choose—nonsexist treatment of jobs for women, humor, meaningful use of new vocabulary, or complex syntax—as a basis for acquiring or borrowing titles needed for a rounded collection.

a. Seek help in finding possible new titles from your school or local children's librarian, from professional journal articles which review new and old titles, or from any other sources.

b. Keep a file of books on your "wanted" list for school purchase, to suggest as gifts to the class by fund-raisers, to suggest for individual parent purchase for children's birthdays, or other such use.

2. If your program includes no formal reading instruction, assess individually the reading skills of the children and plan activities appropriate to the needs of different children.

a. Assessment instruments may be standardized tests such as the Metropolitan Readiness test. However, you can make a series of useful brief instruments, each to be administered individually over a period of several weeks.

b. Decide on your assessment objectives. They might be:

   (1) Identification of letters of the alphabet

   (2) Copying or writing letters of the alphabet from memory

   (3) Name writing or copying or spelling

   (4) Sight word vocabulary

   (5) Some comprehension of rhyming or of phonics techniques

   (6) Vocabulary comprehension

   (7) Other

c. Analyze your assessment for each child and plan activities for each child to further initial reading skills in meaningful ways.

3. Identify deviant or developmentally immature speech of the children in your group.

a. Plan this project with your school or district speech specialist if possible.

b. Develop a clear assessment procedure and objectives using a tape recorder to capture children's speech samples.

c. Identify problems of deviance such as little or no speech, speech which cannot be understood, or problems of gross developmental lag and share these recordings and observations with the speech specialist.

d. Work with the parents and the speech specialist to agree on a developmental, therapeutic, or remedial form of enhancing children's speech development.

CHILDREN'S BOOKS

Bannon, Laura. *When the Moon Is New*. Chicago: Whitman, 1953.
Benchley, Nathaniel. *Red Fox and His Canoe*. New York: Harper, 1964.
Blue, Rose. *I Am Here: Yo Estoy Aqui*. New York: Franklin Watts, 1971.
Brenner, Barbara. *Barto Takes the Subway*. New York: Knopf, 1962.

Bulletin. Center for Children's Books. Chicago: University of Chicago Center for Children's Books. Published monthly.

Caines, Jeannette. *Abby*. New York: Harper, 1973.

Cohen, Miriam. *Will I Have a Friend?* New York: Collier, 1967.

Ets, Marie Hall. *Good Boy, Bad Boy*. New York: Crowell, 1967.

Freeman, Don. *The Seal and the Slick*. New York: Viking, 1974.

Galdone, Paul. *The Little Red Hen*. New York: Seabury, 1973.

Gerson, Mary-Joan. *Omoteji's Baby Brother*. New York: Henry Z. Walck, 1974.

Johnson, Crockett. *Picture for Harold's Room*. New York: Harper, 1960.

Keats, J. E. *Peter's Chair*. New York.: Harper, 1967.

Martin, Patricia. *The Rice Bowl Pet*. New York: Crowell, 1962.

McWhirter, Mary, ed. *Games Enjoyed by Children around the World*. Philadelphia: American Friends Service Committee. Undated.

Meyers, Elizabeth S., Ball, Helen M., and Crutchfield, Marjorie. *The Kindergarten Teacher's Handbook*. Los Angeles: Grammercy, 1973.

Mitchell, Lucy Sprague. *Here and Now Story Book*. New York: E. P. Dutton, 1921.

Politi, Leo. *Moy Moy*. New York: Scribner, 1960.

Showers, P. *Your Skin and Mine*. New York: Crowell, 1965.

Tippett, James S. *Crickety Cricket: The Best Loved Poems of James S. Tippett*. New York: Harper, 1973.

Udry, J. *What Mary Jo Shared*. Chicago: Whitman, 1966.

Vukelich, Carol, and Beattie, I. "Teaching Reading in the Kindergarten: A Review of Recent Sutdies." *Childhood Education* 48 (1972): 327–329.

BIBLIOGRAPHY

Abraham, Roger D., and Troike, Rudolph C., eds. *Language and Cultural Diversity in American Education*. Englewood Cliffs, N. J.: Prentice-Hall, 1972.

American Jewish Congress, Commission on Law and Social Action and Urban Affairs. "The Civil Rights and Civil Liberties Decisions of the United States Supreme Court for the 1973–74 Term." New York: American Jewish Congress, undated.

Anderson, Virgil A., and Newly, Hayes A. *Improving the Child's Speech*. New York: Oxford University Press, 1973.

Arbuthnot, May Hill. *Children and Books*. 3rd ed. Glenview, Ill.: Scott, Foresman, 1964.

Ashton-Warner, Sylvia. *Teacher*. New York: Bantam Books, 1963.

Cazden, Courtney. *Child Language Education*. New York: Holt, Rinehart & Winston, 1972.

Cazden, Courtney. "Some Implications of Research on Language Development for Pre-school Education." *Early Education.* Edited by Robert D. Hess and Roberta Meyer Bear. Chicago: Aldine, 1968. pp. 131–142.

Chomsky, Carol. "Stages in Language Development and Reading Exposure." *Harvard Educational Review* 42 (1972): 1–33.

Chukovsky, Kornei. *From Two to Five.* Rev. ed. Berkeley, Cal.: University of California Press, 1968.

Church, Joseph. *Language and the Discovery of Reality.* New York: Vintage, 1961.

Cohen, David K. "Immigrants and the Schools." *Review of Educational Research* 40 (February 1970): 13–29.

Duker, Sam. *Listening: Readings.* Metuchen, N. J.: Scarecrow, 1966.

Durkin, Dolores. *Children Who Read Early: Two Longitudinal Studies.* New York: Teachers College Press, 1966.

Englemann, S., Osborn, J., and Englemann, T. *Distar Language Program.* Chicago: Science Research Associates, 1972.

Evans, Ellis D. *Contemporary Influences in Early Childhood Education.* 2nd ed. New York: Holt, Rinehart & Winston, 1975.

Fassler, Joan. "Children's Literature and Early Childhood Separation Experiences." *Young Children* 29 (July 1974): 311–323.

Freud, Anna. *Normality and Pathology in Childhood: Assessments of Development.* New York: International Universities Press, 1965.

Galway, Charles. "Nonverbal: The Language of Sensitivity." *Theory Into Practice* 10. Ohio State University, College of Education, pp. 227–230.

――――. *Teaching Is Communicating:* Non-verbal Language in the Classroom. AST Bulletin No. 29. Washington, D.C.: National Education Association, 1970.

Groffman, Erving. *The Presentation of Self in Everyday Life.* New York: Doubleday, 1959.

Greene, Harry A., and Petty, Walter T. *Developing Language Skills in The Elementary School.* Boston: Allyn and Bacon, 1971.

Griffin, Louise. *Books In Pre-school, An ERIC-NAEYC Publication in Early Childhood Education.* Washington, D.C.: National Association for the Education of Young Children, undated.

Hafner, Lawrence E., and Jolly, Hayden B. *Patterns of Teaching Reading in the Elementary School.* New York: Macmillan, 1972.

Harrison, Barbara Grizzuti. *Unlearning the Lie: Sexism in School.* New York: Liveright, 1973.

Hess, Robert D., and Bear, Roberta Meyer, eds. *Early Education.* Chicago: Aldine, 1968.

Huber, Mary B. *Story and Verse for Children.* 3rd ed. New York: Macmillan, 1965.

Jacobs, L. B. et al. *Using Literature with Young Children.* New York: Teachers College Press, 1965.

Kindergarten Bilingual Resource Handbook. Fort Worth, Texas: The National Consortia for Bilingual Education, 1971.

Kjolseth, Rolf. "Bilingual Education Programs in the United States: For Assimilation or Pluralism?" In *Bilingualism in the Southwest.* Edited by Paul R. Turner. Tucson, Ariz.: Universities of Arizona Press, 1973.

Labov, William. *Language in The Inner City: Studies in the Black English Vernacular.* Philadelphia: University of Pennsylvania Press, 1972.

Labov, William. "The Non-Standard Negro Vernacular: Some Practical Suggestions." In *Position Papers from Language Education for the Disadvantaged.* Report No. 3 NDEA National Institute for Advanced Study in Teaching Disadvantaged Youth, June 1968.

Larrick, Nancy. *A Teacher's Guide to Children's Books.* Columbus, Ohio: Charles E. Merrill, 1960.

Lee, Doris, and Allen, R. V. *Learning to Read through Experience.* 2nd ed. New York: Appleton-Century-Crofts, 1963.

Luria, A., and la Yudovich, F. *Speech in the Regulation of Mental Processes in the Child.* Baltimore, Md.: Penguin, 1971.

McCaslin, Nellie. *Creative Dramatics in the Classroom.* New York: David McKay, 1968.

Peal, Elizabeth, and Lambert, Wallace E. "The Relation of Bilingualism to Intelligence." Washington, D.C.: The Psychological Association, 1962.

Stallings, Jane. "Relationships between Classroom Instructional Practices And Child Development." Paper presented to the American Educational Research Association, 1975 Annual Meeting, Washington, D.C., April 1975.

Stauffer, Russell G. *The Language Experience Approach to Teaching Reading.* New York: Harper, 1970.

Tanyzer, H., and Karl, Jean, eds. *Reading, Children's Books, and our Pluralistic Society.* Newark, Del.: International Reading Association, 1972.

The World in Children's Picture Books. Washington, D.C.: ACEI, 1968.

U.S. National Institute of Neurological Diseases and Stroke, National Institutes of Health, Public Health Services, U.S. Department of Health, Education and Welfare. *Learning to Talk.* Washington, D.C.: U.S. Government Printing Office, 1969.

Van Allen, R. "The Write Way to Read." *Elementary English.* Vol. XVIV, No. 5, May 1967, pp. 480–485, and 491.

Webster, Jane. "Using Books to Reduce the Fears of First-Grade Children." *The Reading Teacher* 14 (1961): 159–162.

White, Doris, compiler. *Multi-ethnic Books for Head Start Children.* Part 1. *Black and Integrated Literature.* Urbana, Ill.: ERIC Clearinghouse on Early Childhood Education and National Laboratory on Early Childhood Education. Undated.

Wyndham, Robert. *Chinese Mother Goose.* Cleveland: World, 1968.

Zintz, Miles V. *What Classroom Teachers Should Know about Bilingual Education.* Albuquerque: New Mexico University, 1969.

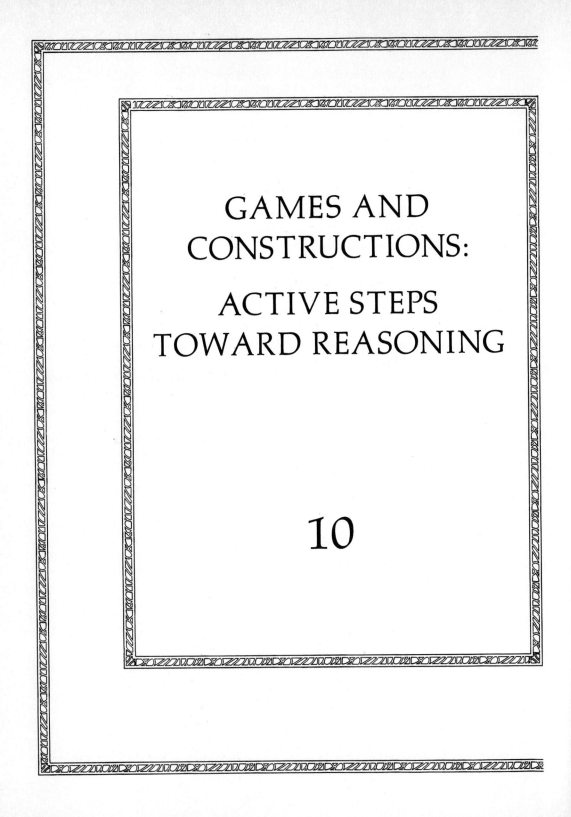

GAMES AND CONSTRUCTIONS:

ACTIVE STEPS TOWARD REASONING

10

According to John Dewey, Plato defined a slave as one whose actions are not expressive of his own ideas but those of someone else.[1] Dewey was pointing up the urgent social problem of how to help people invest their own activity with personal meaningfulness. He saw that when the child is active, he is not merely doing things, "but getting also the *idea* of what he does; getting from the start some intellectual conception that enters into his practice and enriches it; while every idea finds, directly or indirectly, some application in experience and has some effect upon life."[2]

Two very stimulating ways that children's activities lead them to the "idea" of what they are doing are games and constructional activities. Games tease cognitive growth. Inevitably, they lead to rule-making challenges, testing the child's logic. Models and constructions help the child to give shape and structure to his collected impressions and notions and to organize them in some manageable way. If a child has no need to integrate his ideas into some coherent form, they may well remain in a fragmented and unrealized state.[3]

Piaget classified children's games into three general types, that is, practice games, symbolic games, and games with rules.[4] By practice games, he means the playful repetitions of patterns of movement so characteristic of the young child, such as throwing pebbles in a pond. Repetitive practice games seem especially well suited to physical development, since so much physical activity is required. Yet, in every muscular movement the child makes, he also realizes all kinds of relationships—of force to speed, balancing elements, or kinesthetic equivalences, for example. While we

1. John Dewey, *The School and Society*, rev. ed. (Chicago: University of Chicago Press, 1943), p. 23.
2. Ibid., p. 85.
3. Hans Aebli, "Piaget and Beyond," in Joe L. Frost, *Revisiting Early Childhood Education: Readings* (New York: Holt, Rinehart & Winston, 1973), pp. 166–182.
4. Jean Piaget, *Play Dreams, and Imitation in Childhood* (New York: Norton, 1951).

Piaget classified games into three groups: practice games, symbolic games, and games with rules.

mostly see the child's actions, we must not forget how these actions help the child build his ideas of how the world functions and how he can control some of his own functioning. These repetitive or practice games are the means by which associations grow and eventually make symbolism possible and meaningful.

Symbolic games are more readily associated with the growth of logic in the child—if he can play that a block stands for a pillow, he is on the road that eventually leads to abstract symbolizing in words, propositions, and mathematical and other symbols.

The more systematic games with rules are the ones which require logical thinking, at first of a very simple sort, and later, with all the complexity of chess or computer programs.

TEACHING FOR CONCEPTUAL GROWTH

Shaping a concept is a child's own task. However, teachers can help tremendously, and their input is often pivotal to the child's clarification of his growing ideas. Teachers can help a child test a concept to find out what its limits are and whether it may be in need of reorganization.

A teacher and her class of four-year-olds agree that a hamster is dead. But the children, who use the word "dead," don't mean "forever dead." In television cartoons nobody stays dead. If the children bury the hamster, they want to dig it up every day, to see if it's still dead. They find it almost impossible to believe that the animal won't come alive again. They argue about how to make the hamster "undead." A three-year-old tries to explain her parents' divorce to her teacher, saying, "First they fighted. Then, they got un-fighted." But to the three-year-old, this may also seem a momentary state of affairs, since permanent changes in family relationships cannot be grasped at once. With the teacher's guidance, the children talk out their ideas and expectations, and they give them further meaning as they use them in games and in the constructions they build. In the process, as part of a group, the children argue, exchange understandings, and face challenges and tests of their thinking. The social give-and-take and the resolution of conflicts about their ideas help to give their concepts substance and stability where, before, there may well have been inarticulate notions.

Kamii defines discoverable learning

Kamii distinguishes between two kinds of knowledge children have to learn—social and logico-mathematical.[5] Social knowledge is the kind of information a child cannot "discover" but must learn from others, such as the names of objects. Nothing a child can *do* with a table can extract its name. Social knowledge chiefly concerns the arbitrary conventions which social groups agree on and pass on to their children. Logico-mathematical knowledge consists of concepts and ideas and, according to Kamii, is the kind of knowledge children can not "receive" from others but must actively construct for themselves. This Piagetian conception of children's cognitive development goes back at least to Rousseau, who wrote in 1762, "Whatever he knows, he should know not because you have told him, but because he has grasped it himself. Do not teach him science: Let him discover it. If ever you substitute authority for reason in his mind, he will stop reasoning and become the victim of other people's opinions."[6]

For Dewey, school was not a preparation for life, but social living itself, with physical activity the form in which young children's ideas and reflections developed. Piaget stressed the important role of social interactions in helping children to realize that their notions might be different from other children's and thus gradually to become less egocentric.

Discovery learning in the open classroom

Teacher candidates who find themselves drawn to the open classroom, with its informal learning activities and children's freedom to choose their own projects and instructional materials, will find the rationale for their preferences in the Dewey-Piaget theories and philosophy of children's cognitive development. Everything the child does, in his physical, social-emotional, and intellectual activities becomes integral parts of the unified learning which the child makes his own.

Working with young children to help them map out their ideas

5. Constance Kamii, "An Application of Piaget's Theory to the Conceptualization of a Preschool Curriculum," in *The Preschool in Action*, edited by Ronald K. Parker (Boston: Allyn and Bacon, 1972), pp. 91–133.

6. William Boyd, trans. and ed., *The Emile of Jean Jacques Rousseau: Selections* (New York: Teachers College Press, 1956), p. 73.

about the world, the student will find that the antithesis of teacher-controlled order and discipline is not necessarily chaos and disorder. Instead, many classrooms reveal trusted children who are engaged in constructive activities and who share and internalize controls in their busy work-play programs. In such an atmosphere, constructions occur in almost every learning center and games go on everywhere. There are new games, old ones, commercially produced and teacher-made games, or child inventions. Games often develop among the children, but the teacher can often guide the game playing to greater meaningfulness.

GAMES: THEIR FUNCTIONS AND VALUES

Young children's early games look quite formless and random. There may be no rules at all until a disagreement occurs, for example, about whose turn it is. A rule is not treated as final; it can be changed without notice, if it suits the player. The notion of general rules grows slowly as children become less self-centered and begin to perceive other children's needs as sometimes in conflict with their own. Once a rule becomes fixed, it often becomes overgeneralized; the rules may be used where they do not apply. On the other hand, exceptions may undermine a rule entirely. This process by which young children gradually come to understand the need for general rules in games—with exceptions to cover well-defined cases—is a reflection of their total development and has application to every learning situation.

One definition of games stresses the voluntary character of the activity and, for this reason especially, games stimulate more interest than most other types of conventional classroom activities.[7] Coleman points out that the use of academic games is an important way to respond to the challenge of a complex, difficult-to-understand society, and to the problems of children unprepared for abstract intellectual functioning.[8]

Avedon and Sutton-Smith point out that an important type of young children's game—the "central person games"—gives "It," a central player, great power over everyone else in the game.[9] Despite the playful context, games of this type give the young child a brief

7. Elliot M. Avedon and Brian Sutton-Smith, *The Study of Games* (New York: John Wiley, 1971), p. 8.
8. James S. Coleman, "Learning through Games," *NEA Journal* (January 1967), pp. 69–70.
9. Avedon and Sutton-Smith, op. cit., p. 404.

sense of powerfulness. Other game types are chiefly games of chance, of strategy, and of physical skill.

Redl summarizes the functions of children's games to include tension reduction and wish fulfillment.[10] Other functions of games have been identified as development of moral values, of self-sustaining interests, and of character development. Erikson views games as ways for children to make responses which could not be made in reality.[11] Games may also be viewed as ideal vehicles for unsegmented learning because so many developmental threads are intertwined in the game format.

Games serve a variety of functions combining entertainment and learning.

A game has to be fun. If it is not enjoyable, it is not a game. In a game, children can play that they are coping with real life situations. Since it is only a game, practicing to cope with real life problems is safe; all you can lose is the game.[12] In the game format, you can win or lose a game, but there is no grade or other evaluation of your performance. As a practice activity, without threat or pressure, the game invites spontaneity, creative responses, social activity, and unlimited investment of oneself.

Teaching cooperation in games

Games can be played by one player against his own record. Since young children hate to lose to anyone and are not "good sports," competition against others is best muted or omitted. Cooperation should, in fact, be stressed. Children may help each other to win a game or to beat their previous scores. Some teachers who foster very competitive games among children justify this by citing the competitive society in which we live. Yet competition does not pervade all our relationships and activities as adults, nor should it. Family life and community and neighborhood activities require cooperation, participation, and mutual helpfulness. Cooperative teams characterize increasing kinds of work situations where give-and-take and mutual helpfulness, not dog-eat-dog attitudes are appropriate.

Games are well suited to child-child learning situations in which

10. Fritz Redl, "The Impact of Game Ingredients on Children's Play Behavior," in *Group Processes, Transactions of the Fourth Conference*, edited by B. Schaffner (New York: Josiah Macy, 1959), pp. 33–80.

11. Avedon and Sutton-Smith, op. cit., p. 480.

12. Alice Kaplan Gordon, *Games for Growth: Educational Games in the Classroom* (Palo Alto, Cal.: Science Research Associates, 1970), p. 3.

relaxed, good-humored banter and child modelling influence the players without instruction from an adult. What makes a game is a play situation in which the players have rules to follow in order to win the game. Remember, a win does not require someone to lose. If every player increases his score, or has a chance to be "It," all can win! Even rather competitive children learn to enjoy the progress of the group or the team instead of their own personal victories.

Encouraging skill practice through games

The game can provide practice or offer creative efforts in limitless ways. Some games require remembering a series of actions in sequence, as in the song-game, "The Farmer in the Dell." Or the game may stress powers of concentration or alertness, as in "Giant Steps." Games may stress memory, strategy, courage, guessing, or fleetness of foot. Most games for young children tend to be of three types—action, board or table games, and dramatic or role-playing games. Gordon points out that "games increase student motivation, clarify difficult concepts and processes, help to socialize the student, and integrate classes of diverse ability levels."[13] Since learning is the product of the game (though not the intent of the player), games lighten many learning tasks. They also challenge children, who may be quite advanced academically, to use their intellectual gifts in personally gratifying ways. For children who are developing more slowly, or who have various kinds of disabilities, games often provide the continuing kinds of satisfaction necessary to keep motivation and self-esteem high.

Action generates interest

For children's learning and satisfaction, games work because players have to make moves; they cannot remain uninvolved. As soon as a player plays, his interest is aroused in the process. Was it a good move? The feedback is usually immediate, and it comes from the results of his own actions, not other people's judgments. Games are also purposeful; the child knows what his playing is for—to catch the slowest runner, perhaps, or to make "Tic-Tac-Toe." Uncertainty of outcomes holds interest. With some games, there are neither winners nor losers

13. Ibid., p. 18.

but only new ideas. If children play a game to see how many ways they can make a paper airplane sail upward into the air, they all learn more ways than they knew before.

Games produce social learning

The social gains of game playing enhance their value greatly. Children learn:

To take turns
To pick "first turn" by a random method
To be generous to a slow player or humble about one's own speed
To negotiate decisions about controversial plays
To argue points without personal animosity
To remain friendly and helpful
To comfort or reassure an unhappy team member who is dissatisfied with his performance
To support and give courage to a timid player
To learn to follow as well as lead

Games offer possibilities for many social learnings as well as creative, imaginative, or cognitive forms of learning.

While skill-drill types of games seem to predominate in most primary classrooms, fun comes with more open-endedness. Unpredictability about how a game can be won, or what the winners will do to win (as in "Charades"), is far more intellectually demanding than remembering the multiplication table. In fact, it is easier to remember the multiplication table if the purpose is open and personally creative than in skill-drill games. The point to remember is that any personalizing of knowledge—integrating it with strong, unique associations—is bound to increase the motivation, long-term memory, and readiness to use the learning.

Some values are more effectively taught through games than in any other way. As previously mentioned, social learnings are high on this list, among them, socially acceptable ways of handling some forms of aggression, sharing scarce equipment, being honest, cooperating with others, and many other important human values. Games can often reinforce learnings originating in other ways, or they can add the fun element which may be missing from other activities. Young children love games, but all games will not be suitable to their development. Some may be too slow, too fast, too competitive, or too long.

ACTION GAMES

Singing or chanting while playing such old favorite circle games as, "Bluebird, Bluebird, through My Window," "London Bridge Is Falling Down", or "Old Macdonald Had a Farm", all of the children participate actively, although a few or the central person may have most of the action for a short time. Chanting often accompanies or gives the rhythm to games of jump rope, ball bouncing, or hand clapping. Fast-paced rhythmic chanting in unison initiates or paces much action. Collectors of chants turn up perennial favorites which seem to penetrate language and cultural barriers all over the world as has this well-worn counting rhyme used for ball-bouncing games:

> One-a-lairy,
> Two-a-lairy,
> Three-a-lairy,
> Four.
> Five-a-lairy,
> Six-a-lairy,
> Seven-a-lairy,
> More.

Visit school playgrounds during the lunch hour or before the nine o'clock bell rings to hear what chants are current in the neighborhood.

Winick, adapting Montessori procedures, materials, learning activities, and goals, describes in helpful detail many active games to develop sensory discrimination. She stresses visual and tactile discrimination of line, shape, form, length, and other attributes.[14] Gerhardt, focusing on body movement as a fundamental way in which young children conceptualize space, describes many activities, including games by which young children interact physically with the world in discovering time-space conceptions.[15] Gerhardt's games generally require only materials commonly available in classrooms and play areas for young children.

Action games help children form time-space concepts.

The Opies categorize children's outdoor games to include:[16]

> *Chasing*—such as Blind Man's Buff
> *Catching*—such as Giant Steps
> *Seeking*—such as Hide and Seek
> *Hunting*—such as Ringalevio

14. Mariann P. Winick, *Before the 3 R's* (New York: David McKay, 1972).
15. Lydia A. Gerhardt, *Moving and Knowing: The Young Child Orients Himself in Space* (Englewood Cliffs, N. J.: Prentice-Hall, 1973), especially pp. 136–178.
16. Iona and Peter Opie, *Children's Games in Street and Playground* (Oxford, England: Clarendon Press, 1969).

Racing—such as Drop the Handkerchief

Dueling—such as piggyback fights

Exerting—such as Tug of War

Daring—such as Chicken or other challenge to rash action

Guessing—such as Who's That Knocking at My Window

Acting—such as Fox and Chickens

Pretending—such as playing school or adult family roles

Universal forms of action games

Many American versions of these games are listed in the books by Matterson, Ames, Rockwell, and Vinton given in the bibliography at the end of this chapter. Vinton notes that games shared by peoples all over the world include such popular early childhood games as hand clapping, hiding fists, changing fingers, playing with balls, using blindfolds, tag, tug-of-war, and hide-and-seek.[17] She also notes that beans, peas, and marbles are used almost everywhere in children's games. In addition, other universal games for children include pitching, hopscotch, foot races, team and relay races, spinning tops, dice or other games of chance, pencil and paper games, telling "whoppers" or tall stories, circle games, and pantomimes and charades.

Vinton also stresses informality as the key to a game: "the element of freedom to create within the framework of a particular game special rules, different requirements for winning, new ways of playing, or even freedom to evolve their own variations on the basic games."[18] Her comparison of children's creative use of games to the way jazz bands vary a musical theme vividly stresses the children's active roles in rule bending and adapting when playing games. Piaget's description of young children's rule adaptation when playing marbles is a specific case in point.[19]

COGNITIVE SKILL GAMES

Counting and math games are frequently used to stimulate children's cognitive skill development. The commercial catalogs list many games which involve math at various levels of complexity, from Candyland to three-dimensional Tic-Tac-Toe.

17. Iris Vinton, *The Folkways' Omnibus of Children's Games* (Harrisburg, Pa.: Stackpole, 1970).

18. Ibid., p. 256.

19. Jean Piaget, *Moral Development of the Child* (New York: Harcourt, 1932).

Games with geoboards

Geoboards with colored rubber bands or simple metal washers to ring the nails are quick to catch young children's attention. The construction of a geoboard at the carpentry bench requires rather careful nail placement and the counting of rows of nails and thus is a meaningful preliminary activity to geoboard games. One or two children can work together to play such games as the following:

Teachers may buy math games at the appropriate level of complexity or invent their own.

The largest number of nails you can enclose with one rubber band.

Geoboard bingo, using washers and counting coordinates as in rows or columns. Younger children might copy from a picture, while those with some experience might learn to place washers by translating oral instructions into spatial equivalents.

Geoboard Tic-Tac-Toe, to get "three or four in a row."

Create patterns or designs with colored rubber bands, copy each other's patterns or see how many different rubber bands you can use in your design.

Pegs and pegboards can be used in similar ways, to stabilize notions of spatial relationship or sets and subsets or to make, change, or extend patterns of colors.[20]

Note that games with geoboards may be used by an individual child, with two or three children, or as a group activity. Similar use may be made with Cuisenaire rods, Unifix cubes, counting cubes, beans, marbles, tongue depressors, pebbles, or buttons.

Teacher-made games

Teacher-made games with dice or simple spinners and using any available materials for counters present many pleasant, inexpensive activities at whatever level of complexity is needed. Five-year-olds can enjoy counters which have different values depending upon color, so that they have to remember the relationships or equivalences for the various colors.

Attribute blocks offer different levels of challenge as well, including simple sorting and classifying. Children gradually use more attributes to classify on more than one base, for example, size, color, thickness, and shape. Teacher-made games provide for great variation.

20. Helen F. Robison and Sydney L. Schwartz, *Learning at an Early Age*, Vol. 2, *A Curriculum for Young Children* (Englewood Cliffs, N. J.: Prentice-Hall, 1972), pp. 19–24.

They can be made of felt, oaktag, wood, plastic, or cloth. Attributes selected for possible classifying might include length, weight, magnetic attraction, buoyancy, rigidity, porosity, solidity, or any others that are not ambiguous. Sorting is an effective vehicle for peer teaching and vocabulary growth as well as cognitive skill practice. Dienes has excellent games and teaching suggestions, to challenge young children's growing math concepts.[21]

Other math materials

In using Cuisenaire Rods, counting cubes, Unifix cubes, or other math materials, flexible use can lead to firm understandings of the meanings of zero, especially when it means "no move." Other symbols can be introduced into games as children seem ready to identify and use them, for instance, plus and minus signs, words for "go" or "home," or directional arrow signals. When dice are used for games of chance, it is a good idea to start with one die, so as to keep the digits low, until specific children seem able to handle two dice and larger digits or combinations of two digits.

Parquetry-like or pattern blocks are challenging and interesting to almost all children, since they can be used in some way by any child to create designs and patterns, and they offer numerous game possibilities. Children also like to explore Tangrams and mirror cards. How many other activities there are that are far more stimulating and involving than workbooks and drills.

A surprising number of board games win life-long devotees in the early years. In some well-equipped settings, it is not unusual to see five-year-olds learning opening moves in chess, checkers, or Go, Parcheesi, or backgammon. Bright children looking for effective challenges enjoy having to anticipate their next move or to reassess a prospective move after their partner has made a move.

Piagetian-based games

Based on his analysis of Piagetian stages of development, Furth offers many suggestions for cognitive skill games. He includes simple probability predictions using two colors of equal numbers of marbles in

21. Z. P. Dienes and E. W. Golding, *Learning Logic: Logical Games* (New York: Herder and Herder, 1970).

a bag; spatial transformations using clear symbols to stand for objects; sorting, classifying, and visually stimulating observing and thinking; and matching and picture completion tasks.[22]

Some games often played in classes for young children include:

1. HUNT for shapes or letters of the alphabet, or objects. Young children go hunting, with a sample in hand of either the object or a picture of it, while somewhat older children go hunting by matching from memory.

2. MATCH by touch. Children try to find, by touching and feeling a bag they cannot open, copies of objects they see on a board. Shapes, textures, size, or thickness are some of the distinguishing attributes.

3. SELECT objects for a difference wheel so that there are at least four variables (color, thickness, shape, size) and several dimensions for each variable (three colors, thick-thin, three geometric shapes, and for size—small, medium and large). The first player chooses an object and places it in the center ring. The next few players must choose an object that differs by only one attribute from the one in the center ring. Each of these "one difference" objects are placed in the second ring. If, for example, the first object is a small, thick, blue circle, players may select, for the second ring, a circle that is thick and blue but large instead of small. For the third ring "two difference" objects are required. Now, the circle may still be blue but, if so, it will have to be large and thin.

4. PLAY cards. Card games can be commercially manufactured, as of the Old Maid type, or any sets the teacher wishes to prepare that may interest the children. Card games offer many learnings of numerals, counting, number, symbols, and rules of games.

Games with blocks

The block corner has a wealth of game possibilities that are rarely developed. Since most block collections are unitized, not only can games of spatial relationship be developed but also games of quantitative or geometric relationships. In the block corner, such games as the following might be played:

Equivalences. Find how many different ways you can combine a set of blocks as long as the quadlong block or as high as four doublongs piled one on top of the other.

Make a square of quadlongs. Fill in the square with any blocks that fit, then find a different set of blocks that fits.

22. Hans Furth, *Piaget for Teachers* (Englewood Cliffs, N. J.: Prentice-Hall, 1970).

Form a circle out of curved blocks. What is the fewest number you can use? The most?

Make a block pattern on the floor, then copy it in a vertical construction.

Make a big triangle on the floor out of blocks. How many small triangles can you make inside the big one?

Replace blocks on the shelves with one child placing one quadlong block for each two doublongs (or other equivalence) placed by a partner.

Find all the curved blocks and put them on one pile. Find the same number of square blocks or rectangles, matching them one-to-one to the curved blocks.

Materials to make games

Woodworking products can often become game materials—a target board, a counting game, a spinner, or a scoreboard. Paper, scissors, paste, stapler, tape, oaktag, cardboard, and plastic and art materials produce many attractive board games. Student teachers find that children love to help make games with which they can play.

Observing game values

In game playing, students might observe the many ways in which children:

Observe sharply, to identify similarities and differences.

Identify the attributes which differentiate objects.

Associate like attributes, as in sorting.

Classify, at first rigidly, gradually more flexibly and in more complex ways.

Anticipate next steps.

Revise previous moves or recapitulate with self-corrections.

Gain insights.

Reason inductively.

Make deductions.

Formulate rules and generalizations (though perhaps not entirely correctly).

Correct each other.

Challenge each other.

Test each other.

Repeat a game again and again.

Argue and furnish supporting reasons.

Become totally involved in active learning.

All of the above cognitive activities can be stimulated in games, with relatively little or infrequent teacher participation or monitoring once the games are taken over by the children. With occasional groups of children, social learning problems appear to be overwhelming, as when children do not respect each other's turn or stretch out conflict situations. These are the children, usually, who can learn the most from games in self-discipline as well as cognitive skills. A long-term view suggests that such groups should play more games, not less, with more teacher guidance to establish the social learnings, and as much fun and satisfaction as possible for the children in the game itself.

RIDDLES AND WORD GAMES

Jokes and riddles are not understood by young children when the meanings are subtle or hidden or based on adult experience. Child humor is broad, obvious, and literal. Yet young children become playful with language fairly early, and the humor and stimulation which such activity produces should be encouraged. Primitive jokes are replaced very gradually with some double or less visible meanings as children are encouraged to play with, create, or identify linguistic forms of playfulness.

Shultz found that six-year-olds had difficulty "in detecting the hidden meanings of ambiguities which are considered necessary for a successful resolution of the incongruity."[23] He suggests that the ability to discover an incongruity may be related to the Piagetian stage of concrete operations, which is often placed at about age seven or eight. However, he also indicates that riddles are problems to solve and that unresolved riddles may generate unpleasant cognitive tension. This

---

23. Thomas R. Shultz, "Development of the Appreciation of Riddles," *Child Development* 45 (March 1974), pp. 100–105, 104.

kind of tension keeps reminding you that you haven't solved the riddle and annoys you because you can neither put it out of your mind nor think of a solution. Such tension, however, may increase cognitive activity and stimulate efforts to reach a resolution, if only to release the tension. In other words, riddles which children have the ability to resolve may be very stimulating intellectually.

The reason that young children cannot detect incongruities or absurdities is that they are as yet unfamiliar with reality, with the difference between reality and unreality, or the reference may involve material totally unknown to them. In the riddle, "Why did the man go to the North Pole at Christmas time?" the answer, "To see the Christmas seals," would be meaningless to children who don't know what these are.

Yet when simple and obvious riddling begins, as it often does when one child starts to repeat something he heard on the playground from older children, his friends quickly adapt this joking form to their own purposes and understandings. Using Berlyne's definition of play as similar to exploratory behavior, the teacher values the riddle making as the beginning of explorations into linguistic humor.[24]

At first, young children are likely to offer serious, rather than absurd or incongruous resolutions, until they begin to get the idea of the game and recognize the kind of playful response which is in order. A three-year-old girl played a game with her mother on an "I'm big, you're little" theme, requiring her to pretend to reverse roles with her mother. Her mother might say, "If I'm little, can I drive a car?" Knowing that her mother did, in fact, drive a car, sometimes tended to confuse the child, although as she continued to play the game, her ability to maintain the role of reversal became much more stable. As the child sensed the absurdity of the role reversal responses, her enjoyment of the game reached a high point of hilarity. Similar reversal word games, on familiar territory, might center on a child and his pet dog and which one goes to school, wears pajamas to bed, eats with a spoon, or is read to. It is important to develop such a game around a topic that has much material familiar to the child so that the sense of absurdities grows and develops more acutely.

Other types of linguistic humor that children enjoy and understand

24. D. F. Berlyne, "Laughter, Humor, and Play," in *The Handbook of Social Psychology,* edited by Gardner Lindzey and Elliot Aronson (Reading, Mass.: Addison-Wesley, 1954), pp. 795–852, 841.

might be gross exaggeration of familiar experiences, attribution of speech or other unlikely features to objects or pets, or coining nonsense words.

Twenty Questions is a tightly-disciplined format, with its yes-no questions, and young children would find very difficult at first, but, in familiar contexts, they begin to understand the idea. Mixed-age grouping for games like this one, with a tolerant spirit toward the younger members of the team, greatly contributes to the learning by analogy, and sometimes by rule, that children offer each other. My Grandmother's Trunk and its many variants is similarly exciting, in simplified contexts. For children who are beginning to learn to read, the phonics practice of this game could be quite enjoyable and they would, at the same time, be learning the alphabet in order. Mixing younger with older children on a team for this game, with team members allowed to help each other in whispers, keeps the teams happy and painlessly teaches the younger members much useful material.

GAMES AS PLAYFUL ACTIVITY

Since this chapter has stressed games as voluntary, humorous, enjoyable, involving, and self-sustaining, it should be unnecessary to add that the motivation and atmosphere of these games is quickly destroyed by imposition and lack of choice. When choices are respected, there is little danger of embarrassing a child who finds a game too difficult or uninteresting. A child who insists upon learning a difficult game might sometimes have to be deflected to more constructive activity if the teacher senses that the child seems overwhelmed by failure to master the game. Some children, however, who insist upon watching a chess or Parcheesi game they cannot understand may be identifying with older children, or brighter children who can play, and may be experiencing some vicarious satisfaction. Of course, it is always preferable for a child to derive his satisfaction from his own activity rather than from the actions of others. Without encouraging passivity, however, sometimes a tolerance for an observational role leads to participation and activity by children who seem to need to practice in imagination before they venture a difficult assignment. Sensitivity, tolerance, and tentativeness are the chief features of teaching in such situations.

If games add playfulness to all kinds of children's learning, constructions add the workshop or laboratory in which the child can make models, samples, or some projection of his imaginative organization of ideas.

CONSTRUCTIONS

The action that young growing muscles demand, and the shaping and patterning of materials that surging intellectual growth requires, are both well served by many kinds of constructions. Ideas and feelings which may be fuzzy perceptions, cloudy notions, unconscious desires, or unverbalized concepts can all be channelled into work with various kinds of materials. Creative art and other esthetic forms of self-expression (discussed in Chapter 4) offer the other major outlet for physical-emotional-cognitive output.

Inaccurate perceptions and unverbalized concepts can be resolved by many kinds of constructions or patterning of materials.

Constructions are objects that children arrange or put together in some self-determined way. Teachers and other children can, of course, help in suggesting resources and solutions to problems. Teachers often indicate practical needs for constructional activities, such as a bird feeder. Yet, the actual work should be the child's, recognizable to him and others as having some unique characteristics that make it his, even though it serves a classroom purpose.

On a nursery school playground, the concrete used to hold a small drain was badly cracked. A group of children were delighted to go to the hardware store and help purchase some ready-mix concrete. This group plunged into the construction job with bubbling enthusiasm, partly because they viewed the job as very grown-up and saw themselves as performing adults' work. While adults might have done a smoother job, it was clearly the work of children, and they took great pride in showing it off to any visitor. Other teacher-inspired projects may include making birdhouses for the playground, making playhouses and stores out of cardboard cartons, building playground toys or equipment, baking pies, bread, or cookies or other cooking projects, as well as making puppets, sewing costumes or beads, or making slippers, aprons, or hats.

Teacher-directed projects loom very large in some early childhood classes before such holidays as Mother's Day. Most of these are craft projects that children like to bring home but which represent very little of their own thinking, feeling, or constructional work. If the children are permitted only to make copies of the teacher's model, the projects offer the children no opportunity to shape and pattern their own ideas and inventions.

Solving problems in construction

For construction activity to stimulate or advance the child's development, there must be problems for him to solve and ideas to which he gives shape and form. Some teachers totally, and mistakenly, direct these activities because they think the children lack the skills, the ideas, and the problem-solving ability to produce satisfactory products. When this is true, the projects are obviously inappropriate for the children. In early childhood classrooms, the three most active construction centers are likely to be the block corner, woodworking center, and art and craft center. For cooking activities, almost any serviceable table surfaces will do if there is easy access to the sink and ultimately to cooking facilities (though the last may not be needed).

BLOCK BUILDING

School administrators think of wooden blocks as toys for very young children and usually discourage the primary grades from using this versatile material. It is a rare first-grade classroom that is blessed with blocks. Think how the block building noise would interfere with reading instruction. Yet block building could easily and directly improve the reading skills of many children through the patterning and shaping experiences blocks provide and in the planning and sequencing of the building construction. In addition, motivation is enhanced when children experience school satisfactions in appropriate and successful learning activities.

In one public school, several primary classes shared a room that was set aside for building with blocks and other noisy activities, thus insuring that there would be no interference with reading and other quiet learning activities. In classrooms where blocks are valued as much as books, block building and reading often go on at the same time, although sometimes they alternate with each other.

Multisensory block experiences

Blocks provide experiences that can be—all at the same time—visual, aural, tactile, kinesthetic, and conceptual. Wooden blocks have a distinctive feel, sound, shape, and heft. While they have substance and shape, they also have the abstract quality of being units in any design or symbols of any reality. Working with blocks, young children learn both intuitively and verbally about comparative weight, size, thickness, shapes, and corners, and curves and other geometric features such as lines and points, and number and sets. Real meanings grow for such

vocabulary pairs as high-low, stable-tippy, straight-crooked, even-uneven, open-closed, heavy-light, long-short, and thick-thin.

Emotional values of block activities

There are many values in block building. There are emotional values such as the aggressive outlet of banging blocks and crashing constructions. There is self-evaluation too, through contemplating an objective

entity one has made: "I built it! It's mine—don't knock it down."
Pride in workmanship is often evident in the block area. There is
motivation in the appeal of the smooth wood to children's hands and
the ease of pushing blocks around or combining them into structures.
Challenge is often high—to use *all* the blocks, to make a high structure,
to build the airport the class has just visited, or to solve a specific
construction problem such as how to build a tunnel.

Social learnings in block building

Social values are obvious. Who shall be permitted to join the block
building and on whose terms? How does a group agree on a joint
project when each one has a different idea about how to do it and
what it should be? Who should have the responsibility for the large
cleanup task afterward? Should regular block builders give turns to
occasional block builders? Conflicts develop rapidly in the block area
over "turf" when there are separate construction projects in progress,
as well as over a fair division of the blocks. Clearly, the block area is
rich in social learning possibilities and provides the social interaction
children need to begin to work out fair rules of procedures.

Cognitive learning in block constructions

Cognitive values, as suggested above, are numerous. Number concepts
naturally grow, and teacher guidance should take many forms to
capitalize on the high-interest learning opportunities. These include
matching objects one to one, counting, equating sets, making subsets,
combining sets or subdividing them, discovering meanings of area and
perimeter, of squares, of linear measurement, and of many kinds of
patterns.

Patterns often occur randomly when children lay out streets, make
fences, or build houses. Teachers do well to point out the patterns the
builders have made, arousing a conscious interest in further and
deliberate forms of patterning. The first pattern might be a brick-like
road with alternating squares and doublongs. Having first constructed
a pattern intuitively and without conscious decision, children who
receive teacher appreciation and comments about the patterning become deliberate in future constructions and decide just how the pattern

shall be formed. As soon as pattern creating becomes popular, the children begin to experiment, and they find out that patterns can vary in endless ways. In addition to noting patterns made, teachers can elicit patterns, discuss structural problems, ask open-ended questions to stimulate related construction, and encourage verbalization and imaginative projections about the structures.

Dramatic play with blocks

Block building tends to become a focus for dramatic play if the children talk about the structures and generate stories about action and characters. Many teachers complain that the block builders mostly seek to re-create the violence and adult fantasy of television programs. Children who watch violent programs seem to act out violent episodes in their play. Some teachers try to reach out to parents, suggesting that they consider censoring and restricting their children's viewing to reduce the sources of the children's models for violent forms of play. In addition to seeking cooperation from parents in reducing unsuitable viewing and overindulgence in passive behavior, teachers can reduce the effects of television models in block play by stimulating the children to use exciting material encountered on trips into the community, in visits to the classroom from community and other visitors, and from good children's trade books.

This writer has found children very responsive to teacher encouragement and to her valuing the block corner for depicting class experiences, and they often replaced repetitive monster and "bad guy" dramatic play with its guns and violence with more acceptable acting out. If the teacher moves in and out of the block corner, maintaining her presence and interest in the construction activities and stimulating related constructions through open-ended questions and suggestions, block building becomes a challenging and intellectually stimulating activity.[25] Student teachers learning to stimulate block play can practice the art of asking open-ended questions, so they can refrain from dictating the course of block constructions while reminding children to think further about the construction or related constructions.

Another effective way to help children to use block building to express their own ideas rather than the spurious material they view on

25. Helen F. Robison, "The Decline of Play in Urban Kindergartens," *Young Children* 26 (1971), pp. 333–341.

television is to work with a group to plan a construction in advance, encouraging the children to sketch out some of the details and problems and some ways to solve the problems. The teacher might jot down the details if the children want her to, or even make a sketch. Children who choose to plan this way are children who are likely to work purposefully toward the plan. Using a camera to record the finished structure and comparing the photograph with the plan is a further step toward planned, goal-oriented construction. This gives the children specific ways of evaluating their products and planning for further development.

Experiences stimulate block play

Block play becomes more differentiated as the children seek to work out more interesting ideas based on recent experiences and as, from time to time, the teacher invests the area with added objects. Some of the many objects which generate interesting block construction are wedges, pulleys, flashlights, batteries, equipment to rig up lights and bells, tent-like coverings such as large pieces of cloth or long rolls of butcher paper, found materials like large cardboard containers, puppets, costumes and clothing. A discarded wagon wheel mounted on a board soon becomes a ship or airplane pilot's wheel, or a bus or truck. A broken length of garden hose becomes a gasoline station hose, and automobile repair work becomes very popular. Sometimes the children become interested in painting a mural for a backdrop to the block construction, as though to make scenery for a stage production. It is often difficult to know whether to encourage more construction or more dramatization. Yet they inevitably go together and stimulate each other; more complex structures are used in more detailed dramatic play.

CONSTRUCTIONS: WOOD, PAPER, AND PLASTIC

Woodworking, more difficult but similar to blocks, lets the child make some form he has in mind. The skills are usually short of the conception, but if children are helped to use woodworking equipment early, they play with these for the fun of the activity and have less interest in the end product. By the time the child begins to have some control over the tools, he can fashion simple products which have some relation to his idea of what he wanted to make. There is a strong temptation at woodworking to do most of the work for the child to avoid frustration. It is well to resist this. As in block play, the planning ahead, identifying problems and finding some possible solutions, then trying to implement the plans—these activities are where growth and learning occur.

Learning to guide woodworking

Student teachers need to become skillful with woodworking equipment in order to be safe and helpful teachers in the field. It takes time to learn to know tools, the properties of good ones, and what children can safely accomplish with which tools. Hand drills with varied bits can be extremely satisfying for children to use if the handles are not too long and if it is easy to fasten the bits and to change them. In order to teach the young child how to hold a hammer or saw, what size nails to select for various purposes, or how to use a vise, teachers obviously need well-supervised practice opportunities. Other experiences students need include learning to identify the soft woods that children can work with, to avoid hard woods, and some simple facts about wood construction. In addition, students can plan for various kinds of measurement activities that are needed in woodworking and give meaning to the concepts. Also, good safety rules are essential in work with tools.

Woodworking projects often incorporate other materials such as cloth or plastic, art media such as paint or crayons, and all kinds of decorative items. Children often find these varied materials attractive, but since children tend to focus on products, the materials might be withheld until there have been opportunities to develop skills with tools.

Working with paper, plastic, and cloth

Other materials with which young children make constructions that give form and pattern to their thinking include many kinds of paper, shoe boxes, sand tables, cardboard cartons, styrofoam and other plastic materials, papier-mâché, and various kinds of cloth. Possibilities are only limited by imagination. One class made a "listening house" out of a large cardboard container to house a tape recorder. They painted the house, made windows and curtains, and used a flashlight for illumination. Another group made an Indian tent out of butcher paper rolled around chairs. All sorts of stores, houses, communities, and beaches have been constructed, chiefly out of paper and paint. Constructions generally grow out of trips and experiences. Once in a while, the idea for construction is sparked by some materials a parent happens to donate, such as an obsolete book of wallpaper, floor tile samples, rug sample squares, or rolls of felt. Imaginative teachers seem to become virtual squirrels, seeking out possible useful donations whenever possible.

MAP CONSTRUCTIONS

Because geography deals with the physical aspects of the world, many reflective scholars have identified geographic studies as appropriate for young children's first-hand experiencing. Goals for such studies are identified by one source as thoughtful observations, reasoning about geographic observations, some forms of mapping of geographic features, and relating some map symbols to the real landscapes represented.[26] Since the emphasis here is on first-hand experiencing as a basis for subsequent reasoning and representational and symbolic skills and concepts, these studies start with younger children, but later become more systematic and structured in the primary grades.

Observing spatial relationships

Trips within the community are major prerequisites for map constructions, and it is usual to concentrate on the block on which the school is located. Thus many observations can occur before any attempt is made at creating representations of any kind. Children make many focused observations on trips, with teacher guidance to accent important physical features of the area. Discussions and reflections follow to help the children organize their impressions. An excellent beginning at mapping can be made at a sand table by molding the contours noted and using blocks or boxes to represent buildings or

26. Paul R. Hanna et al., *Geography in the Teaching of Social Studies: Concepts and Skills* (Boston: Houghton Mifflin, 1966), p. 111.

*First-hand
observations
are necessary
for developing
the representa-
tional skills
needed for map
constructions.*

other features of the block. This first effort concentrates on spatial arrangements—*where* the objects are with relation to each other and, especially, to the school building. Objects stand for the structures and the features of the block the children have noted on their walks. Children can be challenged to find appropriate representational material— strips of paper or long blocks for streets, a mirror or strips of glass for water, and other objects to stand for telephone poles, mail and fire boxes, empty space, fences, gardens, farms, stores, vegetable stands, gas stations, and the like. This can be a creative effort if the teacher provides many kinds of materials and permits the children to choose those they prefer.

A first effort at representation will produce many questions that then require further observations to fill in forgotten spaces or to reconsider comparative sizes of various features. The teacher must be alert to the children's leads and follow their questions and conceptual efforts. Any teacher plan, at this point, must be subject to change without notice, so she can respond to children's interests and avoid pushing them into investigations that have only adult interest. It is likely, however, that once the children have had some experience in representational work, they will see other opportunities and materials they can use. Plaster of Paris makes an easy-to-use material that takes any shape into which it is poured, and it takes painting well. This material might interest some of the children in making further representations—of the school building, for example, or a house or some well-known public building.

Additional map representations, of a three-dimensional type, can be made on the floor, in the block corner, or wherever it may be undisturbed for as long as the children are interested in it. Once such a representation is made, the children are likely to want to keep it for a long time in order to play with objects and to develop dramatic play. If there is any body of water represented, there is likely to be play with small boats or with make-believe boats, using blocks. Children may wish to play with miniature vehicles on "streets" or "bridges."

Making and reading road maps

Children who ride a great deal in their parents' cars are likely to be familiar with road maps and their use. Such maps, introduced into the area where map representations are being constructed in three dimensions, chiefly serve to remind children how abstract forms of mapping look and how symbols are used on maps. Some children may wish to draw crude maps, pretending they are related to a particular landscape. These first creative mapping efforts can be encouraged without attempting to teach young children more about mapping skills than they are ready or able to use. Just as teachers browse in books with interested children, they can also browse in maps. The major learning that develops in such an environment has to do with the nature of representation. The idea slowly develops that the paper map relates to a real world—the local landscape—and that map symbols stand for three-dimensional real things, just as the objects they construct do.

Three-dimensional representations

Some teachers encourage children to make rather large forms of three-dimensional representations with grocery cartons and cereal boxes. These are delightful end products and are very impressive to visitors and parents, but they take up a great deal of space. If the space problem can be solved, the larger representation makes a very satisfactory dramatic play scene.

Photographs of the immediate neighborhood, or of the various features of the block community the children have chosen to represent are additional aids to connecting the map to the real world for which it stands.

INDIVIDUAL PACE OF CONCEPTUAL GROWTH

Teachers should not expect all children of any given age or class to learn these difficult concepts at the same pace, nor to have the same interest in the conceptualizations. Yet it is usually true that, if exciting activity, reflection, manipulations and constructions are in progress, every child wants to get involved in it in some way. Students who help develop such high levels of involvement are cautioned to wait and see what meanings the different children make of these experiences. Developing concepts are untidy and unstable. Accepting this developmental truth, students may wish to make further plans to produce additional opportunities for children to forge these concepts into functional activities.

SUMMARY *Games and constructions are two very involving activities that help children conceptualize their actions and that help stimulate intellectual growth. Piaget's classification of games into practice and symbolic games and games with rules illuminates the characteristics of games which help children learn.*

Games must be enjoyable but need not be competitive. Game playing supports social skills as well as cognitive development. There are many action and cognitive skill games, as well as riddles and word games, for any purpose and, in addition, teachers and children can devise their own games.

Constructions, or work with materials, enable children to express thoughts and feelings which may be unarticulated or fuzzy. Problem solving and giving shape and form to ideas through independent work with appropriate materials, are ideal for constructional needs. Block building, woodworking, and arts and crafts are usually the three most active construction centers. The many values of block building include emotional as well as social and intellectual payoffs. Teachers can help children work toward more complexity of form, structure, and conceptualization in block constructions. Woodworking and map constructions are additional activities for construction which help give shape and pattern to children's concepts.

✸ EXERCISES FOR STUDENTS ✸✸✸✸✸✸✸✸✸✸✸✸✸✸✸✸✸✸✸✸

1. Select two current commercial catalogs of early childhood materials.

    a. Compile by type of game a card file of the games listed in these catalogs. Classify the games in any way that is meaningful to you— kinds of materials, number of possible players, game content or concepts, or possible age or grade levels.

    b. Select two types of games you particularly like, such as a game of chance with dice involving counting and a game of strategy such as Tic-Tac-Toe. Construct two games similar to these using inexpensive materials and, with the permission of a cooperating classroom teacher, observe how several children play with these games.

    c. Write a brief summary of your observations of the children's use of the games, noting especially their:

(1) social skills

(2) personal satisfactions indicated

(3) skills in following the rules of the games

(4) idiosyncratic use of the game materials

(5) persistence in the game

(6) problems of conceptualization indicated.

2. With the permission of the cooperating teacher, in a group setting for young children where you are welcome and can spend substantial periods of time, plan a series of children's games, some of which are action games, cognitive skill games and word games, and invite children to play some of these games with you. Keep a log of your game experiences with these children, noting especially, for each game:

a. Children's interest and persistence

b. Management or discipline problems

c. How long it took for most children to learn it.

d. Whether any children took over the game, to play by themselves.

3. List three or four constructional projects you think a group of children with whom you are working might find challenging, and discuss the list with your cooperating teacher. With her help, select one project, either in woodworking, three-dimensional mapping, or in construction with a variety of materials, and develop it with the children over a period of several weeks, following their interests and adapting all plans to their use of your project. Keep a log of the project, take photographs of various stages in the constructional project, and report to your college class on this project.

❧ EXERCISES FOR TEACHERS ❦❦❦❦❦❦❦❦❦❦❦❦❦❦❦❦❦❦❦❦❦

1. Review your current program to identify games available to children or developed for various purposes, then select at least two *instructional objectives* for which you would like additional games.

a. Acquire additional games or develop your own to match the needs you have identified.

b. Browse in some of the titles in the bibliography for some suggestions for games or for game components.

c. Start a card file of games, classified in any way useful to you such as social skills, motor skills, or cognitive skills, or more detailed subheadings (which might also distinguish between games with materials and games requiring no materials).

d. As you introduce new games, observe children's use of the materials or rules and, based on your observations, plan to modify or adapt the rules or to offer special forms of skill practice to some of the less mature children.

2. Select a constructional project which seems appropriate for your group and plan to develop it and assess its impact both while it is in progress and afterwards.

a. Design the project, with the participation of children and with parents and volunteers if help is needed in materials or in supervision of children's work.

b. Select your assessment criteria, basing them on your objectives. Some possibilities are task persistence, problem solving, symbolizing various features of the environment, patterning ideas, skill with selected tools, and creativity.

c. Decide on your assessment procedures or instruments. Do you need a checklist? Will children participate by checking their names on a list each time they participate? Will you combine some records of process with assessment of products?

BIBLIOGRAPHY

Aebli, Hans. "Piaget and Beyond." In *Revisiting Early Childhood Education: Readings*, edited by Joe L. Frost. New York: Holt, Rinehart & Winston, 1973.

Ames, Jocelyn, and Ames, Lee. *City Street Games*. New York: Holt, Rinehart & Winston, 1963.

Avedon, Elliot M., and Sutton-Smith, Brian. *The Study of Games*. New York: John Wiley, 1971.

Boyd, William, trans. and ed. *The Emile of Jean Jacques Rousseau: Selections*. New York: Teachers College Press, 1956.

Caillois, R. *Man, Play, and Games*. New York: Free Press of Glencoe, 1961.

Carlson, Elliot. *Learning through Games: A New Approach to Problem-solving.* Washington, D.C.: Public Affairs Press, 1969.

Cremin, Lawrence A. "The Free School Movement: A Perspective." *Today's Education* (September-October 1974): 71–74.

Darken, L. H. "Children's Games: A Bibliography." *Folklore* 61 (December 1950): 218–222.

Dewey, John. "My Pedagogic Creed." In *John Dewey on Education.* Edited by Reginald D. Archimbault. New York: Random House, 1964.

Dewey, John. *The School and Society,* rev. ed. Chicago: University of Chicago Press, 1943.

Dienes, Z. P., and Golding, E. W. *Learning Logic: Logical Games.* New York: Herder and Herder, 1970. (McGraw-Hill).

Elementary Science Study. *Teacher's Guide for Attribute Games and Problems.* St. Louis: Webster Division, McGraw-Hill, 1968.

Fisher, Robert B. *Learning How to Learn.* New York: Harcourt Brace Jovanovich, 1972.

Furth, Hans. *Piaget for Teachers.* Englewood Cliffs, N. J.: Prentice-Hall, 1970.

Gerhardt, Lydia A. *Moving and Knowing: The Young Child Orients Himself in Space.* Englewood Cliffs, N. J.: Prentice-Hall, 1973.

Golick, Margie. *Deal Me In! The Use of Playing Cards in Teaching and Learning.* New York: Jeffrey Norton, 1973.

Gordon, Alice Kaplan. *Games for Growth.* Palo Alto: Science Research Associates, 1971.

Hanna, Paul R., Sabaroff, Rose E., Davis, Gordon F., and Farrar, Charles R. *Geography in the Teaching of Social Studies: Concepts and Skills.* Boston: Houghton Mifflin, 1966.

Kamii, Constance. "An Application of Piaget's Theory to the Conceptualization of A Preschool Curriculum." In *The Preschool in Action,* edited by R. K. Parker. Boston: Allyn and Bacon, (1972), pp. 91–133.

Matterson, Elizabeth. *Games for the Very Young.* New York: American Heritage, 1971.

Opie, P. and Opie, I. *Children's Games in Street and Playground.* Oxford, England: Clarendon Press, 1969.

Opie, Iona, and Opie, Peter. *The Lore and Language of School Children.* Oxford, England: Clarendon Press, 1959.

Parker, Ronald K., ed. *The Preschool in Action.* Boston: Allyn and Bacon, 1972.

Piaget, Jean. *The Moral Judgment of the Child.* New York: Harcourt, 1932.

Piaget, Jean. *Play, Dreams, and Imitation in Childhood.* New York: Norton, 1951.

Piaget, Jean, and Inhelder, B. *The Psychology of the Child.* New York: Basic Books, 1969.

Redl, Fritz. "The Impact of Game Ingredients on Children's Play Behavior."

In *Group Processes, Transactions of the Fourth Conference,* edited by B. Schaffner, New York: Josiah Macy, 1959, pp. 33–80.

Robison, Helen F., Jagoda, Eleanor, and Blotner, Roberta. "Competency-based Teacher Training: Skinner vs. Piaget in Classification." In *Piagetian Theory and the Helping Professions.* Proceedings, Fourth Interdisciplinary Seminar, 1975, pp. 51–73.

Robison, Helen F. "The Decline of Play in Urban Kindergartens." *Young Children* 26 (1971): 333–341.

Rockwell, Anne. *Games (And How to Play Them).* New York: Thomas Y. Crowell, 1973.

Schubert, Delwyn, ed. *Reading Games That Teach.* Monterey, Calif.: Creative Teaching Press, 514 Hermosa Vista Ave., 1968. (Four books as follows: Book I—*Reading;* Book II—*Phonics;* Book III—*Word Recognition;* Book IV—*Word Attack Skills.)*

Starks, Esther B. *Blockbuilding.* Washington, D.C.: American Association of Elementary-Kindergarten-Nursery Educators, NEA Center, 1970.

Vinton, Iris. *The Folkways Omnibus of Children's Games.* Harrisburg, Pa.: Stackpole, 1970.

Wagner, G., et al. *Games and Activities for Early Childhood Education.* Darien, Conn.: Teachers Publishing, 1967.

Winick, Mariann P. *Before the 3 R's.* New York: David McKay, 1972.

CLASS VISITATIONS:

SCHEDULES, ROUTINES, SETTINGS, ENVIRONMENTS

11

While young children's basic needs in groups are similar, early childhood classes vary a great deal in their schedules, settings, and ambience. How classes for young children actually function, day by day, has much to do with their institutional affiliation, their physical facilities, the educational philosophy guiding the program, the unique characteristics of the community, and the kinds of teaching, supervisory, and administrative staffs involved.

This chapter covers operational features of early childhood classes. Suggestions are made for school, classroom, and neighborhood visitations, with guides to indicate types of information to collect. In addition, schedules are discussed in relation to settings, functions, and balance, as well as management of routines and creation of desirable environments for young children.

Observing different early childhood classes in action is one of the most effective ways to gather information about the impact of different settings and arrangements on teachers' and children's behavior. Teacher candidates and in-service teachers in search of imaginative solutions to common problems in socializing young children to group situations find classroom visitations vital to broadening their perceptions of possibilities. They also become sharply aware of the ways in which restrictions may arise from operational necessities or from administrative policies. Restrictions inevitably invite creative responses. It is edifying to discover how wide a range of solutions teachers find to similar problems, since every situation has some limitations with which teachers must learn to cope.

In some settings, it is difficult to comprehend the reasons for the teachers' excessive concern for reduction of the noise level, without experiencing the reactions of supervisors to an excess of spontaneity in the room. In others, the preoccupation with picking up and floor cleaning is understandable when you learn about the power of the school custodian and the many ways he has to let the staff know what is permitted in the classrooms.

Focused observations and subsequent discussions of perceptions and questions enable preservice and inservice teachers to analyze problems cogently, to systematize their overload of information in ways that integrate ideas usefully, and to clarify their understandings of instructional options. Members of a graduate course for inservice teachers sometimes make visitations in small groups with a subsequent report to the class. Recently, such a group received permission to take photographs during the visitation, and their slides greatly heightened audience interest in classroom arrangements, children's work stations, equipment in use, bulletin board displays, and samples of children's work, completed and in progress.

VISITATIONS

Students and teachers can plan ahead to make their classroom and school visits meaningful. Arrangements must be made with the schools to be visited, and decisions have to be made about the major focus of the trip. It is best to communicate to the schools to be visited exactly what the group expects to observe. A well-arranged lunch hour often is the most productive way to include discussions with teachers and staff members. Administrative and supervisory personnel, whose time may be more flexible than that of classroom teachers, are usually gracious in supplying information, conducting tours, identifying specific classrooms or school facilities likely to interest the group, and in articulating school philosophy and policies.

Planning ahead

Planning ahead for the focus and the logistics of a visitation insures meaningful outcomes. Planning ahead by telephone and letter, the prospective visitors should supply all the information the host school will need to fulfill the purposes of the visit. The hosts will want to know, not only the specific purposes of the visit, but also the nature of the group (preservice or inservice teachers), its composition (six teachers, one school supervisor, and one college professor, for example), the expected length of the visit, and probable arrival and departure times.

Visitors should offer at least two possible visitation dates to insure that the time of the visit is convenient for the host school. It is a good idea to stress the *observational* function of the visitation, to avoid long lectures in offices in lieu of first-hand observing. However, there is no doubt that the school head is usually the one best able to supply such basic information about the setting as:

a. Number and age grades of early childhood classes
b. Vertical or horizontal grouping of children
c. Size of classes
d. Staffing of classes
e. Supervision of staff
f. Specialist teachers and their assignments
g. Hours of the school session
h. Meals provided
i. Physical facilities: size and subdivisions of space
j. Special services, that is, medical, speech, psychological, or other services available in the school
k. Extent of mainstreaming of handicapped children, that is, inclusion of handicapped children in regular classes
l. Intake policies and basis for admission as to age, numbers, and needs of children
m. Educational philosophy
n. Forms of parental and community involvement
o. Funding
p. Links with other community agencies, such as a pediatric clinic, art museum, or other agency
q. Special problems of children in the early childhood classes, such as a first language other than English

In selecting a focus for the visitation, the group might consider such possibilities as:

a. Open classrooms versus more structured forms
b. Place of reading instruction in the program
c. Room arrangements
d. Characteristics of art or music activities
e. How meals are managed
f. How parents are involved

Some groups might prefer a narrower focus:

a. Observations of humor in children's play
b. Evidence of fantasy in play situations
c. Handling of conflict situations by staff
d. Peer tutoring by pairs of children

Analysis of schedule and program differences often requires attention to such items as:[1]

a. Entry points, that is, whether children enter the program only at scheduled times or throughout the year
b. Kinds of materials used, from more or less restricted types, or the variety in use
c. Use of time, that is, flexible or highly structured
d. Use of space, that is, single classroom versus areas in more open space
e. Locations of activities, that is, indoors, outdoor, or away from the school site

Plans for the visitation should include a follow-up meeting, either at a subsequent college class or with a school supervisor, administrator, or PTA official to discuss visitors' reactions and questions. A walk—or a ride if the area is more rural or spread out—in the community before or after the visitation should be projected, preferably with a community leader as guide to identify and interpret community characteristics, problems, and strengths. A guide list for such a walk appears at the end of this chapter, in addition to a suggested visitation guide.

Preparing a written guide

When students visit schools or communities, alone or in groups, the preparation of a written guide may serve to direct attention to characteristic features, to suggest questions to pursue, pamphlets or written materials to request, interviews to schedule, and observations to note or to quantify.

Preparation of a written guide for a visitation directs attention to specific objectives to be achieved.

If students plan their visitations in detail, the guide may be adapted or devised beforehand to include the selected features to be observed. Duplicated copies of guides can be analyzed in advance of the visitations to emphasize the purpose of the trip, and students can be prepared to jot down notes during the visitation in order to complete

1. ASCD Early Childhood Council, "Guidelines for the Analysis and Description of Early Childhood Education Programs," in Joe L. Frost. *Revisiting Early Childhood Education: Readings* (New York: Holt, Rinehart & Winston, 1973), pp. 512–521.

the guides afterwards. Completed guides can be discussed, item by item, in a subsequent seminar. Sometimes, a director of a school program is able to join the seminar, helping to clarify students' observations and answering questions that always surface later.

Taking a walk

When students go by themselves to take a walk or a ride in a specific community, a great deal of information is collected just by looking to see what is there. Much more, however, is easily added by entering some stores, making some small purchases, stopping for a cup of coffee, and listening to the talk as well as participating in the conversation. With a community leader to point out a great deal of what is not obvious to a stranger, students develop more understanding about the community, its resources, its strengths, and its problems.

Planning the walk in advance is advisable, however, as it helps to remind students of some characteristics they might otherwise overlook. For example, is there a public library or a medical clinic in the community? What recreational facilities are available for indoor and outdoor activities? What do children do here in their spare time? Where do they play? Are young children generally supervised by adults here, or do they seem to be on their own? What dangers or hazards to young children are noted?

Taking a walk in a community develops understandings about its characteristics, resources, strengths and problems.

What about the appearance of a community? Do the streets and houses look well kept, or are the streets littered and the houses deteriorated? Are there pleasing esthetic features to notice, such as graceful bridges, gardens and trees, interesting waterfronts, views of mountains, lake or ocean, or just blank walls of industrial facilities? What do you see in the shop windows: utilitarian types of objects only or are there also more decorative things?

Are people friendly? Do they help you find your way, or do they hurry on, unwilling to be involved with strangers?

A great deal of information and many impressions (as well as misinformation) may be picked up on a walk through a community. Generally, it is best to check one's impressions with some people who are more knowledgeable and who can interpret occurrences which may be puzzling.

SETTINGS

While most preschool programs developed in the United States outside the public schools, contemporary tax levy funding of kindergartens and state and federal funding of prekindergarten and Head Start centers is placing increasing numbers of young children in public school settings. Some large urban schools of newer design have an "early childhood wing," with its own entrance and outdoor playground separate from those used by older children. There are even some public "early childhood schools," with a second or third grade as the highest grade in school.

Advantages of public school settings

Public school affiliations have advantages and disadvantages. On the positive side are these features:

Public school settings have many advantages for early childhood programs, and some potential disadvantages.

1. Permanent facilities are funded for early childhood use.
2. The tax levy base is often more secure and permanent than other forms of funding. However, this may not apply to five-year-olds in many states, and it usually does not cover children under five.
3. There are usually well-qualified administrators and supervisors.
4. Staff are usually state certified and well qualified.
5. The early childhood classes have access to the school resources for supplies, equipment, special services and, sometimes, specialist forms of instruction as in art, music, and physical education.
6. The presence of classes of older children in public schools is another advantage, for more varied interage grouping and for assistance from older children when teachers need another pair of hands.
7. Teachers can interact and participate in professional activities with a varied staff, with emphasis upon the continuity of the educational experience through the grades.

Possible disadvantages of public school settings

But there are potential disadvantages in public school affiliation of early childhood programs.

1. Large schools may not tolerate young children's spontaneity and exuberance.

2. Rigidities are often imposed on a whole school population without needed exceptions for young children, such as requirements for "lining up" for various reasons or for fitting into school schedules which are not reasonable for young children.

3. There may be some loss of identity for a program which attempts to be humanistically oriented, individualized, and family focused, and which may be different from the school in general. The program may lose its visibility in the community and be deprived of parental interest and involvement because the unique qualities of the early childhood program are obscured.

4. There are too often irresistible tendencies to yield to the pressures from teachers of older children to "ready" children for later grades, instead of concentrating on diagnosed, specified developmental needs.

5. Often the supervision available is expert primarily with regard to elementary education and has little to offer the early childhood classes.

6. There may be considerable isolation from other eduactors and from professional developments in the field of early childhood education.

7. There may also be a tendency to assign staff, whose preparation has been in elementary education, without retraining, just because they are available.

8. The 9–3 hours limitation of the public schools often dictates limited schedules for young children, and half-day schedules for five-year-olds, as though these children had limited educational needs. Working mothers, who have great needs for custodial as well as educational experiences for their children, are especially inconvenienced.

Since American public schools are so numerous, so varied, and so responsive to local communities' needs, they surely contain the best and the worst of early childhood programs. Some settings offer the most advanced complex of services and educational programs, while others seem to reflect little of early childhood thinking about the needs of young children.

Private schools

Some of the very best early childhood schools are operated under private auspices for profit. These tend to serve wealthy families who can afford to pay the high tuition. High fees, however, do not necessarily guarantee excellent programs.

Private schools are likely to start up in any area where there are unmet needs for educational and custodial care of young children whose mothers work. Some are well run by people who care about children and who make a modest living through the school. Whether or not young children are safe and well cared for in centers which are essentially business enterprises depends on the staffing and the adequacy of the premises and the equipment. It is very difficult to mount good programs without subsidies from governmental or other sources because good programs are expensive.

Church sponsorship

Churches have sponsored early childhood programs throughout the country, often leading the way in their communities with exemplary programs that are nonsectarian and serve families very well. Many of these programs are very flexible in hours. Middle-class families who want a play group for their children for two or three mornings a week can often be accommodated in a group that also has a nucleus of children who come daily for a half day or even a full day because their mothers work.

Church- and synagogue-affiliated centers for young children usually charge modest fees because the space used is tax exempt and frequently shared with other groups for other purposes. Scholarships or tuition exemption are usually available for some families who are unable to afford the regular fees.

Parent cooperative nursery schools

Since about 1940, parent cooperative nursery schools have served middle-class families, especially in voluntary associations that initiate and control them. Mostly of small or medium size, such facilities directly serve community needs, with substantial parent involvement in the classroom, in the governance structure, in responsibility for funding and fund raising, and often in maintenance as well. A challenging and, as yet, unresolved dilemma has been how to involve working parents in such a cooperative form of early education—to bridge their needs for closer interaction with their children's schools and to make their potential for governance more real than apparent. While federal funding guidelines for Head Start and day care require parental majorities on policy-making boards, lack of time, knowledge, and sophistication often make parental impact minimal.

Other models of children's centers

Centers with innovative features, here and abroad, suggest ways to resolve problems about parent involvement and to integrate varied services for children.

Examples of cooperative early childhood schools or day care centers can be found in the Scandinavian countries, where these facilities are often sponsored by cooperatives that run industrial plants. In Israel there is the Kibbutz form, largely limited to agricultural cooperatives. The Chinese or Soviet varieties, which may be sponsored by the industrial or agricultural enterprises, are rich sources of ideas for the future development of such centers in the United States. American experience offers a few examples of imaginative forms of early childhood programs—chiefly in day care sponsored by a few large industrial plants. However, when children's centers depend upon corporate decisions for continuity of functioning, there is no guarantee that priorities of the business enterprise will remain unchanged. The placement of such facilities adjacent to or as part of an employing enterprise makes them important models for further study, since they can fill an important need of working mothers to be near their children's centers. Such programs could greatly improve parent opportunities to work with teachers and school staff, to maintain parent-child contacts during the working day, and to exert more influence on the program in many ways. School and family both benefit from more frequent interactions and more basic forms of interaction. The cooperative form of development and governance of schools for young children has great appeal to Americans who value a democratic base for decisions and the mechanisms by which responsibility and responsiveness become operational.

Integrating services for children

One unusual community agency in a large city integrates a variety of funding sources and programs, serving over 350 children in six different programs.[2] These programs include a day care center, a multiethnic and trilingual Head Start center, one group of emotionally disturbed children, a parent cooperative nursery school, a summer play group and day camp, and after-school remedial educational program. Note how each of these groups has different needs, although all of the

2. Louis Berkowitz et al., "A Minicommunity for Young Children," *Children Today* 3 (November–December 1974), pp. 2–6, and 34.

groups are housed under one roof and are offered coordinated services. The hours of the day care center are from 8:30 a.m. to 6:00 p.m., with older children arriving from the public schools after 3:00 p.m. The Head Start center offers half-day programs with high parental involvement. Half-day or full-day sessions are offered the emotionally disturbed children to meet different needs. The parent cooperative functions with parent participation characteristic of such groups, but it is on a full-day session. One unit of retarded children and one unit of orthodox Jewish children are included in the summer programs. The central services, to which all the programs have access, could not be supported for any of these programs alone.

Day care centers

Most facilities for young children are smaller and much less diversified than the program described above. Day care centers—public or private —offer the longest daily sessions. Day care center sponsorship is coming from increasingly more diverse sources—colleges, hospitals, factories, and community agencies of many kinds. There are a few day care centers that either specialize in, or include, infant care. Because of the high ratio of adults to children required, it seems doubtful that day care centers are the best places for care of babies whose mothers work or who require full day care for reasons of health or otherwise. Nurseries or "crèches" for babies have long been available in many European countries, primarily for working mothers. In the United States, the family home start or home care programs or cooperative centers seem to offer better possibilities for more homelike care in smaller settings for infants. If the family care giver receives training, supervision, and educational experiences with others of the same status, better infant care may result.

There are some day care centers that offer some residential care to normal young children, either occasionally to meet special parent needs or on some regular schedule. One schedule is to keep the children in the center through the work week and to send them home for the weekend. Expense, and unresolved problems of continuity in the child's primary family relationships, prevent more widespread use of these patterns. Meeting children's needs in a family crisis may be the next special service to develop on a broader scale. But experience already suggests the importance of *including* children in family experiences, even tragic ones, rather than isolating them and leaving them with great anxiety and vague forebodings.

SCHEDULES

Schedules are designed to accommodate children's needs for food, rest, elimination, and balance.

Classroom schedules are designed as a framework for the group's operation. Schedules are needed so that families know when children are expected to arrive and depart and so that these arrangements can dovetail with the school's operation, with carpools, or bus transportation services. In addition, the schedule is the teacher's way of planning to accommodate children's needs for food, rest, changes in activity, toileting, and use of the indoor and outdoor facilities. Some schedules are posted in the classroom and in the office and suggest rather rigid adherence to preplanned timetables. However, posting the schedule is not a guarantee that it is being followed. It may only imply that teachers are required to post them (or sometimes choose to do so for the benefit of visitors, volunteers, assistants, and supervisors) even though the schedule may not be in operation on any particular day. More rigidity in scheduling is often due to the inadequacy of facilities, such as bathrooms or running water, or playground space. When these must be shared by several classes, joint use imposes rigidities.

Relieving teachers for preparation periods

In an inner city public school, the first-grade teachers were informed that their preparation periods—periods of relief from the classroom for planning and preparatory activities—on three mornings weekly would run from 9:30 to 10:15. This meant that during those periods when the classroom teachers left their classrooms, "cluster" teachers took over as substitutes. Since the cluster teachers spent the day moving from one classroom to another to relieve the teachers, they were unable to sustain the continuity of the program in any room, they claimed, because they could not keep up with that many different instructional plans for the different grade levels. Moreover, the cluster teachers were usually teachers with backgrounds in elementary, not early childhood, education and were therefore less prepared to maintain early childhood procedures and activities.

Teachers find creative ways to overcome restrictions on good schedules.

Knowing that the cluster teachers would fill the relief periods with total group activities, the first-grade teachers thought they might initiate such total group work during the opening period of the day to reduce the differences between the regular program and the relief periods. When the children arrived at 8:45, the teachers agreed, they would have group discussions, singing, and workbook activities, instead of the more usual variety of individual and small-group work choices. The cluster teachers followed this opening activity with more of the same kind of controlled, total-group activities and experienced increasing discipline problems and restlessness. All agreed that the schedules needed changing. However, the principal was unable to change the "prep" periods or to offer the cluster teachers the kind of training that would have enabled them to sustain an early childhood program. Lacking support from the administration, the first-grade teachers decided to avoid total group activities of any kind before 9:30 and to feature the kind of individual or small-group work that could be interrupted during the prep periods for continuation after 10:15.

The revised plan for the day, the teachers decided, would feature three types of activities for the opening period—art activities, table manipulative materials, and store play. For the store play project, they further specified such options for children as painting cartons to make shelves, sorting and categorizing store "stock," writing signs and labels, pricing goods, and writing and pasting prices on containers, to be followed later by buying and selling operations in less time-limited dramatic play and creative dramatizations. Store play, which had been located in the block areas of overcrowded small rooms, was to alternate with block play, with the intention of relocating the store play to another corner of the room in order to free the block area for daily work.

With this change in the scheduling of children's work activities, the teachers were satisfied that the children accomplished more, and the cluster teachers reported less disruption in their total-group singing and story-reading activities. Admittedly, this situation still left much to be desired. Cluster teachers needed to learn how to sustain the early childhood activities which the teachers initiated. Or cluster teachers with early childhood training might have been assigned to the classes. If feasible, the school's prep periods might have been shifted so that the children did not suffer from poor scheduling.

A child's experiences in school include periods with staff other than the classroom teacher, in many cases, but the classroom teacher is the only staff member who can see the child's session as a whole and who can help to keep it in balance.

Solving schedule problems due to inadequate space

In a public school prekindergarten program having three groups of children all in the four-year age range, scheduling problems were related to difficulties in room sizes and lack of sufficient materials. Two rooms were too small and one room was far too big. One solution the staff chose to try, to make the best use of space and materials, was to arrange each room to offer different activities and to rotate the groups among the rooms daily. One room was set up primarily as an art room, one for blocks and manipulative materials, and the large room became the music, movement, and exercise room. In order to rotate the rooms and to move with each group without creating confusion, the staff worked out this schedule, with five minutes for room changes:

8:40	Breakfast.
9:00–9:40	Work period in homerooms.
9:45–10.25	Change rooms. Teaching team moves with the children
10:30–11:10	Change rooms. Work in third room.
11:15–11:25	Clean up. Wash for lunch.
11:30–Noon	Lunch in homerooms.
12:00–12:45	Rest in homerooms on cots.
12:45–1:00	Dress to go home.

Since the staff moved with the children, it was usually the staff rather than the children who found the moving most inconvenient. However, there were other disadvantages. Some activities lend themselves poorly to rigid time blocks. If uninterrupted, long involvement in an activity is discouraged because of time limitations, children "learn" to have a short attention span and then are faulted for lack of persistence in tasks. Other schedules tried by this group, and discarded, included changing rooms, not three times a day but three times a week, spending one whole session in a room at a time. This was found too restrictive of children's choices of activity. The blockbuilders were very unhappy with their infrequent access to block play. Art work suffered for the same reason. Gradually, a modification of schedule developed, with less specialization in each room, more sharing of materials, and more choices for children as to *their* interest in remaining in one room or another. As the staff worked with a consultant to try to make better use of difficult and inadequate facilities, it was agreed that the program criteria would be evaluated for, among other features, the extent of free choices provided the children, provision for some privacy for each child, possibilities for nonconformity, and sufficient nurturance of each child by the same adults. Specific program needs were listed as greater clarity in definition of children's activity options, more predictability by children of the schedules, good rotation and balance of activities experienced by the children, and management of routines without interfering with learning and play activities.

Improving schedules in creative ways

Both examples cited above are realistic types of difficulties teachers encounter in scheduling children's programs to approach their ideals for quality of performance. It can be seen that some features of a situation are outside the teacher's control, although teachers can often work around such constraints to maximize a program's possibilities. Solutions are not always found in a first approximation to improvement. It is, therefore, essential to try out a new schedule and, if it does not work, make further changes. Sometimes, a new schedule fails to work well only because it is new and, therefore, disrupts other chains of consequences that must be reconnected. Or, possibly, everyone needs to work out the best possibilities in a new schedule.

When schedules really do not work, for substantial reasons, teachers must do more than complain. They must document specifically the problems, indicate how these interfere with the program goals, and, if possible, make alternative recommendations. In some cases, it is the administration and not the teaching staff who must come up with better solutions to defined problems.

Scheduling half-day sessions

In half-day programs, which are very common in early childhood centers everywhere, the scheduling problem relates to trying to condense a full-day program into half that time.

One kindergarten teacher, who had been blocking off a half session in mostly brief periods, changed to a large-block schedule in order to implement more involving experiences for the children, since they had great needs for learning English as a second language. In the class, the short-block schedule was as follows:

> Opening (10 minutes). This was mostly show and tell.
> Outdoor play (45 minutes). This was very vigorous, with much running around and little equipment.
> Snack indoor and bathrooming (15 minutes).
> Discussions, total group (30 minutes).
> Self-selected activities or the play period (45 minutes).
> Story or songs (15 minutes).
> Dress for dismissal (15 minutes).

This schedule breaks up the session, with an outdoor period quite early and separate times for stories and discussions that were tightly controlled by the teacher.

Half-day programs challenge teacher ingenuity to create involving experiences for children.

The new schedule started with a ten-minute opening, because the teacher wanted to take care of attendance, money collections, and announcements before the children became too involved in their work. There was also a ten-minute closing period to wind down, get dressed, and be ready for the parents or siblings who picked the children up. In between the opening and closing sessions, there was a two-and-a-half-hour block of time that permitted long periods of involvement or changes of activity for individual or small groups of children at their own or the teacher's initiative. The long-time block also provided the flexibility to spend almost the whole session out of doors in good weather—taking equipment out for the purpose—or spending most of the session indoors in bad weather.

The scheduling of many programs has been changed to make larger blocks of time available for children's work and play activities. This also tends to reduce the incidence of total-group situations substantially and even to relax some of the rigidities that usually surround meal and snack provisions. There will seldom be complete flexibility in the food preparation area, however, because the staff generally work part time.

Despite these restrictions, teachers are often creative in overcoming rigidities in schedules, serving their programs more flexibly, and reducing the pressure on young children to conform to essentially adult requirements. Children's requirements stem from the rhythm of their bodily needs for balance and variety in activity, frequent refreshments to replenish their high output of energy, ready access to toilet facilities, and environments that encourage and stimulate them without producing too much anxiety or pressure.

ROUTINES

Routines are classroom arrangements to provide for children's daily recurring needs.

Routines are classroom arrangements to meet children's basic needs for food and drink, elimination, and rest, in addition to balancing the program to alternate more and less active experiences. Resting seems to be more difficult for most children than other routines, simply because of the stimulation of the group and the exciting activities of the day. Suggestions are made in various chapters to deal with rest problems, and ways of handling rest are summarized in the discussion below.

Daily recurring needs should not require daily recurring planning. As much as possible, planning to take care of children's routine needs should be systematic and regular so that it is chiefly exceptional circumstances that need additional planning and not the day-to-day variety. If the early childhood classroom or area is adequately supplied with bathroom facilities, there can be early encouragement of children's responsibility for their own needs. Initial rules might relate to the need to wash hands before leaving the bathroom and drying hands well.

Encouraging self-care

For the most part, younger children, three or under, need more bathroom assistance than those over four. Some children will need help with their clothing or in the hand-washing routine. There should be very little of either kind of help, if parents cooperate in the kind of clothing they provide for their children and if the bathroom arrangements include low sinks and toilets—or stable wooden steps if the facilities are not of child height. Often, younger children need some rule or reminder not to be wasteful of paper goods. Some children love the water play in the sinks and are reluctant to "finish." But the desire to continue water play is easily accommodated outside of the bathroom to free the sinks for the use of other children.

When routines are well monitored earlier in the school year or early in the children's experience in the group setting, the children themselves usually become self-monitors or insist upon monitoring each other. Toileting is a good example. Occasionally, a child will request adult company in the bathroom, either because it is associated in some way with problems, or because a child's emotional problems may be expressed in the bathroom as well as elsewhere. The age of the children, their ability to assume responsibility for their toileting needs, and the needs of individual children all determine how much, if any, bathroom supervision is required other than checking the area. The need for "eyes in the back of the head," or keeping the entire area where children work and play under rather continuous observation, is as important in areas of toileting as in other areas.

Providing for bathroom needs

It is very unfortunate that teachers in older buildings with poor facilities for bathrooming are sometimes required, or often prefer, to take a whole class for toileting at the same time. This procedure ignores individuality and often creates physical distress, especially for children with sensitive bladders or irregular elimination cycles. It also disrupts learning activities for a whole group and creates discipline problems because most of the class has to wait for one or two children to be toileted at a time. Granting that poor facilities create problems, I suggest that teachers who find themselves in a situation where a bathroom is situated far from the classroom can find better options. One option is to request monitors from older groups, if older children are available. If the early childhood program is in a public school, this possibility is one of the real advantages of the site. Some kindergarten teachers are able to count on a different monitor every period, and the children come to know and accept these monitors. Another is the use of school volunteers, especially older persons who may be grandparents and who are understanding of young children. Another system often used is to trust children more, and send them out in pairs so they have each other for security and so one child may alert the teacher if the other is having a problem requiring some adult assistance. If a large wooden or plastic key is used as a "pass" symbol, staff members who meet young children in the halls know that the children need not be challenged or escorted.

Public school teachers of kindergarten classes often take on the re-strictions and sex distinctions the school insists upon for older chil-dren. Although there is no need for this, some teachers insist upon closed doors, one child at a time, and a system of indicating that the bathroom is occupied, for instance, by reversing an *Open* or *Closed* sign as needed. In most early childhood facilities, bathrooming is treated more casually and without tight regulation. However, some communities may be less permissive about letting boys and girls toilet together and may be more insistent on privacy and sex distinctions. Some children may insist upon privacy and, of course, this should be respected.

Students might remember that the chief reason for casualness and permissiveness in toileting is to create realistic acceptance of toileting functions as natural and universal. With less accentuation of sex differentiation, children usually accept each other without prudery. However, parental sensitivities must be considered. Group discussions with parents often lead to more informed consensus, or at least to agreements about what is acceptable practice.

One disadvantage of group toileting is that it takes time. Unlimited access to the bathroom for the children takes less time and does not unduly interrupt activities requiring large blocks of time and long involvement.

Arranging for independence in snacks and drinks

A similar assumption can often be made for regular mid-session snacks that children can help themselves to when they are ready (unless the snack requires more than simply helping oneself to juice from a pitcher or a cracker from a basket). However, snack periods sometimes afford such delightful small group discussions that teachers may prefer to schedule these when the relaxed talk can be featured. Whether to schedule a regular snack time or let the children help themselves (at least up to a point too close to the lunch hour) depends on the program goals, the group, and the length of the session. If the children stay all day—as in most day care centers—there may be two meals and two mid-session snacks served, in which case there is no need for all food periods to have a group conversation goal. If the snack is the only food served, the relaxed group eating time may be desirable.

Quenching thirst

Some classrooms have a sink and paper cups so that children are free to help themselves to fresh water whenever they like. However, paper cups in this quantity are wasteful, and teacher and parents may prefer to furnish a plastic cup for one child, the cup used only for drinking water so that it is easy to keep clean. Each cup can be designated with the child's name. On the playground a water bubbler is very helpful, especially in hot weather when outdoor play periods are long and children get thirsty. If children have to be sent indoors to get drinks of water, this is an unnecessary strain on both staff and children. An alternative might be to take a large vacuum bottle and a supply of plastic cups out to the playground. It helps to plan ahead so the children can be comfortable without too much difficulty in quenching thirst.

Rest

Rest is needed to help children restore their depleted supplies of energy.

Rest is more easily accomplished if it takes place in an area separate from the work and play areas. With preferred materials and activities out of sight, it is easier for the young child to relax in a place that is designated as a rest area. If no such space is available and the group functions in the same room for all purposes, it is important to create a restful atmosphere. This can be done by lowering shades, turning off lights, eliminating as many sources of noise as possible, and creating a restful ambience through soft music, lack of activity by adults as well as children, and removal of as many stimuli as possible.

If cots are not available for resting, as may be true for most part-time sessions, parents may furnish small cotton rugs. These can be sent home weekly for washing. Sometimes, mats go home and take weeks to return, for various reasons, so it helps to have a few extras as spares. Some teachers manage to obtain plastic mats of different kinds. These can be sponged easily and may be cleaned daily after use so are always available when needed.

Resting with cuddle toys. Some of the younger children, accustomed to a "security blanket" at home, find it difficult to rest without it. The teacher may provide substitute cuddle toys for this purpose or request parents to send something to school that will satisfy the child's need. If children rest more readily with such an object, there is no reason to discourage its use.

Rest for nonresters.   There is always a problem of what to do with the restless child—the nonrester. In a part-time session, such a child can be permitted to do something quietly in a corner of the room or just outside the door in a corridor. A book or a puzzle usually absorbs a nonrester for the relatively short period of the rest. In an all-day program, nonresters create more problems for themselves and the staff. Often, the staff plans on the rest period as a release from active duty to catch up on records, which might otherwise not be written, for conferences with other staff or with parents, for planning future activities, or taking care of other daily needs that cannot be fitted in at other times because the whole group must be attended to. In addition, the nonrester may need rest, although he has trouble relaxing in school. Such a child may become irritable and difficult as the day wears on and he becomes exhausted. If he is encouraged to rest later in the day, his parents may find this late rest period interferes with their dinner and evening plans. The child may be too sleepy to eat dinner or too wide-awake to go to sleep at a reasonable bedtime. Nevertheless, nonresters cannot be forced to rest. They can be asked to lie down for as long as half or more of the rest period and to refrain from waking the other children. Nonresters may be able to listen to soft music on headsets while lying down, or look at books, or play quietly with an assortment of objects. "Resting toys" in shoeboxes may be devised as surprises with rotation of boxes and changes of contents.

If nonresters refuse to lie down, they still should be somewhat subdued during the rest period and engage in very quiet activities. This is where a good children's television program really helps, keeping a child rather sedentary but amused and interested for quite long periods of time. Lacking a television set or a TV program worthy of the child's time, a staff member might read stories to the child away from the sleep area or let him listen to recordings of stories or music.

Restless children who need rest but relax with difficulty can be helped to rest with soft music, a quiet story, stroking the back gently, or sometimes merely sitting near such a child (the child may only want reassurance that someone is still taking care of him). Some teachers manage to quiet restless children with only a soft pat on the head or a whispered endearment.

Occasionally, with five-year-olds especially, the group may not require a rest during a part-time session nor a sleep period during a full day. Where energy levels and vitality are good, the group can be refreshed by rather quiet, sedentary experiences such as listening to a story, singing songs, having an extended discussion (if discussion skills are well developed) or other less motoric activities. This is where balancing the day's activities is important and accomplishes what separate rest periods might otherwise do.

BALANCING PROGRAMS

If the teacher plans a program with large blocks of time for children's work and play activities, this may require more observation of each child's use of time to determine whether each is experiencing sufficient balance. When the schedule runs in shorter time blocks, with separate periods flagged for rest, snack, group discussions, and other types of less active sequences, balance for the group may be more readily determined.

Balancing individual and group needs

Program activities must be balanced for individual and group needs.

However, children have their own rhythms to which they tend to respond without much supervision. With some exceptions, children tend to stop before they are exhausted, rest when they are tired, drink when they are thirsty, and eat when they are hungry. Why not cater to the individual rhythms of the children, provided only that some of the virtues of group living are also experienced by all the children? Group living offers possibilities for social and cognitive learning that are over and above what a child can experience by himself. Hence, early childhood education programs seek to find a balance in this respect as well—between individual and group needs and between the needs of the child to follow his own bent and pace as well as his need to advance his social skills and to benefit from his membership in the group. For example, children need to learn some self-restraint in the interest of group welfare, gradually and successfully.

Balancing activity and rest

Most teachers find, when they evaluate their long blocks of time, that except for one or two children, balance is readily achieved in most respects. The exceptions may be children who seem hyperactive, or have emotional problems that are responsible for the unbalance. Knowing where the problems are, the teacher can allocate her time accordingly, to reduce overstimulating conditions where this is needed, or to use her time in soothing and relaxing the children who need help to achieve balance between activity and rest and between individual activity and group participation.

Starting the day

How to start a session often hinges on whether the children drift in one at a time, come in small groups in car pools, or arrive all at once by bus. When children come one at a time, the teacher can manage a large number of individual conversations if the work period starts as soon as a child is ready to choose an activity. At the beginning of the session, the children are most eager to renew their acquaintance with the teacher, bring her up to date on the latest news, and find out what is planned for the day. The later comers might want to go straight to their favorite play areas and playmates and may be too impatient to stop and chat with the teacher. However, as long as the work period absorbs most children, teacher and children may choose how to get involved, with whom, and for how long.

Ending the day

Some teachers think a group session is a better way to start the day. This can be a very pleasant time to exchange news, to decide what activities will be featured, or to make plans for a walk or a trip. Other teachers prefer to end the session with the whole group discussing the day's events, sharing descriptions of what was accomplished, seeing exhibits of each other's work, and making plans for the next day. Children benefit from opportunities to anticipate work or trip plans as well as from recapitulating what happened. Sometimes both can be featured so as to compare anticipation with actual events. This gives meaning to "today," "yesterday," "tomorrow," or "next week." It also demands that the child organize his recollections or his anticipations sufficiently to discuss them so that others will understand him. This organization of one's thoughts, on request from others, is regarded as a function of cognitive growth.[3]

Balancing by varying schedules

Schedules may differ; they need not be unvaried. Younger children do, however, thrive on regularity and invariance. They need to know what to expect, and regularity makes them less anxious about separation from parent or about demands made on them that they may not be able to meet. Children, unable to tell time or even to understand its characteristics, receive a sense of regular passage of time from expected events occurring in a well-known order. Older children are less threatened by changes in schedule if they are informed in time to adjust to the changes. Younger children, despite the benefits of invariant schedules, also need opportunities to adjust to changes, but it is easier for them when there is plenty of notice, preferably with repetition so they do not forget, and with as much low-key relaxation as possible. Of course, emergencies occur to which children must learn to adjust, such as a teacher's unexpected absence, a parent's unexpected failure to pick up on time, changes in weather or staffing, and sometimes in conditions in the building such as flooding or lack of heat on a cold day.

Flexibility in adjusting to life's conditions is surely essential to survival and should be an important goal of any early childhood program. However, flexibility is not achieved all at once. It grows from small changes, well protected for a minimum of discomfiture, to larger and more frequent changes, with less notice and assistance needed to accommodate them well. One teacher of four-year-olds used to feature an occasional "backwards" day with her class to vary the schedule humorously and deliberately.

The all-day programs are most challenged to include the variety of experiences a child might encounter in less restricted environments.[4]

3. Hans Aebli, "Piaget and Beyond," in Joe L. Frost, *Revisiting Early Childhood Education* (New York: Holt, Rinehart & Winston, 1973), pp. 166–183.

4. Judith E. Chapman and Joyce B. Lazar, *A Review of the Recent Status and Future Needs in Day Care Research* (Washington, D.C.: Social Research Group, George Washington University, 1971).

Late-afternoon television programs, when good ones are available, give the child access to material his age mates are also likely to be viewing and talking about. Respect for moments of privacy and withdrawal are very necessary. Private places can be specially designed, such as a "tent" under a table, a special corner, or one's own cubbie, or the child can himself pick some spot.

By late afternoon, in the all-day program, a child is likely to get his second wind unless he is overtired, and he might be ready for a short renewed session of indoor play or more vigorous play outdoors. Where winters are harsh, space is often insufficient for the kinds of active exercise young children need, either indoors or out. With the tolerance of other teachers and the cooperation of the administrative and supervisory staffs, space for large-muscle activity can often be found in a hall, a classroom vacant at certain times, or in any dual-purpose space. The public schools often have the advantage here of having far more options from which to choose, as an auditorium, gym, music or art rooms, or even administrative office space or meeting rooms. Program evaluation should include the provision of large-muscle activity daily.

Scheduling is one device by which a program takes shape and expresses the intentions of the teacher. The same schedule may not serve the purposes of the staff with different groups of children. With some groups, tighter, more teacher-controlled schedules may be helpful until the children learn how to exert self-discipline, make constructive choices of activities, and increase their persistence and attention span. If the goals are to encourage more mature functioning, the program should at some point show movement in that direction. Growth requires some trial and error, but at least some steps must be forward.

CREATING ENVIRONMENTS

The environment for learning is the total perception the children receive of what the program offers them and what is expected of them. Schedules tell children how fast they have to move, how often they have to respond to other people's decisions, and how much time there is to get involved in anything. The ambience in the classroom is a combination of people, arrangements of things in space, and the sequence of activities. People are undoubtedly the most important factor in setting the feeling-tone of the room. If they are friendly,

Beauty and joy-fulness in the classroom come for the most part from teachers who love and care about children.

understanding, patient, helpful and responsive, time and space are of lesser importance. But school is not just a place to enjoy mothering and nurturance. It is also an important place in which children learn more independence, become more self-reliant, cry less and solve problems more, and make progress in social as well as cognitive skills. To encourage children to lessen their dependence upon adults for their work and play activities, the environment must put things within children's reach, simplify their use of equipment, facilitate keeping objects in good order, and also encourage group use of shared facilities.

Making rooms more attractive

Room arrangements contribute substantially to the environment the children experience. Order and attractiveness and the efficient use of space are the chief means of creating stimulating environments. Teachers must learn to look at a room from a child's eye view, which may be three feet from the floor instead of five or more. A bare room is perceived as cold and controlling to a child. There is very little he can do to it or with it. He must wait for someone to give him something or tell him what to do. Yet a very cluttered room may be intimidating; it is overwhelming to the child because he doesn't know what to do first. In fact, it may be overstimulating if he feels he has to try everything. In the latter case, he won't be able to do more than explore, probably leaving a trail of equipment behind him that will be far more than he can manage to clean up by himself. With less clutter, there is likely to be more clarity. What *is* there can be seen and taken in without tension or strain.

Well-arranged attractive rooms create stimulating environments for young children.

Some teachers like to point out to children what there is in the room to do. This is really unnecessary if the room is well arranged and the child can go around and see for himself. Besides, his own explorations afford him the delight of discovery. "Look," he might tell his teacher (as though she doesn't know), "Look at this!"

Reflecting interests of children and teachers

Every classroom for young children should reflect the interests of the staff and the children. In addition, the classroom should, in some important way, make a statement about the young child's need for beauty in his everyday surroundings. Reflecting children's interests is easy. They produce vast quantities of exciting, fresh, and colorful paintings, interesting and unmistakably immature drawings, and other art products. These are enormously decorative and deserve mounting in interesting ways. Some teachers take the trouble to mount finger paintings or tempera paintings on appropriately colored construction paper, framing them, in effect. Just placing them well on a wall,

bulletin board, or room divider, or on a string across the room or along a wall often makes a very attractive exhibit. Go to a museum and see how the pictures are hung with space between them to give them emphasis and to feature their individuality. Massing the children's work often obscures such uniqueness of product. Some groups collaborate to produce an interesting mural or large papier-mâché figures. Classrooms in which projects are developing grow in interest and attractiveness. See what a big block construction or a store play project does for the room's decor!

Teacher interests are unlimited. Some possibilities are rock collections, plants, terraria, aquaria, photographs, prints of interesting adult art, or handiwork expressed in curtaining, brightly printed doll corner tablecloths, napkins, bedspreads, or dress-up clothing.

Seeking parent contributions to room decor

Teachers can work with staff and parents to make schoolrooms attractive.

If the teacher's hobbies and skills do not include sewing, many mothers are glad to contribute small items for children's dramatic play or dress-up corner. Some mothers are willing to take donated fancy clothes, cut them down so that the children do not trip over long skirts or pants, and sew in small elastic waistbands which stay up on narrow waists.[5] Others may be able and willing to make small versions of working clothes such as overalls worn by many industrial workers, uniforms of firemen or policemen, or distinctive caps for pilots or bus drivers. Parents are often willing to help wash or repaint classroom furniture in bright, fresh colors or even construct equipment or miniature pieces of furniture to make a housekeeping area distinctive.

Teachers, with help from maintenance staff or parents, can transform ugly walls into more attractive ones with painting, large panels of colored construction paper, burlap or other cloth, or with other materials.[6] Unattractive classroom features in older buildings can be masked by furniture placement or by placing panels of various materials in front of them. Animal cages add color and interest to a room but often require attention for elimination of flies or vermin attracted by the animal food.

Using flowers and plants

Scandinavian teachers, in a harsh climate with many dark winter days, insist on a budget for fresh flowers to beautify the children's centers. Some American centers may be able to grow their own flowers for part of the year or, in the more tropical states, for most of the year. Plants, however, can be used almost everywhere all year long to lend beauty and interest to the group setting. A new center for young children in a big city's ugly slum had an exceptionally attractive environment. The center was well designed, but its rooms would have had the cold, functional look of much contemporary architecture

5. Helen F. Robison and Rose Mukerji, *Concept and Language Development in a Kindergarten of Disadvantaged Children*, Cooperative Research Project S-320 (Washington, D.C.: Office of Education, U.S. Department of Health, Education and Welfare, May 1966), pp. 163–164.

6. Helen F. Robison and Sydney L. Schwartz, *Learning at an Early Age*, Vol. 1, A Programmed Text for Teachers (Englewood Cliffs, N. J.: Prentice-Hall, 1972), pp. 19–34.

because of its strong linearity, except for the lavish display of flourishing greenery of many kinds. The sense of beauty generated by the plantings, entirely in pots, exuded a relaxing climate of great esthetic appeal. If teachers do not have green thumbs, there are often parents who can help keep plants alive, transfer them to larger pots as they grow, cultivate and spray them, and make cuttings or otherwise aid in plant reproduction and expansion. Finally, some centers may be able to make connections with florists or nurserymen, to receive leftover or less fresh stock for children's enjoyment. In large cities, where children see so little that is beautiful or that stirs a sense of awe or wonder, the place of flowers cannot be exaggerated.

Applying principles of good design

Modern design and abstract painting suggest some other possibilities for attractiveness and interest in children's centers. The use of color, line, symbols and the novel and unexpected, all combine to create a milieu worthy of young children. Teachers, however, should avoid an overstimulating room, for normal children as well as for children with the usual range of problems. If the center is lucky enough to have a separate area for rest and sleep, this area can be decorated in restful, soothing tones and arrangements.

The most beautiful environment in the world becomes overfamiliar when it remains unchanged. Rooms might reflect seasonal changes in addition to teachers' and children's developing activities and interests. Children love to help decorate a room or to change the decor now and then. Their input can be planned for and encouraged.

Students, in visiting children's centers of various kinds, might look for especially attractive rooms. When a student finds a room she really likes, she might take notes on what she sees and talk to the teacher about how it was done.

SUMMARY   *Operation of early childhood classes is affected by the institutional affiliation, educational philosophy of the program, and characteristics of the children, community, and school staff. Visitations to classrooms and neighborhoods are sharpened by the use of guides, detailed as to features to be observed and recorded. The various types of in-*

stitutional affiliation contribute to differences in functioning and in problems encountered, in early childhood classes for teachers and parents.

Classroom schedules provide a framework for classroom operation, governing opening and closing procedures, providing for routines and daily balance, and contributing to the ambience in the setting. Providing long blocks of time for the program activities requires teacher alertness to individual children's needs to balance high- and low-energy experiences.

The daily recurring routines need to be provided for in regular, systematic procedures. Increasing child independence, flexibility, and ability to cope with changes in routine can also be programmed. Rest periods usually present some problems that require planning in order to meet the needs of non-resters or poor resters.

Teachers create environments for learning—in addition to their schedules—by arrangements of furniture and equipment, the orderliness and attractiveness of the total setting, and by efficient use of space. Early childhood classrooms acquire warmth and interest by featuring children's products (especially paintings), teacher interests that involve collections of various kinds or products of her own design, parent contributions, and children's work in progress. Plants and flowers add beauty to any setting.

⍦ EXERCISES FOR STUDENTS

1. Using the Visitation Guide or suggestions for analyzing settings and operations, plan to visit two different types of early childhood settings. Take brief notes during your visit and complete the forms immediately afterwards.

a. Write a brief analysis of your material, comparing and contrasting the two sites. How are they the same and how are they different?

b. List questions your analysis might generate, for example, *reasons* for routines, schedules, or environmental features that puzzled you.

c. Prepare to discuss these questions in a college seminar with your fellow students or in a group meeting of college instructor, students, and early childhood director, coordinator, or supervisor of an on-going program.

2. Write a brief description of an early childhood group of children in a group setting with which you work regularly.

a. Specify such characteristics of the group as age, socioeconomic levels, language, and other social characteristics. Also note down such program features as indoor and outdoor facilities, length of session, meals in school, and any other material you would need in order to plan schedules.

b. Plan two different schedules for the group, stressing in one schedule children's choices of activity and an "open education" philosophy and in the other a more structured, content-centered philosophy. Analyze these two schedules and select the one you, as a teacher, prefer, giving reasons for your selection and the values you see in that schedule.

3. Visit several different classrooms for young children in an early childhood center or the early childhood classes in a public school.

a. Devise a rating scale for such environmental features as:

(1) adequacy of space

(2) use of space

(3) traffic patterns

(4) room decoration

(5) clarity of room arrangements

(6) use of color

(7) reflection of child and teacher interests

(8) unique features devised by the teacher

(9) other

b. For the room you rated highest, arrange a visit when you can chat with the teacher, discuss the room's attractiveness and efficient learning environment, and find out how it was developed.

c. For the room you rated lowest, write a brief description of the room features and indicate how the room décor might be improved.

❦ EXERCISES FOR TEACHERS

1. Review your own classroom and identify the features you like and wish to retain, those you dislike and wish to replace, and then sketch several room arrangements and materials changes you think might make interesting options.

   a. Invite one or two colleagues to discuss your plans with you in detail, evaluate your options, or to suggest additional possibilities.

   b. Invite some parents to help you, both with planning and re-arranging the environment.

   c. Reassess your classroom after you have made the planned changes.

   (1) Did you retain the values you identified as desirable?

   (2) Did you manage to get rid of features you disliked?

   (3) What values did you add?

   (4) Are there additional values you might add?

   (5) Have you added to esthetic values in every way you can?

2. If you wish to change your classroom operation to more informal procedures, identify aspects of your schedule, room arrangement, and provisions for routines and daily balance that could be changed to feature such values as children's activity choices, child independence in work/play activities, children's collaboration in room arrangements and in clean-up procedures, long blocks of time for work periods, provision for projects that cannot be completed in one day, and clearly delineated learning centers for different activities.

   a. Plan to change your program gradually at identified points over a period of several months.

   b. Keep a log, identifying each change as you make it, problems presented, and solutions tried out.

   c. After a period of about two to three months, assess your classroom operation to determine how much of your plan was implemented and how much remains to be implemented, and devise a time table to complete your plans.

3. Plan to add interest and beauty to your classroom learning environ-

ment by contributing from your own hobbies, or eliciting help from parents, volunteers, or others in the community.

    a. List possibilities for each source—yourself, parents, others.

    b. Plan meetings, class newsletters, telephone calls, or other ways to contact others.

    c. Assess your results. If you do not find them satisfactory, continue this project.

COMMUNITY WALK GUIDE

Features   **Specify**

Type of Neighborhood
   Residential-urban
   Residential-suburban
   Semirural
   Retail stores
   Industrial
   Mixed (specify)
   Other (specify)

Socioeconomic Level
   High
   Medium
   Low
   Mixed (specify)

Location
   Central city
   Suburb
   Other (specify)

Prominent Features
   Major arteries of transportation
   State of repair
   Density
   High or low-rise buildings
   Street cleanliness
   Services available
   Park or recreational facilities
   Other (specify)
   Languages noted on signs and overheard

Community Characteristics
   Population features (ethnicity,
     color, religions)
   Age distributions
   Occupational distributions

Features   **Specify**

Community Agencies
Political
Social
Religious
Economic
Cultural
Recreational
Educational

Community Problems
Employment
Youth dropouts
Youth delinquency
Housing deterioration
Recreational needs
Municipal services
Old-age problems
Other (specify)

VISITATION GUIDE

Features	**Program A**	**Program B**

1. *Title of early childhood director:*

2. *Total number of classes:*

3. *Age groups, number of:*
   a. Under 3 years
   b. 4 years
   c. 5 years
   d. Over 5 years
   e. After-school groups
   f. Interage groups

4. *Average number of children per class:*
   a. Under 3 years
   b. 4 years
   c. 5 years
   d. Over 5 years
   e. After-school groups
   f. Interage groups

5. *Staff:*
   a. Number of teachers per class
   b. Number of paraprofessionals per class
   c. Number of nonteaching supervisory and administrative staff
   d. Number of specialist staff:
      (1) part-time occasional (specify)
      (2) full-time (specify)
   e. Other staff, as maintenance, custodial, cook, bus driver, etc. (specify)

Features	Program A	Program B

6. *Physical Facilities:*
   a. Number of rooms used for children's program
   b. Number of additional rooms (staff, parents, etc.)
   c. Outdoor space (describe)

7. *Funding*
   a. Tax levy
   b. Other (specify)

8. *Special Services:*
   a. Medical (specify)
   b. Psychological (specify)
   c. Health (specify)
   d. Nutrition (specify)
   e. Other (specify)

9. *Child Population:*
   a. "Normal" children only (yes-no)
   b. Handicapped children (specify)
   c. First language non-English (specify)
   d. Income requirements (specify)
   e. Other features (specify)

10. *Parents' Roles*
   a. Board members
   b. Assistants in classroom
   c. Volunteers in school
   d. Fund raising
   e. Other (specify)

11. *School sponsorship*
   a. Board of education
   b. Social agency
   c. Other (specify)

Features	Program A	Program B

12. *Hours of school*
   a. All day only
   b. Half sessions only
   c. Other (specify)

13. *Functions*
   a. Primarily educational
   b. Primarily family-oriented
   c. Other (specify)

14. *Physical Facilities*
   a. Original school building
   b. Well-designed conversion
   c. Other (specify)

15. *Transportation*
   a. All walk
   b. All drive cars
   c. School bus service available
   d. Other (specify)

16. *Cost*
   a. Free to all families
   b. Tuition scale (specify)
   c. Other (specify)

17. *Schedule*
   a. Regular (posted or written)
   b. Casual
   c. Open education (somewhat
      structured)
   d. Open education (very
      unstructured)

BIBLIOGRAPHY

ASCD Early Childhood Council. "Guidelines for the Analysis and Description of Early Childhood Education Programs." In Joe L. Frost, *Revisiting Early Childhood Education: Readings.* New York: Holt, Rinehart & Winston, 1973, pp. 512–521.

Bronfenbrenner, Urie. *Two Worlds of Childhood: U.S. and USSR.* New York: Russell Sage Foundation, 1970.

Berkowitz, Louis, Glickman, Joy D., and Friedman, Ellen. "A Mini-community for Young Children." *Children Today* 3 (November-December 1974), pp. 2–6, 34.

Chapman, Judith E., and Lazar, Joyce B. *A Review of the Recent Status and Future Needs in Day Care Research.* Washington, D.C.: Social Research Group, George Washington University, 1971.

Chisholm, Johnnie Bishop. *What Makes a Good Head Start?* Wolfe City, Texas: Henington, 1968.

Geiger, K. *The Family in Soviet Russia.* Cambridge, Mass.: Harvard University Press, 1968.

Grotberg, Edith. "Early Childhood Education: Institutional Responsibilities for Early Childhood Education." *National Society for the Study of Education Yearbook* 71 (1972), pp. 317–338.

Lally, J. R., and Smith, L. "Family-style Education: A New Concept for Preschool Classrooms Combining Multi-age Grouping with Freedom of Movement among Classrooms." Paper read at annual meeting of American Psychological Association, Miami, September 1970.

Miller, L., and Dyer, J. *Experimental Variation of Head Start Curricula: A Comparison of Current Approaches.* Washington, D.C.: Office of Economic Opportunity, U.S. Department of Health, Education and Welfare, 1970.

Prescott, E., and Jones, E. *An Institutional Analysis of Day Care Programs. Part II.* Pacific Oaks College, Pasadena, Calif. Final Report. Office of Child Development, U.S. Department of Health, Education and Welfare, 1970.

Robison, Helen F., and Mukerji, Rose. *Concept and Language Development in a Kindergarten of Disadvantaged Children.* Cooperative Research Project S-320. Washington, D.C.: Office of Education, U.S. Department of Health, Education and Welfare, 1966.

Robison, Helen F., and Schwartz, Sydney L. *Learning at an Early Age.* Vol. 1. A Programmed Text for Teachers. Englewood Cliffs, N.J.: Prentice-Hall, 1972.

Segal, J. (Ed.) *The Mental Health of the Child: Program Reports of the National Institute of Mental Health.* Program Analysis and Evaluation

Branch, Office of Program Planning and Evaluation. Washington, D.C., National Institute of Mental Health, U.S. Department of Health, Education and Welfare, 1971.

Zigler, Edward F. "Raising the Quality of Children's Lives." *Children* 17 (1970), pp. 166–170.

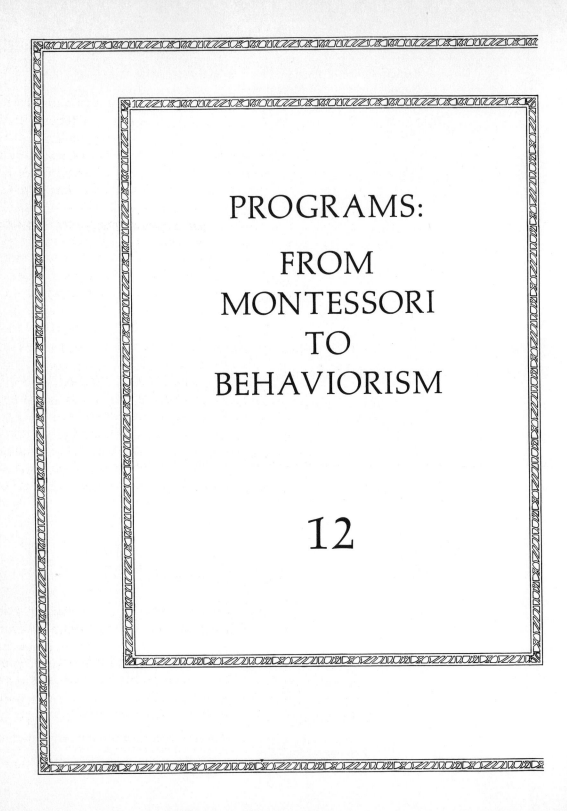

PROGRAMS:

FROM MONTESSORI TO BEHAVIORISM

12

Many parents are more interested in the teacher than the program. Others seek to enroll their children in a particular program which sounds appealing to them. And yet, there are some researchers who say that it is the children—not the teacher or the program—who determine how good the educational results will be. It seems reasonable to infer that children, teachers, and programs all affect each other in many ways.

What about teachers? Don't they have program preferences? How can a teacher candidate learn enough about the bewildering variety of programs in use to decide what he or she really likes? What if she likes one program but is required to implement a different one, one that she really dislikes? These are very realistic problems today when, in many school districts, program adoption often comes out of political considerations and teacher input may be lacking or slight. In one school, a principal accepts a specific program because it has federal funding, offers abundant expensive materials and external teacher training, and frees some school resources of money and time for other purposes. Disgruntled teachers, faced with the requirement to use this program, approach it with distaste and teach it badly, no matter how much "training" they receive. In another school, a group of teachers investigate a program and expend after-hours and week-end time to develop materials and plans for good teaching. Sometimes college professors are the initiators of the first type, sometimes of the second. Other program developers may be allied with publishers, research and development organizations, or private groups selling programs and materials.

The trouble is that most teacher education programs provide little time for visitation and program exploration. Most laboratory experiences and student teaching require placement in one type of classroom for relatively long periods in order to give the student some depth of experience. In student teaching seminars, students often exchange experiences which helps to diffuse insights into programs different from those each student is coming to know. Film and video-tape are also used to offer vignettes of different program types, and, of course, there is a vast literature with program description detail.

This writer suggests that undergraduate teacher candidates keep their options open and try to be more analytical than judgmental about the programs they encounter. Most students like a program because they like the teacher who is using it, and they would probably like this teacher no matter what program she was doing. So it may be pure chance whether students see enough variety in programs, or programs of different types, which are equally well taught. With growing teaching experience, and an awareness of the more difficult questions encountered in the education of young children, teachers become better equipped as graduate students to study and compare programs of different types.

PROGRAM DIFFERENTIATION

The purpose of this chapter is to help students become aware of program differences and the major types that are in operation. Learning to describe and analyze a program is like learning to "see" and analyze a painting. Everyone looks at a painting as he passes it, but few of those who look know *what* to look for or how to understand it. Through informed analysis, students of teaching, unlike casual art gallery visitors, must not only know *what* they like but also *why*.

There are various ways to identify and classify differences among early childhood programs.

Like painting, there are various schools of thought about what is important in a program and how it can be incisively analyzed. Therefore, there cannot be one undisputed form for analysis. The same program can be analyzed from different perspectives or with the use of different categories.

Not only do we lack one invariable base of analysis, but the problem of analyzing programs is further complicated by their tendency to eclecticism. Since so few programs exist in pure form, it is sometimes easier to describe what is going on than to identify the theoretical base. In fact, much more is learned from analysis of what is happening than from what might be intended by the theorists. Many American programs advertise themselves as "Montessori," but they are so eclectic that the observer is hard put to see how the so-called

Montessori programs differ from others not claiming a base in Montessori theory and methods.

American education tends to respond to many different influences at the same time. While Montessori-type materials are found in practically all classes for young children in the United States except those devoted exclusively to literacy, in most of these classes the materials are simply used as additional equipment.

Among the various ways that programs can be differentiated, useful analyses can be made based on degree of structure, on theoretical base or function, educational philosophy, on objectives, on short- or long-term goals, or on observed functioning—that is, what is happening in the classroom. Some analysts distinguish between what they call informal and formal education programs. Others attempt to differentiate behaviorist from nonbehaviorist orientations.

The following discussion considers programs for young children, first, from the different perspectives which contemporary researchers and observers use and, second, from a practical viewpoint suggested by this writer. Students and teachers are cautioned, however, that in many respects, but especially in regard to degree of structure or of informality, the program may tell more about the teacher than the program, since teacher personality usually plays a central role in degree of structuring.[1]

Analysis by degree of structure

Because American programs borrow from each other and any other sources available, one way that programs are being described relates to the degree of structure, that is, whether the program is primarily of low, medium, or high structure.[2] Structure is a deceptively simple word and seems to be capable of an endless number of meanings. The term is used here to mean the extent of decisions that limit the freedom of the teacher or the child to make spontaneous choices. An example from a southern school system, however, illustrates teacher impact upon theory. In this community, the parents and the principal prevailed on the three first-grade teachers to change to "open" class-

1. Eleanor E. Maccoby and Miriam Zellner, *Experiments in Primary Education: Aspects of Project Follow Through* (New York: Harcourt Brace Jovanovich, 1970), p. 31.
2. Ronald C. Parker, ed., *The Preschool in Action: Exploring Early Childhood Programs* (Boston: Allyn and Bacon, 1972), p. 493.

rooms. The senior teacher, close to retirement, was asked to take the grade leadership role. Visiting the three "open" classrooms was an enlightening experience in noting anew how much each teacher shapes her own program. The senior teacher had indeed changed her room, with learning "stations" instead of rows of desks and chairs, but her inherent high level of structure permeated every part of her program as it always had. The two junior teachers were developing programs which had far more openness as to children's activity choices, learning schedules, use of materials, grouping for learning, and content. Because teachers claim they have "open classrooms" is surely no assurance that there is as much flexibility and choice as the term suggests. Low structure, or considerable scope for child and teacher choices, is usually associated with the terms "open education" or "informal education."

Using the terms low or high structure, however, does not avoid ambiguity. One has to look closer to identify what aspects of a program have high or low structure. It is possible to have high structure in content with very low structure in sequence, pace, methods of teaching, grouping, site of instruction, and almost everything else. The Summerhill program as described by its founder, Neill, is just such an extreme of very low structure in almost everything except content. If and when children decide to learn something, the content is traditional and does not share in the interesting innovation permeating other features such as child-teacher relationships and child autonomy in choices of when and how to study.[3]

Differentiation by theory or function

While programs may differ as to theoretical base or function, most programs are in agreement on six features.

Major program types in widespread use in American schools include programs that are primarily developmental, behaviorist, Montessori, academic, cognitive, custodial, and community oriented.[4] However, each example of each type tends to combine some features of other types, and most agree on some fundamental approaches to teaching children. Maccoby and Zellner, analyzing twenty-two federally funded Follow Through projects, found that, despite differences among these programs, all were in agreement on the following six features:[5]

3. A. S. Neill, *Summerhill: A Radical Approach to Child Rearing* (New York: Hart, 1960).
4. Ellis D. Evans, *Contemporary Influences in Early Childhood Programs*, 2d ed. (New York: Holt, Rinehart & Winston, 1975), pp. 16–17.
5. Maccoby and Zellner, op. cit., pp. 23–24.

1. All learning must begin where the child is.
2. Instruction for young children should be as individualized as possible.
3. Failures of learning are attributed, not to the child, but to the methods and materials of the program.
4. A program must have clear goals for planning and implementation.
5. Children need to learn specific school-appropriate behaviors for any program to be successful, such as attention and task involvement.
6. Children must have good feelings about the school and the program.

Developmental programs include many Piagetian types, traditional nursery education, and informal, open-classroom activities. *Behaviorist programs* include the many kinds of behavior modification features, either for learning or social behavior or both. *Montessori programs* stem from her writings and the Montessori teacher-training groups both in American and in European centers. *Academic programs* feature reading and academic subjects almost to the exclusion of all else. *Programs*, here termed *cognitive*, emphasize intellectual and cognitive development above everything else. *Custodial programs* feature the child's physical care and safety—minus an educational program. *Community-oriented programs*, which are largely found in ethnically concentrated areas, may feature the community's culture (for example, American Indians or Eskimo).

Various bases for program differentiation

Evans differentiates programs according to their educational philosophies and learning theories, degree of parent involvement, use of pupil product versus pupil process criteria, the nature of their instructional objectives, degree of child choice of activities, and extent of teacher control.[6] Parker distinguishes programs according to their major goals and objectives, their implementation—how the program is organized, including the children, instructional format, teacher role, grouping, sequencing, and parental participation—as well as the level of structure.[7] Other researchers have defined these terms in various ways.

A practical view of program differences is based on what is happening in the classroom.

Generally, program differences can be found in:

1. *What the child does.* Does he sit most of the time, manipulate objects alone or with others, or wander aimlessly about?

6. Evans, op. cit.
7. Parker, op. cit., pp. 466–506.

2. *What the teacher does.* Is she "center front," telling children, observing, or participating, or assisting children?

3. *What the materials are.* Are they books, machines, or various combinations of objects?

4. *Who makes choices.* Is it always or usually the teacher or the children?

5. *What follows what in the program.* Is there a regular sequence of activities from the time the children arrive until they depart, or how do experiences flow in the program?

6. *Who the children are.* Who is eligible to attend the program and what are the specific criteria?

7. *How children are grouped.* Is there age grouping or inter-age, or how are children arranged within the group setting?

8. *What the program expects to produce.* Are the goals achievement oriented to produce good readers, for example, or process oriented to produce high self-concepts and good problem-solvers?

9. *How parents are involved.* Are parents chiefly consumers, to be educated by professional staff, or do they make policy decisions, participate in the classroom, and evaluate the program?

10. *Source of Funds.* Is the program part of the public school system or private nonprofit, private for profit, community sponsored with public or public and private funds, or otherwise funded?

When students plan visits to early childhood classrooms to see different programs in action, it is helpful to identify features such those listed above.

OPEN EDUCATION PROGRAMS

Most classes for young children today are fairly eclectic, that is, their programs derive from several sources. However, most more or less follow the tradition of progressive education stemming from John Dewey's theories about active education and social activity. The British informal or open education also stems from this tradition, but generally tends to be more relaxed in social tone and less pressured than American schools to bring children up to "required" reading levels. This type of program presents the classroom as a workshop which is well organized for many activity possibilities such as block play, cooking, music, art work, carpentry, dramatic play, and table games.

Features of open classrooms

Open classrooms emphasize exploration, experimentation, construction, playful activities, social interaction, and children's very active involvement in *doing*. Lecturing and "telling" children is not used for instructional purposes in such classrooms.[8]

Open education programs resemble workshops organized for different activities.

Usually, these classrooms accommodate many different activities at the same time. However, some teachers may reduce options to three or four, while others seem to have no limit on the number of activities permitted or available on children's request. Choice of activity is stressed on the ground that the child will be most likely to get involved and stay involved in the activity of his own choice, but teachers may manipulate options to encourage more variety of children's activity.[9]

Reading, writing, and academic content in the program may or may not be featured separately in informal and open classrooms. The purer program types expect that academic skills can best be integrated with other activities and often grow out of needs defined in construction or exploratory activities. Teachers often suggest themes for classroom work, and they play active roles in guiding, encouraging, and appreciating children's work.[10] However, a major feature of such programs is adapting to the child's needs, so that there is great stress on teacher flexibility in noting and adapting to the child's reactions to learning activities, suggested or selected.

Dewey himself, picking out common elements of progressive schools, listed such items as respect for individuality and for increased freedom, building on children's actual experiences, informality, activity instead of passivity, normal social relations and communication, importance of teacher-child contacts, self-initiated and self-conducted learning, and· the "all-enveloping medium" of social cooperation within the school.[11] Dewey's list has endured remarkably well and could easily be applied to any distinctive form of informal or

8. Robert J. Fisher, *Learning How to Learn* (New York: Harcourt Brace Jovanovich, 1972), p. 113.
9. Lillian S. Stephens, *The Teacher's Guide to Open Education* (New York: Holt, Rinehart & Winston, 1974), pp. 244–245.
10. John D. Hassett and Arline Weisberg, *Open Education: Alternatives within Our Tradition* (Englewood Cliffs, N. J.: Prentice-Hall, 1972); and Leonard Marsch, *Being a Teacher* (New York: Praeger, 1973), pp. 108–114.
11. John Dewey, "Progressive Education and the Science of Education," in Martin S. Dworkin, *Dewey on Education: Selections* (New York: Teachers College Press, 1959), pp. 113–126.

open classroom. As a leading philosopher and intellectual, however, Dewey's emphasis on connecting or involving children with major fields and ideas of knowledge—through the activities he encouraged —is receiving less emphasis today than in his own time, when he disavowed the progressive school development because he saw it as mindless and chaotic, perverting his philosophy grossly.

Literacy in the open classroom

Most writers on open education today agree that for most minority group parents in large urban centers, reading and literacy hold the highest priority and must be respected. Advocates of open education programs claim that their approach is far more likely to stimulate and motivate children to read and write and therefore must, in the end, prove more successful than most other approaches. Describing their adaptation (in New York City) of the British Infant School informal methods, Hassett and Weisberg list the salient features of their adaptation to the American scene as: stimulating curiosity to learn through choices of materials and activities, integrating subject matter and using it as a tool of learning, project centeredness, individual and small-group work, learning through activities with natural materials, relating life to school learning, and emphasizing the improvement of the human environment for living.[12] There are infinite adaptations of the Dewey-progressive education-British Informal Infant School approach to be found everywhere. Some teachers and schools emphasize some parts of the approach while others make different selections. Who is to say which is the "true" model?

MONTESSORI

What is probably most appealing to students of Montessori is her great love and respect for children. Her glowing appreciation of young children and her splendid demonstrations of educating children, whether they were economically deprived or retarded, insure Montessori's place as a major star in early childhood education. While Montessori's ideas are in harmony with those of Rousseau, Froebel, Pestalozzi,

12. John D. Hassett and Arline Weisberg, *Open Education: Alternatives within Our Tradition* (Englewood Cliffs, N. J.: Prentice-Hall, 1972), pp. 67–80.

Montessori programs feature materials, freedom, and sensory education, with structural content and methodology.

Dewey, and Piaget, her unique contribution was the development of a complete system of educating young children, including the design of very attractive, useful materials, along with a philosophy and psychology of teaching. The obsolescence of the "faculty" psychology upon which Montessori based her program seems irrelevant to her contemporary followers.

Materials, responsible freedom, and sensory education are the heart of the Montessori program.[13] No one before Montessori, with her medical and psychiatric training, had ever spelled out so clearly why the growing child needs freedom of movement. Child observation is a major teaching skill required to help the teacher know when a child is ready for a specific learning.[14] When a child is perceived as ready, his use of the relevant materials must proceed in predetermined sequence, and teachers use specified didactic or direct teaching modes as a major teaching strategy. While a child in a non-Montessori kindergarten might receive chiefly verbal instructions as to how to use materials, the Montessori teacher usually invites the child to observe her "correct" use of the materials as she instructs him in their use.

Task orientation

Fantasy, dramatic play, and esthetic and self-expressive activities are notably absent from Montessori classrooms, and work orientation is very evident. (It is true that young children can make play out of any task and they probably do in many Montessori classrooms.) Dolls, blocks, and miniature toys are also absent. Tasks are oriented to real life, such as cleaning wood, pouring water, buttoning, and shoelacing, and persistence and orderliness are featured. Each task, however, has a sequence of specified steps to insure correct learning and success.

The task orientation, individual pacing, child centeredness, the sequencing of real-life as well as academic skills, together with emphasis on self-discipline, or "normalization" as Montessori termed it, attracts many parents to this program. Children have choices and autonomy within very clearly defined limits of behavior and learning requirement.[15] Reports of successful reading instruction of very young

---

13. Evans, op. cit., pp. 29–62.
14. Maria Montessori, *Spontaneous Activity in Education* (Cambridge, Mass.: Robert Bentley, 1965), pp. 125–141.
15. Maria Montessori, *The Montessori Method* (New York: Schocken, 1964), pp. 86–106.

children have also attracted those parents most interested in such skill development, although such reports are for the most part lacking in supportive data.

The didactic materials Montessori designed are widely used in American programs and include the number rods (much larger than Cuisenaire rods), the pink tower, and the cylinders. The materials are said to be didactic, that is, they *teach* the child; if he makes a mistake in their use, the mistake is visible and "self-corrective."

When educators freely adapt to Montessori program features such as creative arts, self-expression in dance and music, stories and poetry, and dramatizations, they claim they are only updating the program to what "Montessori would do if she were alive today." Obviously, adaptations are as varied as the adapters.

Lack of social and verbal emphases

The Montessori program is a very individual-task-oriented program. The social interaction Dewey stressed so much for cooperative living is totally absent from the Montessori philosophy. Neither is there value placed on verbal interchange among children or between teacher and child except, in the latter case, for prescribed instructional purposes. Evans summarizes research on American Montessori programs to indicate that these programs seem to develop children's "appropriate attentional responses, persistence, and discrimination sets," but that gains may be greater for children with various defects than for others."[16] Evans also raises questions about Montessori education (as have other researchers) concerning long-term effects, problems of transition to non-Montessori classrooms, and how much of the results are due to the teachers, the materials, or the children.

Impact on other programs

Unlike European experience, American Montessori schools tend to be privately financed and chiefly available to more affluent families. Despite the absence of Montessori programs in most public schools,

16. Evans, op. cit., p. 58.

effects of Montessori programs are to be seen in emphasis on detailed observation of children, use of Montessori-type materials, and matching children's selected learning activities to their present level of development and skill. It can be said that Montessori-type schools tend to permit children's free physical movement within the group setting, although children do learn to be self-disciplined in such free actions. However, the curriculum—the *what* of children's learning—tends to be tightly structured as to content, materials, sequencing, and types of activities.

NURSERY SCHOOLS

College laboratory nursery schools, parent cooperative and community-based non-profit group settings for young children date back to at least 1915 in the United States. Nursery schools seemed to be created either as group settings by college researchers for professional studies on how to care for children on the college campus or to meet the needs of well-educated parents primarily for group social experiences for their children.[17] Kindergartens, established by Froebel in Germany, caught on in the United States at first mostly in communities of German origin.[18] Kindergartens evolved in the nineteenth century as separate educational settings and began to be absorbed in public schools from 1870 on. Gradually kindergartens were established in large urban centers where non-English-speaking children of poor immigrants—the "disadvantaged" of their day—stimulated humanitarian efforts to "assimilate" and "Americanize" them.[19]

Child development base

Nursery schools developed programs very different from kindergartens. Child development was often the focus of observations and

17. Pauline S. Sears and Edith M. Dowley, "Research on Teaching in the Nursery School," in N. L. Gage, ed., *Handbook of Research on Teaching* (Chicago: Rand McNally, 1963), p. 815.

18. Evelyn Weber, *The Kindergarten: Its Encounter with Educational Thought in America* (New York: Teachers College Press, 1969), pp. 18–23.

19. Samuel J. Braun and Esther P. Edwards, *History and Theory of Early Childhood Education* (Worthington, Ohio: Charles A. Jones, 1972), pp. 73–78.

studies of children in nursery schools and the emphasis was on parent education to improve children's developing social, emotional, physical, and cognitive needs. Because nursery schools were not part of public school systems and because the children tended to come from economically and educationally advantaged families, there was no pressure for academic readiness or for early literacy. Play activities were highly valued, as well as art, music, dance, story telling, and story reading. Parents often played major roles, especially in coopera-

tive nursery schools, in making decisions about school policies, as well as in teaching or assisting teachers.[20] Informal education advocates would recognize such nursery school programs as the source of their own programs. There are still nursery schools—church or community

20. Katherine Whiteside Taylor, *Parents and Children Learn Together* (New York: Teachers College Press, 1967), passim.

based, or on a parent cooperative basis—which continue to perpetuate this tradition of child centeredness in free, relaxed environments, with some updating of materials and activities. Such groups tend to be more articulate these days, however, about their being based on Piaget, Dewey, or the English Infant School.

KINDERGARTENS

Kindergartens are quite another story. Educators continue to be perplexed as to the most appropriate stress for this age grade. If the school chooses family, interage, or vertical grouping (i.e., for four-, five-, and six-year-olds or five-, six-, and seven-year-olds), program decisions seem to be easier. With a mixture of ages and levels of development, it seems sensible to provide a range of activities and experiences from very playful to very academic types. Children can then choose or be encouraged to seek personally satisfying as well as developmentally appropriate kinds of school experiences. The kindergartens, which are the entering grade of public schools in most states, suffer from pressures of administration, parents, and primary teachers, to assure "readiness."

Readiness function of kindergartens

As a concept, "readiness" seems deceptively meaningful. Yet look at any five-year-old and you are sure to see that he is always "ready" for something. But what should it be?

Kindergartens became the entering grade of public schools and tended to feature readiness for academic studies.

Public school staffs tend to think of "readiness" as preparation for academic work, often including content that actually initiates the reading, writing, and math programs. Readiness for reading often includes learning to identify and write letters of the alphabet, phonics drill, and sight word instruction. Whether or not initial literacy or preparation for initial reading is included in the kindergarten program, many teachers assume that a prime objective of readiness activities is to accustom young children to sedentary work and self-discipline, required in many first grades.

Other kindergarten programs feature "circle time," "show and tell," and many craft projects as readiness activities to practice public speaking, taking turns, verbalization of information and, of course, a great deal of sitting still and being quiet. "Circle time" now regarded as a group discussion period, stems from the mystical Froebel tradition of creating the unity of a circle in order to experience oneness with God. Since the Froebel objective is no longer followed, the use of circle time needs periodic reexamination for its contribution to good programming. "Show and tell" periods, when children show the class some objects of interest in order to convey some information about the objects, are primarily exercises in public speaking and discussion. This activity also needs objective assessment of its usefulness.

More kindergartens are proclaiming themselves "informal" or "open" programs. This trend indicates a swing away from what used to be a program largely composed of holiday celebrations throughout the year, with some field trips and activities on "community helpers" such as firemen and mail carriers.

Other kindergartens, pressed to produce school "achievers," are so busy in early literacy curricula (usually with the most structured programs available) that just about everything else is excluded. It can be confidently predicted that these will change. *Change* is the only sure prediction. It seems likely that half-day kindergarten sessions of two and one-half to three hours, entirely preoccupied with early reading, will move either to an extended day of about four hours or to the full day of the primary and elementary grades. With changes in the direction of more hours per day are likely to come revived interest in music and the arts, play-oriented experiences and activities, and more child-choice of activities.

The more tightly structured behaviorist kindergartens tend to emphasize academic content more than other goals. However, students should remember how complex program development really is, how many strands come together to shape a program, and how central the teacher is in filtering this program so that it reaches children with a very distinctive flavor of teacher personality and priorities.

SHORT- AND LONG-TERM GOALS

Another way to classify programs includes differentiating those which stress short- rather than long-term goals.[21] Academic content (in the

21. Helen F. Robison, "Early Childhood Education for the Disadvantaged: What Research Says," in Harry S. Passow, ed., *Opening Opportunities for Disadvantaged Learners* (New York: Teachers College Press, 1972), pp. 84–108.

*Whether pro-
grams have
short- or long-
term goals
helps in
differentiation.*
form of early literacy) or other fact-oriented programs would come
under the short-term heading, while sensory-motor, social, cognitive,
language development, problem solving and creativity-nurturance
would be classified as long-term goals. In fact, it is difficult to make
such sharp distinctions because all goals tend to affect all other goals.
Nevertheless, it is possible to identify programs more geared toward
immediate payoff than in development over long periods.

Another way to separate short-term from long-term goals is to
identify "readiness" emphasis, or preparation for the future, as against
the "rich living in the present" emphasis. The former approach tends
to narrow the programs to those features which will lead the child to
be acceptable to the next level of schooling, therefore, the emphasis on
"readiness". The emphasis on the present stems very strongly from
Dewey and child development theorists, who stress the period of early
childhood as a developmental sequence with its own inherent needs
and goals, with no necessary reference to later development.[22]

Other issues which programs resolve in different ways include age
of entrance, grouping, instructional techniques, teacher roles, role of
parents, and articulation with public schools.

DAY CARE CENTERS

Day care centers, originating in the United States especially to serve a
social family need—protection and care of children of working
mothers or mothers unable to care for their children all day—often
play a bridging role with public schools, picking up school age children
after 3:00 p.m. for day care experiences until family members are free
to take the child home.

In the day care centers, teacher training requirements historically
have been far less rigorous than in public schools. In the late sixties,
programs began to approximate those in nursery schools and kindergartens. Program development may be very advanced and up to date
in many centers or given relatively little attention in others. Non-
profit centers in New York, California, and other states where staff
qualifications and educational features are regulated and monitored
often have well-developed programs and sophisticated equipment.
Mostly custodial care results where the children's and families' needs

22. John Dewey, "My Pedagogic Creed," in Reginald D. Archambault, ed., *John Dewey
on Education* (New York: Random House, 1964), pp. 430–434.

are not given centrality in budgeting and in setting standards of acceptable operation.

Day care centers have more complex program requirements than other prescribed settings.

Program requirements are, in many ways, more complex in day care centers than in other preschool settings.[23] The sheer length of the day for the child in the group setting, which can be as long as twelve hours in most cases, or overnight and week-long in a few cases, poses substantial problems.[24] Staff-teaming, and collaborative program implementation in the day care center classrooms to cover the long hours of operation without exhausting child and teacher are among the difficult implementation problems. The differentiated staffing common in day care, with aides or assistants and family workers integrating their efforts with head teachers, may be ideal but lack proven procedures for supervision, evaluation, and improvement in educational practices.

It is important that family needs and values receive adequate attention from the staff, to insure the necessary cooperation for child and family welfare. For example, weary working mothers, or physically enfeebled ones, may experience considerable jealousy of the child's attachment to the center and to specific teachers. Staff sensitivity must be well developed to nurture families as well as children and to seek optimum resolutions of very dire situations which occur.

Day care center programs tend to follow the same continuum of program goals and types as other preschool settings, despite large and more complex responsibilities.

BEHAVIORIST PROGRAMS

Behaviorism rests chiefly on Thorndike's law of effect: Behavior which leads to results that are satisfying tends to recur.[25] Modern behaviorists look to the results; if the desired behavior recurs, the reinforcer works.

Behaviorist programs may be termed "behavior analysis," "token reinforcement," "behavior modification," "contingency management," "operant methodology," or other titles referring to reinforcement of desired behavioral changes. A large group of programs using behaviorist principles are being used, sometimes experimentally, to try to im-

---

23. D. Baumrind, "Will a Day Care Center Be a Child Development Center?" *Young Children* 28 (1973), pp. 154–159.

24. Edith Grothberg, *A Review of the Present Status and Future Needs in Day Care* (Washington, D.C.: Social Research Groups, George Washington University, 1971), pp. 70–71.

25. J. M. McGeoch, *The Psychology of Human Learning* (New York: McKay, 1942), p. 574.

prove learning or behavior with children whose potential is usually considered low because of poverty, physical handicaps, or other reasons.

In some behaviorist programs, it is chiefly the social behavior of children which receives planned reinforcement; in others, the learning of academic content is handled with the reinforcement contingencies derived from learning theory.

Characteristics of behaviorist programs

Behaviorist programs manipulate environmental features to reinforce desired behavior.

Behaviorist programs seek to manipulate environmental features systematically in order to reinforce selected forms of child behavior. Positive and negative reinforcement, and nonreinforcement, are the leading types used, with positive reinforcement and nonreinforcement heading the list. Positive reinforcers, such as food or social approval, are offered immediately after the desired behavior occurs. Nonreinforcement is the deliberate withholding of reinforcement, e.g., planned refusal to pay attention to a child during an episode of undesirable behavior such as crying or sulking. Positive reinforcement tends to increase the frequency, duration, or other features of behavior the teacher deems desirable. Nonreinforcement tends to diminish the behaviors ignored. Reinforcers may be natural behaviors, candy or other edibles, toys, visual or auditory occurrences, social approach, or tokens which may be exchanged for any of the preceding reinforcers.[26]

Reinforcement schedules

The systematic features of behaviorism require the adjustment or variation of the reinforcers to the development of the desired behavioral changes. In the early stages of learning, children are reinforced regularly, but the schedule of reinforcement is likely to change to irregularity once the child approaches some stability in learning. Thus, schedules may vary from continuous to intermittent and from fixed-interval to variable-interval rates of reinforcement. All reinforcers are *contingent*—that is, reinforcement must follow desired behavior and must not be given at random.

26. Don Bushell, *Classroom Behavior: A Little Book For Teachers* (Englewood Cliffs, N. J.: Prentice-Hall, 1973), pp. 83–99.

Goal specification

Behaviorism requires precise specification of desired behavior or of behavioral goals. Reinforcers must be applied only to such desired behavior or to steps which lead to such desired behavior, the latter procedure known as *shaping*. In shaping, if the desired behavior is not immediately manifested, but the child shows movement in the right direction, reinforcers tend to encourage further movement in this direction.

Behaviorism also requires assessment of entry behavior—where is the child now and what can he do? For example, if a child is perceived as physically aggressive against other children, what is the nature of this aggression and of the frequency of its occurrence. The truth of the complaint, "He's always hitting," frequently turns out to be, "He hits another child once a day." Cueing is also used, to remind the child of the desired behaviors to be reinforced. Cueing consists of giving signals, verbal or nonverbal, which serve as directions or reminders to the child *before* he engages in undesirable behavior or commits an error.

Behavioral goals

Thus, the behaviorists generally require a "behavioral goal"—a specific statement of the desired behavior to result from the modification procedures, an identification of current or entry behavior, a plan for behavior modification or specification of procedures for accentuating desired behavior and minimizing or omitting undesirable behavior, selection or identification of reinforcers, and techniques to shape or modify behavior in the direction desired.

Behaviorists tend to use commercially prepared programs like DISTAR or Sullivan Programmed Reading.[27] However, some Head Start, day care centers, and other preschool settings use behavior modification techniques without behaviorally oriented content for social behavior improvement. Often, the behavior modification techniques are reserved for severe behavior problems or for children with

27. DISTAR is produced by Science Research Associates, Sullivan Programmed Reading by McGraw-Hill.

various physical, emotional, or cognitive handicaps for whom other teaching procedures appear to be ineffective.

A great deal of research is available on behavior modification techniques and reflects considerable success in achieving specific goals, whether in improved classroom behavior, social interactions, or various kinds of learning.[28] Most programs that include adequate staff training in the behaviorist procedures report considerable success in achieving specified objectives.[29] However, effects are not the same for all children. Sex, age, socioeconomic status and personality factors, as well as the particular goals of the program, affect the degree of success of modification techniques.

Humanist rejection of behaviorism

Should humanists use behaviorist techniques? Can you use behaviorist procedures in a limited way without contaminating essentially humanist values and techniques? Doesn't behavior modification constitute unethical manipulation of children? Can the ends justify the means? Should children learn to work for external rewards? These are genuinely disturbing questions of ethics and values which are raised by students, teachers, parents, philosophers, and anyone who reflects upon the significance of behavior modification.[30]

While humanists reject behaviorism as manipulation, humanistic features can be used in most behaviorist procedures.

Philosophically, if one espouses humanist values, the manipulation of human beings is generally repugnant. Having said this, however, this writer urges students to candid self-evaluation. Do they manipulate chidlren by withholding or offering affection, approval, or various kinds of rewards? What techniques have they observed, or tend to initiate, in the handling of severe behavior problems in group settings? Skinner actually advocated positive reinforcement procedures as far more humane and effective than aversive, punitive forms of teacher control.[31]

28. K. E. Allen et al., "Effects of Social Reinforcement on Isolate Behavior of a Nursery School Child," *Journal of Educational Psychology* 58 (1967), pp. 231–237; D. Baer and M. Wolf, "The Reinforcement Contingency in Preschool and Remedial Education," in R. Hess and R. Baer, eds., *Early Education* (Chicago: Aldine, 1968), pp. 119–129.
29. L. Ullman and L. Krasner, *Case Studies in Behavior Modification* (New York: Holt, Rinehart & Winston, 1965).
30. Harry S. Broudy and John R. Palmer, *Exemplars of Teaching Method* (Chicago: Rand McNally, 1965).
31. B. F. Skinner, *The Technology of Teaching* (Englewood Cliffs, N. J.: Prentice-Hall, 1968).

Humanistic uses of behaviorist techniques

It is possible, this writer thinks, to enlist even young children in the planned improvement of their behavior in a sequence which leads to internal controls, even in cases of severe emotional disturbance. This —a modified form of behavior modification—would avoid aversive forms of control, yet offer hope when neither social learning techniques nor developmental-relationship procedures seem to work. In selected cases when nothing works—when improved or more mature forms of behavior do not materialize—humane attitudes quickly turn sour for teacher, child, and parent. Usually, in these cases, teachers lack the training and support to establish sufficiently tolerant, acceptant, and positive environments for children who seem difficult to love. Ideally, such teachers should receive the necessary training and supervisory support and the child should receive supportive psychological services. In a world where the supply of services is so short of the needs, it may be more humane to give teachers short-run procedures, which tend to establish a success syndrome to replace a failure syndrome, than none at all.

It happens that there are some clearly humanistic features of the best behavior modification programs, among them the following:

> The teacher must establish the current or entry behavior of the child. Nonpunitive observation and attention is bound to occur, if, on the dimension selected, the teacher truly tries to find out exactly how the child is behaving. Sometimes it becomes clear to the teacher that the child's behavior is not really the problem. Instead, it may be too rigid methods of discipline, unrealistic expectations in consideration of the child's age, history, and current functioning, or other needs such as food or kindly attention. Any form of fairly objective observation of a child is likely to correct distorting perceptions and biases and to suggest ways to ameliorate a child's lot.[32]
>
> Teachers are encouraged to overlook trivial transgressions on the theory that nonreinforced behaviors tend to drop out. No humanist can top this for sheer kindliness and common sense.
>
> Teachers are encouraged to keep good records to show whether behavior is improving or not. How perceptive the teacher sounds when she says, "Look how much this child has improved! He hit a child only once this week instead of at least once every day. He's doing

---

32. Helen F. Robison and Sydney L. Schwartz, *Learning at an Early Age*, vol. 1, *A Programmed Text for Teachers* (Englewood Cliffs, N. J.: Prentice-Hall, 1972), pp. 117–137, 248–254.

better." Without records, the teacher's response is likely to be, "What! He's hitting again? He's always hitting," even though this behavior is really on the decline. It is clearly humane to be factual rather than emotional about children's development.

Reinforcers may be selected by the child (or by the teacher) to accentuate the child's real choices of activity. This is scarcely different from what humanistic teachers do.

"Shaping" procedures may help a teacher avoid abuse and ineffectual punitiveness by encouraging a child every time he takes a step in the direction desired. Shouldn't all children experience elation and approval for small achievements when big ones are scarce?

Fading and irregular reinforcement present problems. If, using external rewards, the teacher really manipulates a child who cannot tell when he will be reinforced and therefore maintains a high level of desired behavior, this constitutes a strong maintenance of external rewards. Unfortunately, most teachers use conditional approval in this way, whether they are consciously behaviorist or not. If the teacher's attention, interest, and benign encouragement lead to the child's internalization of his own behavior goals, the process is regarded as one of socialization, the way adults generally teach children how to behave acceptably in our society.

Clearly, humanistic teachers deplore child dependence on external rewards. Yet most teachers unhesitatingly use such rewards because they consider young children too immature to learn acceptable behavior without approval or reward systems. Some teachers manage to maintain a more logical position most of the time, without approval or reward giving, through social learning or teaching by example, especially in the management of behavior. Combining good social learning procedures with development-relationship procedures would probably work for most teachers with most children. Institutional supports in school and community are required to make such humanistic interactions with children feasible throughout the school.

Humane treatment of handicapped children

Students should realize that they will often have to teach a very disturbed or handicapped child, either one who is being "mainstreamed" by placement with mostly normal children or one who has not yet been identified as in need of specialized services. It is always more humane, in dealing with children with severe or undefined problems, to work positively, optimistically, and with feelings of some success. When children come out of stressful or demeaning environments, teachers are often challenged to "make a difference." Repairing damage, rebuilding inadequate self-valuing, or reversing failure often require complex teaching skills. Teachers should expect the necessary support for such children, inside and outside of the classroom.

Personal value systems

One must construct or identify one's own value system. This writer, humanistic in values and in means of procedures, encourages students to explore the humanistic literature and to personalize its meanings.[33] It is difficult to learn from negative examples of teaching. Yet, even when a student is unable to leave a school placement with a rather negative teacher, it is urgent to avoid imitation by clarifying one's own reactions in a framework of clear values.

SUMMARY *This chapter describes various ways to classify or differentiate programs for young children. One way is to classify programs by degree of structure, regardless of theoretical base.*

Classifying programs by theoretical base or function provides seven categories: developmental, behaviorist, Montessori, academic, cognitive, custodial, and community-oriented. However, programs tend to borrow features from each other and seldom exist in pure form. Other forms of differentiating programs include educational philosophy, degree of parent involvement, nature of instructional objectives, and degree of child or teacher control.

Most forms of program differentiation include such categories as type of child and teacher activity, materials, structure, sequence, characteristics and grouping of children, objectives, extent of parent involvement, and source of funding. Programs and objectives have evolved in different ways in kindergartens, nursery schools, day care centers, and other types of early childhood programs. Some of these differences relate to stress on short-term or on long-term goals or to objectives (which are more complex in day care centers).

33. L. Kohlberg, "Early Education: A Cognitive-Developmental View," *Child Development* 39 (1968), pp. 1013–1062; Don Dinkmeyer and R. Dreikurs, *Encouraging Children to Learn: The Encouragement Process* (Englewood Cliffs, N. J.: Prentice-Hall, 1963); W. Glasser, *Schools without Failure* (New York: Harper, 1969); Carl Rogers, *On Becoming a Person* (Boston: Houghton Mifflin, 1961); and Arthur W. Combs, *Professional Education of Teachers* (Boston: Allyn and Bacon, 1965), pp. 98–111.

Behavior modification techniques are used in many experimental, Head Start, Follow Through, kindergarten, and other types of early childhood programs. While humanists tend to reject behaviorist methods as manipulative of the child and establishing external rather than internal controls, possible humanistic uses, transitionally, of behaviorist techniques, which most teachers intuitively use, seem to be humane in effect.

✤ EXERCISES FOR STUDENTS

1. Make up a checklist of features of program differentiation using any of the ideas included in this chapter.

   a. Use this form to record your perceptions on visits to two very different programs, such as a day care center and a public school kindergarten.

   b. Try to arrange to interview the teacher, supervisor, or someone in the school who can add to your information by answering questions, for example, pertaining to program goals, schedules, child eligibility, and parent involvement.

2. Select a book on open education or on behavior modification and write a report identifying the distinguishing features of such programs. Contrast this list with the features of a program in which you are placed for participation, observation, or student teaching.

3. Arrange to interview at least three parents of your acquaintance with young children on their priorities and values for their children's education.

   a. Based on each parent's response, determine which type of program seems most appropriate.

   b. Justify your decisions, referring to your readings in the literature.

✤ EXERCISES FOR TEACHERS

1. Write a brief outline of the major features of the program you are implementing in your classroom (using one of the classifications de-

scribed in this chapter). Compare this outline with your daily operation, based on a log you keep for at least two weeks.

a. Identify program features you are not implementing, and plan
to include these as soon as you can. Keep a log to help you remember
how close you come to implementing the program you outlined
originally.

b. Identify program features that are not in harmony with your
program outline, and plan to change these to come closer to your
(ideal) outline.

2. Arrange a visitation, if you can, to a classroom where the teacher
is implementing a program different from yours, and include plans to
chat with the teacher over lunch or during a free period.

a. Plan in advance to read material about the program you plan to
visit, and have some questions prepared to elicit further information.

b. Plan also to compare notes on major program features to identify
what impact different features seem to have on such selected criteria
as reading readiness, creativity in art and music activities, children's
self-discipline or attention span, or parental roles.

3. Design a small research project to find out what results have been
obtained on comparing the effects of different programs on children's
progress in various ways. Be sure to consult the Head Start and Follow
Through evaluation studies.

BIBLIOGRAPHY

Allen, K. E. "Effects of Social Reinforcement on Isolate Behavior of a
Nursery School Child." *Journal of Educational Psychology* 58 (1967):
231–237.

Baer, D., and Wolf, M. "The Reinforcement Contingency in Preschool and
Remedial Education." *In Early Education,* edited by R. Hess and R.
Baer. Chicago: Aldine, 1968, pp. 119–129.

Baumrind, D. "Will a Day Care Center Be a Child Development Center?"
Young Children 28 (1973): 154–159.

Braun, Samuel J., and Edwards, Esther P. *History and Theory of Early Childhood Education.* Worthington, Ohio: Charles A. Jones, 1972.

Broudy, Harry S., and Palmer, John R. *Exemplars of Teaching Method.*
Chicago: Rand McNally, 1965.

Bushell, Don. *Classroom Behavior: A Little Book For Teachers.* Englewood Cliffs, N. J.: Prentice-Hall, 1973.

Combs, Arthur W. *Professional Education of Teachers.* Boston: Allyn and Bacon, 1965.

Dewey, John. "My Pedagogic Creed." In *John Dewey On Education,* edited by Reginald D. Archambault. New York: Random House, 1964.

Dewey, John. "Progressive Education and the Science of Education." In Dworkin, Martin S., *Dewey on Education: Selections.* New York: Teachers College Press, 1959.

Dinkmeyer, Don, and Dreikurs, D. *Encouraging Children to Learn: The Encouragement Process.* Englewood Cliffs, N. J.: Prentice-Hall, 1963.

Evans, Ellis D. *Contemporary Influences in Early Childhood Programs.* 2nd ed. New York: Holt, Rinehart & Winston, 1975.

Fisher, Robert J. *Learning How to Learn.* New York: Harcourt Brace Jovanovich, 1972.

Glasser, W. *Schools without Failure.* New York: Harper, 1969.

Hassett, John D., and Weisberg, Arline. *Open Education: Alternatives within Our Tradition.* Englewood Cliffs, N. J.: Prentice-Hall, 1972.

Kohlberg, L. "Early Education: a Cognitive-Developmental View." *Child Development* 39 (1968): 1013–1062.

Maccoby, Eleanor E., and Zellner, Miriam. *Experiments in Primary Education: Aspects of Project Follow Through.* New York: Harcourt Brace Jovanovich, 1970.

Marsh, Leonard. *Being a Teacher.* New York: Praeger, 1973.

McGeoch, J. M. *The Psychology of Human Learning.* New York: McKay, 1942.

Montessori, Maria. *Spontaneous Activity in Education.* Cambridge, Mass.: Robert Bentley, 1965.

Montessori, Maria. *The Montessori Method.* New York: Schocken, 1964.

Neill, A. S. *Summerhill: A Radical Approach to Child Rearing.* New York: Hart, 1960.

Parker, Ronald C., ed. *The Preschool in Action: Exploring Early Childhood Programs.* Boston: Allyn and Bacon, 1972.

Robison, Helen F. "Early Childhood Education for the Disadvantaged: What Research Says." In *Opening Opportunities for Disadvantaged Learners,* edited by Harry Passow. New York: Teachers College Press, 1972.

Robison, Helen F., and Schwartz, Sydney L. *Learning at an Early Age.* Vol. 1. *A Programmed Text For Teachers.* Englewood Cliffs, N. J.: Prentice-Hall, 1972.

Rogers, Carl. *On Becoming a Person.* Boston: Houghton Mifflin, 1961.

Sears, Pauline S., and Dowley, Edith M. "Research on Teaching in the Nursery School." In *Handbook of Research on Teaching,* edited by N. L. Gage. Chicago: Rand McNally, 1963.

Skinner, B. F., *The Technology of Teaching*. Englewood Cliffs, N. J.: Prentice-Hall, 1968.

Stephens, Lillian S. *The Teacher's Guide to Open Education*. New York: Holt, Rinehart & Winston, 1974.

Taylor, Katherine Whiteside. *Parents and Children Learn Together*. New York: Teachers College Press, 1967.

Ullman, L., and Krasner, L. *Case Studies in Behavior Modification*. New York: Holt, Rinehart & Winston, 1965.

Weber, Evelyn. *The Kindergarten: Its Encounter with Educational Thought in America*. New York: Teachers College Press, 1969.

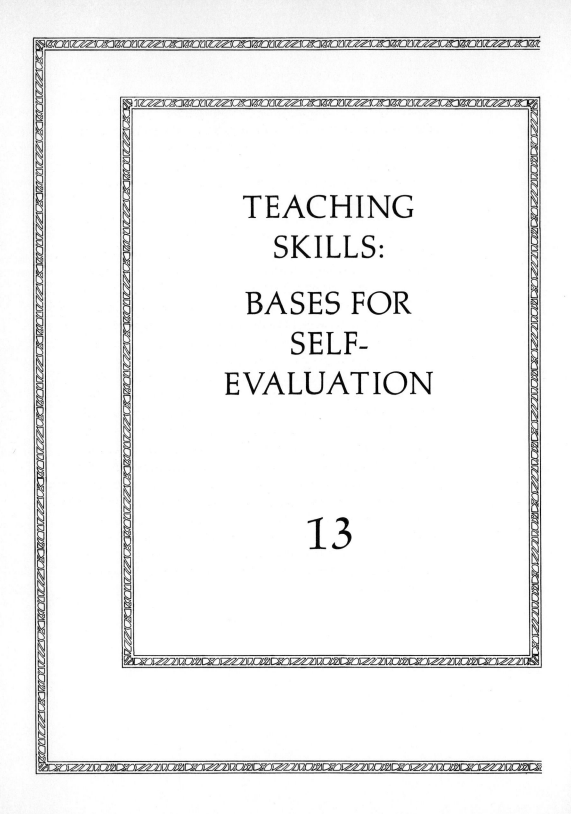

TEACHING SKILLS:

BASES FOR SELF-EVALUATION

13

A professional attitude toward one's own growth in understandings, skills, and views of teaching requires growing
independence, especially in self-evaluation of progress.
Supervisors often differ in their grading and evaluation of
observed teaching. Sometimes they differ because they value
different teaching goals or processes. But they also differ, to
a surprising extent, when they seem to be evaluating the
same skills or aspects of teaching.

Understandably, evaluation of teaching has been somewhat unpredictable because of its subjectivity. Different
observers tended to *like* or *dislike* all or some of what they
observed. Yet subjective evaluations are poor instruments
for stimulating growth because they foster dependency of
the teacher candidate upon others for their opinions and
feelings. During the sixties and seventies, a number of different approaches in research sought to overcome this subjectivity by identifying teaching *behaviors* that could be
specified, quantified, and related, statistically, to each other
and, ultimately, to children's learning. This movement became a vehicle for the newer, rapidly developing national
trend in teacher certification and preparation toward use of
a competency base. Competency-based teacher education
(CBTE) and performance-based teacher education (PBTE)
are used interchangeably in this chapter. However, the
reader should note that in some states, CBTE is measured
only by children's scores on standardized tests of the
achievement type, while in most states the teacher competencies are primarily evaluated by teacher behavior tests
of various kinds without regard to the difficult-to-determine
effects on children.

In this chapter, teacher candidates will find:

1. An analysis of major educational program types and related teaching skills.
2. A description of universal teaching skills in early childhood programs.
3. A discussion of distinguishing features of the CBTE movement.
4. A description of major evaluation systems to analyze teaching.

The reader will note two major types of problems analyzed in this chapter. The first problem concerns identification of teaching skills needed for successful early childhood teaching. The second problem, assuming we can solve the first one, is how to assess the teaching skills.

TEACHER COMPETENCIES AS BEHAVIORAL GOALS

Since the use of behavioral goals is a major component of CBTE systems and is often used even in nonbehaviorist systems, an illustration of such a behavioral goal is given here to indicate how students might find this chapter useful:

> *Given a system for self-analysis of teaching, the student will demonstrate mastery of that system by completion of a self-analysis of one teaching episode which is in agreement by 80 percent or more with the analysis made by the College Supervisor of that teaching episode recorded on videotape.*

It should be noted that, while this behavioral goal for competence in self-evaluation requires congruence with an expert's evaluation, the purpose of achieving such congruence is to establish confidence in the student's ability to self-evaluate independently. When it is difficult to establish such congruence, problems must be identified either in the system of evaluation itself—which may not be sufficiently clear or objective—or in biases of either the student or the supervisor. The more objective the system, the less chance there is for biases to operate in any important way.

EVALUATION SYSTEMS

There are many evaluation systems for studying teaching in use or in the process of development, and usually each system is sufficiently different from the others that data from different systems cannot be lumped together. Some systems yield data only on the *affective* conditions of the classroom, others only in *cognitive* learning, and some limit observation to such specific aspects of teaching as questioning skills.[1] "Program neutral" systems are being developed, although they may never be completely acceptable in all programs.

Systems selected for evaluation of teaching skills generally have built-in preferences which are difficult to neutralize. It seems more objective to identify one's preferences, values, or preferred teaching outcomes and to select assessment systems most closely related to such outcomes. When a system has been chosen, based on a teacher's preferences, the next step is to learn to use the system skillfully.

ANALYSIS OF TYPES OF PROGRAMS

Kohlberg's analysis of early childhood educational programs into three types is a useful way to distinguish the three major value or philosophic frameworks which serve to define program goals. He finds that most programs can be assigned to one of three major categories: Romantic Maturational, Cultural Transmission, and Progressive Developmental.[2]

Romantic maturational

This view stems from Rousseau, who saw the child as innately good and having a need to unfold and discover knowledge for himself in a benign milieu. Teaching in this type of program is chiefly arranging a healthy and stimulating environment, keeping the child safe and

1. A. Simon and E. Boyer, eds., *Mirrors for Behavior: An Anthology of Observation Instruments Continued,* 1970 Supplement, vols. A and B (Philadelphia: Research for Better Schools, 1970).
2. L. Kohlberg and R. Mayer, "Development as the Aim of Education," *Harvard Educational Review* 42 (1972), pp. 449–496.

healthy, and facilitating learning without "telling" or didactic teaching. Good relationships with children are an important requirement here. The Summerhill school in England, established by A. S. Neill, may have the best-known program of this type, with extreme voluntarism for children in their learning activities and strong emphasis upon the encouraging, nurturing environment.[3]

Cultural transmission

People who are "perennialists" philosophically believe that there is a well-defined body of knowledge that must be transmitted to children and that teaching skills to transmit that knowledge can be derived from the goal, that is, successful transmission of specific knowledge. Engelmann's DISTAR program is a well-known example of such a program in early childhood education.[4] Behaviorist theories fit well in this niche, with teaching skills of reinforcement, cueing, learner responses, small steps, and branching.

Progressive developmental

Dewey and Piaget have contributed the main ideas to this philosophic framework, and Kamii's curriculum study—on a Piagetian base—is an outstanding example of this type.[5] Such programs are sometimes termed "interactive" or "transactional." They are based on the belief that the child has genetically given cognitive structures that develop by his own actions on objects in an interactive social environment as he matures. According to this view the child does not receive knowledge but constructs it in the course of his activities, changing and refining these constructions with experience, age, and increasing cognitive growth through various stages of development.[6] The British informal or open education programs belong here, as well as many

3. A. S. Neill, *Summerhill: A Radical Approach to Child Rearing* (New York: Hart, 1960).

4. S. Engelmann et al., *DISTAR* (Chicago: Science Research Associates, 1971).

5. Constance Kamii, "An Application of Piaget's Theory to the Conceptualization of a Preschool Curriculum, in *The Preschool In Action*, edited by R. K. Parker (Boston: Allyn and Bacon, 1972), pp. 91–133.

6. Jean Piaget, *The Origins of Intelligence in Children* (New York: International Universities, 1952).

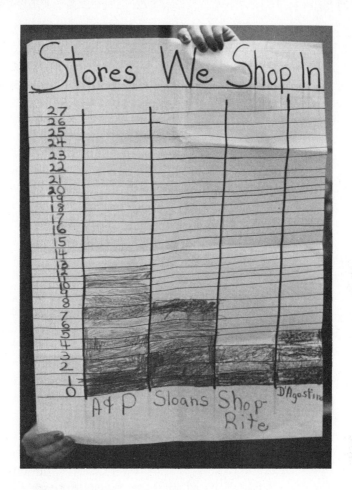

American programs which stress process goals—learning how to learn —rather than the knowledge learned.

Most school programs for grades three and above are of the cultural transmission type, and a majority of primary programs probably are, as well. At the early levels—kindergarten and prekindergarten—there are far more developmental-type and romantic-maturational varieties. Local pressures usually determine which direction the early childhood programs take.

The contemporary CBTE movement is very congruent with cultural transmission programs because of its behaviorist, systems-oriented character. Developmental programs, far more *process*-oriented, are not so easily translated into teaching skills and competencies. However, several interesting efforts are available.

CBTE BASED ON CHILD AS LEARNER

The child as a learner can be central to program distinctions along a continuum.

Attempting to define "teaching skills" in early childhood programs, a study by Anastasiow and Mansergh started with Kohlberg's analysis, then selected what was perceived as the important point of differentiation—the view of the child as a learner. In the study, the authors use a "hypothetical continuum . . . from one extreme of those who perceive the child as a passive receptor (behavioristic; the use of drill and small-step procedures) to the other extreme of those who perceive the child as the active transactor (the use of discovery or guided discovery)."[7] It is interesting that the authors of the study do not regard the use of reinforcement or social learning techniques as a way of differentiating programs; they regard all programs as using these to some extent. Neither is degree of structure seen as a differentiating feature; it is assumed that all programs require structuring of some features.

Anastasiow and Mansergh delineate teaching skills, based on how the child is perceived as a learner, for each checkpoint on the continuum. Thus, at one end of the continuum, congruent with behaviorist theory that the child responds to training by the teacher, teaching skills include techniques of reinforcement, identification of behavioral goals, and specification of small steps of instruction and similar skills.

At the middle of the continuum is the "normal developmental" type, exemplified in many kindergarten programs which stress "readiness" and look to successive grades for their program goals. Such teaching is based, first, on preparation for the next grade and, ultimately, for school success. These programs, according to the authors, stress "teacher-oriented activities to prepare children for formal school, usually first grade."[8] Teaching skills derived from this type of program orientation include, among others, instructional skills and skills of identification of child needs for success in school.

Finally, the cognitive developmental type of program, with its Piagetian base in stages of development, stresses teaching skills relating to knowledge of developmental stages and the arranging of environments to encourage such development.

---

7. Nicholas J. Anastasiow and Gilbert P. Mansergh, "Teaching Skills in Early Childhood Programs," National Center for the Development of Training Materials in Teacher Education (Bloomington: Indiana University, 1973), p. 4.
    8. Ibid.

UNIVERSAL TEACHING SKILLS

Despite these different emphases in programs, however, students should note that all programs for young children have some important common denominators in teaching skills, some of which are so universal that they may not even be specified. One such fundamental teaching skill is the maintenance of a safe and healthy environment. Yet this is not one skill but a group of skills which, together, serve to keep young children in healthy, benign environments. Other required teaching skills include interpersonal sensitivity, planning and evaluating child progress, working with parents to promote home-school unity in child progress, and classroom and behavior management.

Health and safety needs

No program for young children should be tolerated without assurance that the teaching staff possesses skills to assure the health and safety of their young pupils. While there has been a notable absence in this country of detailed monitoring of the quality of early childhood programs except in the public schools, fire and health regulations are generally applied and enforced.

Health maintenance practices.   In most cases, children are required to have a physical examination before admission to a group setting, and children's medical forms are usually required to be kept on file in the school. Students seeking to equip themselves better to understand and implement good health practices might visit a pediatric clinic or discuss child health maintenance practices and problems with a pediatric nurse or a pediatrician. Commonly used medical forms can be secured and studied for the kinds of information requested, and discussion may be held on the range of possible responses.

Practical suggestions are offered for maintenance of children's health and safety.

First aid skills.   Students will want to know about current preventive practices, seasonal occurrence of symptoms of various types, signals of urgency in securing medical attention, and suggestions for "what to do until the doctor comes." A first-aid course is an excellent preparation for teaching young children. However, first-aid practices change with new research findings, so this is an important area for periodic updating of information and skills. Since very few group settings for children offer anything approaching adequate medical services, the teacher must be knowledgeable enough to take the same precautions a prudent parent would take.

Safety practices. Accident prevention and the regular implementation of safety practices are assured through such time-tested procedures as these:

> Use a reliable system of periodic headcounts. Know where all the children are and, if one is not readily visible, go and find him.
>
> Work, always, with eyes facing the classroom so that you scan the room automatically to note anything requiring attention.
>
> Develop a safety check of the room and use it regularly to identify such hazards as slick spots on the floor or playground, splinters, projecting nails, litter, broken glass, and the like. If electrical equipment is used, plugs and wiring should be checked regularly to spot and correct possible fire hazards, energy wastefulness, and accident possibilities.
>
> Involve the children in the safety check, with regular rotation of responsibilities, so that even young children will spot a hazard and call your attention to it.
>
> Model safety practices and praise children's performances when appropriate. For example, to establish the undesirability of handling broken glass with bare hands, point out to the children that you pick it up with a glove or thick mitt.
>
> Develop a very few, clear safety rules with the children and monitor these rules uniformly in the classroom, on the playground, and on walks and trips.
>
> Keep a health checklist and observe each child in the group as soon after arrival as possible, for symptoms of general malaise—unusual inactivity, withdrawal, or unhappy expressions. Look also for any specific symptoms of ill health such as elevation in temperature, rash, cough, nasal congestion, redness of the eyes, or difficulty staying awake. Develop a useful checklist guide with your supervisor, school nurse, or other medical expert.
>
> Keep handy any special health conditions of specific children, including allergies, diabetes, and heart or other medical problem that requires special attention in any way.
>
> Keep handy, for each child, the name, address, and telephone number (at home and at work) of the person to be notified in case of child illness or accident and, where applicable, the name and telephone number of the family doctor or medical affiliation. The school office usually keeps such information on file, but a teacher feels safer, especially on trips, if such data is also in his or her possession.

Plan to hold several meetings each year with parents to discuss health and safety practices and to plan for more unified home-school procedures. For example, plan a meeting on child dental care with a school nurse, dental nurse, or pediatric dentist who can demonstrate and explain approved practices, including diet, tooth brushing, and dental checkups.

In the area of health and safety, teaching skills, as summarized in a CBTE early childhood teacher preparation program discussed below, might include:

1. Knowledge
   a. Knowledge of child development sequences and stages
   b. Knowledge of fire and health requirements for group settings
   c. Knowledge of common symptoms of childhood diseases and health problems and of current approved practices for identification and referral
2. Skills
   a. Skill in identification of children's symptoms of possible disease and health problems
   b. Skill in implementing approved fire prevention and health maintenance practices
   c. Skill in collaborating with parents and community agencies for maintenance of child health and safety

Interpersonal skills

Skills of interacting with others, or human relations skills, are defined in various ways:

Interpersonal or human relations skills can be specified in various ways.

Self-awareness or self-understanding
Empathy for others
Respectfulness toward children and other adults
Personalization of responses
Appropriate forms of communication, both verbal and nonverbal
Accepting other's feelings
Reflecting to others one's perceptions of their feelings
"Reading" others' signals of feelings and perceptions
Adapting one's responses to expected levels of understanding

Carl Rogers' specifications for authenticity in expressing feelings and accepting others' feelings in encounters with others as teachers or therapist will appeal to many teachers of the humanist persuasion.[9]

9. Carl Rogers, *On Becoming a Person* (Boston: Houghton Mifflin, 1961).

A CBTE model defines empathy behaviorally: "(1) attending behavior (maintaining eye contact, physical attentiveness, verbal following behavior in which the individual stays on the other's topic of conversation, (2) reflection of feeling (trainee attends primarily to the feeling or emotional statements of others), and (3) physical empathy (simply assuming the physical posture of the other in an attempt to feel more closely what the other is feeling)."[10]

A summary of interpersonal skills might be as follows:

Knowledge of child development, sequence, stages and major theories including Piaget, Freud, and Erikson

Knowledge of major theories of interpersonal relationships such as those of Freud, Lewin, Adler, and Rogers

Skills of relating to and interacting with children—including subskills of empathy, respect, and personalization—and "reading" children's feelings and messages

Skills of relating to and interacting with staff members and parents, including spontaneity, clarity, empathy, respect, personalization, and articulateness

Preplanning and evaluating child progress

Any educational program worthy of the name requires some elements of planning and evaluation. In some settings, the planning focuses solely on materials and equipment, while in others tight schedules are devised and advance decisions made on grouping children, sequencing the activities, task selection, and assessment details.

Preplanning and assessment skills are required in all programs.

Whether planning and assessment decisions and activities are more or less detailed, more or less inclusive, and relatively formal or informal are usually functions of the setting, program requirements, and staff or administrative preferences. Planning may in many cases be confined to processes or to activities or to such long-term developmental goals as child problem-solving skills. Some plans are contingent, that is, *if* the children demonstrate particular interests or problems, the plans are activated but not otherwise. Other plans *require* eliciting or bringing about desired educative situations, tasks, or activities.

10. *Massachusetts Model Elementary Teacher Education Program* (Washington, D.C.: U.S. Department of Health, Education, and Welfare, 1968), pp. 82–84.

Thus, while planning and assessment skills in teaching have a continuum of requirements and specifications from very broad and permissive to very detailed and required procedures, every teacher of young children needs to be prepared to use such skills in some productive ways. Public schools usually require lesson plans in a particular format, one that is often difficult to use with programs for young children. Early childhood teachers might wish to propose an alternative form or procedure to the administration, one that reflects more productive planning for the program goals.

A summary of planning and evaluating skills universally required for teaching young children could include these skills: (1) Identifying and specifying child progress goals including diagnosis, analysis, and specification of child needs; (2) developing plans to further child progress including selection of activities, materials, experiences, environments, and procedures; (3) evaluating child progress toward identified goals including selection and use of instruments and procedures, outcome goals, and judgments about extent of progress.

Working with parents

Students will find a full discussion on collaborating with parents in Chapter 14. Briefly, examples of teacher skills to promote home-school unity for child progress are:

Skills of working with parents can be specified to promote home-school unity.

1. Knowledge of community characteristics including socioeconomic levels, race, ethnic, language, and religious affiliations and preferences.
2. Knowledge of community resources for children's educational progress, among them, libraries, theaters, recreational activities, parks, museums, exhibits, and industrial, business, and cultural institutions.
3. Knowledge of ways to emphasize school understanding and interest in community cultural distinctiveness.
4. Skill in conducting parent conferences as interactive procedures to reach some agreement on home-school plans for children's educational and developmental progress.
5. Skill in conducting meetings with groups of parents on child development problems and progress, on school and community educational goals, and on forms of home-school collaboration for children's progress.

Classroom and behavior management

All group settings for young children require arranging and managing the environment, the materials, and the equipment—generally termed classroom management—as well as moderating children's behavior in many ways for group living in classrooms. The latter function may be termed behavior management, discipline, social learning, or socialization procedures.

Chapter 4—on self-esteem—includes discussions of teaching approaches to classroom and behavior management that maintain, support, or improve children's sense of self-worth. Since this chapter focuses on teaching skills and evaluating skill development, a summary of teaching skills in classroom and behavior management at this point will serve to summarize and emphasize essential teaching strategies, skills and functions.

Preventing behavioral problems.   If the room is skillfully arranged, a great deal of child dependency on the teacher and child conflicts about use of materials and space can be avoided. Classroom management which minimizes or avoids behavioral problems have such features as:

> Clarity of rules about school behavior expectations
> Children's sense of fair play in equipment use
> Efficient patterns of equipment use
> Increased instructional time available with less waiting time for children
> Greater child independence in involvement and in transition from one activity to another[11]

Practical classroom management skills.   Teacher candidates can develop considerable understanding and skill in management procedures in their student teaching experiences by:

1. Working with the cooperating classroom teacher to improve the orderly arrangement of materials.
2. Helping children to maintain orderly arrangements or to restore materials to their place after use.

11. Helen F. Robison and Sydney L. Schwartz, *Learning at an Early Age: A Programmed Text for Teachers*, vol. 1 (Englewood Cliffs, N. J.: Prentice-Hall, 1972), p. 198.

3. Redesigning the use of classroom space for more productive functioning. Classroom teachers find that children become intrigued when learning center activities take on a new look. Novelty, attractiveness, and fresh appeal are often achieved through a rearrangement of classroom space.

4. Studying children's use of learning centers and behavioral problems distribution to target specific needs for change. For example, observational recording, anecdotal recording, time sampling, or children's completion of checklists daily throughout one week might reveal such problems as:

One feature of good classroom management is arrangement of classroom space for productive functioning.

a. Block corner overuse, with too many children for the space. Alternatives: Enlarge the space, decrease the number of children allowed, move the block corner to a different area with more space, or increase the attractiveness of other learning centers. *Note the procedure suggested above:* Obtain data as to what the problems are, list options for alternatives, select one or more which promise to alleviate problems, and try out an alternative.

b. Too great child dependency on teacher in art center. Alternatives: Improve storage and children's access to art materials to decrease dependency, develop "helper" responsibility so that one child daily plays a teacher role in meeting remaining dependency needs, devise better procedures for preparing art center for daily use and/or for clean-up needs including making available cleaning equipment and training children in its use. Art center problems often include greater demand than supply of easels, sticky jars of paint that children are unable to open, spills which children do not know how to handle, lack of space or equipment to dry wet paintings or to store projects which are not completed. In addition, children waiting turns to paint or to work with clay may become impatient or angry and provoke conflicts in the art center. Clear rules, in addition to attractive alternatives, prevent such conflict situations.

5. Improving procedures during such routines as arrival, snack time, or dismissal. Problems frequently encountered include the following:

a. Confusion about dressing and undressing, especially in bad weather or with heavy winter outer clothes. Alternatives include working with a few children at a time and instructing them in sequence of clothing removal or attire and in small steps to insure mastery of dressing skills; modelling procedures with one child and monitoring other children's performance; asking parents' help early in the semester to buy winter clothing which children can manage more easily and to label all clothing with name tapes; requesting help from older children at school to assist younger children with clothing; developing games and chants about dressing and undressing to help children remember *how* and to help them remain relaxed while they try.

b. Confusion, testing limits, and going out of bounds during transitional periods like the end of clean-up periods leading to toileting, washing hands, and snack periods.

Handling transitional periods. Transitional periods of the above type tend to give student teachers and novice teachers more trouble than any other part of the program. It is not difficult to see why. Children's self-discipline is highest when involvement is highest—for the duration of the many interesting learning activities. As change of activity approaches, involvement declines, the boundaries or limits become more vague, time is suddenly too abundant and empty, and the child who was a model of self-containment goes out of bounds. Resisting suggestion and becoming overstimulated or hostile, the children contribute to the melting of class structures and procedures.

Treating such problems during transitional periods punitively is unproductive, since it only yields fearfulness or anger. More productive alternatives include:

Structuring of transitions until children become more independent and stable.

Choreographing with clarity and relaxed manner the movements children need to make; maintaining a calm atmosphere.

Conveying clear and optimistic *expectations* of children's behavior.

Cueing children to remind them of next steps or of one or two options available before they end their major center activity, for example, "When you finish putting the blocks away, you may go in the library corner to look at a book or come to the music center and sing some songs."

Giving positive feedback to children who stay within bounds so that they know *what they did* that was acceptable.

Redirecting children who tend to go out of bounds so they know *what to do* that would be acceptable.

Note the accent on positive teaching strategies: model, instruct, redirect, cue, emphasize desired behavior. Note also the absence of ridicule, sarcasm, punishment or projections of teacher anger or frustration.

During transitional periods, children forget or become confused about what happens next or their social skills become unequal to the demands made and then their most immature forms of behavior are likely to surface. This is the time when the teacher's most mature skills are needed. Backed by *preplanned* procedures to minimize confusion, the teacher's calmness and confidence in her ability to keep the group in socially desirable limits increase structure and ease children's learning of more subtle forms of group living. These skills transform potential chaos into visible steps in social learning.

Developing alternate management procedures.   Classroom management skills are not acquired spontaneously. Competence in this area results from well-developed procedures, and students need to learn a host of possible procedures so they will have a knowledge base on which to build.

A group of student teachers often finds that each of their classroom placements reflects different methods of classroom management. It is possible, in comparing experiences, to conclude that none of the classrooms provide ideal models. If one classroom provides such a model, the whole group would do well to study it, analyze its components, and simulate some practice experiences. However, since no model is ideal for every teacher and for every group of children, students might complete exercises, such as those at the end of this chapter, to seek alternative procedures for various kinds of groups.

Features of successful classroom management.   Students might remember, in their search for effective classroom management skills, that in working with young children:

> *Physical cues* are often more effective than verbal cues. If children have to place a key on a hook to "sign themselves" into a center or to remove a key to "sign out," the physical cues of entering or leaving a center help children remember the rules and give more structure to their entering and leaving behavior by helping them to define limits physically.
>
> *Reminders or cues* help prevent conflict and forgetfulness of rules. Children's memories may be short when they become involved in interesting work.
>
> *Young children need flexibility* in rule learning. It may be clean-up time, but an unfinished painting demands a few more minutes for completion.
>
> *Time* and *further practice* may be needed when young children are learning rules. If the child manifests any understanding of the kinds of behaviors that are acceptable and the kinds that are not, positive feedback of the acceptable behaviors and further instruction to improve social functioning tend to help children's social learnings improve steadily.

Teacher candidates will recognize these suggestions as reminders that their own knowledge of child development and learning must be applied, especially in difficult teaching situations, where such applied knowledge is most needed. In dynamic classroom situations, it is sometimes difficult to overlook disappointing child behavior or to see its other side, which often reflects improvement but not as much improvement as desired. If students can learn to observe growth and progress and to value the *direction* as well as the *pace* of children's learning, they can become more positive in their views of children as well as in their interactions with them.

Improving child behavior. No matter which theoretical base for behavior management students follow, primarily behaviorist or primarily humanist, they are likely to use some techniques of both. Teachers who profess to be humanistic in their teaching will often use praise or reinforcement—strategies primarily regarded as behaviorist.

Students and teachers will find themselves using both behavioral and humanistic techniques.

Similarly, behaviorist methods are seldom followed without humanistic efforts to establish good relationships with children and to seek causes for their behavior. Desiring intrinsic forms of rewards for learning—wanting children to love to learn—teachers of young children nevertheless find it difficult to omit praise for well-channelled efforts. If teachers trust children and maintain respect and optimistic expectations for growth, few gimmicks are needed.

Stars, gifts, and awards of prizes for children's classroom work are avoidable if teachers seek to strengthen internal motivation to learn. The activity is its own reward for most normal, healthy children. But what should the teacher do to develop interest and productive activity in children who have experienced various kinds of trauma which inhibit self-confidence, expectations of success, or the courage to try to learn? It is possible that children who have suffered damage in some critical aspect of their development may need forms of teaching different from those that healthy children require. While the warmth and personalization of a teacher is often stressed as an important characteristic for an early childhood learning situation, it has been found that some autistic children, who could not respond to teachers, found it possible to respond to a teaching machine. Alleviating or ameliorating developmental problems often calls for much patience, tolerance of regression, and creative responses to situations. However, a teacher is more likely to make a creative response in a productive way if she understands children's developmental problems.

Developmental views of behavior management.   A study of children's fantasies, explored by way of their story telling, found that two- to five-year-olds used eight main themes, from aggression, death, or misfortune to morality and sociability, but the theme of aggression appeared more often than any other.[12] Gardner interprets this finding to reflect children's developmental problems as "related to a host of frustrations and repressed hostilities."[13] The period of development is one which imposes many restraints on the growing child and these frustrate him. The frustrations tend to surface readily and can usually be handled without too much fuss if the teacher is friendly, sympathetic, and helpful. On the other hand, if the children can discharge such hostilities in acceptable play about, for instance, monsters or bad guys, with puppets, blocks, or dress-up clothes, the feelings are not only accepted but also discharged, without harm.

Children's developmental problems are often revealed in their storytelling—a common theme is aggression.

When child behavior is persistently unmanageable, Grey cautions that "a dramatic change in behavior cannot occur solely in the child or at home," but if parents and teachers collaborate, everyone has a chance to change and to help the child make consistent improvement in behavior.[14]

Rogers offers helpful principles in interpersonal transactions, basically:

1. The individual is responsible for himself, and wishes to keep that responsibility.
2. The individual has a strong inclination to grow toward maturity and to become independent, healthy, and adjusted socially.
3. The individual becomes spontaneous in a warm, accepting atmosphere.
4. Simple limits are needed on acts, not on feelings.
5. Acceptance of feelings does not imply approval or disapproval.
6. Avoid use of blame or punishment.[15]

12. E. G. Pitcher and E. Prelinger, *Children Tell Stories* (New York: International Universities, 1963).
13. Richard A. Gardner, *Understanding Children* (New York: Jason Aronson, 1973), p. 97.
14. Loren Grey, *Discipline without Fear* (New York: Hawthorn, 1974), pp. 10–11.
15. Carl Rogers, "Significant Aspects of Client-Centered Therapy," in *Varieties of Personality Theory*, edited by Hendrick M. Ruitenbeek (New York: E. P. Dutton, 1964), pp. 167–183, especially pp. 170–171.

Rogers stresses the person as a whole organism, one who acts from health-directed motives and, therefore, can be trusted to use a helping relationship for improvement in functioning. A similar point is made by White, who says the child's initiative and exploratory behavior is best supported through feeling and communicating respect for the child. White points out: "Evidences of respect go far to make a child feel that he is fundamentally valued, and they soften the pain of such restraints as may be necessary."[16]

White has developed a theory that young children strive for feelings of "efficacy," leading to a sense of "competence" and that thinking, behaving, and feeling are all integral parts of this competence motivation.[17] Viewing a child, as White does, as positively seeking to feel able and competent to function, largely through exploratory playful activities, the teacher can see how positive the child's *motives* are, even though his behaviors cannot always be permitted. Teachers need not feel guilty when it is necessary to set specific limits for all or some children and to constrain their going out of bounds, provided there is no punishment.

Skills for dealing with behavior.   A summary of teaching skills in behavior management would include these major items:

1. *Establishing personalized relationships with children.* This includes:

Teaching skills in behavior management— or discipline— include seven types of teacher competencies.

1. Addressing a child by name
2. Communicating your interest in him as a person and in his activities and interests
3. Recognizing and communicating to him your awareness of his uniqueness in specific ways
4. Increasing your knowledge about his history and family and characteristic behavior so that your interactions with him convey this knowledge in sympathetic ways
5. Initiating and responding in personal positive ways
6. Projecting sincerity and reliability as a mature person who can be trusted

2. *Child study skills,* as detailed in Chapter 4, to increase the knowledge base about a child and to permit diagnosis, analysis, and prescription where problems arise.

16. Robert W. White, *The Enterprise of Living: Growth and Organization in Personality* (New York: Holt, Rinehart & Winston, 1972), p. 219.
17. Ibid., pp. 209 and 327.

3. *Systematic behavior management procedures.* As in classroom management, the *clarity* of classroom rules and the consistency of their implementation, together with flexibility for individual situations and capabilities, are the chief ingredients of successful viable techniques.

For example, in a classroom where hitting is absolutely forbidden (as it usually is), what clear procedures exist to *recognize* and *accept feelings* but to *divert* child behavior to more socially acceptable forms? Feelings are real and cannot be denied. Sometimes feelings can be interpreted. When Bobby screams at his best friend Billy, with whom he is having an unusual fight about block pay, "I hate you! You're not my friend anymore!" it is no use to deny the feelings, even when it is predictable that they will shortly be forgotten. It might help for the teacher to say, "You hate Billy now. He may not be your friend now. But you might want him to be your friend again." In this way, reality is not denied, but neither is it given false and unlikely importance. At this time, both children may be very short-tempered and angry. An alternative to hitting each other must be available and be equal to absorbing the extra energy generated and needing an outlet. Possible options are throwing or "wedging" clay on a clayboard; throwing bean bags at a silly face, trying to throw the bag through a large-mouth opening; donning a small pair of boxing gloves and sparring with an air-inflated figure or a punching ball or large beach ball; playing with wet sand to mold constructions or with water and soap to blow and "bust" soap bubbles. Everyone can add a few more options.

4. *Individualization.* Where teaching skills of individualization successfully engage each child in a high level of involvement, children's feelings of satisfaction in their activities tend to develop more child toleration for other children's interests and activities. It also diminishes needs or opportunities for behavioral conflicts or problems. The more that children develop self-discipline in their activities because of personal interest and appropriateness of the program for their needs, the fewer behavioral problems appear.

According to one study evaluating teaching effectiveness in a beginning reading program, "Individualized instruction requires that the teacher spend time with each child on his program or his products.[18]

18. Ethna Reid, "Evaluation of Teacher Training in a Title III Center," in *Proceedings of the 1968 Invitational Conference on Testing Problems* (Princeton, N. J.: Educational Testing Service, 1969), pp. 31–71.

While many elementary school teachers seem to find this difficult, particularly when the *content* or *end product* pressures are severe, early childhood teachers are usually less pressured for academic results and better trained for individualized work with children.

In some cases, the individualization occurs in a one-to-one tutoring situation. Most often, the early childhood teacher can individualize through brief conferences about activity selection or about products such as constructions or art work. Periodic assessment conferences may reflect to a child some specific manifestations of his progress and sometimes suggest further steps needed.

Early childhood teachers who minimize or omit total group instruction usually individualize their teaching by moving from one learning center to another. They observe all children's activity and engage in individual dialogues to convey individual interest and to note progress and problems as they arise.

5. *Use of positive feedback and forms of conveying child acceptance* are additional techniques which prevent or diminish behavior problems. Even when a child is engaging in activities, some of which are unacceptable, positive feedback emphasizes the acceptable actions. It is possible, also, to indicate the unacceptability of those actions which cannot be permitted. At the same time, if a positive alternative is offered, there is more likelihood of an acceptable change in the child's behavior. For example, on a hot sunny day with water play on the playground, a child may be told that he handles the hose well, that he may not point the hose at children who are frightened by it, but that he may point it at a fence which badly needs washing or at any child who requests it. In such a case, it is helpful for the teacher to stand by to monitor this rule, to offer further positive feedback, and to make sure children are not hosed who do not wish to be.

6. *Productive teaching plans.* Activities planned and teaching strategies selected must involve every child in productive ways, offer variety, furnish balance between high and low activity and structure, add sufficient challenge at various levels, and meet children's physical, social, emotional, and cognitive needs.

Boredom, too little challenge or too much, too much novelty, and too little systematic development of child skills in art, constructions, and explorations can lead to difficult behavior problems. Too much activity or too little can be equally defeating for good program components.

Sometimes, essentially good teaching plans are marred by poor sequencing. If primary teachers are too eager to complete various quiet, less active tasks when the children are "fresh", and children thus spend too long a period in sedentary activities, behavior problems are predictable.

Grouping is sometimes at fault. Working in large groups for too long is too constraining for young children. One problem may be the composition of the group—too many aggressive children with poor skills in social interactions. Often the same activities may be successfully developed in smaller groups where more action and conversation can be permitted.

Before seeking the seeds of problems within the child, the skillful teacher seeks them in the program, in the environment she has created, and in her own style of teaching. Few programs are entirely productive for all the children in the group. Most programs are modifiable or adaptable in various ways to meet the needs of more children. It must not be assumed that the best solution to all serious behavior problems is instant removal from the class. One child, diagnosed as having severe emotional problems by the school's psychological services, was incorporated into a normal kindergarten class of twenty-five children where, with psychological support to child, family, and teacher, the child was undoubtedly rescued from a life of institutionalization. This is not to suggest that the child was "cured" of his problems. But a child who, upon entry, was totally unable to function outside of his home, made great strides toward the normal range of functioning, although still at the weaker end.

7. *Skills of self-evaluation of teaching.* Systems for self-analysis of teaching are discussed in the following section. At this point, it can be said that professional teachers need skills for feedback on their professional performance that free them from complete dependence on supervisors, peers, and parents.

Teachers are often irritated when supervisors emphasize their need to improve specific teaching skills. If the teachers disagree with their supervisors, it is difficult to resolve their differences, and the parties remain unconvinced of each others' positions. Self-analysis techniques offer teachers possibilities for self-diagnosis and self-determined needs for change.

Self-evaluation is not a panacea for all problems in teaching. Personality variables often distort the picture. Some teachers tend to undervalue themselves and their teaching, while others do the opposite. Everyone who looks at a performance does not see the same things. Since personal bias, for better or worse, can obscure rather than clarify the actions to be observed, teachers can augment their self-analysis skills by teaming with a peer for mutual evaluation.

If audio or video recordings are used by the teachers to sample their teaching performances, such records are especially appropriate for objective viewing by others in ways that an unrecorded live performance can never be, and student teachers can practice such evaluations with their peers.

Evaluation by significant others, whether college supervisor, cooperating classroom teacher, or school supervisor, can be further helpful sources of feedback and suggestions for improvement. However, evaluation by others is far less accessible, frequent, or available on demand than is self-evaluation.

TEACHING PATTERNS TO SUPPORT EARLY CHILDHOOD PROGRESS

When based on experience and intuition, many different ways of teaching young children can be effective in supporting early development and learning. As indicated below, research support is so far lacking for most of our cherished preferences. Yet, some approaches to teaching young children appear more promising than others, based on indications from recent research.

Matching teaching patterns to children's needs

It seems likely that all children do not necessarily benefit from the same teaching patterns. For example, a recent evaluation of Follow Through Planned Variation Projects found that teacher praise for math achievement tended to be more effective for first-grade children with low entering ability than those with higher entering ability.[19]

Perhaps the most interesting contribution of this study was its analysis of observational data, which indicated that, contrary to the

19. Jane Stallings, "Relationships between Classroom Instructional Practices and Child Development" (paper read at AERA Annual Meeting, Washington, D.C., March 31–April 3, 1975), p. 7.

Teaching patterns may well make a difference in how effectively children learn.

opinions and findings of others, classroom procedures and teaching patterns "contributed as much to the explanation of test score differences as did the initial ability of children."[20] In other words, teachers do make a difference.

Another pertinent finding of this study was that children who, "for a period of three years, have been in classrooms that use a wide variety of activities and provide a wide variety of manipulative materials" performed better, compared to other programs studied, on the Raven's Progressive Matrices Test, a nonverbal test of perceptual problem solving."[21] This test, largely of spatial relationships of abstract symbols and relations of parts to wholes seemed to show the cumulative effects of very active forms of children's diversified learning experiences.

Teaching style, pattern, model, approach, or behavior are all used interchangeably here to capture the essence of how teachers teach, although these words may be defined in different ways for various purposes. Various systems try to classify teaching patterns.

Nelson, for example, differentiated five general types, that is, emphasis on social interaction, verbal teaching, development of cognitive processes, inquiry and discovery, or interpersonal relationships.[22] Few teachers use one pattern all the time or the same patterns with all children. Yet many teachers favor one of these emphases over others.

Joyce differentiates teaching into four models similar to Nelson's. His models are labelled social interaction, information processing, personal or individual sources, and behavior modification.[23] While he selects a few examples of each model, the social interaction model stems most directly from John Dewey, with its emphasis upon democratic classroom procedures, scientific inquiry, doing, experiencing, and problem solving in group contexts. Information processing, for early childhood levels especially, derives from Piaget's theories about how children develop intellectually. The third model—stressing the individual or the person's self-development—relates most recently to such humanistic sources as Carl Rogers and Arthur Combs. Predictably, behavior modification is Skinnerian, relying upon external conditioning, shaping and reinforcing procedures.

20. Ibid., p. 11.
21. Ibid., p. 13.
22. Lois N. Nelson, *The Nature of Teaching: A Collection of Readings* (Waltham, Mass.: Blaisdell, 1969).
23. Bruce R. Joyce and Marsha Weill, *Models of Teaching* (Englewood Cliffs, N. J.: Prentice-Hall, 1972).

Contrasts of behaviorist and humanist teaching

Broad differentiation frequently contrasts behaviorist and humanist techniques. Behaviorism is usually associated with changing a child's behavior through reinforcement. Humanists tend to reject such procedures as too manipulative of others, preferring to stress instead good relationships, trust, sensitivity, empathy, optimistic expectations, encouragement, and guidance in age-appropriate ways.

Teaching skills for readiness objectives

Some teaching seems to be entirely guided by fears of future demands upon an untrained child or readiness for the next grade. "He must learn to sit still in this kindergarten. Otherwise, how will his first-grade teacher teach him to read?" Other teachers seem to agree with John Dewey that school is not just a preparation for what is to come but is, in itself, an important social life experience. Thus, they stress that living appropriately and fully in any year is its own validity, without premature restriction because of supposed horrors to come.

FINDING YOUR OWN PATTERN

Throughout this book, teacher candidates are urged to be open to new ideas, to study them carefully, and to defer judgment until a base of knowledge and experience accumulates. We all have strong opinions without being able to "prove" we are right. Teacher candidates need to find teaching patterns which *they* can use sensitively and effectively. But students need to learn what is possible and what the range of options is. Narrowly based judgments tend to be dogmatic, restricting the teacher just as much as the children. It seems unlikely that research findings will ultimately validate only one teaching style or model. Instead, we hope to learn how different models help certain kinds of children in certain kinds of contexts for selected goals. Programs in teacher preparation, therefore, tend to stress opportunities to build a repertoire of skills and strategies for more flexibility in teaching and to develop informed choices about which models feel more authentic or effective in the teaching of some or all children.

COMPETENCY-BASED TEACHER EDUCATION

Teacher education programs are moving rapidly toward a "competency base" because of state mandate, various pressures, or conviction. Problems in competency-based teacher education (CBTE) relate to philosophic conflicts, role redefinition, assessment procedures, form as well as content, and complex management problems.

As Elfenbein pointed out, CBTE is a systems approach to teacher education "which includes:

> determining program goals,
> formulating performance objectives,
> analyzing functions and components (defining the parts of the subsystems),
> distributing functions among the components,
> scheduling training and testing of the systems,
> installation and quality control."[24]

She also notes the cybernetic quality of the systems approach, that is, the use of feedback from operations for generating necessary changes or adjustments. In general, the CBTE program derives its goals from a philosophic or value base: What teaching is of the most worth? or a needs assessment base: What do teachers have to do to meet identified child needs and how can they best learn to do this? Very often a course translation base is used, that is, the competency-based program is a near equivalent of the courses it displaced.

Problem with CBTE

Task analysis, or job descriptions, are often used to attempt to determine what a teacher does on the job in order to train a candidate to do those same things well. This method of deriving the goals for the competency base assumes that students should be trained to do what teachers are now doing, but many school critics claim that teachers need to change their behaviors in very fundamental ways. A job description gives a very realistic picture of what *is*. But this particular

24. Iris M. Elfenbein, *Performance-based Teacher Education Programs: A Comparative Description* (Washington, D.C.: American Association of Colleges of Teacher Education, October, 1972), pp. 4–5.

approach to deriving teacher competencies tends to be very conservative of past practices and provides no channel to better ways to teach.

CBTE program requirements

In addition to stating goals, CBTE programs usually include a specification of the competencies or skills the program expects students to master. Attitudes, knowledge and performance skills may be spelled out. Most programs include child development in the knowledge to be learned by students, sociological or political contexts of education, and, occasionally, philosophy. Learning theory, or educational psychology, is also included in most programs.

Each CBTE program is expected to state *which* skills they expect their graduates to master at some level of proficiency. Students are also to be informed in advance just how they will be assessed on competency achievement and for which skills and knowledge. The hope is that if teachers are trained to specific skills and knowledge, they will be better teachers than in the past when program goals were rather open ended and often unspecified. It sounds reasonable to expect that "better trained" teachers will produce children who learn more. But what about a school that is badly administered and where teachers and children may be physically and emotionally affected by poor school conditions? What about a school where there are insufficient materials and equipment for the job to be done? Since children's progress is affected, not only by what happens in the classroom, but also in the school and community, and most profoundly by what happens at home, there is no way to compare teaching results unless all these variables can be controlled.

Another problem facing CBTE programs is what to do about students whose personal style is very different from the performance expected. Sometimes, student teachers and teachers can make drastic changes in their intuitive teaching style. When they do, there is a period when they fall apart, and teaching skills may seem to decline, until they put it all together again.[25]

25. Walter Borg, "Making the Leap from Correlational to Experimental Studies of Teacher Behavior" (paper read at AERA Annual Meeting, Washington, D.C., March 30, 1975).

Use of videotape

CBTE program developers pin great faith on helping student teachers master new teaching strategies with videotape. But videotape is no magic cure, as has already been shown. Fuller and Manning report that students may be discouraged with their videotape performance, undervalue their progress, and feel totally inadequate to come up to the new standards identified. On the other hand, it is just as easy to overvalue one's performance as it is to deny oneself a fair assessment.[26] Students most likely to benefit from videotape confrontation are those open to change and able to make the needed changes, according to Fuller and Manning.

Lack of CBTE data

It should be noted that a large part of the problem with CBTE, in addition to its strong behaviorist thrust, is that it requires us to know answers to questions that are just now being shaped for testing. The major one is what kinds of teaching skills should students master— which are most likely to cause most children to make progress adequately in school settings? Or, to state it another way, what kinds of teaching skills are best for what kinds of learning for which kinds of children under what conditions? This is a complex question to which answers cannot be expected very soon.

CBTE advocates do not deny that there are no answers so far to these major questions. They only say, "Let's find the answers while we develop CBTE programs. Without such programs, we would never be able to test one clear kind of teaching against another for any purpose." Designing CBTE programs, advocates like to say, is like riding the bicycle while you're trying to fix it.

The ferment that CBTE has caused in academic circles has stimulated thorough-going revision and rethinking of teacher education everywhere. Students are becoming partners in this endeavor and their input and reactions are given serious attention by all parties.

26. Frances F. Fuller and Brad A. Manning, "Self-Confrontation Reviewed: A Conceptualization for Video Playback in Teacher Education," *Review of Educational Research* 43 (Fall 1973), pp. 469–528.

Examples of early childhood CBTE

CBTE program development stresses individualization, pacing suited to the student, modularization of learning experiences, and assessment of students at various checkpoints during the undergraduate years and on exit to certify students as having demonstrated identified competencies. Modules are do-it-yourself types of packaged units that give students a great deal of independence and choice among varieties of learning materials, often with tests at various points to monitor progress. Modules sometimes look like workbooks. Assessment procedures have been particularly troublesome because the field is not sufficiently developed to meet current needs for sophisticated, reliable, and objective forms of assessment of teaching competency.

CDA credential

The CDA credential is one example of a CBTE approach in early childhood education.

In the early childhood field, one well-developed competency list has been publicized for what is hoped will be a new credential—the Child Development Associate (CDA). Led by the Office of Child Development in Washington, D.C., a CDA consortium was set up to identify competencies and assessment procedures. The CDA is defined as a role "in which a person is knowledgeable about young children and capable of taking direct responsibility for the daily activities of a group of three- to five-year-old children in a developmental center-based program as a member of a total staff team in child center settings."[27] The CDA is comparable to an Associate of Education degree, awarded by many two-year community colleges. It is expected that a CDA would be supervised by a head teacher or some other qualified staff member.

CDA competencies. Six competency areas identified for CDA training are the following:

1. Set up a safe and healthy environment for young children.
2. Advance their physical and intellectual competence.
3. Build their positive self-concept and individual strength.

27. Child Development Associate Consortium, "Toward an Assessment System: *Efforts to April 30, 1974.*" (Washington, D.C.: The Consortium, n. d.), p. 2.

4. Organize and sustain the positive functioning of children and adults in a group learning environment.

5. Bring about optimal coordination of home and center child-rearing practices and expectations.

6. Carry out supplementary responsibilities related to children's programs.[28]

Generic competencies. These are "generic" competencies, expected of all adequately trained CDA's. In some programs, students find some competencies which are required and others from among which they may choose or negotiate with their faculty advisor. While these six generic competencies are broadly stated, each one includes subcompetencies. For example, for the first competency listed above there are such subcompetencies as, "Take preventive measures against hazards to physical safety," and, "Recognize unusual behavior or symptom which may indicate a need for health care."[29]

CDA assessment philosophy. The "philosophy" of assessment for these competencies rests on these requirements:

Assessment must not only be based on observed teaching but must rest on "performance."

The candidate must know in advance what teaching competencies will be assessed.

The setting for the assessment must be a familiar one for the candidate.

One-shot assessments must be avoided in favor of cumulative assessment over a period of time.

A team, rather than one evaluator, must assess the candidate's work.

Reliability and validity of assessment requires a variety of procedures.

Assessment must offer a basis for diagnosis for further improvement, with a profile of individual performance skills.

The candidate must be involved in the assessment.[30]

This statement is one that many educators have endorsed, yet the requirements will be very difficult to carry out because of the cost. Better procedures for assessment must be devised and tested for all these standards, and more funds must become available for such expensive—albeit desirable—assessment.

---

28. Ibid., p. 2.
29. Child Development Associate Consortium, "Competencies." (n. d., not further identified), pp. 4–8.
30. CDA Consortium, "Dateline CDA," vol. 1, no. 1, (Washington, D.C.: The Consortium, 7315 Wisconsin Ave., February 1975), unpaged.

Critical task assessment. One system for assessment of the CDA competency achievement uses a series of "critical tasks" to be evaluated and assessed. A critical task is a selected teaching task that the test makers agree is important for teaching. It might be: "Increase the child's intellectual and language competence." There might be several behaviorally defined levels of performance of the task, from unsatisfactory to excellent. The lowest level would probably indicate a lack of experience or preparation and the highest level suggest a knowledgeable teacher with very good skills.[31]

Need to sample skill list

The list of teaching skills specified earlier in this chapter as universal teaching skills suggests some of the many areas of competence that are needed by teachers of young children, but it is not complete. No list could be complete. This means that sampling will have to be the basis for assessment procedures. This would be true even if a complete list of competencies could be generated, because of time and money restrictions. Sampling competencies for assessment will require some decisions about which are really the most important ones.

SELF-EVALUATION OF TEACHING

In this chapter, the words "assess," "analyze," "evaluate," and "measure" have been used rather interchangeably, as though they all mean the same thing. Schalock proposes differentiation for three of them: measurement to refer to quantifying something following appropriate rules, evaluation to involve a judgment on how good something is or how much it is valued, and assessment to mean collection and use of information to make specific kinds of decisions.[32] These definitions will be observed in the discussion that follows. In addition, a dictionary definition of "analysis" will be used: "the separation of any

31. National Committee on Employment of Youth (NCEY), "Developing and Testing Procedures and Instruments for the Assessment of the Competencies of Candidates for the Child Development Associate Credential" Final Report. Contract No. FY4 SC003. (Washington, D.C.: Child Development Associate Consortium Research and Development, May 1974), pp. 21–22.

32. H. Del Schalock, "Notes on a Model of Assessment that Meets the Requirements of CBTE," in *Exploring Competency Based Education*, edited by W. Robert Houston (Berkeley, Cal.: McCutchan, 1974), pp. 209–250, especially pp. 211–213.

material or abstract entity into its constituent elements (opposed to synthesis)."[33] Thus, analysis of teaching helps us to break up a complex human performance in interaction with others to identify some parts of the whole with which we can deal in some detail.

Basing evaluations on teachers or children

Some systems of evaluation of teaching look only at what the teacher is doing but, increasingly, efforts are made to include not only the teacher but the child and the give-and-take between them, generally called interaction. Some systems take note only of the child outcomes and, if these are satisfactory, assume that what the teacher is doing must be satisfactory. This is known as a "consequent" assessment, based only on the results in child progress. Teacher organizations and researchers have been quick to point out that there are intervening variables here over which no teacher has control. These include the school context or atmosphere, administrative support and facilitation, the characteristics and needs of the children, the availability of support services, and the availability of needed supplies and equipment. A pilot effort in this direction is being developed by the Educational Testing Service, but the unit of comparison will be schools, not teachers or individual classrooms.[34]

Interaction analysis

Interaction analysis of teaching focuses on classroom events.

Methods in use today for analyzing teaching are varied, but the focus is on the classroom events in which teaching occurs. Samples of teaching must be either "live"—coded or tallied on the spot—or "frozen"—recorded on audio or video systems for later measurement, analysis, and evaluation. Tallies are simple counts to find out "how many," "how often" or other quantitative measures of occurrence. Tallies or codes sometimes preserve the *sequence* in which the various teaching strategies or units occur, but often this data is not available except in a frozen sample or the typescript or transcription made of the sample. Codes, usually parts of category systems, are used to identify various

33. *The Random House Dictionary of the English Language,* unabridged ed. (1966), p. 53.
34. Fred Macdonald, "A Design for an Accountability System for the New York City School System," Abstract of Report submitted to the Board of Education by Educational Testing Service (Princeton, N. J.: Educational Testing Service, February 1973).

parts of the teaching sample by titles such as "eliciting child's verbal-ization," "giving verbal praise," or "rejecting child's response."

Frozen data are very helpful to teacher candidates and to teachers who wish to be involved in meaningful forms of self-evaluation, since there is no other effective way to study one's own performance. It also permits greater objectivity, because it makes possible analysis, measurement, and evaluation by more than one observer at a time. Additionally, observers can view replays more than once to find out whether their views are the same each time.

Research on teaching analysis

Research on teaching has yielded useful concepts and a language of teaching.

A great deal of research has accumulated through the use of some systems to study teaching, although findings are still few and far between. While only tentative knowledge has so far emerged, Dunkin and Biddle point out that the really substantial results are in the many concepts of teaching that have been explored and in the language of teaching that has resulted. Methodologies have been extensively tried out and improved, and better designs and research methods, with many tested instruments, are now available.[35]

Some systems of studying teaching primarily analyze the affective tone of the teacher. Others ignore affect and focus on the content or the cognitive uses of content. It is difficult to locate a system which studies the different aspects of teaching at the same time; it is too difficult to take in everything that is happening at once in complex human interchanges.

The bulk of the research on teaching has occurred at the secondary or elementary levels, although a number of systems have used early childhood as well. Fortunately, there are compilations and descriptions of the majority of systems used to study teaching, and selections can be made of those which feature specific kinds of focus or more than one focus.[36] A problem with many systems is the lack of clarity in the categories they use, overlapping categories, or inadequately defined categories. Another consideration is that if a system has not been tested for validity and reliability, it may have limited usefulness.

35. Michael J. Dunkin and Bruce J. Biddle, *The Study of Teaching* (New York: Holt, Rinehart & Winston, 1974), pp. 355–418.
36. A. Simon and E. Boyer, eds., *Mirrors for Behavior: An Anthology of Observation Instruments Continued*, 1970 Supplement, vols. A & B (Philadelphia: Research for Better Schools, 1970).

Composite system for self-analysis of teaching

Dunay developed a composite system for self-analysis of teaching with six components: (1) measures of teacher and pupil talk, (2) distribution of pupil talk among participating children, (3) division of teacher talk patterns to distinguish instruction from behavior management, (4) division of teacher questions to distinguish convergent from divergent questions, (5) division of teacher responses into constricting or nonconstricting, and (6) division of nonverbal behavior into encouraging or inhibitory.[37] A pilot study with this system indicated that, while many student teachers profited from self-analysis of their videotaped teaching samples, some students required considerable faculty feedback and guidance.

Flanders system to study teaching

One of the most widely used systems at all school levels (including early childhood settings) is the Flanders system of interaction analysis. This deals only with affect, but it has been adapted for various other more specific uses. This system is not difficult to use, and some research supports some of its assumptions about effective teaching. Observers may tally "live" or frozen samples. With only ten categories, the system uses a ten-by-ten matrix to produce both graphic patterns and quantitative measures of classroom interactions.[38] Seven of the ten categories refer to teacher talk—whether it is acceptant, critical, or directive—and three categories refer to child talk. Tallies are made in the appropriate category at the end of each three-second interval during the observation.

Flanders's basic assumption, which appeals to most early childhood teachers, is that effective teachers differ from ineffective teachers chiefly in achieving a higher ratio of what he calls "indirect" as opposed to "direct" forms of teaching. Such higher ratios derive from less teacher talk, more child talk and initiative, more acceptant teacher talk, and less criticism and rejection. (Dunkin and Biddle however,

37. Lillian R. Dunay and Helen F. Robison, "Student Teachers Self-Analysis of Teaching Behavior" (paper presented at AERA Annual Meeting, New Orleans, February 27, 1973).
38. N. Flanders, *Analyzing Teacher Behavior* (Reading, Mass.: Addison-Wesley, 1970).

find these categories overly simple, lacking in distinct definition and in need of clearer conceptualization.[39]

Teacher candidates who wish to try out the Flanders system can help each other by coding "live" during observation of each other's teaching or from videotapes. Training in the use of the system is required to reach a sufficiently high level of expertise in fast coding, so that the results are reliable.

Many systems have more complex categories and have been used mostly by researchers, not by teachers. Other systems of self-evaluation have been used by groups of teachers to code teaching samples and evaluate their own performances on videotape. Some systems are more complex than Flanders's and seek to analyze not only the ratios of teacher to child talk but various cognitive aspects of the teaching as well. Despite criticisms of this system, its use often is helpful to students when analyzing their own teaching.

Cognitive focus on teaching

Taba, and Gallagher and Aschner, developed systems that deal primarily with the cognitive features of teaching samples. Taba studied the cognitive levels of teacher comments and questions and of children's responses in order to help the teacher vary and raise the cognitive levels of interaction in the classroom.[40] Taba used the Bloom Taxonomy of Educational Objectives, which distinguishes six cognitive levels from a factual or simple knowledge level to the highest level —called evaluation.[41] Many informal systems of analysis of teaching use this Taxonomy to flag overuse of factual or memory questions— "When . . . ?" "Who . . . ?" "Where . . . ?"—and to suggest more frequent use of "How . . . ?" or "Why . . . ?" Levels above the lowest recall type of question can call for an example, an analogy, or an application of some knowledge. A translation level would be, "Say it in your own words," which usually shows rather quickly whether a child is repeating from memory or understands something well enough to phrase it himself. Young children's thinking, largely intuitive before

39. Dunkin and Biddle, op. cit., pp. 362–374.
40. Hilda Taba, *Teaching Strategies and Cognitive Functioning in Elementary School Children*, USOE Cooperative Research Project No. 2404 (San Francisco: San Francisco State College, 1966).
41. B. S. Bloom, ed., *Taxonomy of Educational Objectives: The Classification of Educational Goals*, Handbook 1, *Cognitive Domain* (New York: McKay, 1956).

age six, is not sufficiently advanced to deal with all six cognitive levels. Yet they can surely deal with attempts to demonstrate their *own* understandings instead of remembering other people's.

Gallagher–Aschner and Galloway systems

Notions of "convergent-divergent" thinking, developed by Guilford, are used in various systems including the one Gallagher and Aschner devised.[42] Convergence, or "right-wrong" questions, and "divergence", or open endedness where no answer can be wrong, are very useful concepts in early childhood teaching. Examples of divergent questions are:

> How else could this story end?
> What do you think will happen?
> Why do you like this music?
> What did you find out on yesterday's trip?
> What does your mother do that you like best?

Divergent questions not only avoid stigmatizing any child as being wrong but also tend to elicit spontaneous and personal forms of verbalization of material with which the child feels comfortable.

Another system that early childhood teachers might find useful is Galloway's system of assessing nonverbal teacher behavior. In this system, the teacher can assess her own videotape samples, and request peers, or fellow-students to check her codes and evaluation of gesture, tone, locus, stance, and similar features of nonverbal behavior.[43]

Measurement instruments

Some systems use time sampling, critical incident description, or other types of samples. Measuring instruments, in addition to serving purposes selected, also have to meet standards of relevance, reliability,

42. J. P. Guilford, "The Structure of Intellect," *Psychological Bulletin* 53 (1965), pp. 267–293.

43. Charles Galloway, "An Exploratory Study of Observational Procedures for Determining Teacher Nonverbal Communication" (unpublished doctoral study, University of Florida, 1962).

validity, fidelity, and ease of administration.[44] *Relevance* indicates that the feature being measured is important to the purpose. *Reliability*, as suggested above, refers to the ability to obtain a similar finding with the instrument more than once. *Validity* indicates whether the behavior measured is the one intended. *Fidelity* is the extent to which the behavior measured is close to the true behavior. *Ease of administration* refers to how practical and useful the system is.

Most observations of teaching in the past were neither systematic nor reliable. Judgments were made subjectively, and different judges rarely agreed with each other. There was a notable lack of agreement on reliable indicators of effective teaching. What should the observer observe? While teacher warmth seemed so central to good early childhood teaching for such a long time, it was never clear how warmth manifested itself. In fact, rarely was any attempt made to define warmth as a construct, or as a bundle of behaviors distinguishing warmth from nonwarmth.

With recording equipment, better selection of objective indicators of teaching behavior, and more systematic procedures validated through many replications, evaluation of teaching should become a more useful tool for self-evaluation or for evaluation by others.

FINDINGS AND HYPOTHESES

While hard data on teaching is not yet available, researchers are formulating interesting hypotheses and testing some of these in studies of classroom interactions of teachers and children.

Rosenshine's hypotheses

Rosenshine found a few kinds of teacher behavior that he thinks may turn out to be correlated with good results in children's learning, if researchers will test them further:

Clarity of teacher's presentation
Variety of teacher-initiated activities

44. Dale L. Bolton, *Selection and Evaluation of Teachers* (Berkeley, Cal.: McCutchan, 1973), p. 112.

Enthusiasm of teacher

Teacher emphasis on learning and achievement

Avoidance of extreme criticism

Positive responses to students

Student opportunities to learn criterion material

Use of structuring comments by the teacher

Use of multiple levels of questions or cognitive discourse[45]

Flanders and Simon's list of desirable teaching skills

Flanders and Simon made a list of teacher behaviors which they perceived as associated with children's progress:

Accepting children's ideas and opinions

Flexibility in cognitive style; differentially dealing with different children

Using a conceptual framework that includes diagnosis before selecting teaching strategies; assessing children's progress in relation to goals and choosing remedial procedures

Using "advance organizers" or helping children understand new material by prior conceptualization of some important features[46, 47]

So far, teacher warmth has not been validated as having a detectable effect on children's progress. The lack of empirical evidence for this apparently important teacher characteristic (stressed by all early childhood educators) is undoubtedly due to the lack of sophistication of our evaluation and measurement procedures. However, Ryans selected teacher warmth, responsible or businesslike classroom behavior, and teacher stimulation or imaginativeness as characteristics likely to be associated with good teaching.[48]

45. Barak Rosenshine, "Teacher Competency Research," in *Competency Assessment, Research, and Evaluation,* Report of a National Conference, March 12–15, 1974 (Washington, D.C.: AACTE, 1974), pp. 138–153, especially p. 139.

46. N. A. Flanders and A. Simon, "Teacher Effectiveness," in *Encyclopedia of Educational Research,* edited by Robert L. Ebel, fourth ed. (New York: Macmillan, 1969), pp. 1423–1437.

47. For further details on "advance organizers," see David P. Ausubel, "Cognitive Structure and the Facilitation of Meaningful Verbal Learning," in R. C. Anderson and David P. Ausubel, *Readings in the Psychology of Cognition* (New York: Holt, Rinehart & Winston, 1965), pp. 103–115.

48. D. G. Ryans, *Characteristics of Teachers: Their Description, Comparison and Appraisal* (Washington, D.C.: American Council on Education, 1960).

Kounin's discipline studies

Kounin, studying discipline and group management, in kindergarten as well as other school and nonschool settings, found that teacher "desist" techniques or actions to stop punishment:[49]

Produce more conformity and less nonconformity if they have *clarity,* that is, information. This holds true, Kounin says, both for children who were producing deviant behavior and for those who were not.

Produce more conformity and less nonconformity if they have *firmness,* that is, an "I mean it" quality. But this held true only for the deviant children. There was no "ripple" effect, or effect on the nondeviant child or children who were not being directly addressed.

Produce more behavior disruption and more visible signs of children's disturbance, without affecting conformity or nonconformity if they have *roughness,* that is, punitiveness or angry tones of voice.

Other features of teacher style that Kounin measured which correlated significantly with children's behavior in learning settings were:[50]

Withitness and overlapping, or "eyes in the back of the head" so you know what's going on and the children know you know, and, in addition, attending to more than one thing at a time.

Smoothness and momentum, or staying with an activity without initiating actions that interfere with it.

Group alerting and *accountability,* or maintaining a group focus, not attending only to one child, and stimulating frequent performances by children in participatory behaviors.

Valence and challenge arousal, or getting children more involved or curious through enthusiasm or use of stimulating techniques.

Seatwork variety and challenge, or lack of satiation in sedentary activities and sufficient intellectual challenge in learning activities.

SELF-ANALYSIS OF TEACHING

All of the above findings and suggestions are helpful in pinpointing important areas of teacher skill development and in beginning to indicate how to produce more of the results desired. Students and their college instructors may wish to devise or select systems for analyzing

49. Jacob S. Kounin, *Discipline and Group Management in Classrooms* (New York: Holt, Rinehart & Winston, 1970), p. 13.
50. Ibid., pp. 143–144.

videotapes for specific purposes. Based on the preceding analysis of various types of teaching skills, teachers and student teachers might wish to evaluate their own teaching for the purposes that follow:

Practical suggestions are made for self-analysis and improvement of teaching.

1. *Teacher nonverbal behaviors.* Students, or teachers, can begin to understand what negative messages they might unconsciously be sending, by observing sample playbacks of their own work and discussing them with peers, college instructor, or cooperating classroom teacher.

2. *Story reading skills.* A skill list can easily be devised and checked against a videotape. It can include eye-level contact with children, familiarity with the story, showing pictures appropriately, voice modulation and production, articulation and phrasing, involving children in some discussion of the story or pictures without losing the story thread, and maintaining children's interest.

3. *Use of divergent questions* (as indicated above).

4. *Pacing of questions.* A timer might be useful to time the silence between question and child answer, rephrasing of question, or follow-up question. Rowe found that teachers benefitted—as detailed in Chapter 7—through learning to wait long enough, without bombardment or haste, for children's responses.

5. *Behavior management skills.* Students may list their own ideal behavior management skills (or borrow some from Kounin's list just above) and compare these with a teaching sample on videotape. Students can then determine the extent of their skill progress and request guidance from the college instructor or the classroom teacher, if necessary.

6. *Skills of differentiated initiatives and responses to individual children.* This rather subtle and complex teaching strategy can be subdivided into such specific teaching behaviors as use of a child's name, evidencing respect for the child (tone of voice, phrases used, or nonverbal behavior), showing evidence of empathy for a child even when rejecting his request (by giving reasons, stating child's view, or offering an alternative), and responding in ways that are specific to the child and/or his particular initiative.

7. *Responsiveness to individual children in a group without losing the group.* Evidence for this strategy might include:
   a. Facing the group at all times.
   b. Signalling a child nonverbally that his request has been noted, while at the same time responding to another child.
   c. Responding appropriately to each child.
   d. Attentiveness to a child requiring attention.
   e. Initiating interaction with a child who is otherwise alone, uninvolved, or sending a message of unhappiness.
   f. Maintaining group involvement while responding to individual children.

8. *Ascertaining children's cognitive levels:*
   a. Nonjudgmental approach and absence of any evaluative or judgmental statements.
   b. Keeping child active and interested.
   c. Eliciting child's actions and verbalizations.
   d. Probing the child's meanings.
   e. Making errors, then challenging the child to determine whether they are, in fact, errors.
   f. Eliciting the child's predictions before his actions.
   g. Eliciting the child's descriptions of his actions after the action.
   h. Eliciting the child's reasoning for his actions.
   i. Completing a useful recording system to store data secured about the child's cognitive level.

The skill lists may encompass any area in which teaching practice is desired and may extend to guidance and supervision of art media, block or dramatic play, woodworking or music, or any other area of early childhood teaching.

HUMANISM AND CBTE

Teaching is complex and difficult to encompass in any one system of analysis. Many early childhood educators are unconvinced that behavioral analysis of teaching is productive. Yet it is difficult to deny that every profession must have some reliable way to determine who should be regarded as a qualified practitioner. The struggle must be equally difficult in psychotherapy, social work, and other helping professions.

Humanistic views

Combs, committed to a strongly humanistic approach to teaching, has questioned whether novices can learn to do what experts do, since the experts probably use methods which reflect their expertise, and this, novices cannot duplicate. He also fears that novices might become discouraged, facing long lists of competencies, some of which might be incompatible with their personality, situation, or purposes.[51]

Combs prefers to define effectiveness in teaching in terms of the

---

51. Arthur W. Combs, *The Professional Education of Teachers* (Boston: Allyn and Bacon, 1965), pp. 4–5.

uniqueness of the person as one "who has learned to use himself effectively and efficiently to carry out his own and society's purposes in the education of others."[52] He points out that one of the distinguishing characteristics of the helping professions—teaching, guidance, social work, and psychotherapy—is the "instantaneous response." Since these professionals must be alert to respond so quickly in ongoing situations, he proposes a perceptual approach to understanding the behavior of teachers in five ways. These include sensitivity and empathy, positive self-concepts, views of other persons they work with as positive, working with others to open and expand rather than to control, and using methods which are authentic, that is, they are appropriate to the teacher and the situation.[53]

Combs evinced concern for helping students develop their own personalities and grow in personal meaningfulness as the most productive way to produce effective teachers.

Process or product focus of CBTE

CBTE advocates tend to focus on outcomes, products, or some clearly defined endpoint. Mastery of a specified teaching skill, assessed through a criterion-referenced test, is typical of the desired results of CBTE programs. Humanists who are dubious of the feasibility of selecting such endpoints or benchmarks focus instead on the process of growth and improvements in teaching skills.

Joyce, terming Combs's approach "phenomenological," finds it too open ended, personal, and unpredictable for the kind of assessment that CBTE seems to demand.[54]

Here the issue is joined, essentially between those who seek for certainty in assessment (and reject approaches which deny that such certainties can be attained in any meaningful way) and those who are much less concerned with precision in assessment. The latter think that the human element makes predictions and certainties difficult and undesirable. Instead, they choose to focus on the act of growing and becoming for both teachers and children.

52. Ibid., p. 9.
53. Arthur W. Combs and Suzanne M. Kinzer, "The University of Florida's Childhood Education Program: An Alternative Approach to CBTE," in *Exploring Competency Based Education*, edited by W. Robert Houston (Berkeley, Cal.: McCutchan, 1974), pp. 174–5.
54. Bruce R. Joyce, "Assessment in Teacher Education: Notes from the Competency Orientation," in *Exploring Competency Based Education*, edited by W. Robert Houston (Berkeley, Cal.: McCutchan, 1974), pp. 191–208, especially pp. 193–194.

This issue is raised again in Chapter 15 in connection with assessment of children's progress. The same issue appears there as a process versus product orientation. While students ponder the choices, it might be well to remember that when process becomes the focus, the assessment problems are even more difficult, as Joyce indicated, but they are probably not as impossible as he suggested.

Personally, I have learned a great deal from study and participation in state-mandated program development on a CBTE base. My chief reservation is similar to Combs's, that mandating what specific behaviors students must acquire is premature before a useful knowledge base is developed. This seems so because behaviors can always be devised to express any feelings, attitudes, or goals. Human beings are infinitely creative in behavioral manifestations of expression and information. They need to be free to invest this creativity in finding meaningful ways to their goals. Combs says behaviors are symptoms, not causes and, as a therapist, he deals in causes.

Students who find themselves in CBTE programs of one sort or another will have to assess their own experiences and determine their own views about this movement. They will find a great deal that is challenging and stimulating, while they prepare for the next swing of the pendulum forward, it is hoped, to a new and enlightened humanism.

SUMMARY   *For the purpose of planning self-analysis and self-assessment of teaching performance, teaching skills identification is related to types of programs. Competency-based teacher education movements are nationally ascendant, and problems of specifying and assessing teaching competencies concern teacher educators everywhere.*

Some teaching skills are required in any program for young children, but many skills are specific to the philosophical position of the program and its implementation requirements. Universal teaching skills include maintenance of children's health and safety, interpersonal skills, planning for and evaluating child progress, working with parents, and classroom and behavior management. CBTE poses its own requirements, such as for skill identification, choices of teacher training activities, assessment procedures, modularization of training materials, and individual pacing.

Systems to analyze teaching are numerous, but most tend to stress either affective or cognitive characteristics of teaching. So far there is little research support for anyone's list of "effective teaching skills," but there are many suggestive possibilities. Humanists tend to resist CBTE because of its behaviorist thrust, but there are helpful suggestions for designing a humanistic type of CBTE for early childhood education, based especially on the work of Rogers and Combs.

❦ EXERCISES FOR STUDENTS ❦❦❦❦❦❦❦❦❦❦❦❦❦❦❦❦❦❦❦

1. Select a small research project out of a list of such topics as the following:

   a. Major health practices for young children to learn.

   b. Safety checklists in programs for young children.

   c. First aid Do's and Don'ts for early childhood teachers.

   d. Promoting good nutritional practices with young children and their families.

     (1) Secure up-to-date information on your topic from reliable sources, for example, publications by public health services, current texts on nutrition, and school medical personnel.

     (2) Using this data, write a brief summary of the important points you wish to remember.

     (3) Arrange to duplicate your paper, and secure copies of papers written by your classmates after your college instructor has approved the content of each paper.

2. Select one of the universal skills for teaching young children, and list all the individual competencies you can think of that make up this skill including both content knowledge and teaching roles. For one type of knowledge and/or complementary teaching role, find two recent publications indexed by the ERIC Clearinghouse for Early Childhood Education and write a summary of this material, emphasizing how it clarifies problems of teaching young children.

3. Attend a meeting of a local school board. Write a summary of your perceptions of the meeting, noting especially:

   a. Philosophic or value positions expressed or clash of values expressed.

b. Prime concerns of parents manifested.

c. Your own disagreements with any of the above.

d. How you might deal with such disagreements when you become a teacher of young children.

4. Select one system for self-analysis of teaching—the Flanders system, for example, or any other that may be in use on your campus.

a. Make an audio or video recording of two teaching samples of at least ten minutes each in which you are continuously involved in teaching roles with young children. (If recording isn't possible, plan to ask a peer to observe your teaching and tally behaviors "live.")

b. Analyze your recording in accordance with the rules of the system you are using. Write a brief report, listing the major points of your analysis.

c. To your analysis add a self-evaluation and indicate what standards you are using. For example, if your standard is to develop teaching skills giving children *only* positive feedback, evaluate the quality and quantity of such feedback in your recordings. Do you think it was good enough?

d. Further, add a self-prescription on how you can improve any of the teaching skills you observed based on any standards towards which you are working.

e. If possible, work with a peer and evaluate each other's teaching samples and write brief prescriptions or assessments for each other.

❦ EXERCISES FOR TEACHERS

1. Invite a colleague to work with you on self-evaluation of teaching by collaborating with you on selecting and learning to use one of the systems developed for the purpose or adapting any system to *your* purposes. You and your colleague may:

a. Select and learn to use the instrument.

b. Assess each other's competence in the use of the system.

c. Discuss with each other your own assessments of teaching.

d. Check each other's assessments.

e. Assess each other, using the system selected, and plan together for ways of developing the teaching competencies you value.

2. Identify your own program—whether primarily humanist or behaviorist—on the basis of criteria in this chapter, select teaching skills in harmony with your program, and work systematically to master these skills.

a. Specify each skill in as much detail as you can, adding subskills wherever it seems appropriate.

b. Use videotape or audiotape to sample your use of these skills in teaching.

c. Select or devise an assessment instrument appropriate to your teaching characteristics and use this instrument to help you reach the desired level of competence in your selected teaching skills.

d. Consult a colleague, supervisor, or college instructor to help you in this project.

BIBLIOGRAPHY

Amidon, E. J., and Hough, J. B. *Interaction Analysis: Theory, Research and Application.* Reading, Mass.: Addison-Wesley, 1967.

Ausubel, David P. "Cognitive Structure and the Facilitation of Meaningful Verbal Learning." In *Readings in the Psychology of Cognition,* by Anderson, R. C., and Ausubel, David P. New York: Holt, Rinehart & Winston, 1965, pp. 103–115.

Becker, W. C. *Parents Are Teachers.* Champaign, Ill.: Research, 1971.

Bloom, B. S., ed. *Taxonomy of Educational Objectives: The Classification of Educational Goals.* Handbook 1. *Cognitive Domain.* New York: McKay, 1956.

Bolton, Dale L. *Selection and Evaluation of Teachers.* Berkeley, Cal.: McCutchan, 1973.

Broudy, Harry S., and Palmer, John R. *Exemplars of Teaching Method.* Chicago: Rand McNally, 1965.

Child Development Associate Consortium. *Toward an Assessment System, Efforts to April 30, 1974.* Washington, D.C.: Child Development Associate Consortium., n. d.

Clark, H. B. "Teaching Concepts in the Classroom: A Set of Teaching Prescriptions Derived from Experimental Research." *Journal of Educational Psychology*, 62, 1971, pp. 253–278.

Combs, Arthur W. *The Professional Education of Teachers.* Boston: Allyn and Bacon, 1965.

Combs, Arthur W., and Kinzer, Suzanne M. "The University of Florida's Childhood Education Program: An Alternative Approach to CBTE." *Exploring Competency Based Education.* Edited by W. Robert Houston. Berkeley, Cal.: McCutchan, 1974, pp. 173–188.

Competency, Assessment, Research, and Evaluation. Report of a National Conference. Houston, Texas: University of Houston, March 12–14, 1974.

Curwin, Richard L., and Fuhrman, Barbara Schneider. *Discovering Your Teaching Self: Humanistic Approaches to Effective Teaching.* Englewood Cliffs, N. J.: Prentice-Hall, 1975.

Dunay, Lillian R., and Robison, Helen F. "Student Teachers' Self-Analysis of Teaching Behavior." Paper presented at AERA Annual Meeting, New Orleans, February 27, 1973.

Dunkin, Michael, and Biddle, Bruce. *The Study of Teaching.* New York: Holt, Rinehart & Winston, 1974.

Elam, Stanley. "Performance-based Teacher Education: What Is the State of the Art?" PBTE Series No. 1. Washington, D.C.: AACTE, 1971.

Elfenbein, Iris M. *Performance-based Teacher Education Programs: A Comparative Description.* Washington, D.C.: AACTE, October 1972.

Feddersen, John, Jr. "Establishing an Effective Parent-Teacher Communication System." *Childhood Education* 49, (November 1972), pp. 75–79.

Fein, Greta G., and Clarke-Stewart, Alison. *Day Care in Context.* New York: John Wiley, 1973.

Flanders, N. *Analyzing Teacher Behavior.* Reading, Mass.: Addison-Wesley, 1970.

Flanders, N. A. *Teacher Influence, Pupil Attitudes, and Achievement.* U.S. Office of Education Cooperative Research Project No. 397. Minneapolis: University of Minnesota, 1960. (Mimeographed.)

Flanders, N. A., and Simon, Anita. "Teacher Effectiveness." In *Encyclopedia of Educational Research.* Edited by Robert L. Ebel. 4th Ed. New York: Macmillan, 1969, pp. 1423–1437.

Fuller, Frances F., and Manning, Brad A. "Self-Confrontation Reviewed: A Conceptualization for Video Playback in Teacher Education." *Review of Educational Research* 43 (Fall 1973), pp. 469–528.

Gage, N. L., ed. *Handbook of Research on Teaching.* Chicago: Rand McNally, 1963.

Galloway, Charles. "An Exploratory Study of Observational Procedures for Determining. Teacher Nonverbal Communication." Unpublished doctoral study, University of Florida, 1962.

Gardner, Richard A. *Understanding Children.* New York: Jason Aronson, 1973.

Good, T., ed. *Trends in Classroom Observation.* New York: APS, 1975.

Grey, Loren. *Discipline without Fear.* New York: Hawthorn, 1974.

Hall, R. V., et al. "Instructing Beginning Teachers in Reinforcement Procedures which Improve Classroom Control." *Journal of Applied Behavior Analysis* 1 (1968), pp. 315–322.

Hilgard, E. *Theories of Learning.* New York: Appleton-Century-Crofts, 1948.

Houston, W. Robert. *Exploring Competency Based Education.* Berkeley, Cal.: McCutchan, 1974.

Houston, Robert W., and Howsam, Robert W. *Competency based Teacher Education.* Chicago: Science Research Associates, 1972.

Houston, W. Robert, et al. *Resources for Performance Based Education.* Albany, N. Y.: State Education Department, 1973.

Joyce, Bruce R., and Weil, Marsha. *Models of Teaching.* Englewood Cliffs, N. J.: Prentice-Hall, 1972.

Kohlberg, L., and Mayer, R. "Development as the Aim of Education." *Harvard Educational Review* 42 (1972), pp. 449–496.

Kounin, J. S. *Discipline and Group Management in Classrooms.* New York: Holt, Rinehart & Winston, 1970.

Krathwohl, D. R., et al. *Taxonomy of Educational Objectives. The Classification of Educational Goals.* Handbook 2. *Affective Domain.* New York: McKay, 1964.

Mager, Robert F. *Preparing Instructional Objectives.* Belmont, Cal.: Fearon, 1962.

Mager, Robert. *Goal Analysis.* Belmont, Cal.: Fearon, 1972.

Markle, S. M., and Tiemann, P. W. "Problems of Conceptual Learning." *Journal of Educational Technology* 1 (1970), pp. 52–62.

Montessori, M. *The Discovery of the Child.* Notre Dame, Ind.: Fides, 1967.

Montessori, Maria. *The Montessori Method.* New York: Schocken, 1970.

National Committee on Employment of Youth (NCEY). "Developing and Testing Procedures and Instruments for the Assessment of the Competencies of Candidates for the Child Development Associate Credential." Final Report. Contract No. FY4SC003. Washington, D.C.: Child Development Associate Consortium Research and Development (May 1974).

Ober, R., et al. *Systematic Observation of Teaching: An Instructional Approach.* Englewood Cliffs, N. J.: Prentice-Hall, 1973.

Office of Child Development. *Guides for Day Care Licensing.* Washington, D.C.: Department of Health, Education, and Welfare, 1973.

Pitcher, E. G., and Prelinger, E. *Children Tell Stories.* New York: International Universities, 1963.

Redl, F., and Wineman, D. *Controls from Within.* Glencoe, Ill.: The Free Press, 1952.

Reid, Ethna R. "Evaluation of Teacher Training in A Title III Center." *Proceedings of the 1968 Invitational Conference on Testing Problems.* Princeton, N.J.: Educational Testing Service, 1969, pp. 31–71.

Robison, Helen F., and Schwartz, Sydney L. *Learning at an Early Age: A Programmed Text for Teachers.* Vol. 1. Englewood Cliffs, N. J.: Prentice-Hall, 1972.

Rogers, Carl R. *Freedom to Learn.* Columbus, Ohio: Charles E. Merrill, 1969.

Rogers, Carl. "Significant Aspects of Client-centered Therapy." In Ruitenbeek, Hendrik M. *Varieties of Personality Theory.* New York: E. P. Dutton, 1964.

Rosenshine, B., and Furst, N. "The Use of Direct Observation to Study Teaching." Chapter 5 in Travers, R. M. W. *Second Handbook of Research on Teaching.* Chicago, Ill.: Rand McNally, 1973.

Rosenshine, B. "Teacher Competency Research," *Competency Assessment, Research, And Evaluation.* Report of a National Conference. March 12–15, pp. 138–153.

Ryans, D. G. *Characteristics of Teachers: Their Description, Comparison and Appraisal.* Washington, D.C.: American Council on Education, 1960.

Schalock, H. Del. "Notes on a Model of Assessment that Meets the Requirements of CBTE." *Exploring Competency Based Education.* Edited by W. Robert Houston. Berkeley, Cal.: McCutchan, 1974, pp. 209–250.

Sheppard, William C., et al. *How To Be a Good Teacher: Training Social Behavior in Young Children.* Champaign, Ill.: Research, 1972.

Simon, A., and Boyer, E., eds. *Mirrors for Behavior: An Anthology of Observation Instruments Continued.* 1970 supplement. Vols. A and B. Philadelphia: Research for Better Schools, 1970.

Stanley, J. C., ed. *Preschool Programs for the Disadvantaged: Five Experimental Approaches to Early Childhood Education.* Baltimore: Johns Hopkins University Press, 1972.

Taba, Hilda. *Teaching Strategies and Cognitive Functioning in Elementary School Children.* USOE Cooperative Research Project No. 2404. San Francisco: San Francisco State College, 1966.

Taba, Hilda, et al. *Thinking in Elementary School Children.* Coop. Research Project No. 1574, Office of Education, U.S. Department of Health, Education and Welfare. San Francisco, Cal.: San Francisco State College, 1964.

Travers, R., ed. *Second Handbook of Research on Teaching.* Chicago: Rand McNally, 1973.

Ullman, L., and Krasner, L. *Case Studies in Behavior Modification.* New York: Holt, Rinehart & Winston, 1965.

White, Robert W. *The Enterprise of Living: Growth and Organization in Personality.* New York: Holt, Rinehart & Winston, 1972.

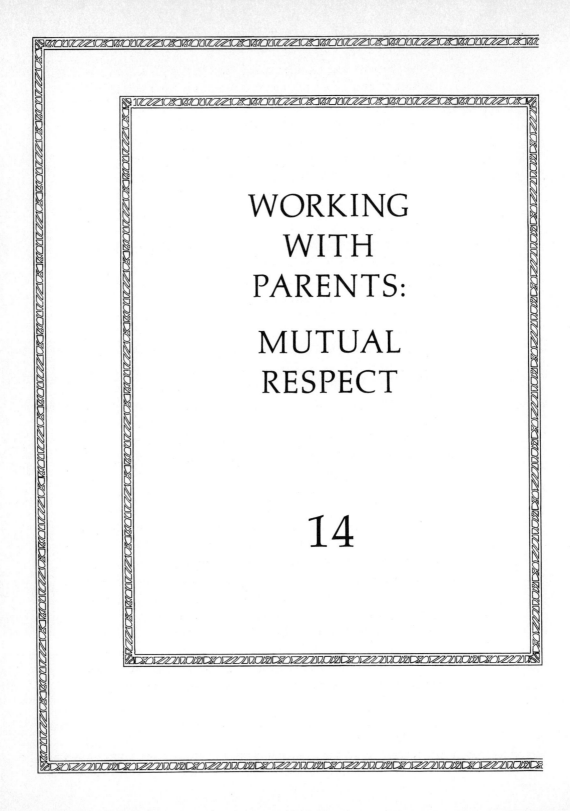

WORKING
WITH
PARENTS:

MUTUAL
RESPECT

14

Since parents are children's first teachers and usually the strongest and most permanent influence upon children's lives, effective teaching of young children is more likely to occur when teachers and parents work together. Yet there are few aspects of teaching which seem more threatening to new teachers than the prospect of working with parents.

It is not difficult to understand the apprehension new teachers often feel. The new teacher is often younger than the parents of the children in the class. She may have ambivalent feelings toward her own parents which may color her attitudes toward school parents. Young adults' surface maturity is readily pierced; struggles for independence and personal autonomy are not won in a single stroke but develop over the years. Too soon, an unexpected challenge or conflict stirs old feelings of uncertainty and anxiety, rigidifying less mature attitudes. The young teacher means to be open, empathic, and welcoming to parents' needs and suggestions but is too insecure to maintain such a stance in the face of unpredictable parental criticism or demand. If the teacher is not a parent, there is also vulnerability because the school parents' experiences are more profound. Yet parents often expect expert advice and counseling on problems of child behavior and development. When they perceive the teacher's lack of experience and/or knowledge of a particularly insistent problem, parents are quick to convey their feelings of dissatisfaction and frustration.

Since the teacher-parent relationship is necessarily complementary, not adversary, inexperienced teachers must emphasize their own strengths in building mutual trust and confidence in working with parents. Lack of experience can be balanced by sincere efforts to acquire information and to convey sensitivity. Parents always sense sincerity of teacher interest in their children. Where there is such honest teacher interest, it is usually easy to tap the abundance of parent information about children. The teacher's strength lies in conveying this interest, developing expertise in interviewing parents and learning to hear them out, learning to identify the useful information offered, maintaining open channels of communication, and putting new information about children to instructional use. Another very important teacher strength must be the use of professional resources—books, journals, research monographs, school and university specialists, and related professionals—to encourage the growth of insight, sensitivity, and wisdom in working with parents.

TEACHER-PARENT RELATIONSHIPS

In many ways the relationship of teacher to parents in the cooperative nursery schools is ideal. Parents or their elected representatives have selected the teachers. Parents either convey their values to teachers or agree together on the value priorities the school will feature. In some instances, parents select a director whose values and ideas appeal to them and then hold the director responsible for staff selection and curriculum development to embody the agreed-upon philosophic stance. In any case, the parental role is dominant in value decisions, while the teacher role is dominant in professional decisions about program, materials, and activities. Often, the school features parent education activities in the form of lectures, seminars, or workshops. Informal meetings are often planned to discuss both general and specific developmental problems. Mutual respect and responsibility are generated by such procedures. Since parents often serve as teacher assistants in the classroom, questions or reservations about program or about individual children's progress become the interest of all parents in the group, and there are many ways in which these differences are aired, discussed, and usually resolved. My own personal experience in such a school left a lasting and positive appreciation of my important role as a parent and of the contributions I made and received in that role.

Good parent-teacher relationships are essential for effective teaching of young children.

But the cooperative nursery school parent tends to be white and middle class, more often suburban than urban. Such parents are generally well educated, articulate, and voracious readers of books on child psychology and development. They are highly motivated to join such a school venture in order to improve their own parenting techniques. Such parents are not overawed by trained school staff, interact with them as equals, and contribute a great deal to easing and strength-

ening relationships between the school and the teachers. Teaching staff who reach out to parents—as they generally do—find they are met more than halfway with receptive, compatible views.[1]

This idyllic relationship, well-established in many small and moderate-sized schools, is found in many suburban public schools but is often absent from big city schools, day care centers, and the many kinds of early childhood group setting that exist. Head Start and day care centers usually feature parental decision making, giving parents a majority of places on governing boards. But the gap between staff and parents is not easily bridged.

Urban kindergarten parents often feel quite remote and alien from the school bureaucracy. Large schools dwarf people; parents feel powerless to affect the school in any important way. But it is an unequal struggle even in small schools. If parents themselves are not well-educated, though they may feel equal to teachers in value and goal orientation, they are frequently uneasy and uncomfortable in the verbal and articulate world of educational institutions.

Visit a busy public school office as a new family comes to register a child in mid-semester. Are there chairs, or is everyone standing in-

1. Katherine Whiteside Taylor, *Parents and Children Learn Together* (New York: Teachers College Press, 1967), pp. 143–172.

terminably, waiting to be helped? What attitude does the school office staff convey? Is it a game—how long will it take before a mother can catch a secretary's eye for assistance? Does the new family sense warmth, a welcome, and helpfulness? Or do they feel that they are being a nuisance, registering "out of season" when obviously everyone has plenty to do without bothering about newcomers?

Warmth of smaller settings

The day care, Head Start, nursery school or other small facility is more likely to welcome the new family and to treat them sympathetically and hospitably. Yet parents in urban settings may feel socially unequal to staff, or beholden to staff, and thus lack the independence to develop an equal relationship. Parents may become confused, angry, or dissatisfied, not having the social skills to penetrate the school's fabric meaningfully or the knowledge about how their needs could be served better. Parents may also be too busy or too tired after work to pursue leisurely conferences with teachers, attend educational discussions, or participate in the classrooms, even where the school actively seeks such parental interaction and participation. Some parents, especially those who have found urban life defeating and demeaning, may be too undemanding because of their own poor self-concepts and pessimistic expectations. They may feel unable to improve their own situations or to make an impact on the powers that be.

Understanding the many problems and problem situations that may undercut sincere efforts to reach out and develop effective working relationships with parents, new teachers must, nevertheless, be prepared to pursue the various means to this end. This chapter is concerned with attitudes, knowledge, and skills which teachers can acquire to insure an acceptable level of home-school cooperation.

ATTITUDES TOWARD PARENTS

The best way to develop the positive attitudes toward parents that encourage good working relationships is to follow the golden rule. Students can help each other, with school and college guidance, to assess their own attitudes and, where indicated, to work for attitude change. Respect for parents must be clearly projected by teaching staffs. A good start toward attitude change is to put oneself in a parent's place. "If I were the parent instead of the teacher," the student might say, "how would I feel, what would I want, and what channels could I use to attain my objectives?"

To feel as a parent might feel, or to acquire empathy for parents, students might volunteer for office duty at a school. Here, parents project their attitudes and concerns clearly in person, on the telephone, and in letters. Based upon such school experience, students can videotape simulated parent conferences with each other, replaying the tapes to assess their performances on such criteria as empathy, objectivity, openness, flexibility, and friendliness. Stopping a tape at a point where improvement in performance is needed, students can "brainstorm" together to find as many different ways as possible to convey desired attitudes.

Two contrasting attitudes toward parents are outlined.

While teachers rarely take extreme authoritarian positions, it is impossible to predict which situation or personality might tend to stimulate a response in an authoritarian direction. Hence, thoughtful consideration of extreme examples may help us resist the temptation to take a negative posture in a difficult situation.

While humane understanding takes many forms, it is possible to illustrate some of its manifestations without exhausting its many attributes. Note the following distinctions between the humanistic way to talk to parents and the authoritarian approach.

HUMANISTIC	AUTHORITARIAN
Open	*Closed*
I know what my perceptions are, but yours may be different and may help to clarify and deepen mine.	I know best, and I'll tell you what I think.
My qualifications to teach have made me aware of how much I have to learn and how listening to others can add to my understanding.	I am qualified to teach; therefore, my ways must be accepted.
My knowledge is tentative and I could use much more.	I base my conclusions on what I know.

HUMANISTIC	AUTHORITARIAN
Respectful	*Arrogant*
You can help me understand and deal with this situation better.	I can help you if you'll only listen and do as I say.
How do you generally handle this?	This is how I handle this, and you should do the same.
From your experience with your child, how do you advise me to meet his needs better?	If you can't handle your child any better, how do you expect us to keep him in school?
Are there ways we both can change our approaches so your child will feel we're both working in the same way?	This is the only way we can handle your child in school.
I would welcome your visitation so that we can plan together after we agree on his needs. Just let me know when you can come.	You can visit during open school week, as other parents do. We can't have parents visiting whenever they feel like it, it's too disruptive.
Personal	*Mechanical*
I would like us to get better acquainted. What do you hope will come from your child's early school experience?	Children are here to prepare for public school. If they can't make it here, they surely won't be tolerated in the big school.
Do you have some hobbies, interests, or skills that you can share with us to enrich our school program?	We can't fit in every idea people come up with. We already have a curriculum that we know is best for young children.
Can you help us on the trip so that the children will really have a rich experience?	We prefer not to have parents on trips. It only makes the children act up.
Knowledgeable	*Ill-informed*
I know your baby is three years younger. How do the children get along?	I haven't had time to read Alison's file; you'll have to tell me all about her history and experiences.
From what I know of your responsibilities, I'm grateful you found the time to come in for a conference.	You missed both conferences earlier this year; it's no wonder you don't know what's been happening.

HUMANISTIC	AUTHORITARIAN
Debby's grown two inches this year and her small muscle coordination is increasing rapidly.	I always get Bobby mixed up with Billy, but I'll look up Bobby's growth record later.

Sensitive	*Insensitive*
If you think it will help us to understand Bobby's current problem better, perhaps you can help us to identify events which might have contributed to it.	I want to know why this happened.
You might have some suggestions and so will we. Together maybe we can figure out what might work.	What do you intend to do about this?
You seem to have problems about getting Barbara out in the morning. Is there any way we can help? Do you need a car pool or another family to share the responsibility of bringing the children to school?	Why is your child always late to school?

Empathic	*Closed*
I know how long it takes to feed the baby and how impatient you must get when you know Bobby's waiting for you to walk him to school.	I don't understand how you can keep Bobby waiting so long to walk him to school.
My friend's child had digestive problems just like your child has. She told me how nervous and upset she used to get when her child wanted foods he couldn't digest. It must be difficult.	Other children have digestive problems too. Why should *you* get nervous and upset about it?
It's very distressing when your child has been well toilet-trained and then has an accident. I remember how I felt.	It's her fault. Why should you be upset?

HUMANISTIC	AUTHORITARIAN
Positive	*Negative*
It's true that Jenifer still hits other children, but it's much less frequent, and only when she's been teased too much. I see progress.	Jenifer is still hitting other children. It's against the rules and she must stop completely.
Billy was very shy when he first came. I can see, by the way he looks at other children, that he's longing to play with them. We're working on ways to help him feel more comfortable with the children.	Billy is shy and a loner. We've seen no real progress yet.

The above examples, contrasting two opposite attitudes toward parents, indicate that teachers with humanistic attitudes are open, respectful, personal, knowledgeable, sensitive, empathic, and positive. Humanistic attitudes are incompatible with dogmatism, compulsion, coercion, and non-negotiability.

DEALING WITH CHILD ABUSE

In rare and extreme cases, a teacher may react with a sense of outrage when she encounters a case of child abuse. Unfortunately, there are some parents who mistreat their own child, undervalue him, abuse him physically, neglect to care for him nutritionally or physically, and reject the child or convey hatred instead of love for him. In such cases, there is a great temptation to be contemptuous and disrespectful to the parents. However, even in such unusual cases, it helps to direct one's energies to remedies and to amelioration.

The question always is how to help the child and the family, how to improve the child's chances for better home relationships, and how to locate resources which might be equal to the family's needs. In the public schools, guidance counselors and administrators usually take on this function. In smaller school settings, directors or specialist staff assistants or consultants, usually handle such problems.

In many areas, teachers and school staff are required by law to report immediately any evidence of abuse of children to the authorities. The trend has been increasingly to identify families "at risk" or evidencing child abuse—not to punish the family but to help them. Many families can be rehabilitated with support from social agencies and monitoring of their handling of their children. Removing children from their families is an extreme step which rarely benefits either, although sometimes no other remedy is possible.

In many cases it is not the family that needs re-education or better understanding but the teacher. If a teacher is new to a community, perceives it as hostile and inadvertently communicates these feelings to the children and their parents, misunderstandings develop and grow into mutual animosities. A teacher may be viewed with hostility by parents through no fault of her own, but this is very unusual. Parents react quickly to teachers' positive sentiments. In fact, parents are as eager as teachers to establish friendly relationships for the benefit of the child.

The more clearly teachers see parents as children's first and continuing teachers, the more effort teachers are likely to make to work constructively with parents. Murphy listed several factors basic to child development which she thought low-income parents often need to understand or accentuate, that is:[2]

A sustained, supportive mother-child relationship.

Patterned, rich sensory-motor activities for children, with intrinsic satisfactions from manipulation and action.

Adapting tolerance to child functioning, keeping his curiosity active.

Flexibility with regularity in home routines.

Stimulating and encouraging environment.

Provision of rewarding adult models.

Some of these factors are missing from poorer homes for economic reasons, others for a variety of reasons, including unfamiliarity with contemporary literature on child development. Some suggestions appear below under "forms of collaboration" for ways in which teachers can help parents in such homes.

2. Lois B. Murphy, "Child Development Then and Now," *Childhood Education* (January 1968), pp. 302–309.

SKILLS IN PARENT EDUCATION

Good skills and attitudes help build construc- tive parent- teacher relationships.

Remembering that the family is the young child's first and most vital primary affiliation group and that parents are a teacher's most powerful allies in the educational process, teachers acknowledge both the importance and the difficulties of constructive work with parents. Empathy and humanistic attitudes were stressed above as necessary to effective work with parents. Respectful *attitudes* and empathy are necessary but not sufficient for this task. *Skills*, combined with humanistic attitudes, are needed for parent education to reinforce healthy child development and learning.

Skills in parent education include systematic ways of maintaining and communicating information and professional behaviors in interpersonal situations. A description of the attitudes and skills required for this demanding aspect of the teacher's educational mission follows.

1. Be well-informed in detail about the child's functioning in school. A brief list of points to be conveyed to parents helps to insure a teacher's accomplishing what she plans to do.
2. Treat parents with respect and as equals, and, in terms of familiarity with the child and his history, as superiors.
3. Have samples of the child's products as specific indications of his functioning levels.
4. Learn to *listen well* and to *hear* the expression of the parent's feelings and requests for information or for action.
5. Accord the parent the courtesy of an appropriate response, another appointment, or an appointment with a school specialist or administrator, if it seems in order.
6. Jot down the gist of a conference, discussion, or telephone conversation for filing and remembering.
7. Provide any objective information the parent wishes or the teacher regards as necessary or helpful.
8. Convey to the parent respect for the child and interest in his welfare.
9. Maintain a professional stance about the confidentiality of material in a child's record or elicited from parents, so that you convey assurance, as a social worker or therapist would, that this material will retain its private character.
10. Be realistic about what teachers can accomplish. Some goals for changing children's behavior can only be accomplished with a unified home-school approach.[3] Other goals may require referral to

3. Loren Grey, *Discipline without Fear* (New York: Hawthorne, 1974), pp. 110–111.

specialists, assistance from the school administration, or other forms of out-of-classroom assistance.

11. Realize that more can frequently be accomplished in a series of conferences with a parent than in a one-shot effort. Acquaintance improves as teacher-parent conferences are held over a period of time, and resistance often melts in the joint realization of mutual problems and equal desire for improvement or resolution of problems.

12. Be able to acknowledge the limitations of one's expertise and information. This includes friendly refusal to give advice outside of one's competence, in marriage or vocational counseling, for example. Some parents are desperate for all kinds of assistance. A friendly teacher is a natural focus for pouring out anxieties, expressing needs, and making requests of all kinds. The teacher can remain friendly without responding inappropriately to such parental needs. Appropriate responses might be referral to the guidance counselor, the school's social worker, or supervisory or administrative staff to find appropriate referral sources.

13. Be articulate about one's professional expertise. Parents are likely to respect a knowledgeable teacher who communicates well.

14. Know several good resources and methods for helping parents to understand the basic factors required for healthy child development and learning. For example, encourage families to secure and use library cards, to request free or low-cost government pamphlets about child care, nutrition, or health practices, or to enter evening adult education or training programs. Prepare a list to distribute to parents specifying such local resources for children as parks, museums, zoos, libraries, and science or industrial exhibits. In low-income areas, know where parents can find information about vocational training, income budgeting, and housing.

OUTCOMES OF TEACHER-PARENT UNITY

Where teachers skillfully implement their respectful attitudes towards children's families, parents feel richly rewarded in a more secure, informed base for child rearing. Pickarts and Fargo, writing out of rich experiences in parent education, list desirable outcomes from work with parents:[4]

Appreciation of the child for himself rather than for achievements or extraneous reasons.

Becoming sympathetic, supportive observers.

4. Evelyn Pickarts and Jean Fargo, *Parent Education* (New York: Appleton-Century-Crofts, 1971), pp. 168–178.

Interest in understanding child development.

Willingness to make judgments based on facts.

Understanding mental health practices.

Self-understanding.

Interest in school activities and processes.

Skills in helping the child adjust to school.

Acquisition of information about child care.

Students will recognize these outcomes as goals, not only for professional teachers but for parents as well. The more teachers and parents achieve these outcomes, the more helpful they can be in their mutual efforts to support children's programs.

FORMS OF COLLABORATION

Teachers of young children usually have more contact with parents than teachers of older children because of the young children's inexperience and immaturity. A young child, for example may need supervision going to and coming from school or may need special arrangements made for his initial adjustment to school. Other ways teachers multiply home-school contact include the following:

1. Programs are arranged to inform parents about the school program or their children's progress or to discuss topics of mutual interest.

2. Parent education programs are arranged, especially on topics of child development, through the initiative of parents, teachers, or both.

3. Parent visitation in the classroom is encouraged.

4. Reporting to parents occurs through oral reports at least once a semester.

5. They work together on various fund-raising activities, to support a nonpublic school, or to raise funds for special purchases of materials or equipment.

6. They work together for political and social purposes such as campaigns for increased school budgets.

7. Parents bring a child to school or pick him up. Such brief, daily,

routine contacts are the chief building blocks in a relationship that is far more personal, informed, and focused on the child than most parent-teacher relationships with older children. Brief interchanges keep the relationship alive and personalized. The mother or father asks, "How's he doing?" or, "Is she giving you trouble? She seems very negative these days at home." Sometimes, the parent alerts the teacher to possible difficulties—physical or emotional. It may be, instead, the teacher who does the alerting, for example, "Have you had his eyes checked? He's squinting a lot lately. I wonder if he needs glasses."

A wise choice of opening activities helps the teacher make the most of arrival times, leaving opportunity to chat with parents for information exchange or to make appointments or plans. A program which is ready to receive children so they may engage in activities of their own choice with minimum supervision is often the best schedule for permitting such parent-teacher exchanges. For departures, either an assistant, a parent volunteer, or, in a public school setting, an older child gives the teacher the leeway to convey messages and to have interchanges with parents.

8. Telephone calls are made by teacher or parent. Parents usually refrain from telephoning except in emergencies or for special purposes. Teachers too often do the same. However, teachers can develop positive relationships with more parents by a regularly scheduled system of telephone calls for the purpose of conveying a positive report. For example, the teacher calls the parent to say, "I thought you'd like to know about something new Billy did today. He felt sorry for Joy, who is unhappy because her mother is in the hospital. So Billy gave up his bicycle turns twice to help cheer Joy up. It was his own idea, but naturally I let him know it was a very grown-up thing to do. You might let him know I told you how pleased I was." Telephone calls should be reserved for such positive reports or for emergencies. A parent must be called when a child is ill or injured, but news of misbehavior at school seldom constitutes an emergency. A face-to-face meeting is always better for talking about behavior problems, because it allows for sensitivity to the other person's reactions and feelings.

9. If the telephone is not available to the teacher when she needs it, or if some parents have no telephones, such positive messages can be sent in writing. A simple form may be developed having the child's name, the date, and a description of something *good* about the child's school development and learning. Sometimes, these might be pasted or stapled to a child's decorative drawing, so the message also features a sample of the child's work.

10. Duplicated messages may be sent home with each child, often pinned to their clothing for security. These may be copies of lunch

menus for the next week, notices of school trips or special events, or notices of school meetings for various purposes.

11. Parents may invite teachers to a social home occasion. Sometimes teachers are invited to a child's birthday party, a family cookout, or a picnic. Some teachers are able to accept such invitations and enjoy them, while other teachers may have heavy family responsibilities of their own. In either case, gracious responses to invitations convey appreciation.

12. In the case of poorer parents who might want or need help in order to support children's developmental needs, teachers can plan ahead to collect needed resources:

   a. Films are plentiful on mental health, physical development, children's fears, problems of social learning, and family conflicts.[5] Most films are brief and sharply enough focused to be useful for group discussion meetings.

   b. Problem-oriented parent discussion meetings are usually the most dynamic, involving kind of resource teachers can provide. In such settings, much is often accomplished in consciousness raising concerning attitudes and in sharing information and experiences in coping with child-rearing problems. Parent training groups to heighten parenting skills, such as those Gordon advocates, can be set up whenever parent interest is sufficiently aroused.[6] Teachers can help to secure leadership for such groups through local community centers or child guidance clinics.

   c. Popularly written pamphlets addressed to parents are available free of charge from many local governmental and community institutions, from the federal government, and from such business organizations as the Metropolitan Life Insurance Company. Teachers can help parents to locate such resources and secure bulk copies for school use.

   d. Other resources include classroom visitations to emphasize positive factors in child development, reminders to parents about some of the excellent programs available on television that focus on aspects of young children's development, and invitations to meet at school with specialist staff, such as a speech pathologist, nurse, social worker, or guidance counselor.

Teachers might remember that the above resources are sometimes needed in homes where the problems are not economic, since middle-class parents are not automatically aware of the major developmental needs of growing children.

5. Mariann P. Winick, *Films for Early Childhood* (New York: Early Childhood Education Council, 220 Waverly Place, 1973).

6. Thomas Gordon, *P.E.T.: Parent Effectiveness Training* (New York: Wyden, 1970).

ENCOURAGING PARENT PARTICIPATION

Aids to collaboration

Many nursery schools, especially of the parent cooperative variety, prepare observation booklets or suggested forms of parent classroom participation so that when parents visit and teachers are busy teaching, the parent receives a guide to possible observation or collaboration. Taylor describes an observation booklet for New Zealand kindergarten parents that specifies nine kinds of focus for parent classroom observations, including making friends, play materials, skill development, creative activities, and developing responsibility and respect for the rights of others.[7]

Suggestions are offered for encouraging parent participation in classroom activities.

Aids to parent-teacher collaboration include meetings to discuss teaching and programs, distribution of occasional duplicated statements on child development and classroom activities (written by school, school district, or consultant staff), and the use of filmstrips, films, videotape, photographs, and other audiovisual media to convey school theory and practice.

Teachers who regularly use a camera to record interesting children's activities and products have rich data sources to share with colleagues, supervisors, and parents. Parent meetings are always well-attended when parents expect to view their children on film, photograph, or videotape. In addition, there is a large collection of informational and artistic material available for educational purposes. Much of the material produced especially for a professional teacher audience is equally useful for a parent or a parent-teacher audience.

Types of parent participation

Where parent participation is encouraged, during classroom visitation in nursery schools, Head Start centers, or public school prekindergartens, the list of possible parent activity often includes these items:

1. Observe one child, your own or another. Jot down any questions about this child you would like to discuss with the teacher during her break.
2. Sit in the library corner. Offer to read a book to a child who seems interested. Let other children join the reading group if they wish.

7. Taylor, op. cit., pp. 168–172.

3. Sit in the block corner. *Listen.* Let the children talk to you about their blockbuilding if they wish. Ask questions but refrain from telling the children *what* to do or from doing any construction for them.

4. Sit at the table for games and table constructions. Chat with children about their work. Chiefly, ask questions, listen well, and praise children for the work they are completing.

5. Observe the art work children are doing. Sit and listen, and chat with them if they seem to want to talk. It is best not to interrupt a child who is trying to complete his work. Write children's names and the date on the backs of their drawings and paintings. If a child wants to write his name, help him unless he can do it by himself. We write in manuscript. Here's an example of manuscript: J o h n n y. Notice we use a capital only for the first letter of a name.

6. If a child seems alone and uninvolved, chat with him and encourage him to find something to do. Play a game with him, if he has no other suggestions, such as Candyland or Chutes and Ladders.

7. At clean-up time, help a group clean up but let the children carry the responsibility and do most of the work.

8. If there is a great deal of traffic at the bathroom, station yourself there for a while to help children who might need some help. Don't be too quick to help: let children try to help themselves.

9. When the children are dressing and undressing, see who needs help. Help as little as possible, however. Show a child *how*, and let him try to do it himself.

10. During *outdoor play*, take a station where children are assembled that is far from the teacher's. Join their games, chat with them, or suggest games if they don't seem to know what to do. Games must be quite simple and noncompetitive. We like *London Bridge Is Falling Down.*

11. When the children are *eating*, join the group. Let the children do as much as they can. Chat and listen.

This is not an exhaustive list, but it indicates the nature of teaching tasks in which parents can participate. It also suggests some early childhood philosophy and values, emphasizing children's actions, self-help, responsibility, and learning through practice. One exuberant mother, visiting a day care center and without such a guide to participation, wore herself out pulling three children in a wagon all over the playground. The teacher rescued her by tactfully suggesting activities the children needed to try out to exercise their muscles and their growing skills. Many parents, who do not distinguish early childhood education from baby sitting or custodial care, are not aware of the school's theoretical grounding in child development. They can be helped to understand this, without embarrassment or contempt.

Parent participation in primary grades

In the primary grades, where teachers never seem to have enough assistance to individualize reading instruction or to supervise children's skill practice in math or other areas, parent volunteers can offer valuable help when assigned to such tasks as the following:

1. Read to one or more children.
2. Listen to a child's oral reading, supply words when the child hesitates, and encourage the child to complete the selection.
3. Help a child check his math answers to activity cards.
4. Play checkers, chess, backgammon, or some other game with one or more children.
5. Help children work on phonics tasks.
6. Work in the listening center and monitor the tape recorder use.
7. Help supervise an art activity.
8. Help supervise some constructional work.
9. Help prepare some instructional materials.
10. Chat with a shy child and encourage him to interact with others.

CONSULTANT SERVICES

Support services are needed in the education of young children.

Where group settings for young children are well supplied with support services, one specialist usually has the primary responsibility of working with parents. Sometimes this specialist is a social worker, but she or he may be an educational director, guidance counselor, assistant principal, coordinator of early childhood classes, or other staff member. Teachers, however, always have a primary function and responsibility to work with parents, because the classroom receives the most direct impact of teacher-parent concerns and problems.

Leadership responsibility by a specialist for work with parents can be of great assistance to the classroom teacher. Such leadership or consultant services may include:

Orienting parents before the child's entry into school, to minimize anxiety and to help the child make as smooth an entry as possible. Orientation usually occurs in group meetings before the beginning of the semester, individually thereafter.

Availability in the school or classroom to help with disturbed children or distraught parents during the initial period of separation of child from parent. This is the most difficult time for a new teacher. When classes are made up by additions throughout the year, there is no need to initiate a whole new class at once. New teachers have to decide, with supervisory and specialist guidance, whether to insist upon a clean break for mother and child or to permit individual adjustment periods with separation according to parent-child tolerance. I personally prefer the latter, with a very few exceptions for children who are clearly secure and adjusted but unable to make the break with parents without help.

Offering consultation to parents on developmental problems or helping to make referrals where more supportive services are required.

Helping on intake procedures, where children must be selected for admission from a larger group of applicants. This may include interviews with parents and child, observation of the child, completion of intake forms on child history, and analysis of medical forms.

Helping to place children in classroom groups based on intake procedures, information collected, and knowledge of philosophy and personality of school staff.

Acting as workshop or discussion leader in parent meetings.

Advising the teacher, after observing a child in the classroom, on ways of handling children with problems.

Speaking for the school in community or professional meetings.

Keeping teachers informed of new research and new professional resources in the field, including professional conferences, journals, pamphlets, and books.

Teachers who find themselves in settings where the above type of services or resources are not available, will need to show initiative and take more responsibility than they would otherwise find necessary. Many teachers actually carry the responsibilities for many of the functions listed above. Assistance from well-trained specialists is extremely valuable and much more can be accomplished with such assistance. Without it, a professional teacher does the best she can.

SPECIAL FAMILY NEEDS

Many families, either with very low incomes or living on welfare sources of income, find their lives fragmented in many ways. Since these families are dependent upon community services, they are required to deal with quite a few different bureaucracies in health, education, and welfare. Until the day comes when integrated services become available, to reduce the large amount of time spent in securing the services needed, low-income families require sensitive understanding of their problems.

Such families sometimes are late in picking up a child after school, because they were "stuck" on a waiting line. When a child is frequently kept out of school because parents are unable to arrange pickup and delivery while they cope with various bureaucracies, teachers often become impatient because the child is deprived of regular attendance at school. Attendance irregularities tend to disrupt a child's social progress and other learning activities. In addition, children are forced to spend time at home in idleness and restlessness, with consequent conflict within the family and general impatience and irritability.

Teachers who are aware of such problems of families who must deal with a number of community agencies may also be alert to ways of helping the family to keep the child in more regular school attendance. This may be accomplished through the cooperation of friends, neighbors, or fellow parents in the class, or in other ways.

In one prekindergarten class, a four-year-old was identified by the teacher as the most difficult behavior problem in the group. Analysis of the situation turned up some obvious causes of problem behavior. The child was wakened at 5:00 a.m. by a mother who commuted to a distant job. He was handed on by two different families to a third family that delivered him to school at 8:30. He was sleepy, irritable, and confused. No wonder this little boy vented his feelings on anyone nearby. In conference between the program's family worker and the mother (in an evening appointment), the problem was resolved by rearranging the child's early morning care. Many problems are far more difficult to resolve, and some are definitely not within the school's power to solve.

Day care centers in big cities frequently find themselves viewed by parents as an oasis in a hostile environment. The day care center tends to accept parents and to try to help or to locate the kinds of help needed. Often, there is a parents' room with comfortable chairs and a homelike atmosphere. There may be a coffeepot ready to pour. Some parent rooms offer other services—sewing machines, books, materials from which to make games and toys for children, samples of puppets, toys and games to copy, or art materials for parent use. Family workers in such centers are very busy responding to parent needs and initiating contacts with parents. In fact, many day care centers emphasize their role as a family-related service more than an educational and custodial service for children.

Parent organization and governance of many of the newer day care centers have often given parents a first opportunity to exercise some form of control over their lives and to plan with others for improvement in the quality of their lives. Such parents, determined to participate in decisions about their own experiences and their children's experiences in early childhood settings may be effective partners in school-home collaboration in their children's development. Teachers may have to learn how to work with these parents, to establish rapport, empathy, and constructive plans for children's experiences at home and at school.

LANGUAGE AND CULTURAL DIFFERENCES

Some students are concerned about social or linguistic and cultural barriers to communication and collaboration with parents. These may exist, but they usually dissolve when parents sense sincerity, integrity, and professionalism. Some parents may be insensitive and too demanding. Surely, some teachers are also. If teachers convey respect and interest, such messages are usually more than reciprocated. Sometimes it is a signal of respect to learn something of another group's language and cultural practices or to request the group to help the program to feature its language and traditions.

A sign of respect for parents which all students should learn to use is to *listen* to them, through an interpreter if necessary, and to *receive* their suggestions and ideas thoughtfully. Another is a *request for their help*—to sing songs, lead dances, supervise ethnic food preparation or make costumes or decorations, to play music, recite poetry, or portray national or traditional events or celebrations. A third sign of respect is the creation of *collaborative* procedures—to plan together for a child's optimum development.

SUMMARY   *Effective teaching of young children is enhanced by parent-teacher collaboration, yet working with parents often seems threatening to new teachers who are young and still ambivalent about their own parents. Ideal parent-teacher relationships tend to flourish in cooperative nursery schools, but it is challenging to create such relationships in big city schools. Large public schools in urban settings seem far less welcoming and sympathetic to parents than Head Start, day care, or nursery school settings.*

Teachers can acquire attitudes, knowledge, and skills to insure an acceptable level of home-school cooperation. Humanistic, rather than rigid authoritarian attitudes, are advocated here, with emphasis upon open, respectful, personal, knowledgeable, sensitive, empathic, and positive communications.

Specific suggestions for effective collaboration with parents include listening to and hearing parents, having realistic expectations, and cultivating patience in working out problems. In low-income areas, sensitivity to parent problems may generate parent education facilities to help families use their limited resources well and to become active participants in the community. Suggestions are also made for forms of parent-teacher collaboration and aids to collaboration. The need for specialist leadership in this area in the school is described, especially to guide the teaching staff and to augment its resources.

❦ EXERCISES FOR STUDENTS

1. Arrange to spend one morning or afternoon a week in a school office, answering telephones, assisting with any clerical work available, but especially observing parents in person and in telephone conversations.

a. Keep a log to summarize your observations of parents in the office experience, specifying the content of parent initiatives. Classify these in some way, such as:

(1) requests for assistance

(2) complaints

(3) requests to visit the classroom

(4) requests for appointments with the teacher

(5) volunteering time or materials

(6) messages concerning child pickup or the like

(7) other

b. Describe the kinds of office responses to parents that you noted.

c. Evaluate the responses you listed in *b*.

d. Summarize briefly your recommendations for possible improvement in school interactions with parents.

2. Attend a PTA or parent meeting at a school, preferably a day care center or nursery school.

a. Describe briefly the events of the meeting.

b. Categorize parent participation in the meeting as to its agenda, personnel presiding or presenting, and parental roles observed.

c. Evaluate your experience and briefly suggest improvement in this school's ways of working with parents.

3. Attend a school board meeting in your own district or in the district where you are currently placed for field or student teaching experiences.

a. Write a brief report summarizing the meeting including the agenda, actions taken, and the nature of the discussions or conflicts observed.

b. Write two brief parallel evaluations, one from the point of view of one of the parents at the meeting or of a school board member and one from your own point of view (written as if you were a teacher employed in a school in this district).

c. Contrast the two positions taken in *b* above.

4. Read one of the titles in the bibliography at the end of the chapter and write a brief review, selecting at least two ideas for collaboration with parents and listing at least five activities for implementing each one.

✣ EXERCISES FOR TEACHERS ✣✣✣✣✣✣✣✣✣✣✣✣✣✣✣✣✣✣✣✣✣

1. With the permission of a few parents, plan to videotape or audiotape a few conferences with individual parents, including at least one parent whose child presents some problems. Explain that you are studying your own performance in parent-teacher conferences for self-improvement purposes.

a. Make a checklist of items you wish to assess in your performance based on suggestions in this chapter or any others you choose. If you use videotape, try to apply the Galloway assessment of nonverbal behaviors.

b. Check your own assessment with a colleague, supervisor, or college instructor.

c. Identify behaviors you determine need improvement and repeat this exercise as soon thereafter as you can, until you are satisfied with the progress you made.

d. If you need assistance in finding out how to change behaviors, consult with a colleague, supervisor, or college instructor.

2. Plan a program of school-home collaboration with new and different features than you have employed in the past. For example, you might:

a. Invite parents to sign up for a specific number of visits and prepare brief guides in writing to indicate what kinds of parent help or participation you need.

b. Videotape a music or art session and invite parents to a classroom meeting to view a replay and to help you plan exciting music and art experiences.

c. Plan different kinds of trips with extensive parent participation.

d. Invite parents to specify talents or expertise which you can enlist to enrich the program.

e. Send home lists of "found" objects needed for projects.

3. Read some of the titles in the Bibliography for this chapter and jot down ideas new to you, to strengthen your work with parents.

a. Review your list monthly to remind you to use interesting ideas in your work with parents.

b. Assess your work with parents at the end of the school year, and write yourself a prescription for improved work with parents.

BIBLIOGRAPHY

Auerbach, Aline B. *Parents Learn through Discussion.* New York: Wiley, 1968.

Child Development and Early Childhood Education. Chicago: Model Cities Chicago Committee on Urban Opportunity, n.d.

Faber, Adele, and Mazlish, Elaine. *Liberated Parents/Liberated Children.* New York: Grosset and Dunlap, 1974.

Gordon, I. J. *Early Child Stimulation through Parent Education.* A Progress report to the Children's Bureau, Department of Health, Education and Welfare, Grant No. PHS-R-306. Gainesville, Florida, 1968.

Gordon, Thomas. *P.E.T.: Parent Effectiveness Training.* New York: Wyden, 1970.

Grey, Loren. *Discipline without Fear.* New York: Hawthorn, 1974.

Honig, Alice. *Parent Involvement in Early Childhood Education.* Washington, D.C.: National Association for the Education of Young Children, 1975.

Lane, Mary B. *Education for Parenting.* Washington, D.C.: National Association for the Education of Young Children, 1975.

Murphy, Lois. "Child Development Then and Now," *Childhood Education* (January 1968).

Patterson, Gerald R., and Gullion, M. Elizabeth. *Living with Children: New Methods for Parents and Teachers.* Rev. ed. Champaign, Ill.: Research Press, 1971.

Pickarts, Evelyn, and Fargo, Jean. *Parent Education.* New York: Appleton-Century-Crofts, 1971.

Taylor, Katherine Whiteside. *Parents and Children Learn Together.* New York: Teachers College Press, 1967.

Winick, Mariann P. *Films for Early Childhood: A selected, annotated bibliography.* New York City: Early Childhood Education Council, 220 Waverly Place, 1973.

Wittes, G., and Radin, N. "Two Approaches to Group Work with Parents in Compensatory Preschool Program." *Social Work* 16 (1971), pp. 42–50.

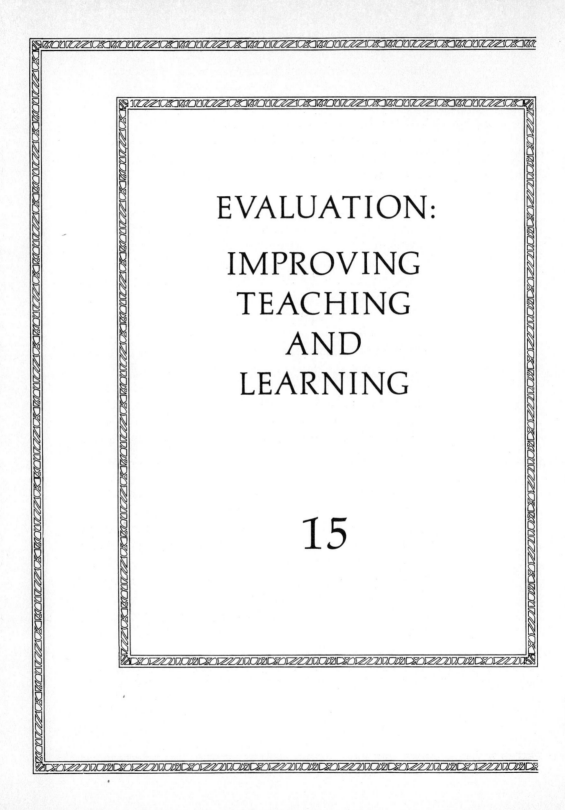

EVALUATION:
IMPROVING
TEACHING
AND
LEARNING

15

Preservice students work hard, and anxiously, to qualify for their profession. They want to complete requirements, pass tests, and demonstrate competence. They realize that the first hurdle, becoming a novice teacher, will open the door to independent practice. They also realize that a great deal of on-the-job experience, with further study and school supervision, will help them attain the status and sense of the seasoned and articulate practitioner. Both here and abroad, many thoughtful writers continue to stress the need for teachers to be lifelong learners as, for example, in this statement, "The idea of permanent or life-long learning is recognition in another form of the impermanency of contemporary knowledge and, at least implicitly, of the evolutionary nature of cultural and social forces."[1]

Since new knowledge seems to grow at an accelerating pace, it follows that the rate of obsolescence of teacher preparation is bound to increase. In western Europe, England, and the United States, there is widespread dissatisfaction with the great gap between the production of new knowledge and its useful application in classrooms.

In the seventies, accountability of teachers to the broader community of parents and local citizens has become a major theme in educational movements for changing and improving the quality of children's experiences in schools. As teacher shortages disappeared in the sixties, impatience mounted over the schools' unchanging practices and absence of quality inservice programs. Equally jaundiced views of preservice preparation sent shockwaves through teacher education institutions and instigated thorough-going revisions of college programs. While the critics of teacher education may be found in every philosophical persuasion, the behaviorists have been dominant among the powers that control educational funds at federal and state levels in

1. James Lynch and H. Dudley Plunkett, *Teacher Education and Cultural Changes: England, France, West Germany* (London: George Allen and Unwin, 1973), p. 178.

the United States. Contrary to American trends, the British educational community has continued its long trek away from perennial values since the end of World War II and toward humanistic goals for young children's schooling. It seems likely that, given time, more of these humanistic values will once again become fashionable in American educational circles.

PRESSURES FOR SYSTEMATIC EVALUATION

Of all the levels of education in this country, settings for young children have remained the most humanistic and child oriented. There is no reason to expect drastic changes in this respect. There will, however, be pressure for more systematic procedures, more articulateness in goals and in evaluation, and more sophistication in teaching skills and understandings of child development.

In all school settings, parents, community representatives, and tax-conscious officials are requiring evaluation. They want to know what their tax dollars are buying. What are children accomplishing in school? They ask whether more could be accomplished with less. These questions are asked everywhere, not only when school budgets are voted but also when teacher organizations negotiate for salary increases and other benefits or campaign for higher state and federal education expenditures.

Launched in 1965 as a massive federal effort to improve the future academic performance and the current physical and mental health of young disadvantaged children, Project Head Start had complex goals that were difficult to define precisely. Evaluations of Head Start, especially those initiated in the seventies, constituted the first extensive systematic effort to identify the payoff of this popular project. While evaluations were generally disappointing, they were subjected to considerable criticism for criteria and methodology used, inadequacy of instruments of measurement employed, and the usual problems of too many uncontrolled variables in assessing human behavioral changes and growth. There will be great interest in the findings of the subsequent controlled variation studies, designed to overcome some of the criticism generated by the Head Start evaluations by reducing some of the variables.

The continuing movement toward evaluation of educational outcomes places considerable responsibility on the classroom teacher—to develop self-evaluation procedures, to find ways to benefit from supervision, and to assess child learning results.

PURPOSES OF EVALUATION

From a humanist point of view, evaluation is most effective when it becomes self-evaluation, facilitates teaching and learning, produces useful records, and guides decisions about curriculum and teaching.[2] Most of the evaluation activities which go on in all classrooms are teacher-initiated, teacher-constructed, and teacher-analyzed procedures for assessing various aspects of children's progress. In early childhood classes, however, the incidence of externally initiated testing and assessment has been rising rapidly. Standardized tests of various kinds are often administered to young children, some of the "readiness" variety and others to assess self-concept, social skills, or other aspects of development.

Screening young children

Young children are often "screened," that is, tested in many different areas such as physical characteristics and growth checks, possible learning disabilities, emotional problem identification, social skill inventory and, of course, for academic and cognitive progress and achievement. Medical or psychological personnel and teachers and supervisors participate in these various screening or test activities. In many schools, teachers of young children are required to write evaluative profiles for each child, either for reporting to parents or for the records. Such profiles usually specify observed aspects of progress and identify needs for further development or for special treatment. Usually, teachers then hold conferences with parents and report orally on children's progress. For fruitful parent discussions of children's needs and strengths, the need for good data for such conferences is obvious.

2. Fred T. Wilhelms and Paul B. Diederich, "The Fruits of Freedom," in *Evaluation as Feedback and Guide* (Washington, D.C.: Association for Supervision and Curriculum Development, NEA, 1967), pp. 234–248, p. 234.

Teachers' needs for evaluation

Besides screening children for problem identification and further diagnostic evaluation, teachers seek data they need in order to make informed professional decisions about teaching. Of course, teachers would like praise and credit for a job well done, as we all would. In the accountability sense, everyone is asking what empirical evidence can be collected to document the results of good teaching.

Teachers want more than praise, however. They know that they need *signals* to change in identified ways and that indicators for change require some *guides* to point to the kinds of changes required. Furthermore, the social scene keeps changing, casting up new concerns or different questions about old ones.

As a new teacher, you are likely to ask yourself many questions about your professional work. You are likely to be overcritical and more than eager to improve your skills. You may ask:

Am I too permissive?

How can I improve classroom discipline?

How can I teach young children without getting overtired?

How can I improve my conferences with parents?

Can I learn to feel more secure when there are visitors in the classroom?

How can I express my values and goals more clearly?

How close did I come to following the curriculum guide?

What kind of teacher image do I project to children, supervisors, fellow teachers, and parents?

Experienced teachers are less likely to be seeking data on problems of discipline, energy control, or self-expression. More likely, they are ready to look at long-range problems, asking themselves:

How can I accomplish more with children who present various kinds of problems and needs?

Which children am I teaching most effectively, least effectively, and why?

How can I keep my professional life exciting and satisfying?

What are my chief current needs for professional growth?

What materials do I need to make my teaching more effective?

What new programs are coming along that I should consider for the children I teach?

How can the supervisory and administrative staff help to remove obstacles and add resources to improve children's learning experiences?

What support services are lacking?

How can the learning environment be improved?

Teachers will find that many of the questions they are asking themselves are being echoed in various ways by the school administration, by school boards, and by parents. Not confining themselves to asking questions, these groups often make suggestions which must be received and duly considered by teachers and schools.

To summarize the major purposes of evaluation, they are:

Evaluative data on child progress provides a factual record of educational and developmental results.

1. To provide feedback on educational and developmental results.
2. Accountability to the wider community to which the school is responsible.
3. To signal needs to change or differentiate programs, teaching methods, or other school variables.
4. To generate data needed to make decisions on teaching and curriculum, or other features of early childhood education, such as need for further resources in health or welfare.
5. To compare educational developments with value orientations, whether the latter change or remain unchanged. In other words to help assess the extent to which goals are in fact being reached.

SPREAD OF THE ACCOUNTABILITY MOVEMENT

Accountability in education is defined in such terms as "the continuing assessment of the educational achievement of pupils in a school system; the relating of levels of achievement attained to the state and community's educational goals and expectations, to the parents, teachers, taxpayers and citizens of the community."[3]

Sabine attributes the growth of demands for accountability in American education to three basic causes, that is, the increasing tax burdens of average families, and their reluctance to accept higher rates, dissatisfaction with schools because of recognition that schools produce

---

3. Creta D. Sabine, ed., *Accountability: Systems Planning in Education* (Homewood, Ill.: ETC Publications, 1973), p. 7.

many youths who fail to achieve functional literacy levels, and the development of management procedures in industry and business to increase effectiveness and efficiency through the systems approach, using modern computer technology.[4]

Other reasons for the rapid spread of the accountability movement include increasing value conflicts among various groups, rising social criticism and reform movements, and dissatisfactions concerning American military entanglements abroad. Also, spilling over to education and other areas of domestic policy are the effects on income and jobs of the worldwide inflationary pressures and the rising levels of education among American parents, which result in increasing concern and interest in improved educational experiences for children.[5]

The accountability movement in education has for the most part centered on public schools. However, with the increasing likelihood that the public schools will sponsor a higher proportion of new early childhood programs (as space becomes available because of the decline of the elementary school population), the movement is bound to affect teachers of young children everywhere. The movement, of course, has also affected federal funding for "child development" programs, although such programs tend to be funded more in response to social demands than to strictly data-based arguments.

Teachers have, of course, always sought to assess the progress of the children they teach. What is new in the current accountability movement is the effort to equate the educational process with production of goods and services in industry and business and to use an "input-output" type of reasoning and evaluation emphasizing the unit cost of the "product."

The "production of optimum results with the resources available" is the definition of accountability attributed to Kruger, who also detailed twelve characteristics of educational accountability, among them, community involvement, technical assistance, needs assessment, management systems, the development of performance objectives, staff development, comprehensive evaluation, cost-effectiveness, and program auditing.[6]

4. Ibid., pp. 7–8.

5. John E. Morris, "Accountability: Watchword for the 70's," in Frank J. Sciara and Richard K. Jantz, *Accountability in American Education* (Boston: Allyn and Bacon, 1972), pp. 18–25.

6. *An Administrator's Handbook on Educational Accountability* (Arlington, Va.: Association of School Administrators, 1973), pp. 20–21.

Humanistic views of accountability

Humanistic educators tend to stress the inappropriateness of wholesale adaptation of business and industrial production models of accountability to educational institutions and functions. Bowers emphasizes that instead of cost effectiveness, accountability should be couched in terms of what a child needs "to realize his fullest potential as a person."[7] He suggests that community consensus on the purposes of education is difficult to achieve and is likely to narrow on constrictive or indoctrinational objectives, incompatible with the broader human potential for development. He sees a need, not for cost-effectiveness accounting with systems analysis and design, but for recruiting more intellectually mature and socially representative kinds of people into teaching. The lack of consensus on the purposes of education, as Bowers points out, is basic to the accountability problem, which forces agreements on the lowest common denominator.

Human values are broad

When teachers try to discover the range of philosophic value preferences, they find rather vague statements. One viewpoint on day care, for example, states that its primary purpose is "to supplement the care and protection that the child receives from his parents."[8] However, an addition to this statement points out that essential components of day care should be "care, protection, education, health supervision, social work, parent participation, and planning and coordination." Another view, cited by Fein and Clarke-Stewart, asserts that successful day care programs have these features:

1. Optimistic assumption of good outcomes because the children are normal—not sick children in need of treatment.
2. Strongly ideological, clearly articulating and highly valuing philosophical and ethnical positions (but these are largely undefined).
3. Assertion of child's capability to make a contribution and requirement that he do so.

7. C. A. Bowers, "Accountability from a Humanistic Point of View," in Frank J. Sciarra and Richard K. Jantz, *Accountability in American Education* (Boston: Allyn and Bacon, 1972), pp. 25–33.
8. *Child Welfare League of America Standards for Day Care Services*, rev. ed. (New York: Child Welfare League of America, 1969), p. 10.

4. Provision of clear examples of mature group membership.

5. Enjoyment of community support and esteem.

6. Provision of a peer society for older children, that stands for adherence to adult values (also undefined).[9]

Problems of cost accounting of human values

However, it is apparent that, while practitioners and writers in early childhood education are concerned with human values, and their open endedness in direction and attributes, funding agencies are stressing cost features and accountability conceptions which are in line with business-oriented ideas. The systems approach, for example, requires the selection of "efficient components" and alternate options for each one. How will such alternatives be assessed for such early childhood education functions as health, safety, encouraging and developing children's feelings of competence, and developing problem solving, creative abilities and behaviors, and positive self-concepts? If and when such alternatives can be tested and costs determined, teachers will surely welcome any data-based information from which to derive better instructional strategies. It must be recognized that a great deal of wishful thinking now substitutes for the solid factual base which would be required if, in fact, a business-type of accountability system were feasible in settings for young children.

PRIORITIES OF ACCOUNTABILITY IN EARLY CHILDHOOD EDUCATION

Options will differ as to whether the cult of efficiency is compatible with a humanistic view of early childhood education. In this writer's view, performance objectives may be feasible, but only with a strong tilt toward *process* objectives. Children are not interchangeable units in a production line, nor are teachers. Many specialists in early childhood education stress, not the equal competencies of each staff member but the ways in which they complement each other. While all teachers of young children will be expected to like working with them and to understand their unique needs and capabilities, surely each

9. Greta G. Fein and Alison Clarke-Stewart, *Day Care in Context* (New York: Wiley, 1973), pp. 290–291.

different teacher can bring her or his own complement of interests, strengths, and skills to round out a strong staff. Since a knowledge base has still to be developed as to children's optimum educational environments and experiences—and the teaching skills which would be required for these yet unknown goals—contemporary evaluation procedures can only be based on experience and value decisions.

Effects of priorities

Desirable teacher characteristics and teaching skills are bound to be specified in various ways by different types of early childhood institutions, programs, and facilities. One brief list of teacher characteristics would probably receive unanimous endorsement: emotional warmth, understanding of children, flexibility, responsiveness, and willingness to become actively involved with children.[10] But surely, every employing agency would require more specificity than this. Similarly, there is great variety of program goals and functions. The United States Office of Education is attempting to evaluate *programs*, through controlled variation studies in Head Start and Follow Through. Predictably, these are beginning to show that different values produce different outcomes. One type of program produces better problem-solving skills while another prizes early literacy.

Specification of goals

Many early childhood programs espouse the same goals, essentially. Custodial care versus educational activities used to be a lively issue in day care. It is no longer an issue except among those concerned with decreasing costs, yet some day care centers have yet to add good educational programs to their custodial care. Commitment to educational programs is not always followed by full implementation. Program evaluation requires agreement upon clear and unambiguous program definitions as well as agreement on goals. There are very few programs where teachers do not have considerable leeway to invent, adapt, or tailor any given program to their own bent. Some programs feature teacher centrality, especially in informal, open environments, and the

10. Ibid., p. 242.

goals preclude rigid adherence to any packaged or preselected learning activities.

Specification of teaching skills

Evaluation of teaching, however, may turn out to be more functional than program evaluation. *People* are so salient for young children, compared with any other element in the educational scene, that it may well be that it *is* primarily the teacher who makes the difference. Teacher competence and morale have already been identified as important features of the success of any program.[11] The major question is whether it is the teacher's personality which makes the difference, the skills and competencies which the teacher learns to use effectively, or the interaction between these two. It seems likely that teachers who work well with children probably work better when they are skilled and knowledgeable. Especially, working with children in groups, it can be expected that intuitive skills are not enough, but need to be developed and set within a framework of principles and theory.

As indicated in Chapter 13, the competency-based teacher education movement (CBTE), requires specification of teacher competencies for all school levels and preservice evaluation of competency achievement. Inservice competency evaluation, now relatively unspecified and unsystematic, is likely to take the same route ultimately.

Contemplating a lifelong career in the profession of teaching, students need to understand and interpret contemporary movements in their field. There will undoubtedly be more program and teacher evaluation, not less. Teachers will have to meet community, taxpayer, and governmental requirements for evaluation. They will have to clarify their own value systems, be able to articulate their beliefs and preferences, and know how, by way of experience and research evidence, to support these values. Teachers may have to shop around for a system which features values they can accept and where choices are possible. They also need skills to evaluate their own progress as a teacher—in specifying program goals and in developing functional and satisfactory ways to evaluate children's progress. Self-evaluation of teaching was explored in Chapter 13. The remainder of this chapter is concerned with evaluation of children's progress.

11. Jenny Klein, "Making or Breaking It: The Teacher's Role in Model (Curriculum) Implementation," *Young Children* 28 (1973), pp. 359–365.

VARIETIES OF EVALUATION SYSTEMS

Evaluation systems can be formal or informal, can be primarily objective or subjective or a mixture of these two features, can include standardized instruments or teacher-constructed procedures, can include long- or short-term goals or both, can include parents, community, or other nonschool personnel in the process, or can include any combination of the above. Evaluation systems may use primarily criterion-referenced tests, norm-referenced tests, or both. The evaluation analysis, and decisions or recommendations based on the analysis, may be the responsibility of the teachers, of administrative staff, of parents and community representatives, or of consultants. However, teacher and school staff involvement are essential to any productive use of evaluation findings and recommendations.

EVALUATION GOALS

It is generally agreed that evaluation must not be too narrow; it should instead encompass the range of goals the school values—physical, affective, and social, as well as cognitive or academic. Yet the narrower the program, the broader the evaluation goals should be, in order to detect side effects or unexpected gains or losses.

Assessing progress toward goals

Once teachers (or administrators), have specified program goals, assessment of children's progress must relate to these goals. Behavioral goals are being required in more and more school settings today.[12] Teachers who find product-oriented goals distasteful should note that behavioral goals can also specify *process*. *Product* goals specifying such outcomes as demonstrated mastery in identification of names of letters of the alphabet are much easier to assess than such *process* goals as evidencing curiosity, creative use of art media, or skills in social interaction with other children. Neither is it impossible to demonstrate to parents and community that where process goals show good progress—for example, in task orientation, attention span, and task-

12. Robert F. Mager, *Preparing Instructional Objectives* (Palo Alto: Fearon, 1962).

completion—long-term goals are assured for children. In addition, content goals for children who become dedicated learners can also be easily achieved in selected areas, when appropriate.

In public schools, the program goals may be preselected but they are usually stated in very general terms. In nonpublic settings and programs, the same situation may be found though, in some cases, there may be a tightly specified program.

Whether program goals are already selected or not, the new teacher will find it expedient to borrow some ideas from other teachers and supervisors and from scholarly sources and inject some interpretations and understandings of her own. No system is so teacher-proof that the teacher's personality or style of teaching is irrelevant.

Teachers who are either attempting to select their own program goals or to understand and adapt those they are expected to follow will find many sources of program description and goal definition, especially in the Head Start and Follow Through planned variation studies.[13] Teaching and learning goals can usually be derived from a good description of program goals given and, in some cases, teaching goals may also be specified to some extent or in detail. Yet many teaching goals can apply to almost any program.

Relation of programs to goals

An example of the relation of teaching to program goals may be illustrated by a program such as Montessori. An important program goal of Montessori education is *motor education*, or physical education, as it is generally called today. Montessori, however, meant more than physical education in general. She was a great believer in specific kinds of physical exercises to prepare particular muscles for educational needs. Popular jigsaw puzzles for young children, widely sold today by commercial manufacturers, have tiny wooden knobs attached

13. See especially Stanford Research Institute "Longitudinal Evaluation of Selected Features of the National Follow Through Program," ERIC 067266 and 057267 (1971), and later studies: Eleanor E. Maccoby and Miriam Zellner, *Experimental Primary Education: Aspects of Follow Through* (New York: Harcourt Brace Jovanovich, 1970); V. Shipman, "Disadvantaged Children and Their First School Experiences." Educational Testing Service Head Start Longitudinal Study," in J. Stanley, ed., *Compensatory Education for Children, Ages 2 to 8* (Baltimore, Md.: Johns Hopkins Press, 1973), pp. 145–195; Ronald K. Parker, *The Preschool in Action* (Boston: Allyn and Bacon, 1972); and Ellis D. Evans, *Contemporary Influences in Early Childhood Education.* 2nd ed. (New York: Holt, Rinehart & Winston, 1975).

to each puzzle piece by which to pick it up and place it. This is a typical Montessori design to give little fingers the kind of practice which she thought would develop the small muscles of the fingers and hand and which would make writing with a pencil easier. Specific exercises, or the use of materials requiring exercise of specific muscles, would be required as teaching goals to carry out this general program goal. But any other program could use the same materials and profess to work toward the same goal. Similarly, various kinds of "real-life" exercises are developed in the Montessori program to help children master the skills for buttoning their clothes and tying their shoelaces. These would also be specific teaching goals in a Montessori program. Yet, many early childhood programs feature these goals as well.

It is not meant to suggest that all programs feature the same goals or that the same teaching goals are pursued regardless of program goals. The sameness of teaching goals often obscures real differences in teaching strategies and program implementation.

In Montessori programs, to return to the example given above, the teaching goals mentioned would be rigorously followed in preplanned Montessori exercises, usually with only one child at a time. Each such exercise is carefully sequenced and followed in detail. By contrast, in most non-Montessori schools, the same activities, such as cleaning, sweeping, zipping jackets, and cooking, are usually carried out casually, without precise order and detail, or in small or large groups or with one child, depending upon the teacher's decision. Montessori programs require teachers to observe children so the teacher can decide when a child is ready for instruction. At that point, the instruction is implemented according to detailed strategies. Which is better, Montessori or non-Montessori approaches? Or which non-Montessori programs? We are learning to frame more productive questions: What values stem from each? Which ones might be more useful for what kinds of children?

Increasingly, early childhood teachers in programs of very different types, are members of teams, not solo performers. The team may include a co-teacher, an assistant teacher, a supervisor, a parent volunteer, or specialists in social work or in the medical or psychological services. The collaborative nature of teaching young children in group settings helps to provide more objectivity in viewing the child, more variety of role models for children, and more variety of expertise in the evaluation process.

LONG- AND SHORT-TERM GOALS

Kamii, in her description of the Piagetian-based curriculum she developed, described long-term goals that were related to the kind of adult ultimately produced by an educational system.[14] Actually, long-term development has been studied very little. Longitudinal evaluation studies are rare because of the expense involved and the tremendous problem of controlling for numerous variables, since everyone's life is affected by much besides education-related experiences. Terman's studies of gifted children represent one of the very few long-term efforts at evaluating outcomes for one particular type of student.[15]

Evaluating long-term goals

Long-term goals have no definite time spans. They may refer to "graduation" end points, or semester or year-end checkpoints. If children spend no more than a year or two in the early childhood level or school, a long-term goal may be defined as an outcome of the period spent in the school.

For young children, evaluation of long-term goals might concentrate on major developmental features such as social skill progress, progress in use of art media, in language development, physical skills, and in conceptual development. Some programs would require the addition of a reading progress goal. An example of one system developed to assess long-term goals is the Georgia model, which specified seven broad objectives for elementary school. One objective—to learn to solve problems—is further analyzed into pupil learning behaviors and includes identification of problems through generalizing solutions. Such teaching behaviors as organizing problem situations and assisting in developing solutions are also specified and relate to these long-term goals.[16]

A regional educational laboratory is making an interesting effort to define behavioral goals in esthetic education. The behavioral features which would be assessed include not only the skill itself, such as paint-

---

14. Constance Kamii, "An Application of Piaget's Theory to the Conceptualization of a Preschool Curriculum," in R. K. Parker, *The Preschool in Action* (Boston: Allyn and Bacon, 1972), pp. 126–127.

15. Lewis M. Terman, *The Gifted Group at Mid-Life: Thirty-five Years' Follow-up of the Superior Child* (Stanford, Calif.: Stanford University Press, 1959).

16. University of Georgia, "Georgia Educational Model Specifications for the Preparation of Elementary Teachers" OE 58019.

ing, but also such aspects as enjoyment, knowledge, and judgment.[17]

A long-term goal of any kind should, it seems, assess not only a child's acquisition of new knowledge or new skills but also his interest in using them and applying them in his own ways. These latter goals turn out to be more difficult to assess.

Evaluating short-term goals

Almost any time period less than that for a long-term goal might be selected for short-term goals. However, since young children make such astonishingly rapid growth, even over rather short periods, some selected short-term goals might be evaluated with some regularity, to identify needs for more or less stimulation or guidance, for changes in approach, of needs for further diagnosis, or others. "He'll outgrow it" and "time is on our side" are truths which fortunately help teachers and parents to tolerate unstable growth periods and transitional periods of development. Assessment procedures, however, are especially needed to differentiate between what are apparently developmental problems and other types of problems in children's growth and learning patterns.

Long-term goals can be segmented into shorter steps along the way, for short-term goal assessment. For example, physical development means different types of skills at various levels of growth. Short-term goals might specify these in some developmental pattern, for example, assessing such skills as running or jumping before skipping and hopping. Whether assessment is to be periodic or systematic, the procedures must be mapped out in advance with appropriate instruments, so teachers can continue to teach while incorporating assessment procedures in their plans. Mager's book on goal analysis might be helpful to teachers in selecting assessable types of goals.[18]

Evaluating cognitive growth

Teachers often say that assessments only work for trivia or such closely defined behaviors that they are not really worth the trouble to collect. Yet Kamii has shown, as did Piaget, that it is possible to sample chil-

17. David W. Ecker, "Defining Behavioral Objectives for Aesthetic Education: Issues and Strategies for Their Resolution." (St. Ann, Mo.: CEMREL [Central Midwestern Regional Educational Laboratory], n.d.

18. Robert Mager, *Goal Analysis* (Belmont, Calif.: Fearon, 1972).

dren's developmental progress in cognitive growth and to plan teaching strategies to match children's actual developmental levels. Admittedly, these are time-consuming procedures, ideally carried out by well-trained specialist staff. But much would be lost if teachers were willing to allocate their evaluation duties entirely to others. A child's characteristic ways of functioning are revealed in great detail in an individually administered, well-planned effort to discover the ways in which he performs. One child turns out to be excessively cautious, unwilling to risk a "wrong" answer even when there has been no suggestion that responses are right or wrong. Another child assiduously "reads" the teacher—wanting only to please, too inhibited to think through his own thoughts, hoping to guess what is wanted. Then there is the sheer delight of a child who is secure enough to figure out his own solution, to stick to it when challenged, and to insist on developing his own version of the problem because he has invested himself so fully in it.

It is only possible to *sample* children's behaviors of the more complex sort. Samples may not be definitive, but they usually suggest the direction of the child's growth, and they indicate some features of his unique ways of behavior. This information is very helpful to teachers who are bent upon individualizing their work with young children.

COLLECTING OBSERVATIONAL DATA

Some teachers like to jot down anecdotes about each child throughout the year, to collect details about his work in the classroom. To do this successfully requires considerable sampling. One method is to keep cards in a pocket for a very few children and after making some jottings during a day, put them at the back of the card pile. If there were fifteen children in the group, and three cards were completed daily, there would be jottings for each child for each week of the year. A better sampling device would be to mix the cards each week so names are drawn on a more random basis instead of in the same order each week. This gives a more differentiated picture for each child, since no child is observed only on Monday or Friday when, for various reasons, behavior might be somewhat different than on mid-week days. Monday *is* different; children seem to have to make a renewed adjustment from home to school, and some children are tired from a too-stimulating weekend or too late a bedtime.

It is advisable that these jottings have a focus. Otherwise, it might be difficult to decide what to jot. The focus need not be *too* narrow but, if it becomes too wide, the system is likely to be abandoned after a while because it has become too burdensome. A good focus for anecdotal records is the social skill development area, including friends made, changed, added, or subtracted, choices of play activities with friends, or examples of social skills and handling of conflict situations.

Recordings of observations when a new activity is introduced provide a wealth of information about children's attitudes and capabilities.

Time-sampling observations—of one or two children, for whom more detailed behavioral descriptions are desired—supplement more casual or periodic check-offs and establish more clearly average rates of occurrence of behavior selected for analysis. Time-sampling methods also help to chart subsidence or increase in rate of specified behaviors, giving the teacher more assurance that the behaviors observed are, in fact, either improving or deteriorating (as the case may be). Where children are being helped to reduce undesirable forms of behavior—temper tantrums or hitting other children, for instance—their own involvement in keeping charts up to date on their behavior, by pasting colored strips on a time chart, may be productive forms of feedback and motivation to continue improving or to reverse deterioration.

Some teachers drown in oceans of observational recording which they have no way to pattern or analyze. To keep one's head above water—and to collect material which is useful—requires some selectivity regarding focus, dimensions, sampling methods, and system. Specific suggestions for observational recording can be found in several of the titles listed in the bibliography at the end of the chapter.

Some behaviors must be recorded when they occur, either because of their unusual character or the urgency of follow-up efforts of some kind. This includes observation of bizarre or deviant behavior, symptoms of physical distress, or any behaviors that are either self-destructive or dangerous to others.

Whenever a new activity is introduced, for instance, finger painting or woodworking, recordings of observations tend to yield rich data about children's attitudes about their capabilities, their willingness to learn something new, and their persistence or discouragement in the tasks. Young children who resist invitations to do finger painting often give intimations of emotional problems which this art medium sometimes causes to surface, especially when they associate the smearing of paint with toilet training experiences that have been negative.

Use of checklists

If observations are to be made of all children, these must be particularly economical of time and effort. Checklist types of records are ideal for this purpose, and some checklists may be maintained by the children themselves, after some instruction. Physical skill development is readily recorded on checklists. If checks are made monthly on a regularly scheduled periodic basis, and dated, the result is a sequential

FOCUS OF OBSERVATION	**RECORDING**
1. Interest and ability in hearing stories read. *Interest* may be gauged by the child's request for a story, or his joining a story group. *Ability* may be gauged by whether the child stays to hear the story without disrupting others' listening.	Week No. 1 Names — Interest — Ability John J. Mary M. /=yes, o=some, —=no
2. Physical skill observations such as hopping, skipping, shoelace-tying, buttoning, pulling on boots and coat, sweater and hat.	Monthly Record SEPTEMBER Names — Clothing — Stapler — Zipper y=yes, n=no
3. Social skill observations, such as taking turns, greeting children and others in socially acceptable ways, accepting helper responsibilities.	Social Skills Names — Take turns — Greetings — Helper jobs
4. Language development, such as articulation, fluency, vocabulary, syntax. This is probably best secured in some elicited activity, such as child story telling or dramatization, or descriptions of pictures, in order to cover the various dimensions of this area of development.	Language Features Names — Articulation — Fluency

schedule of children's skill achievement over the year. Some observations are made and recorded of naturally occurring spontaneous events such as examples of child empathy. However, it is easy to miss an important occurrence by being too busy in a more demanding area of the room. To compensate for such oversights, some observations are recorded from behavior deliberately elicited from each child, in order to have a comparable set of data without any gaps. Child skills which might be recorded either when observed in natural occurrences or when elicited include shoelace tying, paintbrush control, hopping, or skipping.

Observations can focus on almost any aspect of a child's behavior in a group setting. Some examples of some observation checklists that occasionally or regularly can serve a teacher's purposes are shown on page 528.

EVALUATING OPEN EDUCATION OUTCOMES

Studies of open education environments and their evaluation possibilities suggest that some process features can be assessed, for example, "organization of the classroom, nature of the materials in the room, evidence of actual use of these materials in the room, evidence of the individuality of children and teachers, evidence that a classroom reflects aspects of the local community."[19] This source also suggests evaluation of open classroom goals in such areas as resourcefulness, child originality in constructions of ideas and products, child self-perceptions as active organizers and participants in their own learning, child flexibility in personalized and cognitive style, child-child teaching, child-child individuality in expressions of opinion, language functioning in questioning and use of information, and playfulness with language.[20]

Behavioral assessment of affect

Behaviorally-oriented assessment of children generally requires pre-assessment—identifying a benchmark for comparison. The behavioral goals statements themselves contain the essence of the assessment

19. Anne M. Bussis and Edward A. Chittenden, *Analysis of an Approach to Open Education* (Princeton, N. J.: Educational Testing Service, 1970), p. 63.
20. Ibid., pp. 66–69.

goal, since they contain a description of the desired behavior, the context in which it will be assessed, and the level of competence expected.

It is possible to assess an affective goal behaviorally following this formula. For example, the behavioral goal is stated: "The child will, after he has selected a story, enjoy hearing the story read by the teacher in a small group situation, and he will listen to the end without more than two brief interruptions." The affective goal here—*enjoyment in hearing a story*—is assessed behaviorally, that is, by observation that the child stayed to the end of the story with no more than two brief interruptions. The minimum of interruptions could be omitted or changed as desired. But note the *context*. Must he be able to listen to any story someone wants to read to him? No, at first the context is limited to a story that he selects himself. Must he be able to listen in a total group situation? Not at first, because the above context limits the desired goals to a small group situation. Of course, this could be changed to a total group or to a one-to-one situation. This kind of goal determination permits teachers to plan very individually and with realistic expectations for young children's progress in small steps.

Assessing individual progress

Students will find it very useful to learn to make individual goal decisions and to preassess as well as postassess. Progress is a function of two points—where the child begins and where he comes out. Interim checkpoints are useful, but not for all purposes or all children; this would soon be too burdensome. Interim checkpoints are most useful for children with the greatest needs or for those who are most challenging to the teacher. Indications of progress help the teacher to remain positive and optimistic and to be able to convey such optimism to parents from recorded evidence, thereby obtaining home reinforcement of school optimism.

There are varied "profiles," "inventories," or other forms similarly titled that chiefly supply the teacher with ready-made observational checklists and ways of recording judgments and observations of children's functioning. These are especially helpful when they require recording to be based upon specific types of observation. If teachers check off items from memory, the material loses considerable reliability. There is an all too human tendency to create a "halo" effect

—to attribute to a well-liked or particularly attractive child all virtues, whether they are, in fact, present or not.

TESTS

It is not easy to test young children. They react to the tester, the test situation, and to their inner needs with much less inhibition than older children or adults. Test results with young children are notoriously *unreliable*. You can get wildly different results on the same test within a brief period. The *validity* of many tests for young children is difficult to establish. The test may or may not measure what it purports to measure, and what it purports to measure may not be a valid indication of the child's development or learning. Children's self-concepts, for example, are a very relevant aspect of child development. So far, however, it has not been satisfactorily established that any of the instruments or procedures used for testing reliably reflect this construct.

Tests may be too short or too long to measure young children's functioning of various types. Short tests may be extremely unreliable because they sample too little of the child's behavior. Long ones may be equally useless if they cause the child to tune out from boredom or to perseverate from exhaustion (to keep giving the same answer regardless of the question).

Sources of tests

The Head Start Test Collection of the Educational Testing Service is one of the better sources for test selection, with excellent cautions about testing young children.[21] Another good source is the University of California (Los Angeles) Early Childhood Center.[22] The Johnson and Bonmarito book is another good source of tests in the developmental areas.[23]

New compilations of developing or hitherto unpublished instru-

21. Educational Testing Service, *Head Start Test Collection* (Princeton, N. J.: Educational Testing Service, 1971).
22. CSE-ECRC, *Preschool/Kindergarten Test Evaluations* (Los Angeles, Calif.: UCLA Graduate School of Education, Center for the Study of Evaluation, and the Early Childhood Research Center, 1971).
23. O. Johnson and J. Bonmarito, eds., *Tests and Measurements in Child Development* (San Francisco: Jossey-Bass, 1971).

ments are becoming available with increasing frequency and can be found in the ERIC Clearinghouse on Early Childhood Education, on microfiche, or in college and university libraries almost everywhere.

Giving physical tests

Tests may be either informal and teacher constructed, or formal standardized instruments. Tests for physical skill progress are easily devised and given. For example, suppose it would be helpful to know which children can do a somersault. With a list of children's names ready for check-off and a gym mat on the floor, the teacher can invite the children to perform, and she can check the list rapidly. If dozens of name lists are duplicated, any number of quick checklists can be rapidly developed. Also, other physical skills can be checked-off— buttoning, zipping zippers, or copying circles, squares, or triangles with a pencil on paper. The latter is not just a physical skill, since perceptual and cognitive skills are also involved.

Informal skill evaluation

Informal tests, or inviting specific types of performance, may help the teacher gauge the children's progress in such varying types of skill development as the following:

Relevant informal teacher tests are suggested in several areas of child development.

1. Self-care in dressing and undressing.
2. Setting a table for lunch correctly with one-to-one matching of place mat, plate, glass, and cutlery.
3. Shelving blocks by matching blocks to a model, picture, or symbol for each type, by shelf.
4. Adequate handling of art materials without help, including placement of products for drying.
5. Adequate verbal forms of social interaction with other children.
6. Singing a frequently sung song with correct words, adequate pitch, and rhythm.
7. Matching rhythm of clapping to the melodic rhythm of a well-known song.
8. Jigsaw puzzle completion of selected puzzles, timed or untimed.

Assessing Emotional-Social Development.   The above examples of informal teacher tests sample such areas of development and learning

as physical development, math, cognitive, verbal, and are development. Other areas can be sampled—emotional development, for example—for such features as security to try new tasks without fear or
persistence in a task which presents problems to solve. It would not
be difficult to devise tasks similar to ongoing activities, to test such
characteristics. Similarly, social skills may be well worth testing informally in a volatile group in need of considerable social skill learning. Group living in school settings sometimes imposes requirements
upon young children for unreasonably rapid accommodation to school
demands. More realistic goals for social learning might grow out of
preassessments of what children's current skills are. Pacing might
also be adjusted to realistic possibilities of achievement.

Advantages of informal tests

The advantage of informal teacher tests is the selection of material
relevant to the program and the children. School or teacher values can
be featured instead of a test-maker's notions of what children should
be learning. Other advantages are ease of repetitive test sampling to
gauge pace and level of child progress, ease of generating simple checklist types of data out of regularly recurring activities in the classroom
without having to suspend learning in order to test, and the greater
confidence in the *fidelity* and *reliability* of the data because both the
context and tester are familiar to the child.

Disadvantages of informal tests

There are also disadvantages to teachers' testing of their own children
informally. It is easily neglected because of the lack of material in
packaged form. Too many other duties crowd out evaluation needs.
Few teachers have developed the skills needed to devise useful informal types of tests for young children. Moreover, when teachers
test their own pupils, they find it difficult to be objective since their
own investment is so strong. The lack of norms in informal testing
deprives the teacher of standards of comparison. It is difficult to know
whether the class is average, below average, or above average on any
skills tested. However, norms are not needed for many features of
development or learning. To a great extent, the group furnishes its

own norms, not only group averages but also the distance between the most and least advanced children, or the range of functioning.

Many tests, primarily psychological, are not needed for any children except those who manifest considerable deviance in development. Good, systematic observations help to pinpoint needs to test and minimize unnecessary testing. Specialists should probably test those singled out for further screening of various kinds.

Project Follow Through evaluations

It is instructive to note the broad range of evaluation goals and procedures pursued in Project Follow Through evaluations. An interim report lists eight types of measurement impacts on children, four for parents, and two for teachers. In addition, classroom observational data yielded five different scales of process.[24] The eight measures of program impacts on children included their days of attendance, scores on cognitive and achievement tests, skills in math, reading, language

24. Stanford Research Institute, *Interim Evaluation of the National Follow Through Project, 1969–1971: A Technical Report* (Menlo Park, Calif.: Stanford Research Institute, 1973), pp. xxviii-xxx.

arts, and the child's self-concepts and attitudes toward school and learning.

UNOBTRUSIVE DATA

What really counts in the long run, of course, is what effects school has on outside functioning. Does it make any difference that the child is in an educational environment? Unobtrusive data may supply such evidence.

Examples might be lists of children's book borrowings from the public library as a partial indication of interest in reading. Other similar types of data are:

> School attendance figures.
>
> Number of children from the class who attend the local library children's hour on Saturday, as reported by the children's librarian.
>
> Parent requests to the teacher for book titles to buy for children's birthdays.
>
> Children's attendance at park or community recreational facilities, as reported by personnel from those agencies.
>
> Children's patterns of preventing or participating in vandalism or playground littering, as reported by school custodial personnel or police officials.

Often these unobtrusive data are far more convincing and effective, for parents and community and funding sources, than statistics or scholarly reports. One virtue of clear goal selection is to identify the direction in which to seek for evidence of teaching success—in school or in the community.

CRITERION VERSUS NORM-REFERENCED TESTS

Norm-referenced tests used to be almost the only type available for school and developmental testing. Norm-referenced tests chiefly compare groups and individual children to the group averages. Most IQ and achievement tests are of this type.

Recently, there has been a great deal of interest in criterion-referenced tests, which are not comparative at all but simply seek to establish a "yes-no" result, that is, whether or not the child can perform to the criterion or standard selected. Shoelace tying and skipping skills are good examples of criterion-referenced tests—either the child can, or cannot perform the skills. When it becomes clear which skills are especially helpful to the child in school, these are the types of tests teachers will find most useful to devise in their classrooms. Young children who eat meals in school, for instance, may need to be able to consume soup without soiling their clothes, or to dress and undress without assistance. Another criterion might be willingness to take several tastes of all food offered but without having to finish any dish. Such criteria for learning then constitute preassessed goals. They can be used to find out which children can be excused from the learning exercises because they can perform to criterion.

A criterion usually defines the behavior desired without any indication of how to achieve it. If most of the children are refusing to taste most of the food offered for lunch several times a week, what can be done? An obvious first step would be conferences with parents to establish children's preferred dishes and to try to offer these so as to establish good habits and skills of self-care with meals. Later, a teacher can try to improve children's willingness to try new foods. Modeling techniques might be used when trying to establish desirable responses to unfamiliar foods. Additional steps may be needed if progress is very slow in food acceptance.

CHILDREN'S PRODUCTS

In reporting to parents, the most telling forms of evaluative material are children's products. Supervisors and visitors also find samples of children's work a most direct form of information about children's progress. Because the child's work is such an important measure of his school learning and development, some teachers choose to intervene, especially in art and craft products, to make them look "better." Adult tinkering with children's work never really improves it. It only advertises the teacher's lack of confidence in her pupils, and considerable insensitivity to how adult skills can distort children's products.

Children's products have an authentic, fresh quality which cannot de duplicated by older children or adults. In many ways, each product bears its own stamp of individuality. These should be treasured and valued to encourage independent work.

Keeping work samples

Some teachers say they find it impossible to keep samples of children's work, because the children insist upon taking them home. Yet a teacher who really values the children's work usually finds no difficulty in persuading children either to leave all their work at school, for periodic packaging to send home, or to leave at school some of each type of work they complete. The difficulty is usually lack of storage for these products. It is amazing how much children produce even in a week's time at school. Teachers might have to consult with the school custodian or, in smaller schools, with parents about the construction of adequate storage facilities for the different types of products children make. A file of paintings and art work, all on flat paper, might be stored vertically if a simple file is designed for the purpose. Three-dimensional objects need storage of a different kind. Walls, ceilings, halls, and closets must all bear their share of the material.

Secondary sources of work samples

Some kinds of products cannot be preserved. Block constructions, cooking experiences that produce interesting results, and various other kinds of children's work fall into this category. But for products of this type, photographs, stories dictated to the teacher or to a tape recorder, dramatizations, poems, and dances might carry the message instead. These also constitute children's products in their own right and occasions to share children's work in playacting, singing, dancing, and telling stories may be scheduled informally; parents and others can be invited to view voluntary performances.

Assessing work samples

Products should be dated, wherever possible, so that both parents and the teacher can see the progression of the child's development and appreciate the extent of his progress. It is easy to forget how immature and dependent the children are when they enter early childhood classes. Therefore, it is of value to the teacher, as well as the parents and community, to see evidence of change, growth, and learning.

Sometimes, children can be asked to select some of their products for display. At such times, the teacher can take the opportunity to stress to the child his own development, thus reinforcing the child's feelings of competence. In this way, each child can be encouraged to compare his own work with his previous work and to avoid comparisons with that of other children. The teacher's attitude and modeling of valuing each child individually for his own attributes, progress, and pace of development will be caught by the children.

For the teacher, the most important result of evaluation is a sense of how to help children make even more progress while enjoying the results of their work. For children, the most important results of evaluation are their feelings of being able to control their own bodies, being able to cope with school demands, and of being competent persons who can learn and grow. If children emerge from an early childhood classroom with these feelings, teachers in the primary grades should receive them happily, as ideal pupils to teach.

SUMMARY *Teachers need good evaluative data on child progress for productive use in home-school collaboration, as well as for feedback on effects of teaching and for signals or guides to changes in teaching. The accountability movement, growing out of increasing local tax burdens for school support and criticism of schools' accomplishments, requires evaluative data on results of schooling. Humanists and behaviorists differ as to the purposes and methods of evaluation. The latter are pressing for business types of systems analysis, for which the factual basis is as yet nonexistent in early childhood education.*

Evaluation systems to determine child progress may be formal or informal, objective or subjective. Either standardized instruments or teacher-constructed tests may be used. The evaluation may stress either long- or short-term goals and participation may include parents, community, and other nonschool personnel. The school staff itself may analyze the data and make recommendations. Criterion-referenced tests are rapidly overtaking norm-referenced tests in evaluation systems. Program goals indicate what kinds of progress should be evaluated. Process versus product goals is the subject of much controversy.

Evaluation of child progress requires sampling of the more complex forms of change such as conceptualizing or logical thinking. Sources for evaluation may come from various kinds of observational data, tests (both formal and informal), child products, and from unobtrusive data.

✤ EXERCISES FOR STUDENTS ✲✲✲✲✲✲✲✲✲✲✲✲✲✲✲✲✲✲✲✲✲✲

1. Review early childhood test collections in some of the titles listed in the bibliography for this chapter.

    a. Select a test for cognitive functioning—such as the Raven's Progressive Matrices—and one for self-concepts that you would like to try out.

    b. Through your college supervisor or directly from the test publisher, locate a copy of each test selected. Inquire of the public school guidance counselor for the tests you want, since some of these may be available at the school.

    c. After studying the test instructions carefully, request permission of your cooperating classroom teacher and administer each test to three or four children.

    d. Score the tests in accordance with test instructions and write a brief summary of your experiences with the tests. Include how the children scored compared with norms given. Discuss your perceptions of ways in which the tests might not reflect children's actual functioning.

2. Devise a criterion-referenced test in consultation with a classroom teacher with whom you are placed for field or student teaching experiences. Select a criterion which the classroom teacher agrees is appropriate for the group.

    a. Secure the teacher's permission to administer the test to all the children in the group.

    b. Record test results on a prepared form.

    c. Write a brief statement analyzing the results and prescribing specific experiences for children who did not achieve the criterion. Discuss your statement with the classroom teacher.

3. With the concurrence of the classroom teacher, select one *area of children's progress* that can be evaluated by observation.

a. After consulting some of the appropriate titles in the bibliography, make a specific statement of the identified skills to be observed and construct an observational schedule and recording forms.

b. Discuss with the classroom teacher whether your observations require *eliciting* children's activity, observing it when it occurs naturally, or *both*.

c. Complete your planned observations and write a brief analysis of your findings. Discuss this statement with the classroom teacher and in a seminar with your college instructor, sharing your techniques and results with your fellow students.

4. Select some form of information about children's progress, or application of their learnings, that can be secured as *unobtrusive* data. Summarize briefly the information you have selected and the source of the data and discuss these with your college instructor. If these seem feasible, secure the classroom teacher's permission to pursue the data source; report back your findings to the teacher. Share your results with fellow students in a seminar with your college instructor.

✿ EXERCISES FOR TEACHERS ✿✿✿✿✿✿✿✿✿✿✿✿✿✿✿✿✿✿

1. List all the sources of evaluation of child progress in use in your classroom and categorize each one as to its features—that is, subjective or objective, informal versus formal or standardized, and criterion versus norm-referenced. Use the suggestions given in this chapter.

a. Analyze your evaluation base and identify needs for improvement, for example, more objective sources, more criterion-referenced sources, more random sampling in observational material and better recording, or more systematic collection of products.

b. Plan an improved evaluation system that meets the needs you have identified.

2. List specific aspects of children's school functioning about which you would like to have evaluative data for use in parent conferences.

a. For each item specified, find good sources by reading some of the titles listed in the bibliography.

b. Plan an improved evaluation system to yield the data you would like to have.

3. Plan a systematic collection and evaluation of children's products during one week, every month, for a six-month period.

a. Identify an evaluation system you can use as objectively as possible and develop either the *criterion* to be met or the levels of progress to be identified. For example, the criterion might include; "writing one's first name legibly on the product without letter omissions, reversals, or other distortions such as unnecessary capitalization." Each type of product needs its own clear criterion or basis of evaluation.

b. At the end of the six-month period, review your evaluations, your criteria, and/or the grades or levels of functioning you attributed to each product and plan any revisions indicated by unrealistic criteria or evaluative methods.

BIBLIOGRAPHY

Amidon, E., and Hough, J. *Interaction Analysis: Theory Research and Application: Readings.* Boston: Addison-Wesley, 1967.

An Administrator's Handbook on Educational Accountability. Arlington, Va.: Association of School Administrators, 1973.

ASCD, NEA. *Evaluation as Feedback and Guide.* Washington, D.C.: ASCD, NEA, 1967.

Bloom, B. S., et al. *Taxonomy of Educational Objectives: Handbook I: Cognitive Domain.* New York: McKay, 1956.

Broudy, Harry S. "Education 1975–2000." In *The Future of Education.* Edited by Hipple, Theodore W. Pacific Palisades, Calif.: Goodyear, 1974, pp. 21–46.

Buros, O. K., ed. *The Sixth Mental Measurement Yearbook.* Highland Park, N.J.: Gryphon, 1965.

Bussis, Anne M., and Chittenden, Edward A. *Analysis of an Approach to Open Education.* Princeton, N. J.: Educational Testing Service, 1970.

Cartwright, C. A., and Cartwright, G. P. *Developing Observational Skills.* New York: McGraw-Hill, 1974.

Child Welfare League of America Standards for Day Care Services. Rev. ed. New York: Child Welfare League of America, 1969.

Coller, Alan R. *Systems for the Observation of Classroom Behavior in Early Childhood Education.* Urbana, Illinois: ERIC Clearinghouse on Early Childhood Education, April 1972.

Coller, A. R. "The Assessment of 'Self-Concept' in Early Childhood Education." ERIC # ED050–822. Urbana, Ill.: ERIC Clearinghouse on Early Childhood Education, 1971.

CSE–ECRC. *Preschool/Kindergarten Test Evaluations.* Los Angeles, Calif.: UCLA Graduate School of Education, Center for the Study of Evaluation, and the Early Childhood Research Center, 1971.

Dyer, Henry S. "Testing Little Children: Some Old Problems in New Settings." *Childhood Education,* April 1973, pp. 362–367.

Ecker, David. "Defining Behavioral Objectives for Aesthetic Education." St. Ann, Mo.: Central Midwestern Regional Educational Laboratory, n. d.

Educational Testing Service. *Head Start Test Collection.* Princeton, N. J.: Educational Testing Service, 1971.

Fein, Greta G., and Clarke-Stewart, Alison. *Day Care in Context.* New York: Wiley, 1973.

Gage, N. L., ed. *Handbook of Research on Teaching.* Chicago: Rand McNally, 1963.

Gelfand, D. M., ed. *Social Learning in Childhood: Readings in Theory and Application.* Belmont, Calif.: Wadsworth, 1969.

Gordon, Ira. *Studying the Child in School.* New York: Wiley, 1966.

Johnson, O., and Bonmarito, J., eds. *Tests and Measurements in Child Development.* San Francisco: Jossey-Bass, 1971.

Kamii, Constance. "An Application of Piaget's Theory to the Conceptualization of a Preschool Curriculum." In *The Preschool in Action.* Edited by Ronald K. Parker. Boston: Allyn and Bacon, 1972.

Klein, Jenny. "Making or Breaking It: the Teacher's Role in Model (Curriculum) Implementation." *Young Children* 28 (1973), pp. 359–365.

Krathwohl, D. R., et al. *Taxonomy of Educational Objectives, Handbook II: Affective Domain.* New York: McKay, 1956.

Lien, A. J. *Measurement and Evaluation of Learning.* 2nd ed. Dubuque, Iowa: Brown, 1971.

Lynch, James, and Plunkett, H. Dudley. *Teacher Education and Cultural Change: England, France, West Germany.* London: George Allen and Unwin, 1973.

Maccoby, Eleanor, and Zellner, Miriam. *Experimental Primary Education: Aspects of Project Follow-Through.* New York: Harcourt Brace, Jovanovich, 1970.

Mager, Robert. *Goal Analysis.* Belmont, Calif.: Fearon, 1972.

Maryland University Institute for Child Study. *Case Studies of Children in Head Start Planned Variation, 1970–71.* Washington, D.C.: DHEW Publication No. (OCD) 73–1050.

Palmer, J. O. *The Psychological Assessment of Children.* New York: Wiley, 1970.

Popham, W. James. *An Evaluation Guidebook.* Los Angeles: The Instructional Objectives Exchange, 1973.

Raven, J. C. *Guide to Using the Coloured Progressive Matrices.* London: Lewis, 1963.

Sabine, Creta D. *Accountability: Systems Planning in Education.* Homewood, Ill.: ETC, 1973.

Sawin, E. I. *Evaluation and the Work of the Teacher.* Belmont, Calif.: Wadsworth, 1969.

Sciara, Frank J., and Jantz, Richard K. *Accountability in American Education.* Boston: Allyn and Bacon, 1972.

Stanford Research Institute. *Interim Evaluation of the National Follow Through Project, 1969–1971: A Technical Report.* Menlo Park, Calif.: Stanford Research Institute, 1973.

Stanford Research Institute. "Longitudinal Evaluation of Selected Features of the National Follow Through Program." ERIC, 067266 and 057267, 1971.

Terman, Lewis M. *The Gifted Child at Mid-Life: Thirty-five Years' Follow-up of the Superior Child.* Stanford, Calif.: Stanford University Press, 1959.

Walker, Deborah Klein. *Socioemotional Measures for Preschool and Kindergarten Children.* San Francisco: Jossey-Bass, 1973.

Williams, E. P., and Rausch, H. L., eds. *Naturalistic Viewpoints in Psychological Research.* New York: Holt, Rinehart & Winston, 1969.

Wittrock, M. C., and Wiley, David E. *The Evaluation of Instructional Issues and Problems.* New York: Holt, Rinehart & Winston, 1970.

Wright, H. F. *Recording and Analyzing Child Behavior.* New York: Harper, 1967.

NAME INDEX

SUBJECT INDEX

DATE DUE

APR 23 '79	APR 23 '79		
MAY 10 '79	MAY 10 '79		
MAR 4 '80	MAR 4 '80		
MAR 25 '80	MAR 25 '80		
FEB 9 '81	FEB 5 '81		
APR 30 '81	MAY 12 '81		
AP 27 '82	APR 26 '82		
DE 2 '82	NOV 23 '82		
FE 22 '83	FEB 23 '83		
AP 8 '83	APR 8 '83		
AP 25 '83	APR 27 '83		
AP 18 '84	APR 25 '84		
AP 04 '90	MAR 22 '90		
AP 04 '90	MAR 22 '90		
GAYLORD			PRINTED IN U.S.A.